Touring the Low Countries

Map of the Netherlands, 1710

Touring the Low Countries

Accounts of British Travellers, 1660-1720

Kees van Strien

Illustrations selected by Dirk de Vries

AMSTERDAM UNIVERSITY PRESS

The author and publisher gratefully acknowledge the assistance of the Dr Hendrik Muller's Vaderlandsch Fonds.

Cover illustration: Statue of Erasmus at Rotterdam (detail). Engraving, 1694. Photo Coll. University Library, Leiden.

Cover design: Martijn Koudijs, Den Haag
Lay-out: Brassica Producties/Wouter Kool, Leiden

ISBN: 90 5356 305 9

© Amsterdam University Press, Amsterdam, 1998

Contents

CONTENTS

Preface

Following British tourists in the United Provinces and the Southern Netherlands has proved a fascinating and highly rewarding personal adventure. Life in the Low Countries three centuries ago is a subject that has attracted many readers in recent years, but so far they have not had the opportunity to see for themselves what Holland and Flanders looked like in the eyes of seventeenth-century travellers. By 1700 the Seventeen Provinces had long ceased to be a political reality, but the area also known as the Low Countries continued to represent a geographical region often visited by British tourists on their first journey abroad. While doing so, they kept journals or wrote letters to their friends at home, and it is through these documents that we can learn about about their daily occupations and see the sights, many of which are still standing.

After the introduction, which deals with the tourist's motivation and daily routine, the reader is left to enjoy himself and go his own way. Some will start with cities they remember from their own travels, while others try and follow one particular tourist. The itineraries in the chronological list will serve as a guideline. Since most of the accounts presented here have not been published before, specialists in many fields may make interesting discoveries. It is hoped the indexes (which also give the years of birth and death of the persons we have identified) will prove helpful.

Since the descriptions of the cities are the focal points of travelogues of this period, the material has been arranged on the basis of the individual towns. This enables readers to make comparisons and form a perspective. The sights remain the same, but each traveller has his own style of writing. Lord Fitzwilliam, for instance, borrowed most of what he wrote about cities and sights from his guidebooks. Thomas Penson and Joseph Taylor made a greater effort and introduced more travel incidents. The Earl of Perth also enjoyed creative writing. He is continuously chatting to his sister about what happened to him and his wife, and does not care to mention the sights, which his sister can always look up in the guidebooks.

In the texts written by the tourists, names of places occur in a variety of spellings. In the introduction and indexes we retain the British forms only for Brussels, Antwerp, Dunkirk and The Hague. All other towns are referred to by the names used locally. Thus, Gent, Tournai, Brugge and Aachen instead of Ghent or Gand, Doornik, Bruges and Aix-la-Chapelle. However, all versions of the names have been indexed, with cross-references to the keywords.

The spelling, including that of most personal and geographical names, has silently been adapted to modern usage. Annotations in the text are always between square brackets. They consist of corrections of errors made by tourists, usually in connection with names, numbers and historical dates. Some corrections are preceded by = for clarity, as for instance: George [=Henry]. There are also a small number of additions, for instance where the MS has a blank, or where a translation, names or dates have been supplied. Cuts in the text are indicated by [...].

Acknowledgements

I am grateful to a large number of archivists, librarians and other scholars in Britain, The Netherlands, Belgium, France and the USA who have helped trace the material and answered our queries. I am happy to name the following: J. Alleblas (Dordrecht), J. Berghoef (Purmerend), Marten Jan Bok (Utrecht), P.A. Boon (Hoorn), Iain Brown (Edinburgh), James Collett-White (Bedford), A.Th. van Deursen (Bloemendaal), J. Folkerts (Zwolle), Roelof van Gelder (Amsterdam), J. Grooten (Kampen), B. Grymonprez (Leuven), Willem van Ham (Bergen op Zoom), Chris Heesakkers (Leiden), Peter-Jan van der Heijden ('s-Hertogenbosch), Steven Hobbs (Trowbridge), Paul Hoftijzer (Leiden), Norbert Hostyn (Oostende), P.R.A. van Iddekinge (Arnhem), H.M.F.J. Installé (Mechelen), Susan Jones (London / Brussel), W. de Keyzer (Mons), F.W.J. Koorn (Haarlem), Martine Le Maner (Saint-Omer), N. Maddens (Kortrijk), John Marciari (New Haven), Marie Juliette Marinus (Antwerpen), A. Meerman (Vlissingen), W.J. Meeuwissen (Nijmegen), H.J. Nalis (Deventer), G.M du Pui (Amersfoort), A.D. Renting (Apeldoorn), F. Rieunier (Lille), B.J. van der Saag (Gouda), Omert J. Schrier (Nieuw Vennep), Janet Smith (Chelmsford), C.E.M. Strik-Zijlstra ('s-Gravenhage), P.W. Sijnke (Middelburg), J. Toussaint (Spa), A. Vandewalle (Brugge), Peter G. Vasey (Edinburgh), Théo Verheyden (Tournai), G. Verhoeven (Delft), Hans Vlieghe (Antwerpen), Rachel Watson (Northampton), V. Wijnekus (Alkmaar), Jane Zaat (Oegstgeest), K. Zandberg (Leeuwarden), Jean-Pierre and Marie-Jo Zanetti (Tourcoing), Léon Zylbergeld (Brussel).

Particular thanks are due to the owners and repositories of manuscript material for granting permission to publish the texts, full references of which are found in the chronological list of travellers: Birmingham City Archives (Malie, 1722), The Bodleian Library, University of Oxford (Anonymous 1706; Burnet, 1707; Leake, 1711-1712; Rawlinson, 1719), The British Library (Anonymous 1720; Percival 1718, 1723; Scott, 1672), The Brotherton Collection, Leeds University Library (Anonymous 1711), West Devon Record Office (Anonymous 1701), The Fitzwilliam Milton Estates, Northamptonshire Record Office (Fitzwilliam, 1663), Sir Archibald Grant (Anonymous 1712), The Harvey Archive, Bedfordshire Record Office (Talman, 1697-1698), Mr Simon Heneage (Walker, 1671), County Record Office Huntingdon (Anonymous 1699-1700), The Earl of Jersey (Child, 1697), The Lamport Hall Trust, Northamptonshire Record Office (Isham, 1704-1705), Leicestershire Record Office (Tillard, 1716), The James Marshall and Marie-Louise Osborn Collection, Beinecke Library, Yale University (Anonymous 1695), The John

ACKNOWLEDGEMENTS

Rylands University Library Manchester (Prideaux, 1711-1712), Manuscripts Division, National Library of Scotland (Penson, 1687), The Board of Trustees of the Victoria and Albert Museum (Thornhill, 1711), Special Collections Department, University of Virginia Library (Style, 1669), Wiltshire County Record Office (Anonymous 1697; Holford, 1671). For permission to reproduce photographic material I am indebted to the Board of Trustees of the Victoria and Albert Museum (London), the British Architectural Library, RIBA (London), the Koninklijke Bibliotheek (The Hague), and the librarian of the University Library, Leiden, P.W.J.L. Gerretsen, for the use I have been allowed to make of maps, prints and drawings from the Bodel Nijenhuis collection. Special thanks are due to Dirk de Vries, Keeper of this collection, for his judicious selection of illustrations. He has added an extra dimension to this book.

Population, distances and inns

For the very complicated matter of the populations of the various towns, we have consulted the reference works mentioned at the end of each chapter, and checked their data against those given by *Hedendaagsche Historie, of tegenwoordige staat der Vereenigde Nederlanden* (Amsterdam 1739-1803: T.S.) and Jan de Vries, *European Urbanization 1500-1800* (London 1984, pp. 270-272). The figures always exclude the often large garrisons. Distances in hours (Du: *uur gaans*), the equivalent of three English miles, are taken from contemporary guidebooks, which, however, do not always agree. Names of inns come from the various editions of *Reisboek* (1689-1721); those marked with an asterisk* also appear in Thomas Nugent, *The Grand Tour* (1749).

Dates

Our present (Gregorian) calendar, which was introduced in many European countries from 1582 onwards, was not adopted in Britain until 1752. Thus, throughout our period it is necessary to establish whether dates used by tourists are in Old Style (the earlier Julian calendar) or New Style, which until 1700 was ten days later and after 1700 eleven days.

If everybody had followed Thomas Penson's procedure of giving both dates, or had always added N.S. or O.S., like Richard Rawlinson, things would have been easy. John Farrington told his cousin that he set sail from Harwich on 31 August 1710 O.S., adding: 'which now I shall call September 11 N.S.'. However, in order to establish the correct dates, it is often necessary to go through the whole manuscript and resort to a perpetual calendar. Thus, it turns out that Justinian Isham continued dating his journal in Old Style until his arrival in Utrecht; he then adopted New Style. John Leake on the other hand, stuck to the O.S. dates in his British almanac, even though his journey took more than a year. Dates given in the headings always comprise those in New Style.

ACKNOWLEDGEMENTS

Currency

Up till 1971 the pound sterling (£1) was divided into 20 shillings (20/), and each shilling into 12 pence (12 d.) A guinea was 21 shillings. A crown was a 5 shilling piece.

In the Netherlands a large variety of coins were current. The stuiver was a silver coin worth 8 duiten (doits). Six or seven stuivers made a schelling. Twenty stuivers made a gulden (guilder, florin, ƒ1), not a coin but a monetary unit in which most accounts were kept. Thus, 8:14:6 stands for 8 guilders, 14 stuivers and 6 doits. However, Richard Holford kept his accounts in ducatons (silver coins worth 63 stuivers) and stuivers.

In this period the value of a pound sterling in the Low Countries fluctuated between ƒ9:10 and ƒ11. Thus, a guilder was approximately the equivalent of two shillings and a penny (240 to a pound) was worth slightly less than a stuiver.

H. Enno van Gelder and M. Hoc, *Les monnaies des Pays-Bas bourguignons et espagnols 1404-1713*, Amsterdam, 1960.

H. Enno van Gelder, *De Nederlandse munten*, Utrecht-Antwerpen 1976.

A. van Keymeulen, *Munten van de Zuidelijke Nederlanden. Van Albrecht en Isabella tot Willem I*, Brussel 1981.

A Table shewing the Number of Leagues between the most remarkable Cities of the Seventeen Provinces of the Netherlands.

```
Amsterdam
30  Antwerp
 9 27  Amersfoort
18 29  9  Arnhem
65 35 62 65  Atrecht, Arras
48 18 45 47 18  Bergen, Henegouw
25  8 22 27 43 26  Bergen op Zoom
38  8 35 37 28 10 16  Brussels
48 18 45 47 26 22 26 17  Bruges
20 10 17 20 45 28  7 18 28  Breda
22 40 13 14 75 58 53 48 58 30  Campen
20 37 11  8 72 55 35 46 55 28  8  Deventer
15 15 12 19 50 33 10 23 23  5 25 23  Dort
52 22 49 51 13  9 30 15 14 22 62 59 37  Tournay
40 10 37 39 25 15 18  9  8 20 50 47 25 12  Ghent
44 62 35 34 87 80 57 70 80 52 22 28 47 84 27  Groningen
14 17 10 14 52 35 14 25 25  7 22 21  5 39 27 45  Gorcum
10 20 11 19 55 38 15 28 38 10 24 22  5 42 30 46  6  Gouda
11 21 17 21 56 39 17 29 39 12 30 28  7 43 31 52 13  7  The Hague
20 17 14 12 52 35 15 25 35  8 26 20 10 39 27 46  6 12 17  Bolduke
38  8 35 33 14 16  4 21 18 45 43 23 19 13 70 29 28 29 25  Louvain
44 62 35 34 87 80 57 70 80 52 22 28 47 84 72 14 45 46 52 46 70  Leeuwarden
 8 24 14 22 59 42 20 23 32 15 27 25 10 46 34 49 11  5  3 17 32 49  Leyden
47 26 43 34 46 48 31 22 39 29 48 40 34 37 21 08 33 39 41 27 18 69 44  Limburg
75 47 09 63 55 40 55 40 57 56 77 69 66 49 49 97 61 67 68 55 39 97 71 29  Luxemburg
40 20 31 29 46 28 25 18 35 22 43 25 27 33 27 63 26 32 34 20 14 63 37  7 35  Maastricht
34  4 31 33 32 14 12  4 18 14 44 41 19 18 10 66 21 24 25 21  4 66 28 22 43 17  Mechlin
32 14 29 35 34 25  8 18  8 15 52 40 17 22 10 64 22 22 24 23 22 64 27 40 61 33 17  Middelburg
52 17 46 44 31 13 25 10 27 26 58 50 22 22 19 78 38 37 38 32  9 78 41 15 30 15 13 28  Namur
20 16 12  3 61 44 24 34 44 17 17 11 18 46 36 37 14 20 26  9 32 37 22 31 60 26 30 32 41  Nimmegen
52 22 49 51 27 26 20 21  4 32 62 59 37 17 12 84 39 42 43 40 25 84 46 43 60 38 22 12 31 48  Ostend
36 22 28 19 53 24 28 24 40 22 33 25 27 39 32 53 22 28 34 16 20 53 33 15 44 10 22 36 25 16 44  Ruremond
14 18 15 22 53 36 14 26 36  9 28 26  4 40 28 50  8  4  3 14 25 50  6 38 65 31 22 21 35 22 40 30  Rotterdam
52 23 50 52 13 14 31 11 14 33 63 60 38  4 13 85 40 43 44 40 24 85 47 38 54 38 22 19 27 49 14 41 41  Lisle
55 25 52 54 12  7 33 17 21 35 65 62 40  7 19 87 42 45 46 42 21 87 49 35 46 45 21 29 20 51 24 41 43 12  Valenciennes
32 22 24 15 54 26 28 26 40 22 29 21 26 41 32 42  2 21 28 34 16 28 49 33 19 48 14 22 36 29 12 44  4 30 44 43  Venlo
 8 23  4 12 58 41 18 31 41 13 17 15  8 45 33 39  6  7 13 12 31 39 10 39 67 32 27 25 44 13 45 28 11 46 48 25  Utrecht
53 23 50 52 17 18 31 18  9 33 63 60 28  9 13 85 40 43 44 40 22 85 47 45 58 38 22 17 31 50 10 48 41  5 16 44 46  Ipres
21 35 12  6 70 53 33 43 52 20 11  3 24 57 45 31 22 23 29 18 41 31 26 37 66 32 39 39 47  9 58 22 27 58 60 18 16 58  Zutphen
22 41 14 12 76 59 30 49 59 31  3  6 26 63 15 22 24 25 31 24 47 22 28 46 75 35 45 41 56 15 63 31 29 64 66 27 18 65  9  Zwol
```

The Difference of Miles in the several Countries of Europe.

The Circumference of the Globe of the Earth is reckoned at 360 Degrees.

A Degree is

15 Common German Miles.	30 Small ditto.
12 Ditto large.	20 English Leagues.
10 Hungarian.	60 English Miles.
10 Swiss.	80 Scotch.
60 Italian.	48 Irish.
17½ Spanish.	20 Polish.
20 Dutch hours.	12 Danish.
20 Large French.	12 Swedish.
24 Common ditto.	80 Muscovitish Wersts or Miles.

Example of the use of the Table.

Amsterdam

The Hours between any two Cities stand in the Angle under those two Cities perpendicularly and laterally taken.

```
20 | | | | | | 1 Deventer
```

Table of distances, 1744

Introduction

Tourists, guidebooks and travel accounts

Sailing from Scheveningen to Dover on his return to England in May 1660, King Charles II must have had very mixed feelings about his prolonged stay in the Low Countries. Still the Continental experiences of the exiled King and his courtiers may well have reinforced an already firmly established fashion in Britain as in most other countries of northwestern Europe: the foreign journey as an indispensable part in the education of a young man belonging to the higher echelons of society. Next to business and health, this soon became one of the principal reasons for travel abroad. To learn to behave in polite society while visiting foreign capitals was an experience few young gentlemen objected to, and with time and improved travelling conditions, more and more individuals and parties set out for foreign shores. The Grand Tour remained the privilege of the happy few, but after 1660 a relatively large number of Britons could afford the time and expense of a summer's excursion to the Continent. Two or three months were amply sufficient for a combined visit to Paris and the Low Countries.

Of course, travellers, young and old, tried to make their voluntary exile as agreeable as possible. Notwithstanding the repeated exhortations in the educational literature not to mix with compatriots, tourists did so whenever they could. In the Low Countries they met fellow-tourists in the numerous lodging houses kept by English and Scottish landlords. In Leiden, Utrecht and Leuven there were large numbers of British university students; in seaports, particularly in Amsterdam and Rotterdam, tourists took up money with British merchants, and in the garrison towns they met officers and soldiers belonging to English and Scottish regiments in the service of the States. In Holland and Zeeland it was possible to attend divine service in English and Scottish churches, while in Brabant and Flanders visits were made to the many British Roman-Catholic communities, some of which ran boarding schools or colleges. In places like The Hague, Rotterdam, Brussels and Spa, tourists may at times have imagined themselves almost at home.

Indeed, many sightseeing travellers were guided around by countrymen, whose local know-how must have been a welcome addition to the mainly historical information available in guidebooks. Of the latter, there was a fairly wide choice. Lord Fitzwilliam (1663) and Sir Philip Skippon (1663) travelled with *Ulysses Belgico-Gallicus*, written by Abraham Gölnitz (2nd ed. 1655). This book contained very detailed descriptions of the cities in the Southern Netherlands. Fitzwilliam also made use of the Dutch *Beschryvingh der Neder-landen* (1660-1662), which relied

1

INTRODUCTION

heavily on Lodovico Guicciardini's often reprinted description of the Seventeen Provinces (1567). Its 1660 edition, *Belgicae sive inferioris Germaniae descriptio*, contained useful town-plans. Tourists whose Latin had got a bit rusty and who limited their travels to the province of Holland must have found Jean de Parival's *Les Délices de la Hollande* (1651) very helpful. It ran through many editions and was also available in English (Aglionby, 1669, 1671, 1676). Compared to this, the popular guidebooks in English by William Carr were rather slight productions. Far more thorough (four volumes in octavo) was J.-B. Christyn's *Les Délices des Pays-Bas* (1697), reprinted until 1786, and consulted, for instance, by Sir John Percival in 1718. It contained engravings showing the principal public buildings together with plans of the fortifications encompassing the various towns. Another popular guidebook, which included descriptions of cities in Holland and Flanders, was François Maximilien Misson's *Nouveau voyage d'Italie* (1691; English ed. 1699), written for the Grand Tourists.

This guidebook was innovative in that it recommended inns and contained advice on the cost of transport, but the emphasis lay (as with its predecessors) on historico-topographical descriptions. Although Richard Holford (1671) and John Walker (1671), whose daily entries look more like ordinary diaries, do not appear to have copied from guidebooks, tourists who made an effort to compose well-documented travel accounts could not do without them. Dates in guidebooks were more reliable than those given by local cicerones and printed readings of Latin inscriptions on the tombs of great men were usually more accurate than those made by the travellers themselves. Much of Lord Fitzwilliam's text was copied and translated from a variety of guidebooks. He also borrowed several historical anecdotes, mentioning for instance the 365 children born at Loosduinen and Quinten Metsys' change of career from blacksmith to artist.

Guidebooks occasionally contained graphic descriptions which tourists found it difficult to resist. John Ray, whose *Travels* were published in 1673, asserted that the streets of Rotterdam were 'elegantly paved' and 'so clean that a man may walk them in slippers without wetting his foot in the midst of winter'. This statement was gratefully adapted by Edward Browne: 'the streets are so clean that the women go about in white slippers'. Browne's book, published in 1677, became a bestseller, and was probably consulted by the travelling tutor Misson, who visited Rotterdam in 1687. His version was: 'Their streets are so clean that you see the women walk almost constantly in them in their slippers'. In another phrase Misson gave an idyllic picture of the Rotterdam canals, picturesquely juxtaposing the trees, the tops of the houses and the streamers hanging down from the ships' masts. This was borrowed by many readers, among them a British student at Utrecht (1699-1700) and Joseph Taylor (1707).

Travel journals, the most common type of travelogue, come in many forms. Some tourists like John Talman (1697-1698) or the would-be politician Edward Southwell (1696), never got around to working out their notes. Justinian Isham

(1704-1705), with Monsieur Masson looking over his shoulder, had no choice. His fair copy was clearly an assignment meant to teach him history and geography. The journals kept by Lord Fitzwilliam and Sir Francis Child (1697), appear to have been rewritten several times, with the inevitable errors slipping in, particularly in personal names, dates and numbers. The arms painter Thomas Penson (1687) produced at least two surprisingly accurate, calligraphed copies of his journal, which he lent out to more than eighty people. Several of his grateful readers, who liked his jokes, sent him complimentary poems, which Penson added as an appendix.

Other appendices which are regularly found in these journals consist of general observations on the countries visited. They often deal with government or popular customs. John Ray (1663) borrowed many of his observations from his friend Francis Barnham Esq., but Thomas Scott's comments on Flemish customs (1672) are probably his own. Richard Holford (1671) is one of the few tourists from the pre-Misson period to include much practical information. At the end of his journal he wrote down a list of inns and noted the frequency and fares of waggons and barges. Sir John Percival (1718; 1723) provided his travelogues with indexes of persons, places and sights so as to show his young son how such things ought to be done.

Another popular way of presenting accounts of travel is the letter format. Writing letters home is possibly a more natural thing to do than keeping a diary. Letters, even descriptive ones, give their authors more freedom than the journal format, from which scholars sometimes excluded all personal details. With new letters coming in all the time, friends at home could read about the traveller's daily occupations in serial form. This is how the Earl of Perth's sister learned about her brother's experiences in Flanders and Holland. The collection of letters by Joseph Taylor were probably never sent in their present form, but written up after the journey. Inscribing them to his cousin, Taylor did his best to produce a lively narrative of his expedition to the army. Bullets did not hurt him, but as a result of a succession of chance encounters with a lovely English girl, Cupid's arrows did. As it turns out in the end, she was on her way to a convent in Flanders to take the veil.

Reading these texts, we occasionally catch a glimpse of the personality of the traveller-author, but they remain in the background; none of them was out to paint his own portrait. The principal business for them was to present their relatives and friends with a picture of the countries they visited. Thus, we learn about the conditions of travel in the Low Countries around 1700, and through these and the descriptions of the sights we can visualize what these territories and their cities must have looked like to British tourists.

The Low Countries seen by British tourists

Around 1700 the Low Countries constituted the most highly urbanised area of Europe, approximately half the size of England and Wales and with 3.5 million inhabitants far more densely populated. True, Amsterdam, the largest city with 200,000 inhabitants, had less than half of London's population, but England's six provincial towns of ten thousand inhabitants or more were nothing to the Low Countries' thirty odd cities with populations ranging from 10,000-60,000 people. This territory, roughly divided into four distinct political entities (French Flanders, The Spanish Netherlands, the Bishopric of Liège and the United Provinces), was usually perceived by travelling British tourists as North and South.

In this period a traveller leaving London was lucky if he reached Amsterdam, Antwerp or Brussels in less than three or four days. Since few people sailed directly from London, most travellers spent the first full day on the road, covering the seventy odd miles to Harwich or to Dover. If on arrival there, the wind was favourable and the packet boat ready to sail (twice weekly), they needed five or six hours to make it to Calais or Dunkirk, and about 24 to the Dutch coast. In Holland or Flanders passenger services by waggons as well as barges were relatively frequent and punctual. From Hellevoetsluis it was six hours to Rotterdam, and eleven more to Amsterdam. Passengers from Dunkirk to Brussels often travelled by barge via Brugge: 29 hours in all. The journey from Brussels to Antwerp took six hours and that to Spa, by way of Liège, 24.

Since most of our travellers had never been abroad before, they commented on all sorts of details connected with the journey. Skippon was irritated by the formalities at customs, where many hands had to be greased. Passengers paid fixed rates for transport by packet boat, but when going on board or disembarking in little boats they were at the mercy of the sailors. In Holland, waggons were often criticized for their lack of comfort and the noise they made, particularly on paved roads. The postwaggon in which Monsieur Blainville, the tutor of secretary Blathwayt's sons, travelled from Amsterdam to Arnhem had no springs and was 'mounted upon stilts', so that passengers needed a ladder 'to get up into them'. Barges on the other hand, were commodious, cheap and punctual; those in Holland and Friesland travelled at six to seven kilometres per hour, the much larger Flanders scutes, in which meals were served, managed just over five. John Leake, a clergyman who accompanied the vicar of Stepney's son, did not mind his Dutch *trekschuit*, but found it difficult to adapt to the proletariat on board with their screaming children, women kicking off their slippers and putting their feet on the seat next to him, and male passengers making water in the canal.

Remarks on the countryside often remain limited to passing comments on crops and cattle. John Talman, a talented draughtsman, was an exception and also mentioned the fine views he had when touring the undulating country near Arnhem and Kleve. An anonymous tourist in Spa (1720) made a special excursion through 'hilly and barren country' to the village of Coo, three hours distant, where country people 'for a small gratification' entertained tourists by taking away a barrier they had built in the river, so that the water came down 'with utmost violence'. The same tourist was quite taken with Chaudfontaine, 'as agreeable, romantic a

View of Leiderdorp, 1698

place as any that can be seen'. In Holland many passengers in the *trekschuit* between Rotterdam and Delft commented on the low-lying meadows of which, from their slightly more elevated position in the canal, they had an unimpeded view. While travelling on the waggon from Rotterdam to Gouda, Thomas Bowrey noticed the canals separating the fields, and every house, surrounded by water, had its own small boat.

However, the majority of tourists spent their energy on describing the often remarkably neat cities, where after the hustle of travelling, they put up for the night. At Amsterdam, Thomas Bowrey and his friends had their luggage put on a barrow, and in a 'covered sled', drawn by one horse, they proceeded to the White Hart, an English inn behind the Oude Kerk. With fifteen *stuivers* for dinner, prices here were reasonable, but the merchant Bowrey probably wanted something classier, and moved to an establishment where a meal including half a pint of wine cost twice as much. Unlike many of his countrymen who all over Europe complained about cheating innkeepers, Bowrey never grumbled about unreasonable bills, a speciality for which the Dutch have become proverbial. On average, well-to-do travellers seem to have spent about five guilders a day on board, lodging and travelling costs. What made the journey expensive, according to Sir John Percival, were the entertainments the English felt themselves obliged to offer their countrymen whenever they met them.

Since sightseeing was the main business of the journey, serious tourists hired local guides or *valets de place*. Thus, they inspected whatever was 'memorable', as Francis Bacon put it in his essay *Of Travel* (1625): courts of princes, courts of justice, churches and monasteries, fortifications, harbours, antiquities, libraries, colleges, gardens, cabinets and rarities. The top of a steeple provided tourists with a vantage point from which they could try to recognize the shape of each city as it was set out in the guidebooks: Rotterdam was built in the form of a half moon, Dordrecht looked like a galley and Brussels resembled a man's heart.

After these preliminaries, visits were made to the town hall, particularly that of Amsterdam, after 1655 the most impressive civic building in the Low Countries, and the *Great Churches*, whose interiors in Holland were usually covered with escutcheons, hung near the graves of local worthies. Tourists also noticed organs, sometimes a special pulpit, but invariably the richly-carved tombs erected to the memory of admirals, including Tromp and De Ruyter, who had escorted home so many richly-laden East Indiamen. The antiquary, Richard Rawlinson, assiduously copied inscriptions, something which young Justinian Isham did with considerably less enthusiasm. In Brabant and Flanders the churches symbolized the Roman Catholic religion that seemed to have appropriated all the riches of the country. Here an appeal was made to the senses with choral music and incense during divine service, and all sorts of sculptures and rich altarpieces by Rubens, Memling, Pourbus and many others. These paintings were viewed with particular attention by an as yet anonymous tourist in 1720 and by Sir John Percival, who as a young man had visited Italy.

Other buildings of interest in the north were the public houses of correction (Rasphouse and Spinhouse), hospitals and orphanages, and in the south convents and abbeys. Besides these, each city had its own particular sights. Leiden had its university with large collections of *rarities*, Amsterdam the warehouses belonging to the East India Company, Antwerp its magnificent Jesuits' chapel, the Exchange and many private collections of paintings, Gent the diminutive room where the great Charles V was born, and Brussels the royal palace and its armoury. Tourists duly entered their names in visitors' books or, as at Utrecht, in the margins of a medieval bible, one of the items on show in St Mary's church.

Londoners, who after the *Great Fire* (1666) saw their city rise from its ashes and rapidly turn into a metropolis of half a million inhabitants, naturally preferred modern architecture to that dating from earlier periods. However, few travellers comment in detail on newly-built country houses, possibly because these were relatively small compared with the ones under construction in Britain. Gardens, on the other hand, are often mentioned. Visitors to The Hague made daytrips to see the Prince of Orange's House in the Wood and his palaces at nearby Honselaarsdijk and Rijswijk. The gardens here and those belonging to the Earl of Portland, on the road to Scheveningen, clearly merited a detour. Huge sums of money were spent on relatively small plots of ground, unrecognizably transformed into regular geometrical patterns consisting of parterres, arbours, banks, grottoes, garden statues, urns and *waterworks*. But fashions in gardening were subject to change. According to Percival, hardly anybody in 1718 visited Portland's gardens, which 14 years earlier drew all the tourists. Similarly, the garden behind the palace at Brussels was a great tourist attraction in the 1660s, but when Joseph Taylor saw it in 1707 it was 'running to decay'.

The most extensive gardens of the Low Countries around 1700 were at Loo in Gelderland, originally a hunting lodge but much enlarged by William III, who at least in garden architecture was willing to accept French superiority. Numerous tourists thus felt obliged to make a considerable detour (12 hours from Utrecht) across the barren Veluwe, a district which stood in stark contrast with the rich pastures in Holland and which reminded some British tourists of their own country. There were also large gardens at Enghien, south of Brussels in the midst of the war zone, and probably for that reason less often viewed.

No visit to a city was complete without an inspection of the ramparts. At Utrecht, Antwerp and several other towns these served as public walks, but in garrison towns such as Bergen op Zoom and Namur they constituted the principal sight, providing tourists with the latest in the art of military engineering. Justinian Isham liked the defences of Bergen op Zoom, 'Coehoorn's masterpiece', much better than his inscriptions, and Lord Fitzwilliam, himself a military officer, carefully observed the 'works' at Coevorden, a Dutch fortress on the border with Münster. It was 'wholly regular' and did not have 'its like almost in the world'. Tourists also visited the forts near Maastricht or those surrounding 's-Hertogenbosch and Namur. One traveller in 1720 spent more than two hours inside the citadel of Tournai and was impressed by the underground passages that could be filled with explosives, which, during the Allied attack in 1709, had inflicted such heavy losses. Here the guides were usually British soldiers of the garrison, who made sure the less knowledgeable tourists did not mix up their fausse-brayes with courtines and the like.

In view of the constant French efforts to push their borders northwards, these fortifications were an absolute necessity. The treaty of 1659, at which the Spanish King had been forced to hand over Artois together with parts of Flanders and Hainaut, had not put an end to French expansion. And less than five years after the peace treaty of Rijswijk (1697), the war of the Spanish Succession (1702-1713) broke out, after which, in 1713, the Spanish Netherlands became an Austrian dependency. In the three decades during which King William and later the Duke of Marlborough with their huge armies were trying to outmanoeuvre Louis XIV and his generals, thousands of young adventurous gentlemen visited the Allied or Confederate 'camp', only a few miles away from the enemy. Without a French pass or an Allied escort it was risky to travel, for there were always 'French parties' operating far beyond the lines. Although tourists must have seen the desolation caused by war, ruined villages, a depopulated countryside and the centre of Brussels in ruins after the bombardment of 1695, they usually stress the more glorious aspects of war. After 'a glass or two of wine', Joseph Taylor thought himself 'a perfect soldier'. However, having experienced the fatigues of a six-day march with the army, he was happy to resume his less demanding routine as a tourist in Gent.

Getting up early to start the sightseeing programme or to move on to the next town probably meant that tourists turned in early. In small towns there was little to do apart from playing cards, drinking a bottle of wine or keeping journals up to date. However, in larger places there were plays and in Amsterdam, The Hague and Brussels there were even plays and operas in French. Joseph Taylor did not like the opera he saw at Brussels, but he did appreciate the 'comical interludes' and the playhouse itself, built in 1700. Here according to a travel guide, the Prince de Ligne had a *loge*, where he could sit with his friends and drink a bottle or eat supper 'and see the whole representation in the looking glass, without being seen by the actors or the company' (*A Journey through the Austrian Netherlands*, pp. 33-34).

After a visit to the theatre, well-dressed strangers with money were always welcome at *assemblies*. Sir Francis Child mentions these meetings 'of gay young sparks and ladies' in The Hague, according to him the only town in the United Provinces where a gentleman could mix with people of fashion. Here at six in the evening, the *beau monde* toured the Voorhout in their coaches, to see and to be seen. This *tour à la mode* also existed in Antwerp, Brugge, Brussels and Gent, and enabled many an English tourist to get a good view of the local beauties who sometimes looked far more elegant than expected.

Clearly, just as tourists based their ideas about the Netherlands as a country on their guidebooks, they also knew what the natives were like long before they had ever seen them. In the period of the Anglo-Dutch alliance under King William and Queen Anne, the caricatures dating from the three Dutch wars (1653-1678) were still very much alive: the Dutch were boorish (especially towards foreign gentlemen), cruel and ungrateful. For this reason, Richard Rawlinson must have felt ill-at-ease in the egalitarian republic with its complicated federal structure. He preferred the 'more good-natured people' of Flanders, where society, with princes, bishops and the lower orders, was more like that in Britain. True, the Catholic Flemish were superstitious, they had 'too much religion', but in Protestant Holland, as Rawlinson put it ironically, 'that extreme [was] wonderfully well avoided'. The over-praised tolerance of the Dutch in matters of religion was probably due to indifference or based on worldly considerations in an expanding economy, which needed all the immigrants it could get. In Amsterdam John Leake noticed masons and carpenters at work 'during their divine service'. Vendors were going their rounds 'as much as upon any other day' and men and women played at cards 'without the least reserve'.

From the present selection of travellers' accounts, it emerges that foreign travel as a leisure activity for Britons was very much a reality around 1700. John Walker travelled in the Low Countries in 1671. In 1672 he stayed at home and toured Essex, and in 1673 he visited Paris. Thomas Penson sang English songs in the *trekschuit* to Delft, and in Amsterdam crept through the taphole into a large wine cask that served as a tavern. Richard Holford's financial accounts show a donation of two *stuivers* to a 'handsome wench' at the Spinhouse in Amsterdam. Joseph Taylor described in lyrical terms the reception given him by his dancing partner in Rotterdam. And William Mountague, whose *Delights of Holland* was published as a guidebook, explicitly stated that he and his companions had travelled just for the fun of it.

Indeed, the Netherlands were particularly well-equipped to ensure Britons could see everything without making long, tedious journeys. Public transport was readily available, and language was never a serious obstacle, since tourists usually managed to find countrymen willing to help them out. As for the sights, there was something for all tastes. It was pleasant to walk along the tree-lined canals in the neat Dutch cities, or to visit the formal gardens in the countryside. For those interested in antiquities, the Netherlands were certainly not Paris or Rome, but there were Latin inscriptions, libraries and collections of Roman antiquities. Lovers of the fine arts visited town halls, churches and abbeys and admired private collections of paintings wherever possible. Finally, for people keen on things military, there was probably no place like the Netherlands in Europe.

Few tourists make explicit comparisons between North and South, although the differences were striking. They may have remembered Holland as a well-ordered merchants' paradise, where religion, as in Britain, was subservient to the state. In the Spanish or Austrian Netherlands, the people were poor, the country was ravaged by war, and religion seemed to dominate public life. Thomas Penson's light-hearted accounts of his private meetings with a nun in an Antwerp convent and with a prostitute in an Amsterdam music house were his way of epitomizing this contrast.

Extensive comparisons between the Low Countries and Britain are also rare. They mostly bear on religion and social order. Thomas Scott told his Anglican readers not to be too critical of Catholics and not to call superstition what was really devotion. People in Britain would be more devout if there was not so much preaching. John Leake thought that the British Calvinists (Puritans) were unreasonably averse to the use of organs during divine service and invited them to look to Holland. He also made some comments on the position of unmarried women in England. 'Ladies of good family but a small fortune' would be a lot better off if Britain had institutions like the beguinages in the Southern Netherlands.

On their return home tourists finished their travel accounts and handed them to relatives and friends. Of course, they took care not to give them the impression that they now looked down on everything British. With Sir John Percival praise for Dutch cleanliness or the fact that few beggars were to be seen in Holland never becomes open criticism of a filthy London full of mendicants. On the contrary, travel enabled one to be proud of one's country. Thomas Penson told his readers that the most important thing he had learned in his 'short progress' abroad was that England had 'as much to boast of' as other nations. It gave him a good feeling to be back, and he concluded cheerfully: 'Our lot is fallen in a pleasant land'.

Chronological list of guidebooks most frequently used

G. Hegenitius, *Itinerarium Frisio-Hollandicum et Abr. Ortelii Itinerarium Gallo-Brabanticum*, Leiden 1630 (1667).

A. Gölnitz, *Ulysses Belgico-Gallicus*, Leiden 1631 (1655).

M.Z. Boxhornius, *Theatrum sive Hollandiae comitatus et urbium nova descriptio*, Amsterdam 1632.

Louis Coulon, *Ulysse françois, ou le voyage de France, de Flandre et de Savoye*, Paris 1643.

J. de Parival, *Les délices de la Hollande*, Leiden 1651 (1655, 1660, 1662, 1665, 1669, 1678, 1685, 1697, 1699, 1710, 1728).

[L. Guicciardini], *Belgicae sive inferioris Germaniae descriptio*, 3 vols., Amsterdam 1660 (first ed. 1567).

Beschryvingh der Neder-landen soo uyt Louis Guicciardyn als andere vermaerde schryvers ..., 2 vols., Amsterdam 1660-1662.

A. Boussingault, *La guide universelle de tous les Pays Bas*, Paris 1665 (1672, 1673, 1677).

[W. Aglionby], *The Present State of the United Provinces of the Low-Countries as to Government, Laws, Forces, Riches, Revenue [...] the Delights of Holland, collected by W.A.*, London 1669 (1671, 1676).

[Reisboek], *Naeuw-keurig reysboek bysonderlijk dienstig voor kooplieden en reysende persoonen*, Amsterdam 1679. *Reis-boek door de Vereenigde Nederlandsche Provincien*, Amsterdam 1689[2], 1700[3]. *Reisboek door de Voornaamste Koningryken en Heerschappyen van Europa*, Amsterdam 1721[4].

W. Carr [also Ker], *Remarks of the Government of severall Parts of Germanie [...] But More particularly of the United Provinces*, Amsterdam and London 1688 (1727). *An Accurate Description of the United Netherlands*, London 1691[2]. *Travels through Flanders, Holland, Germany, Sweden*, London 1693[3], 1725[6], 1744[7]. *The Travellour's Guide and Historians Faithful Companion [...] England, Holland, Flanders*, London 1695[4], 1697[5].

F.M. Misson, *Nouveau voyage d'Italie, fait en l'année 1688*, La Haye 1691 (1694, 1698, 1702, 1717, 1722, 1727, 1731, 1743). *A New Voyage to Italy with Curious Observations on Several Other Countries*, London 1699 (1705, 1714, 1739).

[J.-B. Christyn], *Les Délices des Pais Bas*, Brussels 1697 (1700, 1711, 1713, 1720, 1743, 1769, 1786; some eds.: *Histoire Générale des Pais-Bas*).

[John Macky], *A Journey through the Austrian Netherlands*, London 1725 (1732).

Thomas Nugent, *The Grand Tour: Or a Journey through the Netherlands, Germany, Italy and France*, London 1749 (1756, 1778), vol. I, *The Traveller's Guide through the Netherlands*.

Seventeenth- and eighteenth-century atlases and reference works

W.J. Blaeu, *The Sea-Beacon*, Amsterdam 1643, reprint Amsterdam 1973.

M. Z[eiller], *Topographia Germaniae-Inferioris*, Frankfurt 1659 (2nd ed.), reprint 1964.

Hedendaagsche Historie, of tegenwoordige staat der Oostenryksche, Fransche en Pruissische Nederlanden, Amsterdam 1738.

Hedendaagsche Historie, of tegenwoordige staat der Vereenigde Nederlanden, 23 vols., Amsterdam 1739-1803.

Blaeu's Atlas van de Nederlanden, Amsterdam 1973.

F. de Wit, *Theatrum Ichnographicum omnium urbium in Belgicarum XVII Provinciarum peraccurate delineatarum,* Amsterdam [c.1698], reprint Amsterdam 1980.

Studies

M. Battistini, 'Le voyage en Belgique du comte Alexandre Segni de Florence en 1666', *Bulletin de l'institut historique belge de Rome,* 1940-1941, pp. 85-147 [with a good survey of Italian travellers in the Southern Netherlands].

Jeremy Black, *The British and the Grand Tour,* London-Sydney 1985.

Anthony Burgess (ed.) *The Age of the Grand Tour,* London 1967.

John Lough, *France Observed in the Seventeenth Century by British Travellers,* Stocksfield, 1984.

A. Maczak, *Travel in Early Modern Europe,* Cambridge 1995.

M. Pfister (ed.), *The Fatal Gift of Beauty: The Italies of British Travellers. An Annotated Anthology,* Amsterdam-Atlanta 1996.

J.W. Stoye, *English Travellers Abroad, 1604-1667,* London 1952 (rev. ed. New Haven 1989).

Eddy Stols, 'Regards étrangers sur les Pays-Bas autrichiens', H. Hasquin (ed.), *La Belgique autrichienne, 1713-1794,* [Bruxelles] 1987.

C.D. van Strien, *British Travellers in Holland during the Stuart Period,* Leiden 1993.

Madeleine van Strien-Chardonneau, *Le Voyage de Hollande: récits de voyageurs français dans les Provinces-Unies, 1748-1795,* Oxford 1994.

The Crossing

Thomas Style, 4-8 (14-18) July 1669

[23] I began my journey July the 4th 1669 one o'clock in the morning, hiring a hackney coach to Harwich. We baited at a place called Witham; lay that night at Colchester, much ruined by our late wars [in 1648]. We saw the cathedral of St Mary. Next [day] by twelve we reached Harwich. The packet boat not yet ready to go off, we crossed over [to] Landguard fort, commanded by Major [Nathaniel] Darell. It contains threescore soldiers and four batteries: the King's battery and Queen's, the Warwick and the Holland. We saw certain wooden scaling ladders taken from the Dutch in 1667. Walking out in the evening we spied the lights hung up, that ships may safely in the night enter the haven, repaired and kept by Sir William Batten, to whom they yield eight hundred pounds a year, each Newcastle man paying a penny a cauldron for their coals before they can have their cockets out of the custom-house.

Wednesday July the sixth about eight o'clock at night, we hoisted sail for Holland, enjoying a prosperous gale till Thursday ten o'clock, which produced a calm and continued so till eleven o'clock at night, when we began to have much wind, which carried us too far northward. About three o'clock in the morning it degenerated into a storm which lasted till eight; extreme violent considering the season of the year and its small continuance. My sea-illness kept me still in the cabin. The tempest growing very violent, I was called out, but being thoroughly satisfied with seeing the waves coming in and wetting our seamen – this little vessel being sometimes on an Atlas of waters, sometimes in an abyss – I was not much taken with the object, the master plainly telling if the storm continued an hour or two longer, he feared the bark was not strong enough to endure such vast [24] rolling seas.

Contrary to our expectation or his, not only the tempest ceased, but we had so favourable a wind as by eleven o'clock on Friday we got sight of the Boreel [Goeree] sands where Sir George Ayscue was stranded. We might know by the seachoughs and pies we were not far from land, who fluttering about our ship, perching upon the mast and yards, sometimes entangling themselves in the cordage, diverted us much. About two we spied Brouwershaven steeple and soon after all Holland. The reason why the land is not seen first is because the sea is a great deal higher. About four we entered Hellevoetsluis haven, escaping almost a shipwreck in the port. For entering with all sail, full wind and tide, we were like to have struck on an anchoring man-of-war, which if it had, our vessel had infallably per-

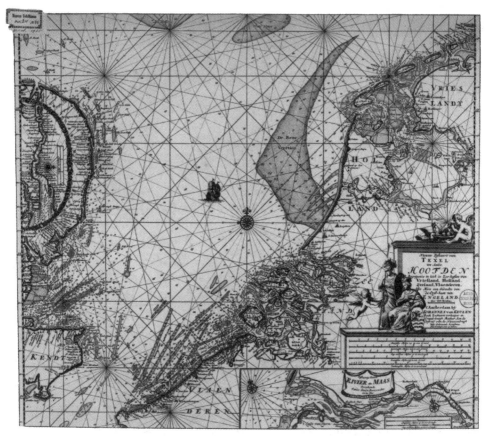

Map of the North Sea, c. 1680

ished. It being withal remedied, we came off only with a small brush. Before one is suffered to come ashore, the master is paid, viz. twelve shilling for my passage, half a crown for the cabin, two shillings head-money. From the ship we went to the inn, called by them the Doelen, to refresh ourselves.

Hellevoetsluis is a little village remarkable for nothing but the conveniency of the haven. Here we found little chariots with horses, ready harnessed, to carry us to the Briel, six miles distant, the States having put a set price; we took two. Crossing the other part of the haven I saw the Royal Charles moored up as a trophy of their late Chatham actions [1667]. About six we arrived at Briel, lodged at one Mrs Notting at the King of England's Head, an Englishwoman.

Thomas Scott, 2-4 (12-14) September 1672

[6r] I had the opportunity to travel through some places of the country of Flanders, wherein, having observed the difficulty that might happen to strangers (by reason of their ignorance of the distance of places and customs of the country and easiest

14

passages, whereby they are commonly brought to great inconveniences), I thought it not amiss to take some notes of what curiosity and time had presented to my view. Which journey was begun from London the second [6v] day of September 1672, by taking water to Gravesend and from thence by post to Dover (being the nearest port for those countries), where we came to next morning and lay there all night, the packet boat to Calais in which we went (being the shortest voyage; not above seven leagues), by reason of the Dutch capers that were at that time on the English shores, not going out till the next morning. At which time going to the pier-side in order to take shipping, we were stopped by His Majesty's searcher, but being advised the night before to take a pass from the custom-house there, we produced it and so went on board without further trouble; only the master of the vessel not going this voyage, we paid our passage, being five [7r] shillings apiece, beforehand.

About four of the clock we set to sea, where, having sailed about an hour, I as well as most of the company, fell sick. But being well-advised by our landlord at Dover, we took with us a bottle of brandy which fetched it off with more ease. Which if some others that were on board had done, they would not have spit up their blood as some did. And the seamen affirm that some, for want of that or other wine, do break their veins by the straining [which] that disease is the cause of. And by experience I found, notwithstanding the many opinions to the contrary, that it is the brackishness of the sea that is the cause of the evacuation.

The wind setting fair, before eight of the clock we cast anchor about two English [7v] miles from Calais, the tide being low, so that we were fetched on shore by small fisher boats. Here it will not be very needless to relate how these rogues exacted on us, making us pay two shillings sixpence apiece for our passage. And when we came nigh shore they held the boat off to get a pack of idle fellows (that stand there) money by carrying us on their backs to land. Nor unpleasant also to relate how one of them was served, there being with us a French doctor, a gross man, who being too heavy for his bearer, the poor man was fain to sink under his burden and caused the doctor to take a purge of salt water, [8r] who, I dare swear, knew a glass of wine was better physic [medicine]. Who, getting up in haste in a rugged manner sent the fellow to grabble for fish, who knew a way to catch them worth ten out. [cont. Dunkirk and Calais]

Anonymous London merchant, 3-5 (13-15) August 1695

[3] On Saturday the third at six in the morning, we took two boats at Billingsgate, and after dining at Gravesend went on board the Anne of Rotterdam, Charles Lousetto master, and immediately sailed to the Nore, where we cast anchor. And after a plentiful supper on board with the other passengers, Mr Fisher and other good friends who accompanied us thither left us and returned to London.

On Sunday the fourth at five in the morning, we weighed anchor and sailed for Holland in a fleet of eighty sail under convoy of two Dutch men-of-war, having a fair gale and dry weather which continued till ten o'clock, and then fell to rain and blew hard, which made every passenger very sick, but especially my son, that is my adopted son Richard Grosvenor. Last night while we anchored at the Nore, the weather was beautiful and calm, and there it was that the porpoises in great numbers entertained us with skipping on the waters, but appeared no more to the end of our voyage, the weather being foul and stormy.

Monday the fifth at six in the morning, our cook espied land, which was some joy to the passengers, though at a great distance, for which everyone as is usual gave him a reward. He was much envied for this discovery by the rest of the crew, having first made it in sundry voyages before. In the night between Sunday and Monday an accident befell us in our sailing which might have been fatal. A Dutch flyboat fell foul on our stern with his bowsprit and bulged twice very hard against us. This noise, which sounded like to guns, awaked all the passengers, and hearing that a ship was aboard, we presently thought we were boarded by the French. Our master soon came [4] to us in the cabin and told us how it was, and that the flyboat got off without doing more damage than breaking off some carved work on our stern to the value of five or six pounds sterling.

At ten o'clock we lay by for two or three hours (the tide being against us), in hopes when the ebb came, to get up the Maas to Rotterdam. But the bad weather increasing, we could not put into that river, so resolved to make the first harbour we could, which proved to be the Goeree, whereupon we anchored before Helvoetsluis at three o'clock in the afternoon, and soon after got a fishing boat to carry us from our ship to Helvoet town, which is a small village but very pretty and is now fortifying with a wall and a ditch.

There we hired two waggons which brought us to the Briel and there lodged the first night [in Holland]. My son Richard still continued very ill to that degree as made me almost repent of bringing him over. But everybody else was well, especially my son Robert, who expressed every day more cheerfulness and courage than is usual for a boy of his years.

The Briel is a fortified city, not very strong nor large, but very pretty. It consists in one or two long streets, has a good stadthouse and two or three churches, whereof one is very large; the other was the English church in Queen Elizabeth's days. The trade of it is chiefly fishing, and it is a port for shipping as Gravesend is in England. The packet boats to England did formerly lie at this port, but ever since the war [1688] have used Helvoetsluis, which lies about two leagues southward from it. Besides the regular fortifications of this town, it is surrounded with very high trees which yield at some distance a most pleasant prospect.

Justinian Isham, 1-27 May (11 May - 6 June) 1704

[1] Monday May 1st O.S. 1704. Tuesday 2nd Anno Domini 1704, being the day appointed for my cousin [Edmund] Turner's and my departure for Holland, and

places being accordingly taken in the Harwich coach, my father and grandfather thought fit we should lie at the inn to be readier next morning. My grandfather's house was chosen for the rendez-vous, from whence we went after supper at about eleven o'clock to the Saracen's Head in Aldersgate [Aldgate], where we lay.

Tuesday 2nd. Between seven and eight o'clock in the morning we took coach in company of another. In ours was one Doctor [Abraham] Silk's, surgeon to Brigadier [Thomas] Farrington's regiment, with his wife. In the other were one Mr Webb and Mr Parrot (who were going to Italy, from whence they designed to winter at Malta and then to Constantinople), Mr Du Gré and Sainclair, his governor, and a Dutch boy. At a quarter past twelve we came to Brentwood, where we dined. About two we took coach again, and at a quarter past six we came to Witham, where we lay.

Wednesday 3rd. We set out between six and seven in the morning and got to Colchester about half an hour after nine, dined and stayed there till half an hour after twelve, and between five and six arrived at Harwich, where we took up our quarters at the sign of The Angel and Town of Rotterdam.

[2] Thursday 4th. I spent my time in walking about, and especially on the seashore, it being the first time I saw that element.

Friday 5th. There being no likelihood of a fair wind, we took a turn to Ipswich by water [river Orwell] in a wherry. We arrived there at about twelve o'clock, having set out at a quarter past seven in the morning, and went to the White Hart. We did not find any diversion in town except that of cockfighting, though there had been before we came great racing and dancing. So we walked about the town, which is pretty large.

Saturday 6th. We set out again from Ipswich by water at half an hour past ten in the morning and arrived at Harwich by two.

Sunday 7th. I went to church, morning and afternoon, which is unusual, for they have but one sermon at Harwich and another at Doverchurch [Dovercourt], two miles from thence, but Mr Samby, chaplain to the artillery, etc., preached in the morning. From Monday 8th to Sunday 14th nothing remarkable happened.

Monday 15th. The wind being at northwest, at seven o'clock in the morning, the Marlborough and Dolphin, two packet boats, set sail for Holland. Aboard of whom they said were near three hundred passengers. After their departure, some horses for recruits were begun to be embarked, which was performed by the afternoon, about which time the convoy [3] came, consisting of two English men-of-war, the Bonadventure and Pool (the latter commanded by Captain Hughes; I had an order from the Admiralty to go aboard), and four Dutch. We thought then of going, but the wind suddenly chopped about to south-east. Towards night, the Phubbs yacht, commanded by Captain [Richard] Byron, came up as far as the town and set ashore my Lord [Lieutenant-General John] Cutts and other officers.

Tuesday 16th. The wind being turned again to northwest, and the Pool lying so far out at sea that we could not conveniently get aboard of her, we made use of the

Marlborough sloop, Captain Cannon commander, which is a free vessel that carries merchants' goods and passengers without a pass as also the mail when there is no packet boat on the side where she is. She was hired to keep along with the convoy. Mr Hambden and his lady, Brigadier Webbe, Colonel Wynne and Doctor Samby were aboard of her. We hoisted sail between five and six in the morning, but about noon the wind chopped about to northeast, so that we were forced to cast anchor off Orford Haven, where we lay all night.

Wednesday 17th. We lay at anchor all day and all night and, it being hard blowing weather, we rolled pretty much, which made most of the passengers and some of the seamen very sick.

[4] Thursday 18th. The wind being always easterly, instead of going to Holland, we came back again to Harwich, which was not very disagreeable to us for we were glad to get ashore anywhere rather than lie so at anchor. We weighed about ten in the morning, lay by for a while, then set sail and arrived at Harwich between one and two. Friday 19th, Saturday 20th, Sunday 21st the wind continued contrary.

Monday 22nd. We returned on board with a south-westerly wind. Between eleven and twelve o'clock in the morning, we set sail, but about two we lay by near Orford, because the commodore's boat was ashore to bring off Lieutenant-General [Richard] Ingoldsby. That night we sailed again, but afterwards cast anchor.

Tuesday 23rd. Between three and four in the morning, we weighed anchor, but dropped it again about seven. This day were several false signals and motions made, and the wind came contrary.

Wednesday 24th. At four o'clock in the morning the anchor was weighed and dropped about six; between eleven and twelve it was weighed again, and cast about one. At seven o'clock at night we set sail, the wind south-east, but cast anchor again.

Thursday 25th [5] We weighed anchor at four in the morning and dropped it at eight, but presently after weighed and sailed; wind south-west.

Friday 26th. Our men espied land. At six o'clock in the morning they cast anchor and at eight weighed it. A calm forced us to anchor again, but after that we weighed, sailed and cast anchor about two hours from Hellevoetsluis. We might easily have got there that night had not the tide been against us, which occasioned some disturbances aboard us, for Brigadier Webbe, who came over in our sloop thinking it practicable, pressed mightily Captain Cannon, commander of the sloop, to endeavour it. But he answering something surlily, which is natural enough to those sort of people especially in such an occasion, the brigadier struck him; at which they closed but were immediately parted, and I think after they came to Rotterdam the matter was made up. The first land I saw of Holland was that of Schouwen.

Saturday 27th. At three o'clock in the morning we left the sloop and went into a Dutch vessel for Hellevoetsluis; we coasted the island of Goeree. Nigh the quay of Hellevoetsluis, where we arrived by five, I was shown the place where lay sunk the

Vigo, an English man-of-war that was driven there by the great wind that happened the 8th of November 1703. I stayed about an hour and viewed the fortifications, which are pretty strong, especially towards the sea, and then set out in a postwaggon for the Briel, which is reckoned about an hour and a half, and came there between six and seven.

This city is walled round, and several new works are adding to it so that they reckon it will be a place of good defence. I saw the Doelen, which is a public house in every city of Holland, with a room hung with a picture or two of the chief officers of the burghers under arms, where the magistrates meet once a year. I was in the church, which is very neat, and up the steeple, which has 318 steps, from whence one has a fair prospect of the island of [6] Voorne, in which Den Briel is situated. I was told that upon one side of the steeple was a watch-house which was blown down with a man in it by the great wind.

Having dined, we took a boat at half an hour after two, which carried us across the Maas to Maaslandsluis, a fisher village two hours from Den Briel. We landed at a quarter past six, there being little wind and contrary to us. So missing of the boat that goes at six o'clock to Rotterdam, we took a postwaggon to carry us thither, which is about three hours. We passed in our way through Vlaardingen, Schiedam, one of the cities of Holland, and Delfshaven. We came to Rotterdam between nine and ten o'clock and lodged at the Crosskeys in Erasmus's place.

James Thornhill, 21 May - 9 June (1-20 June) 1711

[10] The pass for Holland cost us two guineas and sixpence from the Secretary's office, in which all our names were particularly inserted, and more might have been for the same money, as it is a certain custom [fixed duty] and rate. The pass when we came to Harwich we delivered to Mr Bickerton, clerk to Mr Richard Grey who is commissioner there, and who keeps the pass and gave us the following ticket: May 23rd, 1711. Receive on board the Prince packet boat Messrs Edward Strong, Thomas Strong, James Thornhill, Joseph Roberts, John Beaver [servant], George Turner [servant, four] whole and [two] half [fares]. Richard Grey. We gave him a crown as a free gift, and paid each twelve shillings sixpence for our respective passages, and six shillings sixpence for each of our servants [...]

[12] Harwich coach comes Tuesdays and Fridays from the Saracen's Head near Aldgate, per each man sixteen shillings, and lie at Witham. In Harwich passage-boat (45 tun) per each passenger three shillings. Go from Harwich Saturdays and Tuesdays and are in London next morning if a right wind. Tuesday and Friday being the foreign post nights in London, the mail arrives at Harwich Wednesday and Saturday evenings, so that, wind and weather permitting, the packet sails Thursday and Sunday about two o'clock, contriving to be on neither shore in the night time [...]

There are in all five packet boats that go betwixt Harwich and Holland. The

View of Harwich, 1711

Dolphin, the Eagle, the Marlborough, the Dispatch, the Prince. [...] The packets make twenty voyages each in a year, in all a hundred. The packet boat is about sixty tun and carries a hundred men, sailors and all, but on occasion will carry 150 souls. The captain of a packet boat has ten pounds sterling per month, but by letting his cabin, etc. makes as good advantage as some [captains of] men-of-war by the benefit of victualling his ship. [...]

[14] Friday seven o'clock, the Eagle packet boat came out from Helvoetsluis, and arrived at Harwich at three o'clock Saturday afternoon; we saw her come to anchor. We observed their goods under examination at the custom-house, viz. portmanteaus, cloak-bags, etc. Advice: Grease, but do not clog the wheels, give nothing to the customs-men that come on board you when the packet comes in. Have nothing in your pockets that you fear losing. Bleed according to your illness, but take not away too much. When you give your key [of your portmanteau] shake hands with five or ten fingers according to your case.

If you have a night-gown that is fine, wear it into Harwich, and it is safe and just. It is good to take a sharp [quick-witted] postboy from Harwich in order to pass through Manningtree, where the coach is generally searched and then you are past all danger. You may make up and wear six shirts and ruffles, etc.

[27] Thursday June 7th. Wind at north but unsettled. We set sail at three o'clock [in the] afternoon, with Lord Orkney and several gentlemen: Sir Edmund Doyly,

Mr Lilly of The Hague, Mrs Green, a niece of Pennington's at Rotterdam [...], and Mr Marret (whose mother keeps the Flower Pot near the Duke of Somerset's [house at] Charing Cross) in the Prince packet boat in company with the Eagle and Marlborough. They each carried two mails and the Prince packet but one, because it was his turn to go first.

At our first setting sail, the weather threatened us with thunder, lightning and stormy weather, some flashes appearing strongly in the west and south, the sky black. But the wind set us well out for about five leagues, when of a sudden we were becalmed. However, though the wind tacked to a full east for a time, then wavering, still we kept on till about twelve at night when arose so brisk a gale that before nine in the morning we made the Goeree, and landed at Helvoetsluis.

We kept chiefly above deck to avoid sickness and to observe the newness of such a scene. The Marlborough and Eagle went into the dock or head, but the Prince stood off at sea a little way as usual, being the first that was to return for England, so that a large boat took us and our baggage ashore, which we all thought more troublesome than all our voyage from England, it being very close, hot and [the boat] rolled prodigiously: clean without and handsome and inconvenient within.

Sixpence each passenger paid for his carriage ashore, four pence each trunk; for cloak-bags nothing. Then came down an army of wheelbarrows to wheel our things up to any public house. We, as recommended by Mr Lilly of The Hague, went to the Crown, Mr Lovel's. At Helvoet we paid the same for the wheelbarrow carriage as for the boat to come ashore, and indeed, the price is in these cases just what the watermen can get of you. At our entrance to Helvoet we paid sixpence each for head-money.

[28] After our refreshment at Helvoetsluis, we walked with Mrs Green to Nieuwenhoorn and thought to reach the Briel by six o'clock, but the weather being close and hot, and our shoes tired, we took a coach-waggon thence to the Briel, which is from Helvoetsluis seven or eight miles, but a most pleasant way. The coach-waggon held us all seven and cost five and a half pence each, or what they call a bad skilling. At Nieuwenhoorn we drank the beer called the white beer of Liège and a brown beer, both indifferent good. Oudenhoorn we saw on the right going to the Briel.

As we approached the Briel, we were surprised at the beauty of the fosse and the bastions, drawbridge and the whole fortification, being notwithstanding its strength more like the several slopes and descents in a garden than a work to defy an enemy. At our entering the great gate a sentinel, according to custom and for form's sake, asked us whence we came. We told him from Helvoetsluis. 'Ben you van Engeland', says he. 'Yes', we replied. 'Dat is wel'. So we alighted from our triumphal car and walked through this pretty and clean town to Mr Shaw's at the Golden Lion, by the waterside over against the drawbridge, a good house. Civil usage, good pontac, we paid thirty stivers. For strawberries a penny a cup, which held near half a pint. [...]

Then we took boat for Maaslandsluis, about three leagues. The Maas was prodigious rough, whole waves dashed over our heads, which had like to have spoiled our strawberries which we were demolishing. There are abundance of salmon fisheries on this great river. At our landing at Maaslandsluis, our goods were wheelbarrowed, as before, to the commissary's, who keeps the Golden Lion, though we should have gone to the Blackamoor's Head as Mr Lilly desired us. But being [30] so full of people, we went to the place aforesaid, viz. the commissary's. I observed the entry was paved with black and white marble inlaid like large checkers, etc., the side as high as your elbows or higher, done with white galley tiles. The rooms were neat, but it is enough to break your heart to get into the bed and it is dangerous lest your break your neck as you get out again; and [they] are so short that it is impossible for a short man to lie at length. There are leeboards to keep you from falling out in the night, and which can be but on one side because [they are] generally against the side of the room like those in a hospital or a press bed.

The rooms were pretty large, their brass, pewter, earthenware mighty clean and bright, beyond what I have heard before. The very stable there was done with clean galley tiles from the rack staves to the side of the manger which touches the horse's breast. However, the accommodation as to eating was but very moderate: rook-flesh or hung beef and good butter being the fare and cheese with carraway seeds in it, to us not over-pleasant; and moll, a kind of bottled small oat ale, which comes from Nijmegen only, and one end of that town neither, and white wine very sweet, called soete [sweet] wine.

This town consists chiefly of fishermen who go to northern England, etc. herrings, salt fish, etc., famous for hands [sailors]; the women [also work]. Saturday 9. At eight in the morning the commissary's bell rang for the treckschuit to be gone, as it does there every two hours till seven at night, after which you must hire one. We went in for Delft (Schipluiden on the left) and were resolved not to reach The Hague till the evening, which we did accordingly about six at night.

Harwich
Population: 3,000 (c.1825).
Distances: London 71 miles, Den Briel and Hellevoetsluis 90 miles.
Inns, *Reisboek* (1689, 1700 and 1721): De drie Koppen; De Kroon; De Lely; Het Kanon. *Reisboek* (1700 and 1721) also: Den Engels; De Vries.

Dover
Population: 3,000 (c.1700).
Distances: Calais 21 miles, Dunkirk 40 miles, London 71 miles, Oostende 60 miles.
Inns, *Reisboek* (1689, 1700 and 1721): De Stad Amsterdam. *Reisboek* (1700 and 1721) also: Den Engel.

Den Briel
Population: 3,600 (1620), 1080 houses (1632), 940 houses (1744).
Distances: Delft $3^1/_2$ hours (9 miles), Hellevoetsluis 2 hours (5 miles), Maassluis $1^1/_2$ hours (4 miles), Rotterdam 4 hours (12 miles).
Inns, *Reisboek* (1689): De Doelen; Amsterdam*; Dort*; 't Witte Hart*. *Reisboek* (1700 and 1721) also: In Rotterdam*.

Hellevoetsluis
Population: 154 houses in 1732 (T.S.).
Distances: Den Briel 2 hours (5 miles), Harwich 90 miles.
Inns, Nugent (1749): The Three Cups, Mrs Wickham.

Amersfoort

John Talman, 11-12 September 1698 N.S.

[4] From Soest I travelled through spacious roads set with trees. About half an hour before I came to Amersfoort, which is four great hours from Naarden, nine from Amsterdam, I passed by two fine houses opposite to one another. Before I entered the city I passed through two brick gates of which there are four more. Here I lodged. The city is encompassed with a fosse and an old brick wall; of a round figure; bigger than Delft. The houses are not unhandsome, the streets conveniently broad and straight; here are two Presbyterian churches, two Catholic and one Lutheran church. The steeple of one of the Presbyterian churches [Kleine Kerk or Our Lady's Chapel] is one of the finest I have seen in the Seven Provinces. It has three balconies, two in the square part of the tower, which is of brick. From this second balcony the tower rises in an eight-square figure built of stone and open on all sides. On the outside between [the piers of] one of the windows hangs a fine chime of bells. It was very pleasant to see them play; the clapper and the iron bars on which the bells hang being painted red, and the bells kept clean and bright.

From hence I ascended a round stone tower standing in a corner of this building, to the third balcony to which height I ascended by 450 stone steps. Here the woodwork is clothed with lead. From hence I ascended to two other storeys by 60 ladder steps, in one of which are two cisterns of water to be ready in time of fire. Above this place I had a noble prospect of Rhenen, a city four hours from hence situated on the Rhine, of Utrecht also about four hours [5] distant, of Amsterdam nine hours distant, of Naarden, the Zuiderzee, of Arnhem in Gelderland, etc. Here the timberwork is covered with copper. The staircase of this tower is very light, clean and compact. This tower is joined to the church by a handsome brick arch.

Not much farther is the marketplace, by that the Great Church. It stands on one side [of] a square; at the end is the stadhuys, an old building (on the side opposite to the church, over the houses appeared the aforementioned steeple). The church has an aisle on each side [of] the nave, which is supported by stone pillars; the ceilings are arched of an equal height adorned with yellow flowers. The entrance into the nave is through a portico consisting of two rows of pillars, six in a row. They support a sort of a gallery standing on arches that spring from the pillars, all carved. The two doors are adorned with brass rails; in the middle of one of the aisles is a handsome double organ. At some distance behind is painted in grey on a wall St George killing the dragon; the church is dedicated to the saint (and the arms of the city is a cross gules on a field argent).

View of Amersfoort, 1749

In the other aisle is the tomb of [Jacob] Van Kampen [Campen], the architect that built the famous stadhuys of Amsterdam; the tomb is but small, fixed up against a wall. On a black marble stone, about a foot and a half square, supported by two white marble modillions, stands an hourglass with a death's head on it, encompassed with seven little boys, above whom appears a shield in which is a serpent with his tail in his mouth, the emblem of eternity. The monument take drawn from the original. The epitaph which is in Dutch and written in gold letters runs thus: Die aerts Bouer uyt de Stam / Van Kampen rust here under, / Die t'rechtHuys t'Amsterdam / Gebowt heft, t'achste Wonder. Jacobus Van Kampen / obiit 13 Septembris / 1657 [the great architect of the Van Kampen family reposes below this. He built the city hall of Amsterdam, the eighth wonder of the world].

[6] The city is watered by a small river called the Eem, which within the city is divided into two streams, but joining without. After a circular course of about two hours and a half in length [it] empties itself in the Zuiderzee. Here is in this city a garrison of two companies of horse. Belly provisions are very reasonable here.

Going out of the city I passed through three old brick gates. From hence I went through fields for half an hour together full of tobacco, planted on beds about a foot and a half high and great furrows between. The reason is they tell me because this plant, unless it has more than ordinary dung, and to fill up the space between the rows of tobacco, would be too much charge. When they gather the tobacco to dry it they pluck the leaves (leaving the stalk standing), which are of a fine lively green, long and taper, the taste bitter. These they put in great baskets and carry away to the drying houses; then they split the leaves towards the end where it grows to the stalk; after that they hang them on sticks whose ends are held up by ropes.

The houses where they thus hang to dry are long buildings built for that purpose, with openings all round to let in the air. It is observed that the land on which tobacco has grown, they often plough and sow with corn; the stalks of the tobacco they break to pieces and let them lie in the ground, which for two years together will need no dung, and the corn that grows on such land is reckoned the best. I have not only seen fields of tobacco hereabouts, but in several places besides in this province, and they drive a great trade with it.

The next place I saw was a little village called Hoevelaken, upon the entrance of the province of Gelderland, about an hour from Amersfoort. Here in this province I had first a sight of rising ground. I passed through roads, on each side beset with wood and watered with clear streams, which with many other brooks run into the Eem, a little before that river enters Amersfoort.

Here I saw the manner of carrying the corpse to the grave, which was thus. First came a waggon with the corpse, at each end sat two women, clothed in long black robes with hoods to each, hung over their faces. Next followed twenty men in black, two by two, [7] after them the waggons full of women, and then came some more men on foot, in mourning like the former. This is the manner when they carry the corpse from one town to another. [cont. Arnhem and Zutphen]

John Farrington 19-20 November 1710 N.S.

[260] At five minutes past twelve we left Loo for Amersfoort. We had both bad way and bad weather; it blew and rained very hard so that we were forced to keep close under the cover of our waggons and be content to pass almost eight hours without any prospect. We reached Amersfoort at eight that night. Lodged at the Doelen or the tavern which the magistrates use, where we were well used. We had good lodgings, but it was so late we could get but indifferent provisions.

Wednesday November 20 we walked on the ramparts of the town, but there are no great matter of fortifications besides a ditch and pretty high brick wall. Their other fortifications or outworks were levelled when the French took this city in 1672. From the tower of the Great Church [=Our Lady's Chapel], which beside the ladders is 350 steps high, we had a good prospect of the town and country round about it, as far as the [state] of the weather would permit.

This city is far from being so small as the gazetteer represents it, who in my opinion errs egregiously both in the accounts he gives of cities as in their distances, too, in which, measuring geometrically, he often falls short near an half. It is as large as Nijmegen or Zutphen, neither of which are small cities. It has two large Calvinist churches, one Arminian [Remonstrant] and one Lutheran, and four small Popish chapels. The trade of the town is chiefly in tobacco plantations, which we saw from the top of the tower, as also the houses where they cut it. The town is situated pleasantly enough on the river Eem; it is well enough built; the stadthouse and churches are the chief buildings in it. While we stayed here, the weather continued fair, but no sooner did we get into our [261] waggon, but it began to rain and continued so to do all the day.

Population: 6,000-7,000 (1660-1720).

Distances: Amsterdam 9 hours (25 miles), Deventer 11 hours (30 miles), Naarden 4 hours (12 miles), Utrecht 4 hours (14 miles), Zwolle 14 hours (41 miles).

Inns, *Reisboek* (1689, 1700 and 1721): De Doelen*; De Witte Swaan*; De Vergulde Swaan*.

Further reading

Rerum Amorfortiarum scriptores duo inediti, Leiden 1693.

H. Halbertsma, *Zeven eeuwen Amersfoort*, [Amersfoort-Veenendaal 1959].

Ach Lieve Tijd, 900 jaar Amersfoort en de Amersfoorters, B.G.J. Elias (ed.), Zwolle 1987.

Flehite, tijdschrift voor verleden en heden van Oost-Utrecht, 1964-

Amsterdam

William Lord Fitzwilliam, May-June 1663

[15v] Amsterdam is one of the most famous cities of the world. It lies in Holland of which it is the fifth town. It lies as if it were in the jaws of Neptune. The river Amstel runs by it, from whence it is called Amsterdam, which is as much to say as Amstel's dam, the river Amstel's bank, etc.

This is now the chief magazine of Europe, as Lisbon is of the Indies; but truly this town may claim this title as much as the other, for whatsoever the Old or New World produces may here be found. The town is divided into old and new, both of them of late very much augmented and yet they are to be made a quarter bigger [so] that it will be, when it is all built, bigger than Paris or London. It is surrounded with above thirty very well-made bulwarks and great ditches; besides that, in case of necessity, she may set herself wholly in water whensoever she pleases. The arms of Amsterdam have been formerly a little ship called a kogge, wherein did stand two Holland counts. Now their arms are crowned with an imperial crown, bestowed on them by Maximilian, King of the Romans, and are supported by two lions.

Amsterdam is governed like all other towns of Holland by a mayor or schout, four reigning burgomasters and four [eight] non-regent, nine scabini and thirty-six senators, those are the chief magistrates. Besides these, there are many other inferior dignities, and several charges likewise in the Admiralty and military court. Their church government consists likewise in the secular power, only the ministers and elders govern under them.

This town, lying in marshy ground, is very unfit for to be built upon, wherefore if any great fabric is to be erected, there must be first driven into the ground an infinite number of stakes and great pieces of wood, above forty or fifty foot deep and [16r] those very close one by another, which costs an infinite deal of money and as much and more than the whole superstructure. Yet for all that, there are abundance of rare buildings both profane and religious.

In the old part of the town there is the Old Church, a great and stately building, having a very high steeple and very rare chimes on the top of it. Before the choir in this church are these following words written:

T misbruyck in Godes kerck allenghskens ingebracht
Is hier weer afgedaen in 't jaer tachentigh acht.

[The abuses gradually introduced in God's church,
have here been removed in the year 1588].

Before the burgomasters' seat these words:

Twist, hoverdy en Overdaet
Doen dat geen huys seer langh en staet.

[Discord, pride and extravagance
result in a house not standing very long].

The great organ of this church has few or none like it in the Netherlands. On one side of the choir is the tomb of the famous sea captain Jacob of Heemskercken [Van Heemskerk]; on the other side is the tomb of another valiant sea-hero called Cornelis Janson [Janszoon] of Amsterdam, called otherwise Cock ['t Haantje]. Upon the windows you will find many old pieces of painting of Philip the Good [the Handsome] and his wife, Christ's nativity, and Mary's and Elizabeth's salutation. Behind the choir is a new piece which represents King Philip [IV] of Spain's coronation [=inaccurate] and his signing with his own hands the peace with the Seven United Provinces [1648].

The other chief church is called New Church, the first founder of which was one William Eggaart [Eggart], steward to William [VI], the 24th Earl of Holland, and merchant of Amsterdam. It was burnt anno 1645 and rebuilt by the city. On one side of the choir, you will find between two pillars the tomb of this William Eggart with his coat of arms and epitaph in Low Dutch. Within this church is a most curious wrought pulpit, all of wood but very neatly carved. The door and entrance of the choir [16v] is made of great brass rails. Here is likewise a very great organ, which is supported by great marble pillars. The windows above two doors are finely painted; one represents Earl William giving the city of Amsterdam a new coat of arms, the other Maximilian, King of the Romans, crowning them with an imperial crown. Behind the pulpit is the tomb of the famous sea-hero John of Gaalen. He lies cut out in marble and his epitaph is as follows:

Generosissimo Heroi
Johanni à Galen
Essensi [...]

[to the generous hero
Johan van Galen,
born in Essen ...]

Upon some other windows there is painting-work representing the peace of the United Provinces with the King of Spain. Besides these two [17r] churches, there is Nieuwe Zijds Chapel, Old Zijds Chapel, the oldest church of Amsterdam,

Town hall, 1663

Westerkerk, on the top of which stands Maximilian's imperial crown, Southkerk and Northkerk. Besides these, there are many lesser churches, as the English, French, High-Dutch. Many sects have their meeting places; Lutherans, Arminians have here likewise their churches. The Jews have a synagogue; here live many thousands of them. In one of their houses, we saw a circumcision and in another Solomon's Temple and court, the children of Israel's journey in the wilderness of Egypt, all this very prettily made of paper or suchlike thing, and very conformable to the story of these things of the Old Testament.

The convents and cloisters, of which there has been here a very great quantity, are turned into profane or religious and pious houses. The Reguliers convent, which is before the Reguliers port [gate], is now a physic [botanical] garden. By St Joris Chapel is a place called It Pant [Het Pand], where all sort of rare carved wood-work is to be seen. Within St Peter's Chapel there is flesh to be sold; above it is the anatomy house. St Lucy's cloister is now an orphan house, all the rents of this cloister and of the Carthusian are given to this house. St Joris Hof is a dwelling place for aged citizens, who for a little money are maintained here with their wives as long [17v] as they live; this has been formerly the Paulinianen kerk and convent. Out of the old and new nunnery and St Peter's and St Elizabeth's hospital is made a famous great hospital for men and women, for all sort of sick persons of either sex, for wounded and maimed soldiers and for poor travellers, who are here maintained three days for nothing. This place is called 't Gasthuys.

Besides this, there is another hospital for old men and women, called the old men's house, in which there is a well of fresh water, which is a great rarity in Amsterdam. Another house there is for leprous persons, another for madmen, which has two courts wherein there are about forty or fifty huts. There is likewise a house for French orphans and places for to maintain poor housekeepers and poor widows. Besides these pious houses, there are many houses of correction, viz. the Spinhouse for women and the Raspelhouse for men. Upon the gate of the Raspelhouse there is carved out in wood a loaded waggon drawn by lions, bears and wild swine, with this motto: Virtutis est domare quae cuncti pavent [it is deserving to bridle that which everybody fears]

Here are many public houses as the Exchange or Beurs, a very great and stately building but not so good as that of Antwerp or London. They sell likewise some things above it. The East India Company has many noble houses without and within the city, which are well-filled up with all sort of precious merchandise. [18r] To this company belong the best ships of Holland. Upon their own cost they wage war in the New World. The West India house is likewise worth a man's sight. It stands now upon the Old Sconce [Oude Schans] on the river IJ. Here has likewise the Groenlandish Company a house, who by catching of whales gain a great deal of money.

But above all, the town house of Amsterdam deserves to be seen; it is one of the wonders of the world. It did rise like another Phoenix out of the ashes of the old one, which was burnt anno 1652 in three hours' time. The money in the bank, all the papers and town's writings and some other things were saved. This present [house] is a thousand times more sumptuous than the former was. It is built of a fair white stone and very much according to the exactest rules of architecture. Only the entrance into it and the place where it stands cannot escape man's censure, for they are not proportioned to the bigness of the fabric.

The east frontispiece, all of marble, represents Amsterdam as a crowned woman, having sea and land and all what is in it under her feet. The west frontispiece is not yet finished, nor the tower on the top of this house. Within the house you see nothing but marble: the ground whereon you tread and the pillars and all other ornaments are of marble rarely cut out, and all adorned with precious pictures. All the rooms are big and large enough. In the burghers' hall you tread heaven and earth under your feet, that is to say, the earthly and heavenly globe is curiously [18v] made upon the ground of that hall. Below this hall are the prison, the Bank of Amsterdam and other little chambers. This house has cost an infinite deal of money and perhaps will cost as much more, before it is finished. By this house stands another, where all merchandise is weighed, which brings every year to the town about two hundred thousand guilders.

The Admiralty deserves in the next place to be seen, and is one of the most curious things of Amsterdam. Here is kept all ships' provision; not the least rope is wanting. With this provision they set out completely a ship. When it comes back from its voyage, it must give an account of everything it has received. Is anything lost or spoiled negligently or maliciously, they to whose charge such things are committed are severely punished. Otherwise, they are supplied with new things instead of the old or lost ones. Every ship has its provision apart, and so upon the least occasion may be made ready. Upon the top of this house, there is always sixteen hundred tuns of rainwater kept, which by pipes and cocks can be conveyed through the whole house, which is very necessary in case this house should be set on fire. It is a hard matter to get into this place; by the means of one of the Lords of the Admiralty, called Mr of Alteren, Heer van Jaarsvelt, who went with us, we saw it.

By this house, on one side is the haven, which extends itself as far as the place called the Old Heeren House [Oude Stadsherberg] and further, where you see the bravest ships, both for traffic and war, and abundance of little pleasure boats: a forest in one word upon the water. [19r] On the other side of the Admiralty there is the new East India House, and here the city is begun to be augmented. The fortifications are almost done and several houses are already built. Here are two public houses called Heeren Logements, where all great persons and ambassadors are entertained. Here is likewise a public house called the Schouwburg, where twice a week comedies are represented. Here are two good schools and a *gymnasium* where the three faculties are read, to which belongs a very good library. Besides all these buildings there is a pesthouse out of the Heyligeweghs port [gate]. Many houses and gardens called dools [doolhof, i.e., maze], where the common people take their recreation, in which you will find all sort of puppet play and good waterworks.

Here are divers marketplaces of which the fish-, corn- and oxen marketplaces are the chiefest. Here are likewise many fair and great streets, amongst which the Heerengraft, Keysers and Princengraft with the Cingle [Singel] and Warmer [Warmoes] Straat are judged to be the chief. The latter is counted the richest of Amsterdam. Most of the streets are planted with trees and through them runs water, which if it was fresh it would make Amsterdam the Paradise of the world. Yet these ditches, although they are not pleasant, yet they are very convenient, for by their means merchandise may be brought up by water to everyone's house, which saves abundance of charges. Over these ditches there are everywhere fair bridges. At last Amsterdam has four landgates called Haarlemmer-, Heyligeweghs-, Reguliers- and St Anthony's port. On the water there are two gates. Out of the Haarlemmer- and Reguliers port are many saw-mills; and this is all which I observed at Amsterdam. [cont. Noord-Holland]

Richard Holford, 8-10 (18-20) August 1671

[9v] Amsterdam so called from the river Amstel. We came thither Tuesday about seven at night, to the house of Mr Wood, an Englishman, at the White Hart, near the Old Kirk. Wednesday we saw their New Town which has been taken in, and rivers cut and stately streets built, and a stately wall and river without it. This new

town is about as big and stands upon as much ground as the old. Here are two very fine streets and good houses built, all to be let for two and a half per cent profit to weavers on purpose to invite them from Leiden [...].

[10r] We also saw several almshouses, most neatly prepared for boys and girls, with the schools, tables and lodgings apart. Mr Astrey saw a wench as tall as himself that had no hair upon her .... We also saw the Admiralty offices, incredibly well furnished. At the corners of their streets they have in many places statues and at [blank] they have placed a man in armour with a sword in one hand and a bishop's crosier over the armour, and underneath written in Dutch: the Bishop of Münster [...].

[12v] They have an excellent way to give light to passengers in the street in the night by candles set in the streets at ten or twenty yards distance. [...] We drank with Mr Goodhand at the New Stads Harbour [Herberg], and thence went to the Long Cellar, where I now saw the etc. [whores]. Thursday we went to Sardam [Zaandam] by water to see the building of the ships, and Mr Goodhand affirmed to us that the builders in the time of the late war [1665-1667] offered the States to launch every day a new man-of-war, if they might have six months' warning.

We after saw the Bethlehem [Dolhuis], a very sweet, cleanly place and full of distracted people. Then we saw the Spinhouse, another very fine, clean building and well kept, where are a great many handsome sluts put in for their ill living, etc. and [13r] are made to spin, make band, etc., lace and other suchlike, according to their several capacities. After that we went to the playhouse and there saw their acting; all their clothes of the fashion of ours in 1665, but richly laced. The stage so far in that they strain their voices extremely. Afterwards we went to the East India house, where we saw all their stores and a very great number of ships, four or five new, one whereof almost finished of a thousand tuns, called the Makassar. Their ropehouse is three hundred fathom long and all other buildings proportionable [...].

[13v] They are very curious in observing their time and to that purpose have chimes every quarter, and the clock strikes every half hour. The first time they call half, as half twelve, is half an hour before twelve, and is on a small bell; the second time is whole, as whole twelve and then the clock is upon a greater bell.

Their women are generally well, indifferent handsome faced, but not at all well-shaped, and suffer their bodies and feet to go at liberty. They seem very modest and look upon a bare breast as a great impudency. The merchants' wives and [14r] daughters adorn themselves with jewels, and are commonly very fine. [cont. Utrecht]

John Walker, 11-12 (21-22) August 1671

[3] Amstelodam[um], the metropolis of all Holland, was the next place we came to. A city of a boggy and unwholesome situation but extreme populous and large, so

that I conceive it little inferior to London and on the Herengraft and some other parts thereof far exceeding in building. Many of the merchants' houses are of the Corinthian order (in imitation of the Italians), the lower rooms generally paved with marble and on the top battlements set with figures, insomuch that it is usual to lay out ten or twelve thousand pound sterling upon a single house.

On the 12th our curiosity was diverted with a sight of the stathouse, a very costly work. The inside is [4] illustrated with variety of painting and carved marble, but the frontispiece comes far short of the rest of the work. Yet the Dutch have this salvo for it, that it was contrived for strength as well as beauty, their chief bank being lodged within it. If any be so curious to inquire further into this structure, he may procure the book of cuts of the several places and rooms belonging to it [by Jacob van Campen, published 1661]. Their Beurs is but mean and no way to be reckoned with the worst of our exchanges, but the trade of this town is so great one would think the wealth of the world were brought hither.

Here are hospitals of all sorts and sexes, for they think nothing more pernicious to the government than to suffer the meaner sort of people to live in idleness. The chimes go very delightfully most part of the day and about seven of the clock in the evening the organists repair to their respective churches and play all variety of tunes to divert and recreate the people. It is usual to have two or three of this sort of instruments in every church.

In the New Church we beheld a most glorious screen of burnished brass and a pulpit which they say stood them in fifteen hundred pounds sterling, the carving running up into a pyramid of great height. Brass in lavers or fonts are frequent with them. This town affords them a relish of all religions amongst which is a famous Jewish synagogue. The natives throughout Holland are for the most part Calvinists; their ministers are allowed of and paid their salary by the States-General and in case they are disliked, they send them their wages with a new pair of shoes, which is a certain sign they are discharged from their cure.

The inconveniences of this place are many, but one of the chiefest is that they have no fresh water but what descends from heaven, which they are forced to preserve underground in little brick houses plastered with paris. They admit of few coaches upon wheels for fear of shaking and loosening the foundations, but gliding in the manner of our sledges at Bristol. No building anywhere without piles. The grafts [canals] for the most part smell noisome in the morning, but custom makes it natural to the inhabitants. They are very strict in their laws, yet have [5] they several licentious houses as the Longen Celdur, or Long Cellar which is the tarpaulins Whetstones Park [red-light district], where they meet every night between seven and nine, and truck for love or money. Three or four stivers is a common price for a doxy.

We lodged at an Englishman's (one Browne, who lived over against the Oude Kerk) and made this observation that we were more imposed upon by our own countrymen than any other persons.

Exchange, c. 1650

Thomas Penson, 30 July - 6 October 1687 N.S.

[28] July 20/30. [After a journey in the night-schuit from Leiden] So about six in the morning we arrived safe at the famous city of Amsterdam. I soon found out my good friend Mr Joseph Norris, a watchmaker upon the Dam, and also Mr [Gerard] Valck, a bookseller, his neighbour, for whom I had letters. [29] I took up my lodging at the house of Mr Carmichell at the sign of the Two Lions in the Bantammer Street, where I had good entertainment and very civil usage. And indeed, I think my land-lady was as handsome a Dutchwoman as any was in this city.

The Great Tun was the first thing I was shown, together with five or six persons more, men and women. We crept in at the place of the taphole and being entered, found a table and benches ready placed. We sat and drank a can of wine and every-one made their mark or set the impression of their seals, of which there were many thousands (for this great tun is as eminent as the Great Bed of Ware is in England).

But before I proceed farther in these my slender observations, for ornament sake I have here placed a touch of the arms of this famous city as they were given to them by the Emperor Maximilian in the year 1488. [30] [large sketch of arms of Amsterdam] I am not ignorant that here appears bad heraldry, viz. a pale sable [black] on a field gules [red] (it being directly against the rules of good armoury to lay colour upon colour or metal upon metal). But it being the gift of an Emperor let it pass.

[31] This great city Amsterdam is a place of vast trade as appears by the great numbers of merchants who daily resort to the Exchange, which place is very large and spacious. Here also they observing the same method which I have before mentioned at Rotterdam, of shutting up the Exchange doors after the bell has done ringing. And as they are exact to their time, so they are to their places, for the pillars are numbered by figures, so that each merchant knows where to find his correspondent. And it is not without just reason that the Exchange thus speaks of herself as I have seen the picture thereof in sculpture with these verses underneath it:

> De Beurs spreekt.
> Roemt Ephesen op haar kerk
> Tyrus op haar markt en haven
> Babel op haar metzel-werk
> Memphis op haar spitze graven
> Romen op haar heerschappij
> All de wereldt roemt op mij.

That is:

> [32] The Exchange speaks
> Boasts Ephesus of her church
> Tyrus of her market and haven
> Babel of her masons' work
> Memphis of her high mountains, etc.
> Rome of her lordships
> All the world boasts of me.

The stathouse I have often viewed, which is a brave building and curiously adorned both without and within. It is the more wonderful being so great a building on so sandy a foundation as Holland, which is a place recovered (by the industry of the people) out of the sea. Nevertheless, this famous city perhaps may compare with many cities in the world for great numbers of stately and lofty buildings. But as all their foundations are secured by piles or masts of ships drove into the ground, so is this. For my curiosity [33] led me (upon the view of this vast building) to make a more strict inquiry than is common, for my own satisfaction. And though I will not pretend to decipher each particular of this stately structure (as well because I would not make the perusal of these my *Short Travels* too tedious, as that I must acknowledge it to be a work not suitable to my genius), but here I shall beg leave of your patience to take a short view of this so eminent a building, which is said to be the wonder of all nations.

This stathouse or city-house is erected upon a foundation which before the first stone was laid, consisted of thirteen thousand six hundred fifty-nine masts or piles, which is drove into the ground by engines (as I have seen an example of the foundation of a bridge which was to be laid when I was there). At this engine I saw about [34] one hundred and twenty men at work, ramming in the piles (which is about thirty or forty foot long) in great numbers and so close that at last they go so tight into the ground as a wood peg can be drove into a thick plank.

This building contains in breadth, from out to out, 282 foot, in depth 235 foot and in height (without reckoning the tower, which stands in the middle) 116 foot. At each corner of the upper part of this stathouse is a great leaden cistern, which contains an hundred tun of water which they have always in readiness in case of a dry season. For they have no fresh water in this city but the rainwater which every house also saves by such (though smaller) water-backs which is on the top of each house. In the lower part of this building is a very strong prison for criminals, a place for arms and a watch-chamber for [35] the Burgers and soldiers with a dwelling place for the goaler. Also many other conveniences too long here to mention, etc.

Having ascended the stairs I was let by two large brass gates into the great hall with a stone floor, wherein is wrought with much curiosity two large terrestrial globes and one celestial. I believe each are in the diameter about twenty foot; the letters and lines being of brass and all the other parts of natural stones of divers colours, so neat and truly inlaid that it looks as pleasant as if painted on paper or parchment. About this stately hall is distributed in divers places (but on the same floor) their several chambers or offices proper for each particular business that happens to come there, either for the administration of justice or mercy, viz. the Justice Chamber, the Secretary's Chamber, [36] the Orphans' Chamber, the Shippers' [schepenen, i.e. judges] Chamber, the Assurance Chamber, the Burger-masters' Chamber, the Shippers' extraordinary and reckoning Chamber, the Treasury Chamber, etc., all which doors are adorned with figures and histories (carved in white marble) proper for each office. Also festoons of fruit and flowers and instruments of music and other ornaments, so finely and tenderly performed that they would delight any curious eye to behold them. Nor is the outsides only thus beautified, but the insides also affords brave paintings of great masters, etc.

But descending the stairs again, I was conducted to the dire place where sentence of death is given to such malefactors as forfeit their lives to the law; who after a full trial and examination being found guilty, are here brought to receive their dreadful doom. [37] The entrance into this place is by a pair of folding doors of brass being formed in a strong open work. On the one door is wrought Jupiter's thunderbolt, on the other two swords in cross and in the middle a prodigious serpent. The inside is composed altogether of white marble wherein on the left hand I beheld four lofty pillars, the upper part of which were with great art formed for naked women (only so far as modesty permits) with drooping heads and kerchers [handkerchiefs] in their hands in such apt postures for weeping that I could almost imagine they cried aloud. Their heads were the capitals of these pillars, supporting the cornice, which is composed of death's heads, bones, serpents, adders, wings of dragons and what else looks dreadful. Between these pillars are finely carved these three stories. In the middle is the justice of Solomon concerning the live child and the dead one. On the one side is the story of Seleucus, [38] who caused one of his own eyes to be put out to save one of his son's, who had transgressed the law. And on the other side stands that of Brutus and his two sons, etc. At the upper end of this dire place is the seat (made also of white marble) for the judge or person who is to pronounce the sentence of death, etc.

There are many other things which might be taken notice of, but I think this sufficient in this place because I design to compose this work in as short a compass as I can. But before I leave this stathouse I must say something of the tower, which is placed in the middle of the top thereof, wherein is continually maintained very fine clock-work or chimes, which go of themselves at their fixed hours. The small bells hanging round the outside of the tower, which when they go, they play so true and with such brisk airy tunes that they make extraordinary pleasant music. And not only here but in divers other [39] parts and places of Holland as Rotterdam, Leiden, Delft and Haarlem I heard the like pleasantness from the bells, but more especially at Utrecht, which I shall mention hereafter in its proper place.

The Great [New] Church upon the Dam is of a very large extent and has in it many remarkable things, some of which I took more than a short view of, viz. the monument of the famous Admiral [Michiel] De Ruyter, at the upper end of the church, within the choir which is enclosed with a partition of brass, in marble finely performed. Also the marble monument of Mr John [van] Galen, one of their grand captains at sea, which stands behind the pulpit. Likewise divers other monuments for admirals, vice-admirals, etc. which remain in this church. Nor is there to be found in all their churches any curious monuments but only such as are for their sea admirals and commanders, [40] for the preservation of whose memory they spare no cost.

The pulpit in this church is curiously adorned with carved work and on the top of the sounding board is erected a towering building, which advances a great height, being ornamented with abundance of figures, which are so truly wrought that it is admired for a great masterpiece. And I think I heard the value of it (if I am not much mistaken) was three thousand pounds, but it is well worthy to be taken notice of by all travellers that go hither.

The lofty organ I there heard divers times; not only together with the people's voices in singing of psalms (who all sing by notes) but also alone at an appointed time, when some persons of quality were to be obliged by the organist, who for the space of near two hours made variety of excellent music. On the top of this vast organ is divers ornaments finely carved, but in the middle [41] thereof is placed the figure of a young virgin sitting with a songbook in one hand and the other lifted up, which is so artificially done that sometimes I could fancy I heard her pleasant voice, but she is placed so high that I might be deceived.

For the painting in the glass windows perhaps here is the finest in the world, as witnesses the story of the Emperor Maximilian delivering to them the arms of Amsterdam (being adorned with an Emperor's crown as I have already depicted them). The figures are boldly painted and much bigger than the life, which looks lusty and brave though it is placed so very high.

And not in this church only, but also in the Old Church, which stands near the middle of the Warmoes Street, I beheld delicate glass painting. And likewise the brave monument of Admiral [Jacob van] Heemskerk and another monument for Vice-Admiral [Abraham] Van der Hulst, together with several others, which would be too long to particularize. [42] This church has to it a vast high steeple, the tower whereof overlooks the whole city. And therein is kept a nightly watch, who if they perceive a fire in any part thereof, do immediately give notice by their doleful sound of trumpet. But so long as the city remains safe and well, they express it by pleasant soundings for the better part of the night, which has many times been very grateful [agreeable] to me.

The New Lutherans' Church is a fine building [1668-1671], the whole body thereof being circular. The top of this church is covered with plates of copper, which covering was the gift of the King of Sweden. The pulpit also is well worthy observation, round which is fairly carved several stories of Our Saviour's life and also that of his Crucifixion.

The Western Church is eminent for a very high steeple [43] in which is kept very pleasant clockwork or chimes. And on the top thereof is an Emperor's crown in copper of a prodigious bigness.

Many other churches I visited and viewed which I thought worth seeing, viz. the Southern Church; the Northern Church; the Eastern Church; St Olof's Chapel, which is thought to be the oldest church in this city of Amsterdam; the French church; the Arminians' church; the Anabaptists' church and the English church, which seems to be ancient. On the back thereof is the Begyne Hof, or a religious place for devout women of the Romish faith. They have neat pleasant houses and gardens adjoining to them. And although these nuns wear the religious habits, yet they are permitted to go abroad anywhere about the city. Nay I was informed that if they have a [44] mind to marry (by application to the Lords of the States) they shall also have leave to quit the nunnery at their pleasure. But if there be any nun that is likely to be worth a great fortune, the cunning priest takes care to send her to Antwerp, where the Lords have no such power over them.

The Krijtbergen or the Jesuits' church I was at on the 21st day of August, at which time was sung Te Deum, for a victory obtained against the Turks. I was favoured with a place in the gallery among the music by the interest of Mr Daniel Penning, a gentleman I met with in this city, with whom I was well acquainted sixteen years before in England, who also did me many more favours whilst I stayed at Amsterdam. Nor did I only visit the Christian churches, but also the Jews, whose temple or synagogue is a magnific building, to which I repaired more than once, being [45] informed of some of their great days on which they performed some extraordinary ceremonies, which seemed to me more like madness than order.

Having done with their churches I shall next say something as to their manner of burials, several of which I have seen and have been an invited guest to two myself. In the morning of that day the deceased is to be buried, the bier is set in the street just against the door. Between twelve and one of the clock comes the aanspreekers or servitors who are to officiate at the funeral. They usher in the guests, directing them into what chamber they shall go, etc. The company being come, the corpse is brought forth and set on the bier. The top of the coffin being flat there is set thereon a rigid frame, thus [sketch in margin], over which is laid the pall or covering, being a good piece of black cloth.

Then the corpse is [46] taken up upon the shoulders of fourteen men in mourning cloaks (which are commonly the best friends or nearest neighbours of the deceased). Thus (the people being orderly coupled and the whole company in black cloaks), the Aanspreekers go before the corpse each bearing in his hand an hour glass, and they move slowly and solidly to church, where they use no manner of ceremony or service over the grave, but immediately proceed to bury the corpse. And those fourteen friends that bear the body thither do also fill up the grave. And so the whole company return, in the same coupled order, back again to the house of the deceased, where the tables are plentifully adorned with flagons of wine and rummers [large tall glasses], which the aansprekers hand about to the company very freely. For their custom is never to serve any wine about, till the corpse is buried and the people returned home again.

Their prefixed time for burial is two of the clock in the afternoon exactly, to be at [47] the church where the corpse is to be interred. Which if they exceed, for every hour after, the friends of the deceased forfeit fifty guilders, each containing twenty pence of English money.

Here it is also to be noted that the women do never go to funerals, no not so much as of their children, as I have observed at the burial of a child. The coffin was covered with a piece of black cloth (which was set down the middle with knots of black ribbon). The corpse was carried by a man in a mourning cloak, who was followed by two other men also in cloaks, and that was all.

Hospitals or places dedicated to charitable uses are many in and about this famous city. There is for instance [48] the hospital for old men and old women that have been citizens. Being fallen to decay and past their labour, they are received into this place, where care is taken of them during life. But at their coming in, they are obliged to bring with them a good bed, three blankets, two pillows, three pair of sheets, six shifts, two stools and cushions and divers other useful things. Also two guilders in money, which is to be given into the hand of the nurse, who is to have the care of them.

Rasphuis, 1662

The hospital in the Kalver Street for poor orphans is a large building and therein is kept a thousand poor children. Their coats are composed of two colours, the one half black and the other red. [49] There is also another hospital wherein is kept fourteen hundred children.

The hospital for poor widows or women unmarried [Diaconie Oude Vrouwenhuis] is very pleasant with fine gardens and walks in the middle. It contains a great number of women. In each chamber is two beds and in each bed lie two widows. In the midst of the chamber hangs a lamp which burns all night, that if any of them happen to be taken ill they have a light ready. And so many are placed in each chamber that one may be helpful to the other.

Lazarus Huys or hospital for fools, etc. This hospital contains a great many men, women and children of that sort which we commonly call naturals. They are here kept by themselves in a handsome place and pleasant air, but are very troublesome to those who have the care of them. And although their several actions and antic postures [50] may afford diversion to the beholders, yet as a thoughtful man cannot but pity their misery, so also ought he to be touched with a thankfulness to God that he is not cast in the same mould.

Also in the madhouse (het Dolhuys) are divers miserable objects whose several actions I shall not venture to describe any farther than to say they were such as are generally to be found among madmen. Only there was one woman that had so much English as to say Our Father, and she told me the Dutch to it. Over the gate as you enter into this hospital stands the arms of this city largely carved in stone and in the midst of the garden there is advanced on a pedestal the figure of a naked woman well-carved, in a posture of raving madness, having one hand tearing her hair and the other her body.

[51] Places of correction are two, viz. the Rasphouse for men and the Spinhouse for women. The Rasphouse. This place is more dreadful than our frequent executions in England and yet but a medium between the whipping post and the gallows. And although slender corrections are performed here (such as if a man finds his son stubborn, rather than trouble himself, will send him here to be whipped), yet there are also for greater offenders heavier punishments. Their chief work here is rasping of wood, as log wood and brazil for the use of the dyers, of which each two prisoners are obliged to rasp the quantity of three hundred pound weight every week during the whole time of their confinement, which is limited according to their crimes, as upon examination I found one prisoner was [52] condemned to remain there for the space of five and twenty years without bail or main-prize. He was a young fellow but had killed a man. Another for twenty years, other ten or five, some more, some less according to their crimes and the circumstances thereof.

Sometimes they have sullen, stubborn rogues, who will not perform their task, whom they order after this manner: they have in this prison a convenient cellar whereinto the tide comes and therein stands a pump which will convey the water out again. The prisoner being put there, if he will not work at the pump, must be drowned. And really I was informed that there has been fellows put there, who would let the water come up to their chins before they would handle the pump.

The Spinhouse. Here I found also the women were not [53] without faults, by this place, which was prepared on purpose for their discipline. Their chief work is spinning flax and wool, which seems to be a work pleasant and easy enough, but only that which makes it a punishment is that each person must perform a certain task every day, and that they are constrained to endure the confinement for a month or a year, or more according to the time limited [specified], which is always suitable to their offences, whether it be whoredom, thievery or other misbehaviour. The prisoners work abovestairs in a very stately, large, light room which is kept very neat and clean. At the entering into this place are some large stone pillars, over which is written in gold letters as follows:

> Schrik niet, ick wreek geen quaat, maar dwing tot goed.
> Straf is mijn handt, maar lieflijk mijn gemoed.

That is, [54]

> Do not complain, for I desire not your hurt but your good.
> And although my hand is heavy, yet my heart is loving.

But although they have these prisons and useful places for punishing vice, yet there are also in this great city other places, which visibly encourage it. Particularly the Long Cellar, which (I was informed) is tolerated by the States for the use of strangers and travellers, whereunto they may repair and have a woman to live and lie with them, so long as they stay in the country. And they will also tell you they shall be very just to you, taking care of your linen and do whatsoever is necessary to be done for you, as if she were your faithful wife (but trust them who will, for me). I was divers times there, being curious to know the customs of the place and [55] was directed by a friend in England to a captain of a ship that trades thither, to find him every day upon the Exchange or at night in the Long Cellar. But I found him on the Exchange daily and he was so kind to go with me and show me some of the customs of the country, which perhaps I had not known but by his acquaintance. But I used it with such prudence as I thought might become me, being a stranger there.

I found the women generally very loving to Englishmen and would rather be a companion to them than any others. When I entered this cellar (which is a long place and where they always burn candles), I found divers women walking about, very neat and clean dressed. So soon as I was sat down, there came one of them to me and sat down by me and kissed me saying: 'Mijn Heer ghy sal met mijn slapen de nacht', that is [56] 'Sir, you shall sleep with me tonight'. I was no sooner set but the servant brought me a rummer of wine, for which (according to the custom of the place) I presently paid six stuyvers. Then I sat and talked and drank with my lady a little while. Soon after I saw another which walked by me, I thought much handsomer and to be preferred before the first, so I beckoned her and the other soon left me. This also was very free in her embraces and offered me all the kind things I could desire, inviting me home to her lodging, whither I went with her. Where so soon as I came in, her maid filled a large rummer of wine and set by me on the table. We tippled that off and was very merry with singing, etc. and had another filled. Nor could I ask anything of her that she did not freely impart to me. And entreated me to stay all night, which I as decently refused as I could, with a [57] promise to come to her on the morrow, which visit I ever after omitted. Thus, my curiosity led me to tread the serpent's path, but was not stung, which I must own as a blessing from Heaven since neither importunity nor opportunity was then wanting.

During my stay at Amsterdam arrived their ships from the East Indies, whose seamen are called the Lords for six weeks (Heeren van zes weeken). Most of their clothing is of the painted Indian silks and some of them do wear long rusty basket-hilted swords, stuck into a leather girdle about their waists and make very comical figures. Their pockets now being full of money, they lord it about the city and extravagantly spend their gelt. They are frequently reeling in the streets before noon and some (accompanied with their whores) will have a black boy to bear his hat before them or to go by the side of the coaches, which are thus [sketch in margin], without wheels and drawn by one horse upon a sledge. And I have seen [58] in the Long Cellar one of them (having gotten his wench by him) throw down a piece of money of eight and twenty stuivers, to pay six for a rummer of wine, would not trouble himself to count over his change but with his hand swept it into his coat-pocket, right or wrong.

Thus, in about six weeks' time (at the most), having lived like lords, their money becomes very low and perhaps a little in the landlady's debt, from whom they obtain nothing but frowns and sharp words. Then they begin to look simply and scratch where it don't itch and after all, finding no other expedient, must tack about and take another voyage to the Indies, for three years at the least and sometimes four, five or six years' time before they return. And it seems it is the policy of the States of Holland to give them any liberty while they are on shore and let [59] them live as they list. Unless they commit some signal outrages in the street, etc. they are not molested. And by this means the States never want seamen to go that voyage.

And indeed, their policy is very notable in drawing money from the people in divers manners, as for example whosoever is without the city gates after nine o'-clock, must pay a stuyver for his entrance, which very tax alone continually produces a prodigious deal of money. Again in their fairs the States build the booths for the rope-dancers and other shows, and place to each an officer with an iron money-box. And all the money that is taken in a day is put therein. And at night the players must repair to the stathouse, where the box is opened and the money divided into three parts, whereof the Lords of the States take [60] one and the players the other two. Also their collections for the poor in their churches (as I was informed) is all paid in at the stathouse. Nor is there any eminent house of trade or commerce in the city, either public or private, but there hangs one of these poor's boxes which perhaps is opened but once in a year. Likewise their passage money either by land or water, the tax on bread, beer, etc. and many hundred other ways, insomuch that it is observable that if a poor man go into Holland and have nothing of his own, but beg for his living, the States shall get forty or fifty guilders in a year by him.

I was shown the warehouse in the Kalver Street, where all kind of cabinetmakers' work is sold, as fine tables, stands, drawers, [61] presses, etc. To this place every workman in the city must bring his work that is finished and those people that are minded to buy, come hither, where a person constantly attends to sell or tell the price of anything that is there. So that a man sees at once all the choice things of that kind that are in the whole city. But at Amsterdam kermis (or fair) there was shown a wonderful curious rich cabinet, a complete piece of work made at Leiden; it was twelve years making and valued at five thousand pounds sterling.

As to their markets I viewed them all and shall only name them, viz. the fish-market, where I bought brave salmon for eight pence the pound; the two flesh-halls; the apple market; the flower market; the rag market; the pipe market; the butter market and [62] the dog market, which made me laugh heartily. I went divers market days, which is every Monday morning. There I beheld (with great diversion) dogs to be sold of all kinds, from the great mastiff to the lady's lap-dog and also cats and young kittens, etc.

Now having treated of the curs there I must not omit (by way of caution) to speak of the Jews who are nicknamed Smouses. They are the money-changers and stand frequently upon the bridges with bags of Dutch money under their arms, and if they see a stranger will say: 'Heb ghy wat gelt t' wesel myn Heer?', viz., 'Sir, have you money to change?' I say, let him that goes to Holland take care of them, for they will cheat a man to his face, although for my own part I think I was cozened but of a double stiver in the change of a guinea. [63] But it so happened that a gentleman who lodged in the same house with me at Amsterdam, brought home a Jew with him into my chamber to change twenty pounds English money for Dutch. And though the gentleman had a competent knowledge of the money himself (being a trader there), and thought it was right, but when he came to tell over the money again, and the Jew gone, there wanted near four pounds and indeed, it is accounted their common practice.

The playhouse I sometimes visited, being willing to see what diversion the heavy-heeled Dutchmen could afford on the stage, which I found to be but very indifferent. The stage is prettily adorned but the altering of their scenes is such a tedious business with them, that it mightily baulks [64] the fancy of the spectators. I saw there a French opera and amongst other plays in Dutch, that of the besieging of the city of Leiden by the Spaniards, which is accounted the best they have and is only acted about the same time of the year when it was actually besieged, which was in September 1574. Over the gateway of the playhouse is thus written in large letters, viz.

De wereld is een speel-toneel;
Elk speelt zijn rol; en krijgt zijn deel.

that is:

The whole world is but one theatre
wherein each plays his part and is gone.

[cont. Utrecht]

Sir John Percival 6-10 (17-21) July 1718

[78v] There are scarce any manufactures established in Holland but what are likewise carried on with [79r] great success in this populous city. Here they fabric cloth, camlets and all such sort of stuffs. They likewise manufacture silks, gold and silver brocades, velvets, ribbons and gilt leather. They dress leather after the Turkish and Persian way. They refine vast quantities of sugar, borax, camphor, sulphur, wax, snuff and oil. They polish marble and saw wood by means of mills at forty times a cheaper rate than we in England can afford this work. They build numbers of ships of different size for other nations. And I have heard that at Sardam, a village four

miles long and near adjoining to Amsterdam (inhabited chiefly by shipwrights), they will, after three months' notice, fit out every day a ship of four hundred and fifty tun for as long as desired. Indeed, the quantity of timber and hemp brought from Norway, Muscovy, Lower Germany, Pomerania and the provinces bordering on the Baltic Sea is incredible. The hemp is manufactured into cordage and sail cloth at home, of which their storehouses are always replete. [...]

[81v] During my stay in Amsterdam I paid a visit to the famous Monsieur [Jean] Le Clerc, by birth of Geneva but settled many years ago in Holland. When first he went thither, he preached in the Calvinist church, which is the church established. But discovering himself in his sermons and writings to hold Arminian tenets, the magistrates gave him his choice, either to preach pure Calvinism or else to quit his pulpit, whereupon he went wholly over to the Arminians, who chose him pastor and professor of divinity.

This gentleman is allowed to be one of the best critics in languages and divinity now living; in mathematics he is not so eminent. [82r] His writings have been greatly esteemed, and I have heard the present bishop of Rochester, Dr [Francis] Atterbury, say that Monsieur Le Clerc's reflections on incredulity and our English Dr [Samuel] Clerk [Clarke]'s *Metaphysical Demonstrations of a God* were writings unanswerable. This is a great confession from a prelate, the avowed head of our High Church clergy, which set of men have almost to a man scarce used Monsieur Le Clerc with common charity, imputing to him Socinianism, though openly denied by him, and spending their rage against him on all occasions, though he frequently makes honourable mention of the Church of England in his writings, and has always maintained a close correspondence with some of her most sober and learned divines.

It must be owned that the ephemerides or journals published by him have been one great occasion of the ill opinion conceived against him, because therein (his purpose leading him to give an account of books, and withal to add freely his own opinion of them) he mentioned the works of Mr [John] Locke with respect and spoke the best he could with a reserve to truth of the *Rights of the Christian Church*, a book which some years ago made great noise in England, and gave no less offence. But it should be considered that as to the writings of the first of those authors, Locke's *Treatise of Human Understanding*, there never was a modern book of greater vogue [82v] in England for a time, insomuch that it was diligently read, approved and recommended even in the University of Oxford, till such time as Bishop [Edward] Stillingfleet wrote against it.

And as to *Rights of the Christian Church*, it is not to be wondered that Mr Le Clerc, who is an Arminian, should speak well of those principles he found therein conformable to his own, though in other places he agrees not with the author. In my conversation with him, he blamed extremely the manner of preaching by book, a custom used only with us in England, which he attributes to the clergy's laziness. The original of it was, as he thinks, the injunctions put forth at the beginning of the Reformation, obliging the ministers to read the homilies.

Dr [Frederik] Ruysch, that noted physician, having quitted Leiden now resides here. But his famous collection of anatomical preparations, which I saw at Leiden in my first travels, is much diminished, a considerable part being dispersed in foreign countries. Very lately he made a present to our Royal Society of a body preserved in pickle, which is very curious and far exceeds in its use to surgeons and physicians the waxwork that came not long ago from France, and was publicly shown in London. The liquor wherein he preserves the bodies is a secret not yet communicated to the world, but answers perfectly well the design. I remember he showed me in 1708 [83r] at Leiden a child of his own, which he thus had preserved above thirteen years and which looked as fresh as when alive. [...]

[86v] The organ in this church [Nieuwe Kerk], among variety of other stops, contains a vox humana which imitates perfectly well the tenor and bass of a man's voice, as likewise the sound of a bass viol and several other instruments of music, so that an artist such as the present organist is, though blind, can alone entertain the hearers with a complete consort of vocal and instrumental music. I have met with many travellers who never heard it, which I much wonder at, being one of the greatest and most pleasing curiosities that offers itself abroad.

Within this church there are two handsome monuments where Admiral Van Galen and the famous Ruyter lie buried. The first was killed by a cannon ball in 1653 and the latter in 1676 by a wound he received in the haven of Syracuse in Sicily. He was born at Flushing in 1607 of very poor parents and was first put servant to a seaman of the neighbourhood, and before he was ten years old he received the pay of a mariner; and from that time rose gradually from pilot, captain, commodore and vice-admiral to be admiral-in-chief of the United Provinces. His tomb is of fine marble, enclosed with iron [87r] rails, through which his statue is discerned, lying at length on a bed of honour. His head is supported by a cannon, one hand upon his breast and the other holding a truncheon; underneath is a long epitaph in Dutch. [...]

[87r] Of the Rasphouse, Spinhouse, Madhouse, etc. I shall say nothing, being so [87v] very well-known. Neither shall I describe all the several houses for orphans, widows and old men. I will only speak a few words of one hospital worthy the curiosity of strangers to see, as well for the charity that appears in the ample provision made for a vast number of helpless creatures, as for the neat and careful manner in which they are used.

The hospital is erected for the maintenance of old women. There are others of the same nature, but this is the principal, built upon the Amstel in the finest and most open part of the town. The house is very convenient and large and cost fifteen thousand pounds sterling the building. In it are maintained 467 poor women, admitted when past fifty years of age. They must be of the religion established by law. It is observed that out of these there die annually about sixty. Those who by age or infirmity are judged to draw near their end, are removed out of their cells, which hold some four, other two beds and lodged together in a long gallery, kept as neat

De NIEUWE KERCK is begonnen A° 1414 volbouwt en toegewyt de Maget Maria en S! Catharina A° 1470.
TEMPLUM NOVUM fundatum eſt A° 1414 penitus Exſtructum & dedicatum S.° Catharinæ A° 1470.   F. de Wit Fecit.

The New Church, c. 1690

and as sweet as possible. The best attendance is there given them, till at last when judged irrecoverable, they are sent into the sick chamber, where they breathe their last. They are maintained in clothes, meat and all other necessaries, and several of them, old as they are, employ themselves in making [88r] tape, course lace and suchlike things, which brings them in something that helps to ornament their chamber and makes them live more at ease.

This house was built entirely by charitable contributions and is supported no other way than by collections made principally at the church doors. The money arising annually this way, if I have been rightly informed, amounts to 35,000 pounds sterling, which sum, if added to the other public provisions and establishments made for the poor, and the private and unknown charities of particular persons, of which last no estimate can be made, rises so high that I may venture to affirm the inhabitants of Amsterdam are the most charitable society of Christians this day in the world. It is said that 1,800,000 guilders, making eighteen tun of gold, or 180,000 pounds sterling, is yearly thus collected and carefully distributed. [...]

[88v] I bought here of Mijnheer Jacomo de Witt, a painter, the nephew of the merchant at Antwerp whose collection of fine paintings I formerly mentioned, a

49

small closet piece of Our Saviour and the twelve Apostles for an hundred guilders. He paints very skilfully and understands the inventing, drawing and colouring part extremely well. He is about twenty-three years old and if he goes on as he sets out, may become as eminent a painter as any of his time. I saw at his house a ceiling well-executed, consisting of several large pieces not yet finished and bespoke by Mijnheer Cromhorst [=Cromhout], one of the burgomasters. He carried me to see two collections of pictures in the hands of private persons, among which were several by very good masters.

In the first collection there was a sketch by Raphael of the famous Ascension [Transfiguration] piece which that great painter painted at Rome for the church at St Pietro Montorio. There were likewise some pieces of [Philips] Wouwermans, Mrs [Rachel] Ruysch, [Adriaen] Van der Werff and other Dutch masters.

The other collection belonged to Mijnheer C[l]ock, an eminent clock maker, where I saw a fine Magdalen by Serini [Sirani], a [89r] scholar of Guido Reni, a large painting with many figures by Vanbal [Henrick van Balen], the landscape part by [Jan] Breughel, several good pieces of flowers and fruit, a fine picture of Our Saviour and the twelve Disciples by [Nicolas] Bertin, a Frenchman, and several others of Ostade, Teniers, Rombats [Rombouts], all eminent masters in their way.

These were all the collections of this nature I visited during my stay at Amsterdam. There are others, but my acquaintances, which I made when formerly in Holland, and who would have introduced me to the sight of them, happened at this time to be out of town and it is very difficult for a mere stranger to get access into private houses, the Dutch being, in this respect as in others, much more reserved than the French or Italians.

Richard Rawlinson, 18-24 September 1719 N.S.

[16] Arrived at eight at night at Amsterdam, where I paid for entrance at the gate one stiver. From thence through the High Street of the town I came to the White Hart, behind the Old Church. [17] Tuesday, 19 September 1719 N.S. This day I saw the stadthuys, the Spinhuys, the Rasphuys, hospital and at night the Hof of France, which are public brothels licensed by the High and Mighty States.

Wednesday, 20 September 1719 N.S. Saw the gallows and wheels on which were hung and laid the bodies of several criminals executed for various crimes, after justice done before the stadthuys removed hither. They stand in a place near the river [IJ], very boggy and moist. Those which were hanged were hung on a gallows triangular of iron across three pillars of stone, in chains over a very spacious and deep well, into which their rotten carcasses dropped. Those on the wheels had several pistols over their heads to denote that they were assassins. On a pillar next the well hung a kettle, which heated set fire to a house and burnt it to the ground; this was performed by a woman whose body is exposed on a wheel near.

From thence [18] we went into the Exchange, where we saw a collection of natural rarities, of antiquities, medals, medallions, statues, inscriptions and paintings or prints of the faces of all the plenipotentiaries concerned in the treaty of Utrecht [1713], instruments for casting of medals, etc. These were brought from Utrecht by Nicholas van Chevalier, who has printed two catalogues in folio and octavo; the first with portraitures of his principal rarities, to which I refer for further satisfaction. For this we paid six stivers, as we did eight for passage to the gallows, etc. Dined with Mr Le Conte and saw the Lutheran Church, which had three storeys of galleries, and in the nave a vast number of chairs for a numerous congregation. Saw some statues near the Port Leidens, one of Pan, an antique, the other a

---

Population: 140,000 (1650), 200,000 (1680), 220,000 (1720).
Distances: Alkmaar 5 hours (20 miles), Amersfoort 9 hours (25 miles), Antwerp 30 hours (91 miles), Gouda 10 hours (30 miles), The Hague 11 hours (28 miles), Haarlem 3 hours (7 miles), Leiden 8 hours (19 miles), Rotterdam 14 hours (37 miles), Utrecht 8 hours (23 miles).

Inns, *Reisboek* (1689) gives over 90 inns and begins as follows: Het Oude Heerenlogement*; Het Nieuwe Heerenlogement*; De Doelens [not 1721]; De Munt [not 1721]; 't Rondeel in de Doelestraat [only 1689]; De Nieuwe Stadsherberg; De Oude Stadsherberg* [in the Ykant*]; De Eerste* [1721: Engels ordinaris; Mr Clark*], Tweede [1721: de middelste], Derde* [1721: or Schild van Vrankrijk], Vierde [not 1721] Liesveldsche Bijbel, De Beurs [not 1721], De Smak [not 1721], or Koning van Sweden (these six in the Warmoesstraat); Het Huis van Jeremias (Gaarkeuken in de Servetsteeg) [only 1689]. Several other lodging houses at the end of the Warmoesstraat, in d'Oude Teertuinen, 't Witte Hart, achter de Oude Kerk [only 1689], etc.
Reisboek (1700) gives over 80 inns, including most of those mentioned above; names not appearing in 1689 are: Vredenburg, aan 't eind van de Oudezijds Voorburgwal; De Groote Koning van Vrankrijk, Zijn Roomsch Keizerlijke Majesteit, De Brug van Londen, or d'Oude Prins van Oranje (these three on the Zeedijk), etc.
Reisboek (1721) gives 40 inns; names not appearing in 1689 and 1700 are: l'Etoile d'Or*, La Ville de Lions* (both in the Nes); De Stad Edenburg; Het Wapen van Deventer*; Groningen en Ommelanden*; 't Wapen van Overijssel*; De Eendracht en Parlement van Engeland*, Au Pontac* (two French ordinaries in the Kalverstraat); 't Keijzers Hof of 't Wapen van Emden* (on the Nieuwendijk); Keysers Kroon*, Hof van Holland*, Graaf van Holland* (these three in the Kalverstraat); Wapen van Zeeland*, ordinaris en gaarkeuken (Rokin).
Nugent (1749) also mentions: The Queen's Head (Johnson) in the Warmoesstraat; Green near the Exchange; 'Clark's (the English Bible) is the only one fit for the reception of genteel company as having very neat and convenient apartments, a good ordinary, and all other accommodations at reasonable rates'; Het Schild van Vrankrijk, on the Pijpe Markt; Het Wapen van Leyden, on the Singel; Het Gulden Vlies, behind the Stadhuis.

Germanicus or Venus with fine buttocks, Pan, Apollo; the three last copied at Rome and sent hither to be sold, though they have as yet met no good market [...]

Saturday, 23 September 1719 N.S. Went to visit the Admiralty House, which we were not able to see as it is not at present shewn to any without the burgomasters' leave. From thence we went to the playhouse, where we saw the comedy of Don Quixote and a foolish farce of the humour and tricks of a Dutch bawdy-house, which began at four and continued to after eight at night.

Sunday, 24 September 1719 N.S. Saw one Romish chapel and the confirmation of marriages at the stadthuys, for which we paid [21] two sest'halfs [5½ stuivers] of which we were cheated by an impudent fellow. After dinner saw the New Church, wherein are interred some admirals, to whom the States have in gratitude erected monuments which may be seen in the account of Amsterdam and the third volume of the *Histoire Métallique* [*de la République de Hollande*, Amsterdam 1690]. Saw another Romish chapel, well adorned, and the Persian church, which is small, and its altars are adorned with three crosses and a piece of the Ascension.

Further reading

J.I. Pontanus, *Rerum et urbis Amstelodamensum historia*, Amsterdam 1611 (ed. in Dutch, 1614).

M. Fokkens, *Beschrijvinge der wijdt-vermaarde Koop-stadt Amstelredam*, Amsterdam 1662, 1663, 1664.

[O. Dapper], *Historische beschryving der stadt Amsterdam*, Amsterdam 1663.

F. von Zesen, *Beschreibung der Stadt Amsterdam*, Amsterdam 1664.

C. Commelin, *Beschryvinge van Amsterdam*, Amsterdam 1693-1694, 1726.

Le guide d'Amsterdam, Amsterdam 1701, 1709, 1720, 1722, 1734, 1753, 1772, 1793, 1802.

H. Brugmans, *Geschiedenis van Amsterdam*, I.J. Brugmans (ed.), vols. 3 and 4, Utrecht 1973[2].

Ach Lieve Tijd, zeven eeuwen Amsterdam en de Amsterdammers, B. Bakker (ed.), Zwolle 1988-1990.

G. Mak, *Een kleine geschiedenis van Amsterdam*, Amsterdam 1994.

Ons Amsterdam, 1949-

Amstelodamum, maandblad voor de kennis van Amsterdam, 1914-

Jaarboek Amstelodamum, 1902-

Antwerp

William Lord Fitzwilliam, April 1663

[9r] [coming from Brussels and Mechelen] Antwerp lies likewise in Brabant and is an imperial marquisate, the fairest and most well-built city of Europe. It is situated on the river Scalde [Schelde] and on even, plain ground. Its figure is like a half-moon or rather a bow whose string is the river Scalde. Formerly, before Amsterdam began to flourish, it has been the most famous emporium [storehouse] of Europe. It is very great and strong, being surrounded with brave, great and admirably well-made ramparts and bastions whose latitude and other measures are very proportionable one to another. The walls are all planted with trees and [have] the most pleasant walks upon them that ever can be imagined. Brave, broad and deep ditches and great sumptuous gates round about the town.

The castle, which His Catholic Majesty [the King of Spain] keeps as a bridle to keep the city in awe, is one of the most exquisite pieces of fortification that ever was made. By the governor's leave we came to see it; its ambitus amounts to an Italian mile. It is surrounded with five bastions extraordinarily well-made of brick and stone; all the ramparts are undermined and upon the top of them we found above sixty pieces of ordnance (which to touch is almost crimen laesa majestatis [the crime of lese majesty]). The ditches are very broad and deep, full of water. On one side of the castle runs the river Scalde. For outworks it has very few: some ravelins and half-moon pieces, nothing else. Within its circuit are great and large magazines and ammunition houses, spacious walks, great stables and houses for the governor, soldiers, bakers, brewers, wine- and alehouse keepers. It is a little town by itself; it has everything within its walls. Here we saw some leather little boats which the Hollanders did use for to surprise with this castle [1624].

The river Scalde is by this town more than five hundred Antwerpish ells broad and almost twenty-two high [deep]; at high water it is twelve foot higher. Anyone that considers this must necessarily admire Parma's bridge [9v] which [in 1585] was made over this river about Lillo, at a village called Oordam, not far from Antwerp but where the Scalde is more than 2,400 foot broad and at least sixty high at low water. Here you will find the cleanest, fairest and broadest streets, the most handsome and uniformly built houses, a matter of twenty-four great marketplaces, a very magnific Exchange having four gates leading to it. The pillars which sustain the upper part of it are all of a different work, none like another.

We did lodge in the best street of the town, called the Mere [Meir], which formerly has been a standing water. By the means of an Englishman, called Mr

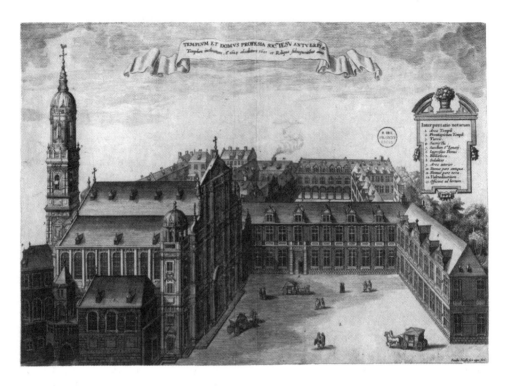

Jesuits' chapel, c. 1650

Hartop, we saw the best painting-work of this town in which it does excel any other town of the Netherlands. Our Lady's Church is the cathedral of this town, a very big and fair building, very richly adorned with gold and silver, chiefly with pictures of an inestimable price of the most famous painters that ever lived in the world. Many pieces of Rubens, Van Dyck's and Quinten's making. Quintinus [Metsys] was but a smith by his profession, but out of love for a woman (who it seems would not correspond to his affection as long as he was a smith) he went to Rome to learn to paint, and in a very short time he grew so skilful in that art, that he surpassed all the painters of former ages, and perhaps them who are to follow; all his pieces do evidence it, chiefly that picture of his which hangs over the altar of the Three Kings' Chapel of this church. Besides this chapel there are sixty-five more, all very richly adorned.

To this church belong two steeples; we were upon the top of one, which is above 620 stairs high. From it you may see towns at least sixteen leagues distant of Antwerp. Here we found about sixty-eight bells, great and little, the bravest chimes of Europe, abundance of very little singing bells (as they are called) which, by a strange kind of machine on which a fellow plays just like upon [10r] an organ, are made to play and that all sort of tunes and airs. On the churchyard we saw the tomb of famous Quinten, smith and painter. His hammer and other instruments on one side, and his pencil and other painting instruments on another. Here is likewise his iron well, which he made with no other instrument but a hammer. Here are four parish churches more, many religious houses, hospitals and bridewells or houses of correction.

The Jesuits' church and college we saw. The church is one of the most rich and rarest pieces of architecture of the world. All of it is made of Asiatic marble. It is supported by thirty-six pillars, most richly adorned with pictures of the most famous painters. Many pieces of Breughel and Rubens' making; of the latter, the father who showed us the college told us a very pretty story. A good Capuchin came to reprove Rubens for painting so many naked women and thereby making so many men to sin, how he could answer this before God? Rubens told him that he would lay all his crucifixes, Mary's and saints in one scale and his naked women in another, and he hoped the holy ones would outweigh the others. The college has been formerly the English merchants' house. Anno 1585 the Jesuits came to settle themselves; there are a matter of a hundred in number. We saw likewise their library, none of the best nor of the worst, one of its apartments holds no other books but them which have been written by their own order. Afterwards we saw their vaults or cellars, wherein there is their burying places, each body having a cave by itself, and for some great person that has a mind to be buried amongst them.

Here is likewise a very great and well-built town house, not so rich and good as that of Amsterdam. Here have also the Hanseatic towns a great and stately house [Oosterlingenhuis]. For traffic, now it begins to decay because there is no trade; before the great rebellion it was a very famous place. Here is likewise a glass-house, a place where they coin money, a house where they make rare [10v] tapestries, Plantin's press, now belonging to Mr Moret, his nephew [son-in-law] who immediately did succeed Plantin. Here you will see all sort of characters and letters at least a hundred, and twelve presses every day at work. Here is likewise a very famous water-house, which furnishes all the brewers with good water. Here is likewise a tour à la mode, where men and women meet one another in their coaches all the afternoons. This tour is made upon the Meir and so from one street into another.

In the old town of Antwerp justice is administered sub dio, under the canopy of the heavens. Upon one of the gates of the old town stands the statue of Priapus, very much defaced; it has been formerly the God of this town. Now the Virgin Mary stands above it, who is the true patroness.

Upon one of the watergates just by the river, stands the statue of Burbon [Brabo], formerly lord of this place where the town now stands. It has been only a passage for ships of which this lord did use to exact a very unreasonable custom [toll] and they that did not pay it, or used to cheat him of it, he used to cut off their hands and to throw them into the water. From hence, say the good people, the town is called Antwerp, *hand* being a hand and *werp* to throw, that is as much to say as throw the hand. In this posture, having a hand in one of his hands and in the other a sword, he is set upon the above mentioned gate as likewise upon the iron well made by Quintinus, and this is all which I did remark at Antwerp. From hence we went to Bergen op Zoom. [cont. Bergen op Zoom and Breda]

Thomas Penson, 29 September - 6 October (9-16 October) 1687

[73] [Rotterdam] On Thursday 29 of September 1687 O.S., being the day of St Michael the Archangel [74] about four in the afternoon, I embarked for Antwerp, we having on board two other Englishmen, several French and Dutchmen, three women and three young children. On Friday about nine in the morning, we sailed by Dort and afterwards by Willemstad and Breda, and that night came to anchor off Duiveland. On Saturday, October 1st, we passed by Zierikzee and came that night in sight of Ter Goes, where we lay till Sunday. Then sailed by Bergen op Zoom and came to anchor that night off [Zuid-] Beveland. On Monday we sailed till we came off the Polder of Lillo, where we had the misfortune to run on the sands and there lay till low water.

Our voyage proving longer than was expected, our provision was ended, having already made three meals on boiled mussels which our seamen got with the small boat, nor [75] had they any more brandy on board to sell us. We called a council of the whole ship's company to advise what to do, and finding that nothing but a spring-tide could carry us off (which would not relieve us under five or six days longer), at last it was resolved that some of the ship's crew should go before us and we would endeavour to make to land on foot over the sands and through the shallow waters, which in many places proved almost up to our middles.

Thus, having stripped our lower parts, [we] set forward with bag and baggage, both men, women and children and travelled the compass of three English miles (which with the difficulty of picking our way to avoid being caught by the toes by the great crabfish, which lay on the sands), and were sadly tired with carrying ourselves and baggage after this unaccustomed way of travelling. And at last when we were hardly able to creep, had a high bank to climb, but by helping one [76] another (God be thanked) we got on shore about three of the clock in the afternoon. We congratulated each other with a hearty welcome and lay down on the ground to rest a little while.

It was between Bergen op Zoom and Lillo where we came to land and espying a roadway, took it. And at a good distance in a bottom, discovered a house of one of the boors or country farmers, to which we marched with what speed we could, which was but slowly for we were very faint. We told the farmer our sad misfortune, who plainly saw we spoke the truth by the pickle we were in. He readily conducted us into his house and brought forth the brandy-bottle. His wife being sick on the bed, moved with compassion, caused the maid to set before us the beef, the bread, the butter and cheese and also made her son and servants to give us water and towels to wash our feet, etc.

Having rested and refreshed, we offered him money for his kind civilities, which he [77] refused. Then we desired the farther favour of his waggon to carry us to the next town (which was the fort of Lillo), to which he readily consented and immediately gave order to get the horses ready, which was done and we paid him what he demanded for that service. Thus, having returned our thanks to him and his good wife, and given money to his servants, we parted with our kind stranger, whose name we enquired, which was Keyser de Marine, which may be interpreted The Emperor of the Sea. But we all consented he should be made an Emperor on the land.

Our great chariot being prepared and clean straw laid therein, we ascended, some by way of the wheels and some up a ladder, so with our long team and charioteer riding by, we merrily rode on in triumph to the fort of Lillo, where they did not oppose our entry, for they could not believe we came to storm the fortification. [78] We got thither about six at night, where we refreshed, shook off our straws, dismissed our chariot driver, took a short view of this fort (which is a strong place) and procured a boat to carry us to Antwerp. But in the way were examined and searched by the Spanish officers (for we were now in the dominions of the Kings of Spain). About eight o'clock at night we arrived safe and well at the brave city of Antwerp.

Thus, after four nights hard lodging on the planks on shipboard and that severe travelling over the sands, we at length came to good beds, which was very acceptable to us. The two Englishmen and myself kept together and the other persons went their several ways according to their occasions. We took up our lodgings at the sign of King James of England's Head, near the Exchange, where we rested and feasted. During my short stay in this city I [79] continued my observations as before and had the favour of Mr Adrian Peninghen (a gentleman that lived here, to whom I brought letters from Amsterdam), he was pleased to walk out with me every day.

First I was shown the Exchange, which (is said) was the first exchange in the world. It was built in the year 1531. But the trade of this city is so much decayed that the grass grows thereon and the number of people daily resorting thither, I found, seldom exceeded fourscore or one hundred. I viewed the fortifications and measuring the walls of Antwerp, found them more than two and twenty yards broad. Thereon are pleasant walks and brave lofty trees planted in good order.

The churches in all these Romish countries are well worth seeing. I visited many of them and shall only name some and so pass forwards, viz. the churches of St George, St Michael, [80] St Andrew, the temple of the Virgin Mary, all [of] which are brave large churches and well adorned with good paintings, carving and gilding. But more especially the Jesuits' church is so wonderful that I should want words to tell of it, every part thereof being so richly beautified that it is much better seen than described, wherefore I shall advise all that are curious, to go and see it as I have done.

Also I was conducted (by my courteous friend) to the chapel of the Blessed Virgin without the city [N.D. de Joie at Beerschot], which is a place eminent for working of miracles and curing diseases. This chapel is hung roundabout with the pictures of several persons with their names and the times when they have been wonderfully restored to their health, out of divers distempers and infirmities, by invoking the Blessed Virgin. Some who have had withered hands, others sick or lame or afflicted with pains in [81] divers parts of their bodies, all cured and restored without applying any other medicines or cordials than calling on the Virgin Mary. Nay, they tell you farther that some have had their houses on fire, and by this means only, the fire itself has extinguished. In all their churches are pains and diseases cured, too, but in this more especially. Many people upon occasions do with great pains and charges travel more than a hundred miles, to meet with a miraculous and sudden cure by obtaining the favour of the priest to intercede for them to the Blessed Virgin.

Nor is it here alone, but in most of their churches, both in Flanders and France I observed the altars hung about with plates of silver, wrought into the forms of several parts of the body, as the head, the heart, the hand, the breast, the foot, the leg, etc.; so that, what part soever is afflicted with any pain or disease, by [82] calling on such or such a saint (and that piece of silver hung upon the crucifix or on the figure of the Virgin Mary at the altar), the people are healed of their infirmities. But the subtle priest takes care that none of this be lost, and in convenient time unloads the Virgin and her Son, and so makes room for more of the same metal. Though I must confess that the poorer sort of people were also admitted to the benefits of the prayers of the Church. Yet their zeal is so great, that though they could not procure a plate of silver or gold to hang on Our Lord's shoulders, yet they impressed their infirmities on wax in like manner. But I fancy the priest did not pray half so fervently for the latter as he did for the former. And by this trick alone there is yearly a vast treasure insensibly drawn from the people. [83] But although in some of their ceremonies they may be charged with superstition, yet they are free from slovenly indecency, their ceremonies being performed with so much devotion and adoration.

The English nunnery I visited, being accompanied by my friend. At the gate I was let in by a servant, who directed me up one pair of stairs, which led me into a fair light chamber (adorned with the pictures of many devout women). On the one side thereof was a large double iron grate and by it hung a cord, with which I was ordered to ring a bell. Soon after came one of the nuns and called: 'who is there', to whom I answered: 'Madam, a person from England travelling through these countries and desirous to see what is worthy my observation, and especially this place'. She bid [84] me welcome and enquired how the King [James II] did and how all things were in England. I told her very well and in peace and quietness when I came thence, and recounted to her the time, which she was very glad to hear and wished 'God bless him'. Her garments were all black and her face veiled and she also said: 'Sir, you were pleased to require more than we can admit of, viz. to see us: which by our order we are forbid, for we must not unveil our faces. But be pleased to sit down and I will call one of our worthy matrons'.

When she came, she enquired from what part of England; I told her London and said if there were any of the ladies of this place that had any service to command, I would readily do it at my return thither. She answered there were none from London, though all Englishwomen. [85] She also entreated the favour of my name and my religion, to both which I truly answered (that my education had been of the Reformed Protestant religion according to the Church of England), to which she was pleased to reply: 'I am sorry' and farther added: 'Sir, you seem to me to be a person of understanding and ingenuity, etc., it is a pity you should remain out of the pale of that Church wherein salvation is only to be obtained'. I told her that since I came abroad, I had had some conferences with persons of the Romish faith and had received ample satisfaction in many things from them, and that at my return to England I should have opportunities of farther inquiries. To which she heartily advised me and did not doubt but thereby I might be made happy.

After this and suchlike discourse, I was inclinable to take my leave, telling her I feared I should trespass too long on her [86] patience and goodness. To which she answered, no, I was welcome, and [she] said because I was an Englishman, she would farther gratify my curiosity by letting me see a novice which at that time remained there, and immediately gave directions that she should be brought to the grate, which was done.

There soon appeared (as an angel of light) a delicate, proper, young, beautiful lady, all in white garments and barefaced, whose graceful presence was delightful to behold and yet struck an awful reverence, considering she was devout and religious. And having paid my respects and fed my greedy eye a short moment on this lovely creature, I thus spoke: 'Madam, may Heaven bless and enable you in your undertakings, which to us that are abroad in the world seem so hard and difficult. For we account it no less than being buried alive to be immured within [87] the confines of these walls.' To which she answered: 'Sir, the world is much mistaken in their harsh censures of these religious houses, not considering the felicities we here enjoy in the service of God. And although for my part I may forsake this place when I please, being now but in the year of my noviceship, yet do assure you, Sir, I find so great satisfaction and contentment in this manner of life (being daily present with these devout women in holy exercises and prayers), that I would not change conditions with any princess or noble lady in the world.'

Here I thanked them for their favours to me and taking my leave they assured me that at the altar they would recommend me to God Almighty in their prayers, that He would preserve me in my travels and restore me safe to my friends and relations; so we parted. [88] Thus, I have faithfully set down what materially passed between us.

Anonymous London merchant, 13-20 and 24-27 September 1695 N.S.

[19] [coming from Dordrecht] At seven o'clock we cast anchor and lay by, the weather being stormy and raining hard all night long, which made several of the passengers very sick and me among the rest. At five the next morning we sailed again and in two hours came up to the Tholen in Zeeland, where we tarried half an hour, but the rain continuing we did not go ashore. This city looks very finely built with two or three churches and is fortified with a broad river and a good wall round it of earth having several guns planted thereon. About a league from it lies Bergen op Zoom, which is also another fortified city in Zeeland [Brabant]. But the winds being good for us we made the best of our way for Antwerp and made no stay there.

Our passengers in this voyage were mighty civil and distributed their wine very liberally to each other. I did so likewise with my English tobacco which was acceptable, there being none good in all our travels except Spanish, which is very dear, and yet the people are greater smokers than in England. One [20] fellow happening to break his pipe off close by the head after he had filled it, put the head halfway in his mouth and smoked it saying he would save the fire in it, which seemed very pleasant. The Dutch are mighty singers of psalms, both at home and in their churches, half the time of this voyage being spent by them in singing either psalms or ballads.

The Scheldt which we sailed on from Dordt to Antwerp is narrow in some places but in others very broad, having sometimes no sight of land. Many pretty villages lie as we pass both on the coast of Flanders and Zeeland and Brabant. On the last lies Lillo in sight of Antwerp, a strong fort where all ships stop to be examined and pay a toll to the Dutch. Here I was minded to go on shore, and the schipper, who went alone asked me to go with him, but the wind and rain kept me on board with the other passengers. After two hours' stay at this fort, we sailed again to Fort St Marie. There we were searched again by the Spaniards. I landed here with some other passengers and walked with my rice-sack and greatcoat two leagues to Antwerp, where I arrived at six o'clock at night on Wednesday the 14th September.

Antwerp is a city in Brabant lying on the Scheldt which separates that country from Flanders. The city is bounded on one side with the river and a broad wall on the other, for four or five coaches to go on. This wall is well-planted with lime trees and fine walks between them. Without the wall is a very broad ditch and bastions to secure the town. Without the ditch are pretty gardens adjoining which makes a pleasant prospect from the walls.

The stadhouse is built of stone and is bigger than Guildhall in London. Here are five parish churches which seem to be as big as our cathedrals, besides forty or [21] fifty abbeys and monasteries, all [of] which have very fine chapels. Some of them I saw, as also several nunneries and drank good beer in one or two of them. St

Sailing route from Rotterdam to Antwerp, c. 1710

Mary's, St Jacob's, St George's and St Andrew's are all the most beautiful churches I ever saw. The altars, the images, the painting, the multitude of candles, lamps, organs and reliques are too numerous to set down; sometimes twenty or thirty altars in one church, all dressed up very costly in a different manner. These altars do belong to the several trades or fraternities in the city and some of them to Lords and families in the country, who use them as occasion requires.

But the Jesuits' church here, though small, exceeds all other. It is of stone without and covered with brass, but all marble within: the pillars, the altars, the galleries, the floors, the chapels are of such massive, carved, inlaid and polished marble as would dazzle the eyes of any beholder. The altars are all very rich; the biggest was set round with bay trees and flowers. In one of its chapels stands the Virgin Mary and Our Saviour in her arms, all hung with pearls and bedecked with diamonds of a great value, and by it hang a great many relics. It is impossible to describe the painting and carved images in this church or the extraordinary cost of this famous structure.

During my stay at Antwerp a procession was made for a deliverance from a great sickness sixteen years before [1678], wherein sixteen thousand died, which so lessened the inhabitants that the rent of houses fell much and continues so. In this procession the several companies go in their gowns with lanterns and flamboys, then the priests and friars with wax lights and crosses and some carrying images of Our Saviour and the Virgin Mary, for whose honour, being the patroness of this city, her image is set up in all churches and in the corners of most streets and also in the shops of most traders in this city. In this [22] procession the host is carried by a priest under a canopy, with music and singing going before, and the people crowding on all sides.

At another time the host was carried to the house of a sick person, many boys and priests attending in surplices with lanterns and wax lights at noonday and music going before it. This host coming out of a church, I drew near to see it, not knowing what it meant. A person in ordinary habit came up close to me and said 'Le Grand host est avenue' [the great Host has arrived], whereupon I walked off but the host following, everyone in the street kneeled down, and seeing that, I hastened away, but still looked back to observe the ceremony.

After I had viewed the town everywhere and walked on the ramparts and seen the citadel, which stands without the town and is strongly fortified having grass ground and sheep and cattle within it, and also walked some miles without the town where we had eels, wine and good beer, I went at eleven o'clock at night on Tuesday the 20th instant in a ship for Brussels going down the Schelde to Willebroek and from thence on the canal of Brussels. After changing our ship five times and going six miles by waggon (one of the sluices being broken), we arrived at Brussels on Wednesday the 21 instant, being a fast and St Mathias [Matthew] day and thirty miles from Antwerp. [cont. Brussels]

[24] [After a visit to Brussels and the army] On Saturday morning [24 September], upon viewing a church, there happened to be a funeral of a citizen in one of the choirs of St Mary's. An empty coffin covered with black was set in the middle, the body had been buried two or three days before. The choir, the altars and the priests were all dressed up rich; about twenty wax flambeaux burning about the corpse, and a multitude of smaller candles lighted. After [an] abundance of ceremonies at the altar, the priest came back to the coffin and walked round it several times, casting incense and sometimes holy water upon it, a little boy standing at the feet with a high cross in his hand, while the priest read the office at the head in Latin. This being done, all the priests and people walked out to the place of burial and then went quite away leaving the coffin alone in the choir, which was soon after removed.

The same afternoon I was carried to the abbey of St Michael, the finest abbey in the town. Here are thirty-six friars called the Heeren de Michel and an abbot, whose habit is the finest white English cloth. One of them showed us their church, their apartments, the lodgings of the abbot and his chapel, the library and gardens as also the dining-room, which is famous for its curious painting. Here we had plenty of good strong beer and the company of several of the friars till their supper came in; then we retired. This is a most splendid building and might serve very well for a prince's palace for the bigness and beauty of it.

[25] On Sunday, after a plentiful dinner at Mr Wellens, I went with him and his brother and Mr Vandenborg to see the citadel, which seems to be very strong and has a good garrison in it. Here we saw the chapel and then drank wine and beer in the gardens among [an] abundance of citizens who resort thither on Sunday for diversion.

On Monday I walked with the same company four miles out of the town where we saw [an] abundance of country seats and gardens belonging to merchants and gentlemen. Among these one of them was curious, consisting of fine arbors, a wilderness and many images. The walks are of sand but no gravel. In our return the peasants were getting in their oats and buckwheat, which was very late this year by reason of the rain. The last they call French wheat and is used for brewing and is thrashed in the field to prevent its shaking off. Their land here is exceeding rich being tilled and dunged one year in four, but the land in Flanders on the other side the Scheldt in the Pays de Waas, is much better and is tilled only one year in seven.

In the afternoon I went with the said three gentlemen to see the stadhouse, wherein are several chambers and offices. The chiefest are the senate room, where the council of the town meets, without whose consent no money is given to the King of Spain or his Governor General of the Spanish Netherlands. This and all the other cities concur therein or else no money is given. In this great room is a large picture of the present King of Spain, Charles II aged about 33, and many other pictures of the Dukes of Brabant. The next is the courtroom of the schepens and burgomasters which resembles our court of aldermen in Guildhall, with the addition of a small chapel and an altar at one end of it, where mass is said to the court, upon the opening a large pair of brass doors very finely cast. From thence we went to the kitchen of the stadhouse, where we drank a pot of my Lord Mayor's Rhenish wine.

At this moment a fire broke out in a great house [26] close by the stadhouse, a company of the city being then at dinner in it. This is a house where the operas are acted, part of the actors' clothes being burned. A vast multitude of people upon the ringing of a bell was got together who brought buckets and three or four engines and soon quenched the fire. This happened near the house of Mr Wellens. His maid came and told him by mistake that his presses were on fire, which made him fly from me in such a fright as I never saw any man. After this we went to see an idol in one of the parts of the old town which the people anciently worshipped as also a church which has a street going under it and in another place one street going under another. From thence passing through a fishmarket we bought a hundred smelts, six flounders and fifty or sixty oysters, which made us a mighty supper that night. The next morning, being 27 September, I took ship and returned to Dordt [Dordrecht].

St Michael's abbey, 1720

Anonymous tourist, 29-31 July 1711 N.S.

[6] Wednesday the 29 to Antwerp, which is a stately well-built town; the Exchange here is very handsome, built after the manner of that at London, but nothing near so large. The front has three storeys of pillars of different orders. But above all is the finery and sumptuousness of their churches, which are wonderfully adorned, insomuch that the five parish churches and twenty convents are a great many times more worth than all the town besides. The Great Church has a fine tower steeple, built after the manner of that at Boston, but much finer. In the body of the church are [an] abundance of little altars besides the high altar, which is finely painted by Rubens representing the Assumption of the Virgin, to whom the church is dedicated. And in the cupola is the same, but it is so high that one can hardly see the painting, and it is said not to be by Rubens himself.

In one of the small autels [altars] is a small madonna of Rubens, very fine, and at a pillar in the body of the church is a small dead Christ of his also; and at another autel is the piece of the Last Judgement [the Fall of the Angels], done by Van Neck [Frans Floris], and upon the buttock [thigh] of one of the figures, the fly done by the smith that married his daughter. But above all is that valuable and so much talked of piece of Rubens representing Our Saviour's descending the cross, the fellow whereof (but I think not so fine) representing Our Saviour's ascending the cross is in the [7] parish church of St Walburgh. In the academy of painters is Rubens' wife and child excellently painted by himself, and Van Neck at study [Saint Luke painting the Virgin] by Frans Floris, with some pretty good landscapes and flowers by Rijsbrach [Rysbrack], Verbruggen, Boul [Boel] and others, but nothing extraordinary.

There is also a piece admirably done at a place called the Doel, or great tavern [Kolveniershof], in a room kept for great feasts. The picture [by Bosschaert] represents Mars, going from Venus. War represented like a fury pulling him away and Venus with little cupids hanging about him. It is said six hundred guilders has been bid for it, but they do not agree whose hand it is; some say a painter called Long John [Johann Boeckhorst] others Vit. Bordence [Willeboirts, alias Bosschaert], and Mr Boul [Boel] told me it was one of his name and family that painted it.

In this town one may see all bigotry and superstition imaginable. In the great place [Meir] is a crucifix modest enough, but in the corners of most of the streets is some ridiculous thing or other, sometimes a madonna showing her child, sometimes crying over him, sometimes God the father, and in one place a pyx with the host and under it written (as a gentleman that understood Dutch interpreted it to me) HERE RESTETH THE ALMIGHTY. In many places you find such unnatural representations of the crucifixion as would create laughter, and in two places, to wit at the Dominicans [8] and at St George's parish church, is purgatory represented in figures painted and coloured after a strange ridiculous manner. And in another place I saw the Pope and clergy at prayers and the angels pulling the people out of the flames. And in several places an image representing Our Saviour dead and lying along [at full length] in a shroud strewed with flowers.

At St Michael's convent is the largest picture I ever saw, representing [an] abundance of building and people and Our Saviour curing the paralytic. And the altarpiece, representing the offering of the Magi, is done by Rubens and very fine, but I think the boys upon the camels are brought so forward that it a little disfigures the rest. And the foolish fable of St Veronica with [the impression of] Our Saviour's head upon her handkerchief is represented in [an] abundance of places, but nowhere well. To this order [Norbertines] also belongs a nunnery where twenty-two nuns work waxwork for sale.

There are several other orders here but above all for strictness are the Carthusians who are only to the number of eight and live in their cells, consisting of three little rooms, an outlet and a little garden, without speaking to each other; only once a week and on holy days when they dine together. They never eat any flesh, nor fish neither upon certain times; but one of them, a very facetious, pleasant man entertained us very civilly and showed us their chapel, which is the worst I saw. That monk is a young healthful man and has been there nine years, seemingly with a great deal of pleasure and satisfaction. [9] He told us the master of their order is at a cloister at Grenoble, and is of a great age, having been master above eighty years and that out of the eight at Antwerp there had but one died in thirty years, when he professed. So great is the advantage of all their sparing diet towards the continuation of life.

But what exceeds all orders in learning, grandeur, riches as well as politics is the Jesuits here. Their chapel is one of the finest things in the world though not very large. The front westward is extremely fine-built, of several orders, but the inside exceeds everything. The walls are adorned with pictures and carved work, and the middle aisle, which goes up to the top (whereas the two side aisles are galleried over), stands upon two storeys of marble pillars of the Doric order, each pillar consisting of one entire stone. The altars, which are five in number, are exceeding fine and rich and adorned with the finest carved work in marble I ever saw. The roofs, both under the galleries and above, are adorned with pictures of Rubens valued at an extravagant rate. The interpreter said they were every other Van Dycks, but I thought that improbable, and Mr Boul, the painter, told me they were all of Rubens.

At the high altar they say is a very fine piece, but, it being St Ignatius' day [31 July] when we were there, it was taken down and in the stead was placed that saint's image, very rich, which I did not think so well worth seeing, but that [10] loss was made amends for by the music which was very good, both upon the eve and the holy day. Here I observed that under the saints' pictures there is written: 'Corpus sancti ... ex coementerio sancti ... colitur die ... mense ...' [the body of saint ..., from the cemetery of saint ..., is venerated on the ... day of the month of ...], which I don't well understand how it can consist with their pretence of not worshipping saints in reality. I was told that at Christmas there has often been a farce or play acted, representing the whole New Testament for the benefit of certain poor monks. I am promised the play-book.

John Leake, 7-11 (18-22) June 1712

[29r] Upon the return of the tide we went forwards [from Dordrecht] at our usual slow rate. We sailed over a large mass of waters called the Hollandsch Diep, which were occasioned by an inundation of the sea in the time of our Queen Elizabeth [St Elizabeth's Day, 1421]; there were above sixty villages drowned in one night. We were showed Geertruidenberg, Willemstad, 's-Hertogenbosch [probably Oudenbosch], Breda and Bergen op Zoom, which last place is fortified as well as art and Dutch fears [of the French] can make it. Having thus spent the best part of two days in coasting the several islands of the province of Zeeland, on Saturday the eighth instant there arose a brisk gale at N.N.W., which brought us into the Schelde and in a few hours set the fair city of Antwerp before our eyes.

In going up this river we were twice visited and examined for contraband goods. The first time by the subjects of the States-General upon our leaving their territories, who came off from Fort Pearl. And a second time by the subjects of the Emperor upon our entering the marquisate of Antwerp. We were [30r] civilly used by both of them and permitted to proceed on our route. About four of the clock in the afternoon we came directly before Antwerp, which we saluted with the guns of our yacht; and after having had permission from the magistrates, we all safely landed there. We went directly to the Red Tun in the Egg-market and made that our quarters.

We had scarce looked round us in this beautiful and venerable city, before we perceived our scene of objects considerably changed from what we had been used to in Holland. We had now no longer the Dutch boor and skipper to converse with, but a people of a civiller and more complying temper; we had lost our watery ship-cities and seemed to tread original terra firma. As trade and wandering is the business and delight of the Hollander, so religion and a profound rest appeared to entertain the Fleming. Here the churches are more frequented than the Exchange and the number of monasteries and other religious houses were an overbalance for the gasthouses and hospitals of their neighbours. In short, the conduct of the Hollanders seems better suited towards making a figure here, and their management may entitle them to the wisdom of children of this world. But whether the Antwerpers by a counter practice may not by their pompous works of piety be more acceptable hereafter and have a greater interest in the court above is a question resolvable by none to whom the sincerity of the heart is unknown.

After having taken a turn upon the pleasant walks that are upon the walls of this city, we went to view the citadel. Upon our entrance into it, the commanding officer upon duty, seeing us to be strangers, ordered a sentinel to wait upon us all over the castle and to give us such informations of the fortifications and garrison as [31r] we should require. This citadel is at present in no good repair. I presume the largeness of it may be one reason why it is suffered to fall into decay. There were three Spanish regiments in garrison in it when we were there. The Dutch, though they have a regiment of blue guards in garrison in the city, are not permitted to come armed within the walls of the castle. We were told that to garrison this place as it should be, would require ten or eleven thousand men; so that at present it seems in no danger of suffering the inconveniences of a siege, its own bulk making it not very manageable upon such an occasion.

The next place we went to see was the Burse, or Exchange. It is a fine, square building, and at its four entrances you take a view of four principal streets. It is neither so long as the Exchange at Amsterdam, nor so large a square as ours in London, and at present the number of its merchants is so small as to be conveniently enough contained, at full 'change, within the compass of one of our walks. We took also a transient view of their other famous buildings, such as their bank, the English Hall, which was formerly the place where our merchants had their staple for our woollen manufactures, the Portuguese Hall, their stadthouse, market-places, etc.

The next day we were brought acquainted with an Irish father of the Augustin order, who showed us the conveniences of his cloister, and did us the favour to come and dine with us, as did the Fathers Wood and Welsh of the order of Jesus, who invited us to a noble consort of music that was to be held in their glorious chapel in honour of their founder. This order began to have footing here first in 1562. The magistrates gave them leave to inhabit and teach school in that place which was known by the name of the English Hall. It is impossible to have [32r] your senses or curiosity higher gratified than they are upon their entrance into this church. The inside of it is one entire piece of Asiatic marble. Here are thirty-six pillars which support this proud building.

Its paintings, which are the several representations of the sufferings of this society in this country and elsewhere, are the products of Brugelius' [Breughel] and Rubens' pencils. In short, we were given to understand that no building either in Italy or elsewhere exceeded the beauty and richness of this divine structure. After our agreeable entertainment in this place, the Fathers Wood and Welsh courteously offered themselves to show us the other curiosities of this city. Upon my going out of the Jesuits' chapel and casting my eyes upon the front of it, I found this inscription: Christo Deo, Virgini Deiparae B. Ignatio Loiolae, Societatis Autori, Senatus Populusque Antuerpiensis Publico et Privato Aere Ponere Voluit [The city council and the people of Antwerp have been prepared to erect this building with public and private funds, for Christ God, the Virgin Mother, the Blessed Ignace of Loyola, the founder of the order of the Jesuits, in 1621].

Our reverend guides told us that there were above two and forty churches, monasteries, hospitals and other places dedicated to pious uses in Antwerp. Father Wood, who was confessor to an English nunnery there of the order of Saint Tiresia, carried us to see our countrywomen, who seemed well enough pleased with their retired condition. They were very poor and very modest; they are not permitted to converse with any men except through a close grate, palisadoed with iron spikes of a foot long and veiled. However, being in company with their confessor, we had an opportunity of conversing with them face to face, which was a favour we could not have enjoyed under the conduct of any other person. We purchased some pictures, flowers and purses of these ladies, made them a present of a supper of fish and finally took our leaves of these recluses, who promised us their good wishes and prayers for the prosperity of our journey.

[33r] The next place we went to was the cathedral church, dedicated to the Blessed Virgin. It is a large and noble structure and adorned with a curious high steeple from which I took a charming view of the whole city and the adjacent country. There is a dean with 24 canons and other priests who perform divine service in this church. Antwerp was erected into a bishop's see by Philip II of Spain anno 1467 [1559].

The churches of St Michael and St James ought to be seen by the curious traveller who has any taste of architecture and painting. It was in one of these churches that we observed a pompous epitaph inscribed to the memory of one of the gunpowder traitors [1605] named Brooksby.

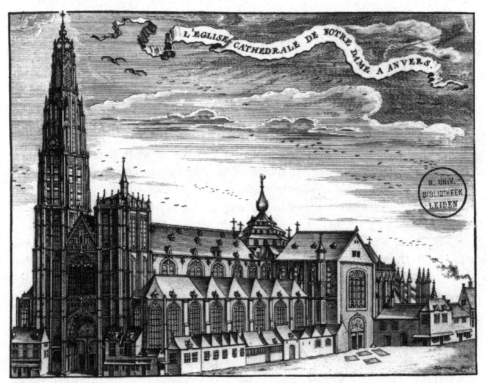

Cathedral, 1720

After we had satisfied our curiosity in seeing churches, chapels, altars and monasteries, we were conducted by our guides to the painters' academy, where we were delighted with several original paintings of the best Flemish hands. We saw also an excellent bust of the Elector of Bavaria cut in marble. From hence we went to the Emperor's Mint, where we were civilly entertained by the director of it who had formerly served our Kings Charles and James II in the same capacity.

We had now nothing of moment left unseen but the late famous Christopher Plantin's printing house, which is a place admirably well suited for the accomplishing of the ends of its erection. It has been for some time [since 1589] in the possession of the Moretus's, and it is managed at present by a gentleman of another name, because of the minority of a child of the above family. However liberally the commonwealth of letters may have been furnished with books in all tongues and faculties formerly from this press, at present it is wholly employed in sending into the world breviaries and missals.

[34r] June the 10th we took out our passes and on the 11th early in the morning, being attended by the Fathers Wood and Welsh, we took our places in the Mechlin [Mechelen] coach, after having returned our hearty thanks to the said gentlemen for their kindness and civility to us during our stay at Antwerp. We left two of the

company which came with us out of Holland behind us, and Mr Wright, Mr Clayton, the two Mr Warkhouses and myself were the persons who set forwards together for the army. [cont. Mechelen and Leuven]

Sir John Percival, 19-22 June (30 June - 3 July) 1718

[40v] From hence we went to the cathedral or church of Notre Dame, a very large structure and reported to be 500 foot long, 240 broad and 340 high [117 metres long, 65 wide and 123 high]. From the top of the steeple (noted for its beauty and height, being seven fathoms higher than the Monument in London, as one that measured both assured me), I took a view of the city and river and could plainly discern Bruges, Ghent, Mechelen, Breda and some other cities situated in Flanders and Brabant [...]

[41r] Francesco Floris, another painter of good reputation, was born in this city anno 1520. There are several of his pieces in this church, one whereof, representing the battle of St Michael, is in my judgement well executed with respect [41v] to the expression, the characters and attitudes or actions. There is a good piece by Hupotorf and a descent from the cross by Van Dyck, but these are far excelled by two pictures of Rubens, the first of which, over the gunners' chapel in the south aisle, representing the descent from the cross, is counted the most perfect of all his works. There was more than ordinary care taken of it when finished, by enclosing it within two folding doors, the insides whereof were likewise painted by the same hand. Nevertheless, no picture in the church is so spoiled as this very one, occasioned by the neglect of a painter, employed by the late King of France to copy it, who leaving the original exposed to the air, it is now so perished that several of the figures can scarce be distinguished. The other piece is over the high altar and represents the Assumption of the Virgin. It is painted upon board and extremely well preserved. The death of the Virgin is painted on the back. These two pictures have been frequently engraved and are justly celebrated [...].

[44v] [The collection] of Mijnheer Luit [Licht], a clergyman, consists chiefly of birds, fruit and still-life painted in miniature, of which he has a great number, excellently well-done. On one of the best is the name of Crabiche, a person now living, but I could not learn of what country he is or where settled. This gentleman has likewise a few paintings in oil by Rubens, Van Dyck, Corregio and others [...].

I walked one evening to the citadel, built by the Duke of Alva to bridle the citizens after their rebellion in 1566 [1568]. It stands on the south side of the town, upon a rising ground and within cannon shot of the rampier. The form of it is a regular pentagon, surrounded by a wet ditch of narrow breadth and a glacis. [45r] In former time it was esteemed a place of great strength, but is now no longer so. However, it may still answer the end for which it was erected, namely to bridle the citizens.

There is in the midst a handsome place of arms, from whence the governor may see what is doing at every attack and send the necessary succour, and there is a large chapel, in which we saw the tomb of the Marquis Del Pico, a former governor, who from a private soldier raised himself by his merit to the dignity of grandee of Spain. It is of marble and the carving upon it greatly esteemed. He is represented in a leaning posture, looking up to heaven; the carver's name Schomaker [Gillis Schoenmakers]. I found some persons opening the grave to bury the body of the Marquis of Terracina [Terrazana], late governor, who died the day of my arrival. He had enjoyed that post above twenty years, and the year that the Allies took Ghent [1706], having deserted the Spanish interest and surrendered the citadel to the Imperialists, the Emperor continued him governor.

Anonymous tourist, 20-24 May 1720 N.S.

[13v] Set out [from Brussels] with a berline at eight o'clock; dined at Malines à la Grue, came to Antwerp at six, eight leagues. The finest and most agreeable country we yet saw. See St James' Church, pretty good, with sixteen chapels. At the door of one of them see the tomb of Rubens without any ornament. In the chapel is a picture of his, where his wife and two daughters are painted. Good altarpiece by Van den Borch [Boeyermans]. See the ramparts, the finest work of that kind perhaps in the world. Four or five rows of trees. [14v] See Mr de Koning [de Coninck] and Mr Petier. This last treated us the next day very handsomely. See Mr Coqueel's mother and Mrs Bertryn, wife of John Arnold Bertryn and Mrs Wyngarden's daughter.

See the town house, two good rooms, one excellent picture of Abr. Jansse[ns]: Neptune and Cybele. The Exchange, the first of the kind, very neat with four doors and as many straight streets answering to the doors. They showed us an immense giant by which they mean to represent Bruon [Druon Antigon, a giant] or Draon [Silvius Brabo, the king who defeated the giant], see Misson, an elephant, etc., which are shows they used to carry about in their procession to please the people. At the bottom of the giant's statue are these words:

> Bellua anhelantis Lybiae nutrita sub axe
> Bellatura tuis adsum Dux maxime castris.

> [A beast nurtured under the skies of panting Africa.
> Here I am, greatest Leader, to fight for your camp].

See the remains of the church of the Jesuits, the main altarpiece and two chapels show how beautiful the whole must have been. Fine pictures of Rubens, both there and in other places of the college. The library takes up five rooms with galleries in them. Very good books in them. The cathedral very large and beautiful, dedicated to Notre Dame. Two masterpieces of Rubens and Van Dyck, the best Rubens ever made in his own judgement: the Assumption of the Virgin and the Descent from [15v] the Cross. The tomb of Plantinus, Anno Aetatis [aged] 75, 1589. Balth.

Moretus A[nno] Aet. 67, 1641. J. Moret Gener. Plant. 1610 [Plantijn's son-in-law].

The steeple of it very fine, went up; see the country round at a vast distance, and the Hamborough House [Oosterlingenhuis], which was a factory belonging to the Hanse Towns, etc. At the great door [of the cathedral], see an epitaph made to the honour of Quintinus Mattii [Metsys] one hundred years after his death, and the well near it (see Misson), but there is some difficulty in the years, for the well is made in 1552 and Mattiis died in 1529. In the cathedral they show a picture of his father-in-law, Frans Floris, where Mattiis after his stay of two years at Rome painted a fly, etc. We see another picture of his at the painters' room, very good.

See Plantin's printing house and that of Moretus who owns it, very fine. They print now in this once so famous house nothing but missals in black and red and the prints belonging to it. But in another room they preserve the letters of all languages which Plantin used formerly. In the yard are the busts of Lipsius, Plantin, Moretus, etc.

See the abbey of St Michel, very handsomely situated at the Schelde's bank. In the refectory of the abbot's apartment are some very good pictures. The apartment is very handsome. [16v] Went to the Dominicans, where there is a grotto that has something solemn, said to be made after the model of that of Jerusalem over Our Lord's sepulchre. In the church a fine picture of Michelangelo of the Virgin with Our Saviour, at the right of the great altar, and the Council of Trent by Rubens, as also Our Saviour scourged by the same. The beheading of St Paul, done by Van Borchman [Boeyermans]. Bought some artificial fruit of the nuns Norbertines.

See the collection of pictures of Mr De Licht, extremely remarkable for miniature. Perhaps never had any one single man so many excellent pieces representing to the utmost nicety fruits, flowers, fishes, reptiles, etc.

Antwerp is a fine large, beautiful town; the streets very broad and straight but not very well peopled. The Scheldt is a great ornament to it and was formerly the occasion of their great riches, but now, as some will have it, the Dutch have sunk some ships to spoil it, but however are masters of it by the many forts they have that command it.

Sir John Percival, 24 August - 2 September (4-13 September) 1723

[12r] There are about twelve booksellers' shops here and the famous printing shop of Plantin still subsists in the hands of Mr Moret.

The art of painting is much on the decline. Vanall [Jacob van Hal] is the most eminent history painter and he but indifferent; Sneyers [Peter Snyers] copies well in divers manners and does well in fruit. I saw at his house two good [12v] heads of Philip of Spain and his queen by Rubens. Old [Pieter] Rysbrack, who has five sons all of them painters or sculptors of whom three were then in England, is the best for landscape, but his figures are bad.

The most eminent sculptor is Vervout [Michiel van der Voort or Vervoort]. He showed me some excellent work and was upon finishing the statues of St John and

St Paul for the parish church of St James. He models extremely well and studied long at Rome and is about fifty years old.

Sir James Tobin brought me acquainted with Mr Skelders [Schilders], father and son. The latter speaks our language well, having been long in England. They are both very well-bred gentlemen and live in one of the best houses in the town. They are bankers and of the best family there. I saw a Madonna and Joseph by Van Dyck, painted soon before he left Rubens, and wherein you see more of his master's manner than in those he painted afterwards.

A mile out of town they have a very handsome garden, large, well-entertained and full of choice fruit, though all made out of a field since the year 1716. By the favour of this gentleman I saw the collections of paintings and other cu- [13r] riosities of several gentlemen, as that of Mr Gillis, who has several basins of silver gilt and an ewer, all [of] which are set with ancient seals, cameos and precious stones. He values one of them at five thousand guineas and desired I would speak to the Prince at my return to buy it. I did so, but those things were not his taste and besides Sir Andrew Fountaine, who is a good antiquary and with whom their Royal Highnesses advise on such occasions, being their vice-chamberlain, told me he had seen it and that he asked a hundred times too much. This gentleman showed us likewise some good paintings, among which are a fine head of Gerard Dou by himself, a piece by Breughel and a half length of Marquis Spinola by Van Dyck.

Mr Skelders carried me to see the great collection of paintings of Mons. de Wit [Jacomo de Witt], I mentioned them in my former travels. That gentleman dying last year, they were speedily to be sold by his widow, and it was a particular favour that we saw them. He was an eminent wine merchant and his cellars are well worth seeing, being high and well-arched and containing on each side a hundred tuns of Rhenish wine, each holding five French hogsheads. I tasted some forty-five years old.

[13v] Mr Du Pret [Jacques de Pret], my banker, a gentleman of very good breeding, styled for his integrity the Aristides of Antwerp, and for his knowledge in affairs put at the head of the Ostend Company by the Emperor, carried me to see Mr [Michiel] Peeters's fine collection of paintings. He is a gentleman of very good estate and has besides a good cabinet of books and many natural rarities as eggs, insects, minerals, birds, shells and suchlike, brought from several parts of the world. Among his paintings are many of Van Dyck, Rubens, Breughel, [Francisque] Mil[l]et, Bourguignon [possibly Pierre Bourguignon], [Nicolas] Poussin, etc. The principal were a hunting of wolves by Sneyders [Frans Snyders], a Roman charity and prodigal son by Rubens, St Peter crucified with his head downwards, a Madonna with an adoration of Our Saviour and some other pieces at length by Van Dyck and an old man's head by Langjans [Johann Boeckhorst, alias Lange Jan]. He has besides some works of Tintoretto, [Pier Francesco] Mola and Guido [Reni], but I perceive the gentlemen of Flanders are not so curious of Italian paintings as those of their own country. He did not know their names.

Mr Dupret carried me to see Mr Lunden's collection; they are not many but good.

He showed [14r] me a noble landscape by Rubens, the only one of that master remaining, as believed, in Flanders. He has also four heads of his ancestors by the same hand, one of which, in the dress of a country lass after the Roman way, is much the finest performance I ever saw, the air and skin was never equalled even by Van Dyck.

There is a gentleman who paints for his diversion after the manner of [Adriaan] Van der Werff of Rotterdam. He showed me a Diana and Iphigeneia well enough finished. His name is Latombre [Latombe]. I likewise saw in a private house a good picture of [Jacopo] Bassan[o] and four family heads by Van Dyck.

It may be easily believed that having time upon my hands, I did not miss making a general review of the churches, which bating the few private houses I have mentioned is all that can entertain a stranger where no court is kept nor gentry dwell.

Population: 66,000 (1690), 43,000 (1755).
Distances: Amsterdam 30 hours (91 miles), Bergen op Zoom 8 hours (24 miles), Breda 10 hours (30 miles), Brussels 8 hours (24 miles), Gent 10 hours (31 miles), Leuven 8 hours (24 miles), Mechelen 4 hours (12 miles), Middelburg 14 hours (42 miles), Rotterdam 18 hours (52 miles).

Inns, *Reisboek* (1689, 1700 and 1721): De Tinne Pot*; De Roozekrans*; De Vette Gans*, De Bijkorf (on the Eyer-markt); *Reisboek* (1700 and 1721) also: De Beer (on the Eyer-markt), De Laboureur*, Brussel* (on the Meir); Kleyn Parijs*, Amsterdam*, De Bonte Koe* (near the Bier-hoofd).

Further reading

L. Guicciardini, *Descrittione di tutti i Paesi Bassi,* Antwerp 1567 (numerous editions until 1660).
A. Sanderus, *Chorographia sacra Brabantiae,* Bruxelles 1659-1660; 's-Gravenhage 1726-1727.
J.B. Gramaye, *Antiquitates Belgicae,* Bruxelles-Leuven 1708.
An accurate description of the principal beauties, in painting and sculpture, belonging to the several churches, convents, etc. in and about Antwerp, London 1765.
K. van Isacker and R. van Uytven (eds.), *Antwerpen: twaalf eeuwen geschiedenis en cultuur,* Antwerpen 1986.
Antwerpen in de XVIIe eeuw, Antwerpen 1989.
Antwerpen in de XVIIIe eeuw, Antwerpen 1952.
Jaarboek Koninklijke Oudheidkundige kring van Antwerpen, 1911-

Arnhem and Zutphen

John Talman, 13-14 and 18 September 1698 N.S.

[7] About an hour from Arnhem I passed by at some distance a little town called Velp. Travelling on, I came into a most pleasant shady road, set on each side with four rows of trees. On one hand were hills, whose gently declining sides were adorned with corn, intermixed with verdant pastures for sheep; on the tops of the hills were woods. On the other hand I had the prospect of several pretty gentlemen's seats, environed with plantations. Besides I had the sight of several towns.

Passing on still, I saw at a little distance Rheden. Here the city Nijmegen, three hours and a half distant from hence, came into view. Not much further I came to a fair house called Middachten, belonging to the Heer van Ginkel, now Lord of Athlone and general of the Dutch horse. The house has the river IJssel on one side, and some hills covered with wood on the other. The house is a square pile of building, four storey high, built after the Italian mode, with a handsome stone front. In the pediment, which is round, I observed carved out in stone a scutcheon charged with an elephant, [8] supported by two griffons. The house is moated round with a broad moat, over which is a fair arch. Behind and on each side [of] the house is a garden; before is a court surrounded with old building on three sides. The draft of it may give more satisfaction [sketch].

Leaving this place, I came to an angle of the IJssel, which for its often turning and winding is also called the *slang* or serpent. It is broad and has high banks. Here I had a prospect of the city Doesburg on the other side of the IJssel, distant almost an hour. Travelling on I passed by at a little distance a village called Ellecom, then I went through a wood situated on a rising ground, from whence I saw Dieren, one of King William's houses, which stands at the end of the wood.

Travelling through ploughed land, the next place I saw was Brummen, a little town which I passed through in my way to Zutphen. This place is a great hour distant from Dieren. From hence I passed through flat arable land, and in a great hour's time came to Zutphen, five great hours from Arnhem, where I lodged.

This city is situated on the river IJssel, which just before the city divides itself into two branches, over which are two wooden bridges, the first 103 paces long and ten foot broad, the second 150 paces, built on six boats. I entered the city through four brick gates. This is a large city in the Lordship of Zutphen.

I went up the guard-house [Wijnhuis] tower, which is a handsome building of brick. It stands in the chief street, which is broad and crosses the whole city; otherwise the streets are narrow and dirty. This tower on each side has a high flight of

De groote Markt en Wynhuis te ZUTFEN.

Zutphen. The marketplace and Winehouse, 1741

steps which lead to the first storey. To the first balcony the tower is square, to the second eight-sided, with four fair stone pillars that stand at some distance from the building. On the four pillars stand four stone pyramids. From the second balcony, in four of the sides are windows, on the other [sides] four half-pillars supported by modillions. The clockwork is fixed in a large frame with four fair iron pillars of the Doric order at the corners, about half a foot diameter. These support a cornice suitable to the rest of the work; the tun on which the music is set is very large, about five foot diameter. The tower is ascended by 164 steps.

Here are four Presbyterian churches in this city, but it being rainy weather I had not time to stay. Here is a garrison of two regiments of soldiers, one of foot, the other of horse. The city is well-fortified, encompassed with a broad ditch, with bastions and mounds of earth. This city is governed by fourteen burgemeesters and a senate or vroedschap.

I went out of the city at four old brick gates and over a drawbridge, and from hence I travelled through low land and came to an angle of the IJssel. From hence I rode through roads on each side set with trees, but by reason of much rain the roads were covered with water. I passed by a goodly, old, brick house, at some distance from the road, pleasantly encompassed with trees, belonging to Major Keppel, by which name the house is called. [...]

[19] From hence [Nijmegen] I took place in the treckschuit for Arnhem. Here we changed the boat three times. About midway we passed by a little town called Elst. The church steeple is a handsome brick building with three balconies after the old fashion. This canal crosses an island, formed by the Rhine dividing itself into two arms, whereof one is the Waal and runs by Nijmegen as aforesaid, the other is the Rhine which runs by Arnhem. We were three hours in our journey.

Arnhem lies on the Rhine, over which is a wooden bridge built on twenty-two boats. Arnhem is the largest city in Gelderland. At our entering the city [we] paid toll. The city is in [the] form of an oval, fortified with bastions and mounds of earth; the ditches are broad and deep [20] and partly full of water. It is encompassed with an old brick wall. Two or three of the gates are of stone adorned with pilasters, the rest are of brick. They are six in all, and most of them are treble. The houses are most of them old; the streets narrow. The most remarkable thing is the church, it is a large Gothic building, mostly of stone in [the] form of a cross. In the choir is the tomb of Charles, Duke of Gelderland [...]

[21] The church is handsomely arched and carved, most of the windows are full of painting. The tower is ascended by 238 stone steps, besides 22 of wood. Here are two cisterns full of water to be ready in time of fire, and they raise the people on such occasions by blowing such a trumpet as they have at Nijmegen. The clock chime consists of above forty bells; the tower has three balconies, round. From hence I had a view of the stathouse and the palace where the high court of justice for this province is kept, this city being the chief of Gelderland. Here in this city is an hospital for the maintaining eighty aged persons, as well men as women, etc.

On the heath, a little without the city, called Mooker-heide, I saw an encampment of twenty-five thousand men, horse and foot, most of the forces belonging to the United Provinces. Among whom were six regiments of Scotch and two regiments of Switzers. These were ordered to rendez-vous in this place. Because they were nigh, the King had a mind to make a review. The camp was in two lines: between every regiment was left a broad lane; every regiment was eight tents deep or thereabouts, and something more in front. Behind each regiment was a line of lieutenants' and ensigns' tents, and behind them were fixed the pavilions of the higher commanders as colonels, etc. At the front of each regiment were the sergeants' tents, in a line immediately before the common soldiers' tents. Before each sergeant's tent stood his halberd, fixed in the ground. A little distance before these were the arms. The pikes were set one against another in [the] form of a pyramid; the muskets were set against a stake and covered with a case made for the purpose. Before them were fixed in the ground little flags in which were signified to whom each regiment did belong.

At [22] some distance from each regiment lay the watch, consisting of four or five tents. At each end of the infantry were the cavalry. The order of their tents was much the same with those of the infantry, only behind each line of tents, I mean athwart, not parallel with the front, were the horse. The camp was not entrenched, there being no great apprehension of an enemy. When the infantry left the field to retire to their camp, the cavalry went at the front and brought up the rear. The livery of the Dutch forces is white-lined with red, and turned up with the same, with red stockings. The cavalry wear a black bunch of ribbons over the button of their hats, etc. The Switzers were in blue turned up with yellow. Instead of pikes, I observed they had halberds, or rather what you call bartesaan in Dutch. So much for the camp.

Anonymous Utrecht student, 1 September 1699 N.S.

[10] [From Utrecht] we went in a postwaggon to Arnhem with some Scots and English gentlemen, hiring the waggon among us. We passed by a little town called Rhenen and along the Betuwe, a very low and rich country. At night we came to Arnhem, which is a pretty town. The fortifications were not very considerable, yet what there is is in very good repair.

Next morning we went about a large mile out of the town to see the camp that was formed there for about twenty-five thousand men, horse and foot, the King being to take a review of them on the great heath by Arnhem, which he did about noon. They made a very good show; they were most of them Dutch troops that were drawn out of their garrisons in the frontier towns. We returned to the town in the evening.

John Farrington, 16-17 November 1710 N.S.

[245] I little thought to have dated two letters from Nijmegen, but some accidents will sometimes happen to travellers contrary to their inclination, and indeed, unless there sometimes did so, they would hardly relish the pleasures they meet with, no more than a person could have so just an idea of the Dutch neatness, unless he had seen the Westphalian nastiness as a foil to it. However, being delivered by the return of the post, as soon as we had dined, we took a postwaggon for Arnhem, and about half an hour [246] past two, Mr Van der Marsch and we set out together.

We passed the Waal over the flying bridge and there we entered our waggon. The way [to Arnhem] lies all along by the canal, where the treckschuit or the horse-boat goes, but it is the most narrow, weedy and foul canal I have seen in any of the provinces. Arnhem is eight [three] hours from Nijmegen; we came to that city about forty minutes past five, and now begin again to pay passage money and gate money, as is the custom in Holland. Lodged at the sign of the Pauw, or Peacock, a good house enough, the best in the city.

On the 17th, as soon as it was light, we hired a guide and went to see the city. The fortifications are not very strong, but several new works [1702] are designed by the late famous engineer General Coehoorn. The walks on the walls round the city are very pleasant, the streets of the city generally broad, and the town is well enough built. It is situated on the river Rhine, the religion is Calvinist, but the toleration of other sects is unlimited. The Calvinists have two churches, the Lutherans one, and the French Protestants have a church there likewise. The chief buildings in the town are the court of the Heer van Rozendaal, the court of the late King as stadtholder of the province, the Arsenal and the churches, which are very good. There are several large houses, which have a very genteel look. Their trade is chiefly merchandise in corn, the government is in the hands of twelve burgomasters, two of which are presidents or reigning burgomasters during one year.

In the Great Church is the tomb of the last duke of Guelders, which is a very good one, his effigies lying on the top of it. He died in the year 1538, as some old Latin rhymes or verses tell. There was also his effigies in wax, [247] and his coat of arms and other usual ornaments. The Arsenal [Bussenhuis], which is a good building of itself, is remarkable for the forty-four field pieces that were taken from the French at the battle of Hochstädt [Blenheim, 1704]. They are all of them brass, and some of them formerly belonged to England.

There is another large church [St Walburg's] in the city, which has not been made use of these hundred years and is now turned into a magazine for corn. The Papists in this town are not considerable for number or estates. The weather was very good and the wind at east. About half an hour after eight we left Arnhem and took waggon for Zutphen.

In our passage to Zutphen we turned out of the road to see the house of the Heer van Rozendaal, which stands about an hour from this city. The house is part of an old castle that seems to have been a very strong fortification heretofore. In the house there is not much to be observed, only its antiquity and some good pictures, as two of the late King William and his Queen, and two more of the present King of Prussia and his Queen. The house is very pleasantly situated and has a very good look with it. In the courtyard are several large bird-cages with the arms of the Earl and a coronet on the top. The arms are a spread eagle, the motto

Ut aquila ardua quaerit

[like the eagle he tries to reach the peaks]

The most remarkable birds in the cages are two Chinese cocks and hens, very finely spotted, a large black peacock and pea-hen with yellow bills, which are indeed very strange birds, but not nigh so fine as ours.

[248] The gardens, which are the most admired in this country, are really fine and large, well-planted with several rows of trees, which lead up to several summer-

t Huys te Rozendael van de Binnenplaats aen't Inkomen, met een gedeelte van de Gallery en Voljeeres

Rozendaal, 1718

houses. On the left of the house are several ascents, where are some cascades, fountains, box-knolls, the spread eagle well-laid in brick, etc. From thence we walked into the plantations, where are nine large ponds, twelve foot above another and in the lowest are four cascades and several fountains. Several arbours, where they may rest themselves or be sheltered from the weather. There are several very good stews for fish; in one are [an] abundance of large carp, in another smaller feeding; in the third are jacks and in the fourth perch. These are separated by palissades from one another to prevent their mingling.

In one of the summer-houses which is built upon a hill are a great many humorous prints and one especially of the Lifeland boor who conducted the King of Sweden's army [Charles XII] through the woods and snow in the year 1700, when he raised the siege of Narva. The device of letting down a table from the ceiling, or rather a cover to prevent spoiling the table in the room, is a very pretty contrivance and discovers a rose upon the roof, that all things may be done under it, as our proverb as well as theirs requires in a private conversation. When that is not let down you see the arms of the family, handsomely painted.

There is another garden on the right hand of the avenue or walk to the house,

80

which is also adorned with fountains and is very pleasant. On both sides [249] [of] the road is a canal and on the left hand within the canal is a little fountain which turns a small papermill, that will make sheets of paper about the bigness of those that are used for billet-doux, which the Earl uses for his diversion. The house and gardens upon the whole are worth the time we took to see them.

About an hour and a half from thence you come to Dieren, a small village in itself, but famous for the King's house, that is situated nigh it. This house is now as well as Loo contended for by the King of Prussia and Prince of Friesland. The country round about this house is very good for hunting. The alleys that lead up to it are well-planted. The house itself is a large quadrangle with a good front every way. On the left as you enter is the apartment of the late good Queen Mary. In the antechamber are several pieces of tapestry, as of slaying the first-born in Egypt, the eating of manna, David and shew-bread, Moses and Aaron, etc. The furniture of the chamber is removed by the Prince of Friesland.

In the King's apartment the room they called the dining-room was but ordinary for a prince, though it would have made a very good one for a gentleman, but the rest of the apartment was very fine. In the first room were a set of curious tapestry of flower pots made in flourishing and bright colours, very good pictures of pheasants, partridge and other birds. The furniture of this chamber is of sky-coloured silk laid with gold, and the frames of the chairs carved and gilt, very fine marble chimneypiece and window stools. In the closet are a set of very fine hangings of the Queen's own work. The [250] prospect from the King's apartment into the country and gardens is very pleasant. The gardens are but small but very neat; in the middle a large pond with grottoes round about it.

Under the King's apartment is that of the Earl of Albemarle, which is also very good. Having seen the house, we dined at the village on such provisions as the place would allow. We had some cold-baked meats and a piece of boiled beef, sauced with sugared turnips. About half an hour past two, we set out for Zutphen, which was three leagues distant from it and came there at three quarters after four in the evening. Lodged at the sign of the Crown, civil host and good usage. [cont. Overijssel]

Arnhem

Population: 6,000 (1650), 4,550 (1700), 5,600 (1750).

Distances: Deventer 8 hours (20 miles), Nijmegen 3 hours (10 miles), Utrecht 12 hours (32 miles).

Inns, *Reisboek* (1689, 1700 and 1721): De Toelast; De Roode Leeuw*; De Paauw*; De Goude Wagen*; De Konstapel; 't Kartouw; De Koning van Deenmarken*. *Reisboek* (1721) also: Reurmonde*; 't Frankfoorder Posthuis*; De Vergulde Zwaan*.

Zutphen

Population: 7,000 (1650), 5,000-10,000 (1750).

Distances: Arnhem 6 hours (19 miles), Deventer 3 hours (8 miles).

Inns, *Reisboek* (1689, 1700 and 1721): 't Wynhuis*, De Wildeman*, De Roode Toorn*, 't Groote en kleine Veldhoen, 't Wapen van Overyssel*, De Keizers Kroon*, De Stad Messina*, De Druif.

Further reading

J.I. Pontanus, *Historiae Gelricae libri XIV*, Amsterdam 1639.

A. van Slichtenhorst, *XIV boeken van de Geldersse geschiedenissen*, Arnhem 1653.

Arnhem Zeven Eeuwen Stad, Arnhem 1933.

Ach Lieve Tijd, 750 jaar Arnhem, de Arnhemmers en hun rijke verleden, P.R.A. van Iddekinge (ed.), Zwolle 1982-1983.

W.Th.M. Frijhoff (ed.), *Geschiedenis van Zutphen*, Zutphen 1989.

Ach Lieve Tijd, 1000 jaar Achterhoek en Liemers, H. de Beukelaer (ed.), Zwolle 1996.

Arnhem de Genoeglijkste, kwartaaluitgave van het Arnhems Historisch genootschap 'Prodesse Conamur', 1980-

Bijdragen en Mededelingen, van 'Gelre', vereniging tot beoefening van Gelderse geschiedenis, oudheidkunde en recht, 1898-

Arras and Douai

John Leake, 20 June (1 July) 1711

[43r] Upon our entrance into Douai, we were obliged to give a strict account of ourselves before we were suffered to be quiet in our inn. We had just time enough before night to traverse the town, take a transient view of the public schools, the Jesuits' church and Scotch fathers' convent. The latter place is but small and far from being a magnificent structure. Upon the outside walls of this house was a petition inscribed to one Margaret, Queen of Scotland, vid. a saint, to pray to God pro conversione Scotorum [for the conversion of the Scots].

This place was erected into a university not long since [1560] by the [44r] King of Spain upon the model of that of Louvain, and being favoured by the Popes with the grants of many privileges, it has continued in a flourishing condition ever since its foundation. The staple of the corn trade of these parts is in this city, which is no inconsiderable merchandise, as the great estates got by the practices of it here sufficiently testify. [cont. Kortrijk and Lille]

Anonymous tourist, 8-13 (19-24) August 1711

[12] From Lille we went August the 8th to Douai, a town of no great fame, but that it is an university, the cloisters and schools and colleges making the greatest part of the town. [13] In one of the latter belonging to the English [we] were civilly entertained by Mr [John] Berrington [Berington], a Herefordshire man and Mr [Edward] Dickinson [Dicconson], brother to the gentleman who owns Stanton [Standish near Wigan]. The former showed us the town and church, where I saw nothing worth remarking, besides in that belonging to the Minims a fine altarpiece, representing Our Saviour presented in the Temple, which is much after Rubens manner I thought very fine, but was told it and the altar piece in the Jesuits' was done by one Arniaen. In the Minims also is a very fine head of a cardinal.

In another of the churches [St Amé] is an altar said to be miraculous and that once upon a time a priest having let fall a piece of a consecrated wafer, Our Saviour came and appeared for several days together upon the altar, sometimes in the shape of a child and sometimes in the shape of a man, and all the country came in and saw it. In memory whereof there is an image of a child and a man placed in the place where it is said the apparitions stood. There is also the English Recollets, where Sir Henry Fletcher is building a chapel.

View of Arras, c. 1700

On Wednesday 12 we came under the escort of General Lan[d]sberg to Marchiennes, a little fortified town, where there is a fine college of Jesuits. On Tuesday 13th we came to the Duke of Marlborough's quarters [before Bouchain] at [blank] which is a country seat [14] belonging to the canons of Cambrai. [cont. Mons and Tournai]

Anonymous tourist, 26-29 July (6-9 August) 1720

[47v] Set out for Aire, three leagues. Found there the same inconveniency, none being willing to receive strangers for fear of billets de banque, which officers force upon them. Aire is a little town, well fortified with a citadel, but which lies very low. There were three attacks made by the Allies [1710], the real one near the gate of Arras. The town suffered very much. The cathedral dedicated [48v] to St Pierre is quite ruined. N.B. In all the country hereabouts the houses in the villages are made of mud covered with straw.

In the afternoon set out for Béthune, five leagues off. See there Mr Mansall, a prévot of the canons of St Bartholomew. The town something bigger than Aire; may be put under water on one side. The gate of St-Omer very strong. Mr

[Antoine] Vauban governor, nephew to the late famous engineer [Sébastien de Vauban]. See the church of St Vaast, built by the English in 1553, when they were masters of this country. The architecture of the steeple very handsome. Lodged at the sign of Grand St Martin.

27 July. Set out for Arras, six leagues. Went out of our way a little to see the abbey of Mount St Eloway [Mont-St- Eloi], Austin friars, canons of the order of St Austin. Were very civilly received and treated at dinner. As they are placed on the top of a hill, they have been forced to make [49v] a well of four hundred foot deep, out of which they draw the water by means of a horse. The rope is four minutes going down. Their gardens handsome; in one of them a fine echo. A very beautiful terrace which commands a prospect over the country. The ground walled in; is larger than Béthune. Here our army was encamped and the French army about Arras, a league off. Came to Arras, lodged at Petite St Paul, very well.

In the little marketplace see a building called St Chandelle, a pretty dome, built by the English in 1215, handsome architecture. In the church of the Carmes de Chau [Déchaussés] a pretty pulpit of iron gilded. See the gardens of Mr Vauban within the fortifications. Abundance of very good fruit. From thence one discovers the strongest part of Arras, where they are making a new contrescarp with stones they dig out of the fosse.

The abbey of St Vaast (St Vedastus), very ancient and very rich of the Benedictine order, a large church. On the right hand as one goes to the sacristy is the descent from the cross by Rubens, incomparable. [50v] They bought it for a pistole of a waggoner by chance. Fine ornaments of embroidery for altars. Fine treasure; variety of relics inlaid in gold and precious stones of a very great value. The library very large and complete. We were shown a rituale Duranti [by Guillaume Durand] with these words at the end: Presens rationalis divinorum codex officiorum venustate capitalium decoratus, rubricationibusque distinctus, artificiosa adinventione imprimendi ac caracterizandi, absque calami exaratione sic effigiatus. Et ad eusebiam Dei industrie est consummatus per Joh[annem] Fust civem Moguntinum [Maintz] et Petrum Bernkheim [=Gernsheym], clericum diocesis eiusdem 1459 sexto die Octobris [the present book, offering a survey of the divine services, decorated with elegant capitals, and ornamented with red initials, has been given this form through the ingenious invention of printing and of carving characters, without writing by pen. And for the worship of God it has been carefully finished by Johann Fust, citizen of Mainz, and by Peter [Schoeffer] of Gernsheym, a clerk of the same diocese, on October 6, 1459].

As the arms of St Vaast are a cross and a bear, they are obliged to keep a bear alive, which we saw. See the cathedral of Notre Dame in the city. Went to the citadel, a regular pentagon with tenailles between [51v] each two bastions and a contregarde covering each bastion. It lies much too low for the town and is commanded by a bastion from the town. It has a greater extent than either that of

Tournai or Lille. The governor's garden between the citadel and the city, where people come to walk, is pretty handsome. His name is Artagnan.

Arras is a large town but narrow streets, a fine large marketplace with piazzas round it. Well fortified it is divided into town and city. The city is a place of liberty, such as Westminster, where the bishop has a particular jurisdiction. In winter a good deal of nobility, particularly when the States of the province assemble.

29 July. Set out for Douai, six leagues, at five o'clock. Stopped at the abbey of ladies at Nevelle [Avennes, then at Bellemotte castle]; pretty gardens and a fine prospect to Arras, which it is distant from about a league. See the abbess, etc., very civil. Came to Douai before dinner. See the seminary; English secular priests; nothing remarkable. [52v] From thence to the Scotch Jesuits, whereof there are seven fathers in all. [They] are building a house for pensioners. In their church a noble picture of Raphael, representing the angel fighting with the devil. They were civil to us and treated us with wine; were so kind to go along with us the next day through the town. Saw the English Recollets, a pretty church built by Sir George [=Henry] Fletcher of Hutton Hall in Cumberland. There they show us a live tortoise.

The English Benedictines in a house belonging to the abbey of St Vaast at Arras; a tolerable library. See the arsenal room for arms for fifty thousand men, now only for fifteen thousand. Fine cannons, cast in the famous foundry in this town. The library of the Flemish Jesuits very large and handsome, well stocked with books, but few modern and no manuscripts. A very good garden.

Arras
Population: 16,000 (c.1650), 15,000 (1700).
Distances: Cambrai 7 hours (20 miles), Douai 4 hours (12 miles), Lille 8 hours (25 miles).
Inns, *Reisboek* (1689): The Arms of Holland*.

Douai
Population: 13,000 (1700), 21,000 (1750).
Distances: Arras and Cambrai 4 hours (12 miles), Lille 7 hours (20 miles).
Inns, *Reisboek* (1689): A la Place Royale*.

Further reading

A. Sanderus, *Flandria illustrata*, Cologne 1641-1644, 's-Gravenhage 1732, 1735 (*Verheerlykt Vlaandre*, 's-Gravenhage 1732, 1735); reprint Antwerpen-Amsterdam 1981.

J.B. Gramaye, *Antiquitates Belgicae*, Bruxelles-Leuven 1708.

L. Trenard (ed), *Histoire des Pas-Bas français*, Toulouse 1972.

Bergen op Zoom and Breda

William Lord Fitzwilliam, April 1663

[10v] From hence [Antwerp] we went to Bergen op Zoom, a town lying likewise in the dukedom of Brabant but is a marquisate by itself and is now under the States of the Seven United Provinces dominion. We arrived here at a very good time so that we had time enough the same evening to see the fortification of this place, which by art and nature seems to be invincible. [11r] It is situated near the river Schelde (where it is very broad) and in a plain open country; no hills but a good store of sand round about it. Where it is thought to be weak and to give some advantage to the enemy, there it is fortified with a very great piece of horn [Scots hornwork], before which the Spaniards did once [in 1622 during the siege by Spinola] lose a great company of soldiers. The town is fortified with good strong walls, nine or ten bastions, some of which seem to be too little and too far distant one from another. But this defect is easily remedied by the little towers which stand upon the courtine, which defend one another and the bulwark also.

Besides the great hornpiece there is a little one; some spurwork and half-moon pieces. Towards the river is a sconce of a very great strength [Beckaff], which defends the haven of this town. Three sconces more there are towards Steenbergen. Three or four gates lead you to this town, besides two other ports which serve for to make excursions upon the enemy or to receive secours from friends. The walls I think are of earth and some of the parapets; others of brick. The ditches are broad and very deep and full of water; some sluices belong likewise to this place.

The town of itself is very neat and well-built. The governor is Prince Fritz of Nassau [George Frederik van Nassau-Siegen], by whose leave we saw it. Here is the Protestant religion only professed; the Papists are connived at. Besides the Dutch, the English and French have here their churches. Here is a princely house to be seen; a fair great market and the Great Church, in which there are some tombs and monuments very well worth a man's curiosity.

From hence we went to Roosendaal, a very great country town, [11v] and so to Breda, lying likewise in Brabant and belonging to the Prince of Orange, who is baron of it. Here we saw the Prince's castle, which is but an old building, not very magnific but convenient. One large gallery is within it, besides an infinite number of little chambers, which were, at our being there, all ungarnished. The castle is made of brick; the bridges of wood. It is surrounded with ditches full of water and with four bastions, which, with the thirteen others which defend the town, make up seventeen in all, all of earth and very well-made. Great and broad ditches under

Het HOF des Princen van Oranje te BREDA.

Breda. The Prince of Orange's castle, 1743

them; several outworks for to defend them, as pieces of horn, spurworks and half-moons. By the castle is the Prince of Orange's garden (called Falckenberg [Valkenberg]) which is very curiously made and a pleasant wood in it. Here is likewise his tennis-court, and the governor's garden is made in a hornpiece, which is very pretty and pleasant.

Below the walls of the castle we saw where the turfboat, like another Trojan horse, entered the town and so took it from the Spaniards; the history is well-known. The walls of this town are all planted with trees, which serve for a very delightful walk. Within the town we saw the Great Church of St Margaret's [St Mary's], where we found the tombs of several persons of quality, amongst which a Prince of Nassau (who they say had been the first Prince of Orange) was the chiefest [Engelbert II, Count of Nassau]. Here he lies with his lady all in marble, his tomb being supported by four kings and round about it, the arms of all those towns of which he had been lord. This is one of the most curious tombs that can be seen in the Low Countries.

In this church there is written in great capital letters when it was taken and re-taken both by the Spaniards and by the States. [12r] Here the Papists have likewise no public exercise of their religion, only secretly permitted. A little convent of nuns is likewise suffered, who have a little chapel within their limits. The streets are here very fair and big; the houses well-built. A river called the Mark passes through it, which is defended a league of the town by two sconces, on each side one. This river brings all the vessels to the town, which are always searched by these two castles, chiefly the turfboats, that the town may not be taken once more by a turfboat.

A quarter of a league out of the town, we saw the Prince of Orange's house of pleasure, called Speelhuys. It lies in a little wood, very pleasant; it is wholly round and of brick, not at all stately but yet very pleasant. A league of the town we saw a pretty wood, consisting only of pine trees. That wood in a siege may do a great deal of hurt to the town, otherwise it is very pleasant; there are fair walks within it. In Breda there is good beer brewed, the best according to my palate in the Low Countries. We did lodge at the Cardinal Infanta. The night before we went from hence, we did ask if there was not a clapperman or bellman belonging to this town, as there are in all the towns of the Seven United Provinces. He answered us that there had been one, but a matter of a year ago he was cast off, by reason that good wives would not let their husbands in quiet and rest. At what hour soever, soon or late, the bellman did call, they did put their husbands in mind of their conjugal duty, so that hereby a good old burgomaster and some other old citizen, having married young wives, had been almost undone. This he confirmed with his own experience, although he and his wife could make up a hundred years and above. [cont. 's-Hertogenbosch]

Thomas Style, July 1669

[39] Having stayed a day here ['s-Hertogenbosch] we hired a chariot to Breda, eight hours distant, for they reckon all by hours in the Low Countries. The highways extreme[ly] pleasant, beset with fruit trees. The ways somewhat dangerous by their being extreme[ly] high and elevated. We came to Breda between four and five; lodged at an Englishman's, the sign the Cardinal Infanta.

[40] Breda, situated on the river Mark, famous for the King's [Charles II] so long residing here [1660], for the last treaty of peace concluded with the Dutch [1667], is a great barony belonging to the house of Nassau. It is triangular; the bulwarks set round with oaks and ashes in number fifteen; the ditches seventy foot broad; fourteen ravelins. The palace of the Prince of Orange is built castlewise: a drawbridge, a quadrangular court piazzaed. Underneath I saw a triumphal chariot, extremely old, all gilt; [it] formerly brought a French princess, married to some of the Nassauian family, there kept for a memorial. We saw the large room where peace was concluded between the Dutch and us, the Prince's dining room, the famed ceiling in fretwork of gold and azure. In the late Princess's [Mary Stuart, wife of William II] chamber, hung with crimson velvet, I spied in a window cut with a diamond this: Mutare vel, timere sperno. Tout ou rien [I scorn change or fear.

Everything or nothing]. Underneath written: Anne Hyde. A little below, I suppose by the same hand: En Parole de Prince [my princely word].

The garden vast, whereof half of it is a well-disposed grove. In the middle a rotundo or pantheon of tall trees, where the King [Charles II] in summer often used to sup. The Prince [William III] here served a huntsman's apprenticeship when his tender years could not permit him the use of greater forests. On the east side of this pleasant wood is a great fish-pond edged with freestone resembling a lake, where carps come with a whistle and fight for loaves. Two steps lower is the parterre or garden, being boxwork representing the Prince's arms and names [monogram]; beyond this several close walks. The house is moated round.

The next thing we saw was St Mary's Church, where the two Swedish ambassadors were successively buried; a third being sent to conclude the tripartite agreement with us and the Dutch [1667]. The image of Our Lady still preserved; a fabulous story of it. The object most worthy of remark is the Prince and Princess [41] of Orange's tomb, [Engelbert II, Count of Nassau] grandfather [ancestor] to this present prince. It is looked as a chef d'oeuvre, the Princes being laid along in their winding sheets upon a table of black marble. At the four corners four Caesars kneeling, upon whose shoulder rests a covering of black marble the same breadth and length as that of the bottom. On the top of all lie the princes' diadem, sword and armour, wrought in white marble [alabaster]. This is in a particular chapel.

Further on are several other monuments known more by the name of founders than by that of their families. I was so long looking on these antiquities as my companion, Mr Coxe, [was] gone out of the church and I locked into the church alone [that] I could make nobody hear. At last I knocked at the library door; there came out a minister to whom in Latin I related my misfortune, which he soon remedied, letting me out by a private wicket. My re-encounter made us but sup the more merrily, though towards the latter end there happened a quarrel between two Dutch captains about [ambassador] Sir George Downing's sending over [John] Okey and [Miles] Corbet [1662]. They would have referred it to us being English, which we refused. After supper we had a message from Captain Botteler, who hearing we were English sent to invite us next day, the haste of our journey not permitting us to receive his civility. The governor is a Frenchman named Monsieur de Hauterive. Next day we were up betimes going towards Dort. In the morning we took a Dutch gentleman into the chariot to ease us in the price.

A mile from the town we passed a wood of the Prince of Orange, consisting of fir trees affording a delicate shade. In the way we saw them dig turfs; it is full three year before it is fit to burn. First it is digged in a black moorish ground; all the winter exposed to the snow, frosts and rain; the summer dried by the sun; in the excessive heats often watered. Thus continued three years, the merchant here comes and buys it by [42] the perch. So rich a merchandize as whilst I was at Leiden a turf merchant died and left his son three tun of gold, every tun valued at ten thousand pounds.

About six we came to Bergen op Zoom, stayed half an hour at the gates which were shut and the bridges drawn up, which always is done when they change the guard in all towns of war. At last having liberty to come in, we were lodged at a Frenchman, the sign of the Three Horse-shoes. In one window I found cut with a diamond: Franciscus Barnham per hoc oppidum in Angliam profectus est [Francis Barnham has travelled to England by way of this town].

Bergen op Zoom, situated on the river Zoom, which Charles V erected into a marquisate in 1533, is at present so fortified by nature and the Hollanders, the present possessors, as by all people it is esteemed impregnable. Towards Antwerp side there is a half-moon which extends itself to the fort of Kinkin Pot [Kijk-in-de-Pot]; besides they have one side by a canal open to the sea. They have two secure ports where vessels may ride without danger. There is in all fourteen redoubts, twelve ramparts, so many counterscarps and two long ravelins.

In the town we saw the Duke of [Frédéric-Maurice de La Tour, Comte d'] Auvergne's palace, who [in 1662] married the princess of Bergen [Françoise von Hohenzollern] and in her right possesses half the town. The Hollanders here, for fear of a surprisal, keep in continual pay three thousand men. The governor is Prince Maurice [Maurits-Lodewijk] of Nassau [-La Lecq-Beverweerd]. At supper we had some of the commanders' and captains' companies. We were all at supper made participants of the word that night, which was *North Holland*, a civility usual among soldiers.

Next morning we were up by five, intending to reach Dordt, a great day's journey. We met upon the way, being Sunday, a great many travelling into the King of Spain's dominions to hear mass. We passed a little ferry or canal called Lint [Dintel], which separates Brabant from the territory of Dordt [Holland]. Two mile further a great misfortune happened to us through the ignorance of our charioteer, who mistaking the way endeavouring to turn, overturned us. The chariot fell over and over into a dry ditch, for so are all the Brabant and Holland ways elevated, twelve or fourteen foot high, just room enough for two waggons or [43] chariots to pass. God be thanked I got no hurt but Mr Coxe strained his arm, the Holland gentleman had his wrist out of joint.

Whilst our chariot was mending, we got to a neighbouring cottage, where the country people stared on us like Columbus when he first landed in America. Our machine mended, our bruises rubbed with brandy, we got into it again and arrived at Dordt at seven. I know not by what accident, as generally misfortunes are sociable and one attends another, we were lodged in a very bad house, nasty chambers, ill diet, worse drink, nothing good but the resolution we took of staying there no longer than necessity required. The first thing we did was to send for the chirurgeon, who confirmed us in the opinion Mr Coxe's arm was but strained.

Richard Holford, 16 (26) August 1671

[24v] We left Dordt Wednesday morning at seven and came to Moerdijk by boat. There we baited and took a cart for Breda and in our way crossed at Breda Haven a ferry and came to Mr Hurst's, an Englishman at the Prince Cardinal, near the castle [...].

[25r] We went afterward up into the tower, a very high, substantial, brick tower, very stately, 365 steps high. We saw the mills with which (with great care) they make their linseed oil. On the east and south part of the town, just within the walls, are long rows of little tenements for the soldiers [...]. This is in Brabant and is the domain of the Prince of Orange, and worth to him at the least £10,000 per annum. The fortification is most admirable. We left it about nine Thursday morn and came through the Buss, a stately wood of curious, straight fir trees, as full as one can stand by the other, and is at least seven leagues round. A noble, pleasant sight and worthy admiration.

Anonymous Utrecht student, 9 October 1700 N.S.

[13] Next day [at Dordrecht] we went to the waterside by waggon about a league, and then went by boat across the water. At night we got to Breda. Next day was the anniversary thanksgiving for their deliverance from the Spanish yoke, and there were sermons in the churches suitable to the occasion and at night illuminations and fireworks. In the Great Church I took notice of this in great letters over one of the doors: aMbrosI spInoLae / VIgILantIa / breDA eXpUgnata [Breda has been captured by the vigilance of Ambrosio Spinola in 1625]. And at one end of the church this: Auxilio solius Dei ... [With the help of God alone, by order of the Confederate Netherlands, does Frederic Henry, Prince of Orange, capture Breda on 6 October (while Ferdinand of Austria, Infant of Spain in vain came to its assistance with a formidable army), after it had been besieged from 23 July until the assault on 19 August, 1637].

The castle or palace belongs to King William, who is Baron of Breda. It is four-square with a large court in the middle; it has a moat round it. There is a fine gallery where are painted many of the King's family with their alliances by marriage. There are four large rooms hung with tapestry very good though old, in which are wrought the [14] several princes and princesses of the House of Nassau since Adolph, who was Emperor, down as far as the King's father [William II], all on horseback as big as the life with several of the memorable actions done by most of them. There is an old tower, yet standing, just by the house, whereof the common people have a prophesy that as long as that tower is standing they will not be freed from taxes.

The town is pretty large and well fortified. As we went out of the town beside the common way – gelt as they call it, we paid again a particular toll to the King as Baron of Breda.

Bergen op Zoom. Coehoorn's fortifications, 1706

Justinian Isham, 23-24 April 1705 N.S.

[30] Thursday 23rd. About nine o'clock in the morning we set sail [from Goes] with a pretty fresh gale, and after some time came into the Eastern Scheldt [Oosterschelde], and about half an hour after twelve to Ter Tholen, a city of Zeeland but a miserable place, being twelve hours from Middelburg. After some stay we went in a covered cart with one horse to Bergen op Zoom, an hour off. We ferried over a little rivulet [Eendracht] by the town and passed through Halsteren, a village standing upon a hill, which was the first of that nation I had seen for a good while. It [Bergen op Zoom] is I think in Brabant. We spent the rest of the day in seeing the town which is well enough. The marketplace is large and upon it stands the church, the stadhuys and the Grand Guard. One canal comes [from the Schelde] into the town.

Friday 24th. [31] Having obtained permission from the commander of the town to see the fortifications, he sent a soldier along with us, and the engineer one of his men, to show them us. Towards Brabant Coehoorn has done his masterpiece, there being such a number of fine works. Each bastion has on both sides its lunettes. Underground are a vast many galleries, casemates and mines, in which subter-ranean works consists chiefly the strength of the place. All round about the town, as I was told, might have been put under water, had it not been in one place where is a rising ground, which, though they have levelled as much as possible, will not yet do. Towards the waterside are only the old fortifications, and as the others are not yet finished it will cost the States a vast deal more. The works are carried on by one Monsieur Le Lubigny [Longuehaye].

In the church are several monuments worth seeing. The first I saw was of a governor of the town [Louis de Kethulle], who the fellow that showed us said had been page to Prince Maurice. He being in the camp [before Deventer in 1591] when a Spanish general challenged any that would fight him, accepted the cartel [provocation] and at first blow cut off the Spaniard's hand, for which action the government of the town was bestowed upon him. He stands in plasterwork in a niche and his wife in another. Above that he is represented on horseback in boss [high relief] with a hand lying by him. [...]

[32] Another monument is one of Edward Bruce, Baron of Kinloss, a Scotchman, who being to fight a duel saw Death's head in a looking-glass, so that he was sure to be killed, which fell out [1613]. He is in marble, lying upon his tomb with Death unto him. [...]. But the finest of all is of [Charles] Morgan, an Englishman, governor of this place. He lies in marble on a tomb of the same with a lion and a helmet at his feet. Just by, [in a niche] stands his wife, and on one side of her is their son and on the other their daughter. Morgan's wife lies now interred at Delft in Holland. For the inscriptions I had not time to take them. This church was a great deal bigger, but a great part of it was pulled down, and as I was told, the walls were higher than the church is now. I saw some leaden coffins of the marquesses and governors of Bergen that were found in the demolished part.

Anonymous military officer, 25 June (6 July) 1706

[2v] From hence [Rotterdam] I went June the 23rd for Breda by sea and landed at Moerdijk in my way thither, and June 25th arrived safe here. This is a noble, fine town; a very large and noble marketplace, large streets and fine pieces of architecture [3r] in almost every street here. That which is most to be admired is the King's house, built [1684-1695] by King William, and the church at the lower end of the marketplace; a description of both which follows.

The King's House. You are led to it by a square place, regularly planted with green trees and fine houses on each side. Through the walks you pass in a direct parallel line to an old large gate, over a ditch by a drawbridge, and over which being passed, you see on the left the King's house, being a most noble building surrounded with another ditch and a drawbridge over which you must pass to the palace, which has a lovely prospect in the front as ever can be seen, being a garden full of pleasure and admiration. [Going] into this garden you pass by on the left a tennis court, built after the English manner, and arrive at a gate, where by ringing a bell you are admitted into a sort of an oval court, planted with large trees, through which you pass to a very neat gate making a most glorious and rich show and yet not costly, being more [3v] for show than expense, but yet extremely fine, at the top of which is the name of the King in a cipher, over which is the English imperial crown.

Through this gate you pass into a very large and fine grove, leaving on the left hand a very fine and curious aviary in which are fine large pine trees growing about seventeen foot high within the wires. Here are all sorts of birds called singing birds, with pheasants, partridges, quails and the like, with both rabbits and hares. I myself saw a leash of hares feeding at one time appointed. [Next] to this aviary is a private garden with a burrow walk, directly in the middle, which is very pleasant. Betwixt these you pass into the grove, which is one continual shade, the sun not being able to penetrate the trees which are of a very great height, and planted extremely regular, in which are planted abundance of seats for the ease, pleasure and convenience of the spectators, which are abundance.

At the upper end of this grove are two very long and fine walks which run the whole length of the grove, garden and palace, from which at once you have not only the prospect [4r] of the palace but likewise of the ramparts, which enclose the whole as well as it does the town, the garden, the grove, the fish-ponds, the aviary and great part of the town. As you walk along those walks, you pass under several summer houses archwise, full of seats in the middle, [on] most of which these two mottos. The first is a scroll of paper supported by four angels, very well painted, with this motto: Hinc lucem et munimentum [from here one receives light and protection]. On the right hand of which is an eagle holding in his claw this motto: Hac itur ad astra [this way he flies to the stars].

From this you descend eight descents into the garden where you find a hundred images planted very regularly at the corners of beds of box, which are very beautiful. In one grows the royal arms of England, so plain to be distinguished in each part as if it were painted. In another that of the States, in another a sun-dial, in another several curious and artificial knots, as indeed all the whole is grounded. In the middle of the garden is a very large image of Hercules' [4v] flaying of the lion. On the ends of the garden are large high hedges of hornbeam cut very even, in the middle of which are round holes cut, in which are planted several images in imitation of Caesars' heads, which gives a very pleasant prospect. There are likewise very fine fish-ponds walled in, which seem to be very well stored by the great quantities that are seen upon the surface of the water, both of great and small fry.

The church is a noble structure, built all of stone, but within very fine, beyond ours in England as is very strange, but I can impute it to nothing but their bigotry, by reason they are full of the finest of paintings after the Romish fashion. The steeple of this church has 448 ascents, which make 224 foot in height; upon which a man watches continually night and day, and as soon as the clock strikes ten in the evening, he sounds a trumpet and so continues to do every hour in the night, to give notice he does not sleep. And likewise to see no enemy appears, [5r] neither if there is any fire in the town.

This town is a large fortified town having only four ways to come into it, which are called ports, with ditches, drawbridges and ramparts planted with cannons. The four ports are these: the Antwerp port, the Boschport, the Ginneken port and the Waterport.

Sir John Percival, 22 June (3 July) 1718

[46r] Breda is ten hours by computation from Antwerp, but our berline brought us thither in six. As it is a frontier town, the Dutch keep a particular eye upon it and have rendered it extremely strong with ditches and outworks, maintained in exact order and repair. Besides, in case of a siege it may be lain [46v] under water.

The Popish inhabitants are computed at four times the number of the Reformed, which last are about 2,400. Yet the magistrates are under no apprehension; for remaining easy in their civil rights and being allowed the exercise of their religion in private houses, they [i.e. the Catholics] live peaceably and contribute with cheerfulness to the common defence of their country. The government suffer them not indeed to bear civil employments, being sensible of the mischievous effects of allowing magistrates, or those who serve the State in offices of trust, to profess a different religion from that established by law, insomuch that it is not allowed even so much as to the Arminians. But in the army they make use of their Papist subjects, which endears them to the love of their country, seeing they are permitted to serve it in posts of honour and profit, and it might be dangerous to refuse this to them on account of their numbers. [...]

On Monday the 23rd June, we set out from Breda in a postwaggon at five in the morning, and about nine arrived at Swoll [Lage Zwaluwe], a small village on the banks of the Biesbos. The country we passed is so low a flat [marsh] that there is no travelling through it, even in summer, but over the dikes and rampiers [ramparts], cast up to fence against the waters. Swoll is the last town of Brabant, which province is here separated from Holland by the sea above mentioned. The passage from hence to Holland is frequented in summer, but not in the winter season, for when it blows anything hard, the waters grow outrageous and dangerous.

Formerly there was a great tract of land where now we see the [48v] Biesbos, but in the year 1421, the sea broke down the banks and washed away a hundred thousand inhabitants. We found here a narrow passage bark ready to sail and, the weather and wind favouring, entered it.

In our way some passengers showed us the place, nine miles distant, where the late Prince of Frieze [Johan Willem Friso] (whom I knew in 1706, when I made my first travels) was lost as he endeavoured to cross from Brabant into Holland [1711]. He was a hopeful prince and behaved himself so well in the field that the army had conceived the greatest esteem for him. But the trading part of the Seven Provinces dreaded him, apprehending that he would one day arrive to be stadholder, to which office they were much averse, by reason of the power annexed to it. The little concern they showed at his death gave occasion to some to think he had not fair play for his life, but the following extract of a letter written on that melancholy occasion, will satisfy men that it was only the will of God that so he should perish.

Bergen op Zoom
Population: 2,500-5,000 (1675-1750).
Distances: Antwerp 7 hours (20 miles), Breda 7 hours (20 miles), Dordrecht 10 hours (28 miles), Middelburg 8 hours (26 miles).
Inns, *Reisboek* (1689, 1700 and 1721): De drie Hoefyzers*; Den Helm*; Het Naghtegaalken; De Swaan, bij de Wouwsche Poort*.

Breda
Population: 5,000-10,000 (1675-1750).
Distances: Antwerp 10 hours (30 miles), Bergen op Zoom 7 hours (20 miles), Dordrecht 5 hours (16 miles), 's-Hertogenbosch 8 hours (23 miles), Rotterdam 9 hours (26 miles).
Inns, *Reisboek* (1689, 1700 and 1721): De Prins Kardinaal*, d'Oranje-appel* (op de Markt); d'Oude Prins*, achter de Kerk; De Drie Mooriaanen*, in de Brugstraat; De Swaan, op de Havermarkt*; 't Hof van Gelderland*, in de Nieuwe-Straat; Diest, in d'Antwerpse Straat; De Swaan, bij d'Antwerpsche Poort. *Reisboek* (1721) also: 't Leggende Hart (op de markt); De Witte Leeuw*, op de Boschstraat.

Further reading

J.B. Gramaye, *Antiquitates Belgicae*, Bruxelles-Leuven 1708.
T.E. van Goor, *Beschryving der stadt en lande van Breda*, 's-Gravenhage 1744.
J. Faure, *Histoire abrégée de la ville de Bergen-op-Zoom*, 's-Gravenhage 1761.
V.A.M. Beermann et al., *Geschiedenis van Breda*, vol. 2, *Aspecten van de stedelijke historie, 1568-1795*, Schiedam 1977.
W. van Ham and C. Vanwesenbeeck, *Gids voor Oud Bergen op Zoom*, Antwerpen [1983].
Ach Lieve Tijd, acht eeuwen Breda en de Bredanaars, M.W. van Boven (ed.), Zwolle 1985-1986.
Ach Lieve Tijd, 700 jaar West-Brabant, de West-Brabanders en hun rijke verleden, H. de Bruijn-Franken (ed.), Zwolle 1994-1996.
Jaarboek van de geschied- en oudheidkundige kring van Stad en Land van Breda 'De Oranjeboom', 1948-
De Waterschans, mededelingenblad van de Geschiedkundige Kring van Stad en Land van Bergen op Zoom, 1968-

Brugge and Sluis

William Lord Fitzwilliam, 6-7 July 1663 N.S.

[38v] [coming from Gent] Bridges is [after Gent] the second town of Flanders, it lies in a champion [level open] country, three miles of the sea. There are no natural rivers but all artificial, which run by and into this town. Amongst these ditches there is a very excellent great ditch, which runs directly into the sea, upon which ships may come out of the sea into the town. And to this belongs a good sluice which separates the seawater from the sweet. This town is very fairly built, although the houses are a little dispersed one from another. Here are many good streets [39r] and a fair marketplace. Most of the houses are of wood and built according to the old fashion.

Here are very good churches amongst which St Donaas and Our Saviour's are the chiefest. They are well-adorned with gold and silver and precious pictures. In Our Lady's Church we saw a great [St] Christopher made all of one tree. The Jesuits have here likewise a fair church; the form and outward shape of it is like all other which belong to them. In St Basil's Church it is said that there is kept the true blood of Our Saviour, preserved by Joseph of Arimathias and sent hither by a Count of Flanders [in 1148]. Our devotion was not so great as to make us go to see it, yet it was so fervent and ardent that it did engage us to go in pilgrimage to Jerusalem, at least to a chapel of it, which was transported from thence to this place, the true model of the church and sepulchre of Our Saviour on Mount Calvary. This town is indifferently strong. Formerly it has been very rich and proud. Here are very fair women, the fairest of Flanders. Here are likewise good capons.

From hence we went to Damme, a stronghold only a league from Bridges and two of Sluis. By art and nature it seems to be impregnable, lying in a plain country, and by the means of sluices it can drown the country round about it in twenty-four hours. It is surrounded with seven good big bastions of earth, as likewise the ramparts and parapets are of a good height and thickness; a brave fausse braye and some pieces of half-moons [39v] and spurworks round about the walls. Within there is nothing of remark but a fair spacious place, a little town house and few houses. The next day we went from Bridges to Sluis.

Sluis has been formerly one of the chiefest towns of Flanders. Now it is a little but very strong town belonging to the States of Holland [States-General]. It is situated on the seaside, being almost surrounded with water. This makes it very strong besides the good fortification which makes it almost impregnable. It is environed with eleven or twelve bastions, a very strong castle within the walls and on the mouth of the haven. Within this castle there is a well which is very curiously made and affords the most sweet water (for all it is so near the sea), that can be drunk. Not far from the castle, amongst a row of trees which formerly has been a pall-mall, there is the governor's garden, which is very pretty and curiously made. On the other side of the haven over against the castle, there has been another strong place and from it to the castle there used to be extended a chain for to hinder ships from entering the haven. This chain was cut in pieces by a ship which had a saw at the bottom. The chain is yet to be seen in the town's house, which is a very pretty place in respect of this town. Here is an excellent haven.

On the other side of [40r] the haven towards the Spanish fort called St Donaas, there is a very strong outwork of some bastions; on the seaside is Cadzand and other little forts; over against on the other side of the sea there is a Spanish fort called St Jacob's. St Donaas, which lies towards Bridges, is environed with four bastions very strong by art and by nature. It is but a quarter of a mile from Sluis. In the time of war it has exacted contribution money of Sluis, and when the Hollanders did use to shoot from their ships into Dunkirk, the Spaniards would most commonly send back their balls from St Donaas into Sluis.

Sluis has gotten its name of many sluices which belong to it and by whose means she may drown the country round about her and set herself wholly in water, by which means she seems to be impregnable, and had not been taken by Prince Maurice [1604] had he not starved the town. Here we were entertained by an English captain called Buttler by whose means and the governor's permission we came to see this town. From Sluis we returned the same night to Bridges. [cont. Oostende and Nieuwpoort]

Richard Holford, 22-23 August (1-2 September) 1671

[34r] We came to Bruges Thursday night at seven and lodged at the Porte d'Or. Saw nothing that night, but the morrow we saw the cloister of the English nuns (one whereof the lady abbess is Madam Bedingfield, the other lady abbess is Madam Brouncker), a great many English nuns and some very handsome.

We saw the Jesuits' church, a most curious and strong building, very light and beautiful, and at the upper end three altars, the middlemost very rich, and two great brass [34v] candlesticks at least twelve foot high, set upon marble pedestals about eighteen inches high. Very excellent pictures and a most neat and curious pulpit, artificially placed and most exquisitely carved to admiration. The statue on which the pulpit stands kneels on two carved books, so artificial that it will deceive the eye at a small distance, and the cover of the pulpit a curious carved scallop shell, not to be described.

We saw the cloister of the Dominicans and in their chapel the new St Rose [feast day 30 August], lately canonized. Her canonization was celebrated and the chapel yet adorned and in the midst, on a large pedestal placed Faith, Hope and Charity, supporting a canopy and over them under the canopy the Saint. The manner of adorning their churches for such ceremonies mighty pretty, pleasant and cheap.

We then saw St Mary's church, a very large and beautiful building, the spire whereof seems to stand awry, for which they tell a story (and show a monument of a skeleton in the churchyard) that the builder of the steeple perceiving the [35r] same to stand awry, pulled it down once or twice, and not being able to place it upright, threw himself from it. This seems to be but a story, but they yet pray and have a mass for his soul, therefore it is thought he fell down by accident. [...]

John Walker, 30-31 August (9-10 September) 1671

[15] [Having left Gent] On the 30th instant in the evening we reached the delightful town of Bruges, situated in a flat plentiful part of Flanders, watered by the river Reya, a dark and slow-running stream. Here (as at Ghant) we were not permitted to enter till we had given in our names.

This town represented to us [a] great variety of objects; many religious houses and churches. In that of the Virgin Mary we beheld an incomparable draught of Michelangelo's, showing Christ when he was taken down from the cross; a very costly tomb in great brass figures of the Duke and Duchess of Burgundy; a pair of exceeding large brass candlesticks standing before the altar in the choir, above twelve foot in height. In this church is the effigies of St Christopher, cut out in stone of a wonderful magnitude.

After this we went to the Jesuits' college, who civilly showed us the library, school and theatre and invited us to see the tragedy of Martin Spira (acted by their young scholars the next day), but our occasions would not suffer us to tarry so long. From hence we repaired to the abbey [Ter Duinen] of St Bartholomew or Bernard (for wanting the language we did often mistake). This we found to be a handsome regular building and a stately cloister. Here they showed us the heads of two ancient abbots, Oswold and Grimbold, cast in silver and of great proportion. The prior was very respectful to us, walked about the garden and presented us with grapes and other fruits, sprigs of myrtle and suchlike favours.

But the obligations of the lady abbess of the English nunnery were above all things else. Her name was Brighurst, a comely well-spoken woman. The house of the nunnery had been a palace belonging to the governors of the Netherlands, a good old building. The abbess favoured us with a sight of some of her nuns, amongst which was a sister of Sir Francis Englefield's in Wiltshire. In the chapel was buried the heart of the Lady [Mary] Teynham of that family with an inscription over it. The abbess, being willing more and more to oblige us, was pleased to grant us the favour to hear her choir of nuns. Whilst we were discoursing, a nun came and tendered her a key upon the knee, and after that rose up and tolled a bell, which was no sooner done but we heard the nuns began to convene in a gallery overhead. After this we heard a [16] most harmonious consort of viols and violins with the organ. Then a ravishing voice of a nun singing in Italian a treble part alone; the rest now and then keeping the chorus; next one of them played singly upon the lyra viol and ran very delightful division. And last of all, one of them played upon the trumpet marine to admiration. This favour was the greater because it was performed before the time of vespers.

Having hitherto pleased our fancy with divine objects, we deemed it not amiss to take a relish of secular things in the close. We walked about the walls of the town till we came to a place called the garden of the archers, viz. Hortus Sagittariorum. It was indeed a very curious waterwork, where all sort of artificers were at work as in that at Bruxelles. On the outside of the rails are several horsemen, their horses disgorging water, Neptune riding upon a dolphin, Fortune, standing with one foot upon a globe, turned round all the time by the force of the waters. Opposite to this is an archer standing with a drawn bow in his hand, the water ascending into his body and streaming out at the end of his arrow. In the midst of these knacks stood a basin with a golden ball in the middle, which was forced out of its centre by a stream of water ten or twelve foot high and so kept up for a long while, with divers other pretty remarkable diversions.

From hence we went off about three of the clock in the afternoon and took boat for Ostend. [cont. Oostende and Nieuwpoort]

Thomas Scott, 27-28 September (7-8 October) 1672

[22v] [After an uncomfortable night outside the walls of Gent] But the day at length to our great comfort appearing, about nine we took boat for Bridges in which, though on the benches, we made amends to nature for its want of sleep the night before, till about noon being called to dinner, which came not very [23r] unfavourable; passing the afternoon by cards till we came to Bridges, where getting up somewhat early Saturday morning, we took a short view of the town.

First we are led to the waterworks, being puppets of tin imitating several trades, having their motion caused by the water. From whence, in our way to the marketplace, is the friary of the order of Capuchins, in the door whereof is erected an artificial rock, wherein are the images of our Blessed Lady and St Francis so lively wrought that at the first sight you would take them to be really so, which (it being service-time) was all we had sight of.

[23v] Not far from this stands a church having nailed to the doors thereof several horseshoes dedicated to a farrier, the founder thereof, and at one certain day in the year all the country [people] bring in their horses to be blessed there; such is the superstition of that religion. From here we are led to the town hall [Lakenhalle, woollen drapers' hall], which, being in the nature of a bridge the water running lengthwise under it and a spacious building, is not without remark. Near to this stands an ancient building which our now Sovereign Lord, the King [Charles II], was pleased to content himself to live in [1656-1658], in the late unfortunate troubles in England.

SACELLUM SACRI CRUORIS.

The Chapel of the Holy Blood, c. 1725

Not far from which is erected a neat chapel called [24r] the Chapel of Blood, from a glass of blood therein kept, believed to be Our Saviour's real blood. Which to me seems a great contradiction of their faith who can have it every day by virtue of five words speaking [at the eucharist]. And I am apt to believe that if it were examined, there would appear to be as much of this as there were of that Saint's teeth in England, which were supposed a present remedy for the toothache, but being called in by proclamation by King Edward VI appeared to be a ton at the least.

The last place our time would permit us to see was the English cloister of nuns of the order of St Francis. The Lady whereof, entertaining us with wine, biscuits and discourse, [24v] understanding we were going for England, desired us to deliver her several letters here, which having received, we parted. And being not permitted to enter further than the gates, we saw not anything of curiosity but the sight of her ladyship and her holy sisters the nuns (the habit of whom being known to many of England and too tedious to insert, I shall omit).

About ten of the clock we took boat for Newport where arriving about noon [four], and being informed that the packet boat for England went off the morrow night, being Sunday, and conceiving it a speedier though [25r] more dangerous way than the way by Calais (by reason of the Dutch capers cruising on those seas), we resolved on that passage. In order whereto on Sunday about seven in the evening, by reason of shutting the ports, we went aboard the vessel, which about twelve set sail. And about three on Monday [afternoon], by reason of contrary winds, arrived at the North Foreland, fifteen miles from Dover, the intended port, and within two miles of Margate in the county of Kent, but by the way were frightened by two French capers, which at first we supposed to be Dutch.

Joseph Taylor, 2 (13) September 1707

[31r] Dear Cousin,

I am at last got safe again into the Dutch territories and employ my first leisure hours in giving you an account of Bruges, which I last came from. The city is very beautiful, being adorned with many noble buildings, fine houses [31v] and spacious streets. The steeples are high and ornamental, two of which may be seen at several leagues' distance. That belonging to Our Lady's Church is whitened for a beacon to the mariners at sea, which is done at the charge of the Hollanders. There are several markets, but the cornmarket, the flaxen-market, the Friday-market or Spanish parade are the chief, as also several halls, of which the woollen-drapers' is the finest, being built over a river so as ships may come under it and unload.

This town derives its name from the vast number of bridges it has over the river and canals, of which they told me there were 360, most of stone. The principal churches I visited were St Salvator, which has a noble marble portico belonging to the choir, and in an altar I saw the picture of Our Lady with the angels carrying up the Holy House [of the Virgin] to heaven. Amongst the many fine altars that of De la Rosa, all of polished marble, is the most remarkable, which has a picture representing Saint Silvester [Hippolytus] torn to pieces by wild horses. There is likewise fixed to one of the pillars the picture of St Joseph at [32r] large, and [in Our Lady's Church] the effigies of St Christopher of a prodigious size, cut out of one entire tree, bearing a proportionable figure of Our Saviour upon his shoulders. In Our Lady's Church the beautiful tombs and the monuments of the barons of Sterkhuison [Gruuthuse, Princes of Steenhuyse] and the rich robes of Philip the Good and other princes are worth observation. The finest altar-piece is that of Our Lady's and Our Saviour carved in marble by that famous artist Michelangelo.

In the Jesuits' church is a handsome pulpit with carved work in imitation of ropes to support it. The like carvings is at one of the altars, supported by four marble pillars. The several pictures of Our Saviour worshipped by the Wise Men, Joseph and the Virgin Mary travelling to Jerusalem, Our Saviour lying dead and the women bewailing him, Our Lady received into heaven by Our Saviour and St Ignatius praying to Christ, who appears to him in the clouds, are very well done. In St Anne's Chapel I saw a Resurrection, indifferently well designed, but it stands too near the view. I also visited the famous Chapel of Jerusalem and the model of Our Saviour's tomb, built by a nobleman [Pierre Adornes] of this place, who had travelled [32v] twice thither in order to have it more exact. On one side of the altar is the figure of Our Saviour lying along [at full length] in a little vault with a lamp continually burning. There are stairs on each side leading up to the tower, on which there is a great ball, wherein twelve persons may easily sit.

The famous abbey of Bernard called Dunes is a noble pile of buildings scarce finished; it was first founded on the seashore [at Koksijde], from whence it received its name; which for more conveniency was removed to Bruges [1627]. It is four storeys high with spacious arched galleries and large gardens. It happened to be a holiday so, the abbot being abroad and the rest of the fraternity at their diversions in the garden, by the favour of one of the religious, who was a very good-humoured man, I saw all the rarities. When I came into the library I enquired for *Monasticon Anglicanum* [by Sir William Dugdale], on purpose to try whether he would show it me being an Englishman, but he told me it was not there, though afterwards I with a little searching, found it amongst the rest of the English histories. In his chamber he showed me [an] abundance of good prints, particularly two of mortality and diverted me with his flageolet [33r] to which a number of birds round the room joined in consort and made a great deal of harmony. And indeed, by all his actions he seemed to be a virtuoso, above the common genius of that useless part of mankind.

In a dining-room I saw the picture of King Charles [II] and his two brothers, who in their banishment resided at Bruges [1656-1658] and also the pictures of all the other abbots. In another room I was very much entertained with three excellent pictures done by Van Dyck of the descension of the Holy Ghost in the Pentecost, of a soldier placing a crown of thorns on Our Saviour's head and of St John Baptist and of St John the Evangelist at full length. They told me they were mortgaged to the King of France for a vast sum of money, which with much reluctancy he returned to the abbey upon repayment of it. There is likewise a very good night-piece, four landscapes and two heads done with a great deal of spirit and many other pieces of painting of more than ordinary elegance. The boards of the floor are remarkable for their great length, and the hangings of needlework [33v] are very curious, wherein is represented the Ascension and the angel's appearing to the Virgin Mary.

From thence I went to see the house where King Charles resided, and afterwards to the Augustine nunnery, where there are forty-five nuns professed. Having no recommendation here, I enquired for the lady abbess and told her I was just come from Brussels and the army, and being upon my return for England, should be glad to do the ladies service, if they had any commands to lay upon me. She desired me to walk into the speaking-room, where in a short time she brought me word that the ladies had no occasion to give me trouble, but if I desired to see any of them, she would intercede for me. I told her I was altogether a stranger but should be glad to have the honour of speaking with the last that came thither, not in the least suspecting who it was, upon which she retired. And as soon as I had sat down in a chair, who should enter but the pretty Mrs Vaughan and her sister and another lady. This put me into an inexpressable surprise, and indeed, the ladies seemed [34r] to be in no less confusion.

They became their habits extremely well and had their former charms, though their fine hair was shaved. The youngest of them first spoke to me and said, 'Sir, you may be well surprised to see us here, but it was what we designed when we left England; and what we told you to the contrary at Brussels was only to turn your discourse from further enquiry'. By this time I had power to tell them I was glad to see them well, though through a grate, and since so much virtue, beauty and good nature must be cloistered, I began to preach up the pleasures of a retired life, free from the cares and perplexities of a troublesome world. In such discourse we spent some hours, till a bell rang and then they rose up and took their last farewell, telling me they must stay no longer, and so, wishing me a good voyage, retired, desiring if ever I came into that country again, that I would not forget a visit to my fellow travellers.

After [34v] this odd encounter, to divert myself I went to see the waterworks, which by a certain engine turning a chain with a great number of buckets artificially disposed, receives and discharges into a cistern water enough to serve the whole town. I went afterwards to the Grand Tour, where the fine ladies with rich equipages were as numerous as at Brussels or Ghent. [cont. Oostende and Nieuwpoort]

[36r] The next morning I set forward for this place [Sluis] by a postwaggon, the canal being out of order. The carriage was two permission shillings a man. I had the company of a merchant's lady, who had been at Bruges to bring her daughters from the nunnery, where they had spent two or three years for their education, and what with their comical relations of the several passages in the nunneries and the entertainment of their diverting songs, [36v] the journey seemed abundantly less tedious than I expected. [cont. Zeeland]

Sir John Percival, 15-17 (26-28) June 1718

[28r] The Jesuits have here a very handsome church, which was begun in 1646 and finished in three years' time [1619-1641], at the charge of the citizens of Ghent [Brugge], who for that purpose laid a duty of a penny per quart upon their beer. The front is well-designed and plain after the Roman style of architecture, not charged with improper carvings nor crowded with improper ornaments after the French taste. The roof is supported by stone pillars, which form three aisles, of which the main one is spacious, high and every way well-proportioned. The prospect to the high altar from the principal entrance at the west door is magnificent, and struck me more than anything I afterwards saw of like nature abroad.

The altar like others of the country is finely ornamented with marble columns of different sorts, busts and statues; those of Saint Ignatius [of Loyola] and Saint [Franciscus] Xaverius are finely carved. The last died in China, anno 1552 and was canonized in 1622; a finger of him is here preserved as a relic of inestimable value. The side aisles are covered with large historical landscapes representing for the most part the miracles of this apostle, and they don't forget to make you take notice of one in particular [28v] by [Jacob van] Art[h]ois, who was in best esteem for this manner of painting.

In the sacristy we were shown a number of rich vestments and ornaments for the altars on noted days: the silver and gilt plate set with diamonds and other precious stones belonging to these altars are here in great plenty. We saw likewise the theatre, where the scholars, educated in the college to the number of a hundred and fifty, are by representing plays, habituated from their childhood to a graceful action and proper confidence. This they do every month, but for their other learning there are five large school rooms, through which they pass successively, and wherein they are taught the rudiments of language, grammar, syntax, composition of Latin verse and lastly rhetoric.

The Jesuits are certainly the most learned religious order in the church of Rome, and the advantage they have of educating gentlemen's children after a better manner and method than other seminaries is one great reason why they subsist and are able to support themselves against the hatred of all the other orders and the resentment of many of the laity who detest them for intermeddling in matters of government and secular affairs [...]. [29r] Neither their morals nor discipline are so severe as that of other orders, for which they are envied by them. But it recommends them better to the nobility and the rich laity, who generally live more freely than the vulgar. And it must be owned to their commendation that none are more civil, sociable and genteel in their behaviour than these fathers, especially to strangers.

[29v] From the Jesuits' church we went to pay a visit to Mrs Blunt, the sister of Sir John Guise of Gloucestershire, a lady of very good sense and remarkable wit, but of very strong passions, who from the most zealous Protestant became three years ago as rigorous and bigoted a Papist (her husband being always one) and was then settled at Bruges, partly to avoid her friends' importunity and reproaches and partly to breed her children with liberty in the same persuasion. She was not at home, but we found her at the English nunnery of St Clare [=Augustines], where a sister of the Duke of Powis is lady abbess [Thérèse Joseph Herbert]. After some conversation with this lady, Mrs Blount introduced us to two gentlewomen of good family in England and whose relations we were acquainted with, Mrs Jerningham by name. They were sisters and had been nuns some time.

From hence Mrs Blunt carried us to the cloister of Carmelites chaussés. It is a begging order as well as the Carmelites déchaussés, but not so disagreeable, the latter going barefoot. They have a very handsome church, built after the manner of that of the Jesuits before described, but not so large. The friars, on that lady's account, for whom they had a particular esteem because of her constant attendance on their divine service, received us very civilly, showing us some rich ornaments in their [30r] sacristy, of which they were very conceited. They afterwards carried me into their private room, reserved for the reception of strangers, where I was obliged to sit down at table in company of three or four of them, who drank bumpers of white wine to the prosperity of England, their convent, my friends, their father guardian and suchlike indifferent healths. The ladies in the meantime waiting without in the sacristy, this apartment being sacred from women, as are the libraries of convents. It was with difficulty I could get away, and at parting I dropped a piece of money into the charity box near the church door, the begging orders being allowed to accept benevolence that way, though forbid to receive it in the hand. [cont. Gent]

Anonymous tourist, 5-8 May 1720 N.S.

[4v] Set out [from Nieuwpoort] at two o'clock in the common boat for Bruges; convenient boat enough; came to Bruges at eight o'clock, seven leagues. Bruges, a pretty neat town of a good extent. Fine cathedral. Went to the bishop's palace, fine tapestry hangings, viz. the history of Joseph; fine pictures; the present bishop is [Henri Joseph] Van Susteren. Were introduced by Mr Linch, a magistrate of the town, into the town house, where a fine picture of the Emperor and another of the Duke of Bavaria. Over the judgement seat is a fine picture of Cambyses [King of Persia] ordering a bad judge to be flayed alive. See in the hospital of St John two very fine pictures representing the Virgin Mary, the beheading of St John, and the whole apocalypse in very fine colours on wood not at all faded, though made in the year 1479 by Johannes Memling. The transparent veils upon the women's heads are very remarkable in [5v] these two pictures as being incomparably made. Memling had been in the hospital himself and presented it for an acknowledgement.

The Jesuits' church is extremely fine; the great altar railed in by fine marble parquet. Twelve very fine pictures, six on each side of the church. Lodged à l'Hotel du Commerce, good house but dear. Went upon the tower of the clock, from whence a very fine prospect. See the chapel of the English nuns, indifferent. To Notre Dame, a very fine church. Two magnificent tombs of touchstone [black marble] with fine work of brass gilded; the one for Charles the Hardy, Duke of Burgundy, who died upon the field near Nantes [Nancy]. The other of his daughter Mary, sole heiress to the Seventeen Provinces, married to Maximilian of Austria [1477].

Seen there also an admirable statue in white marble of the Virgin Mary, done by Michelangelo, upon the altar of a chapel. Seen the college of [one of] the four bodies [making up the County of Flanders], called 't Free [het Brugse Vrije], a beautiful room where there is fine carved work in wood over the chimney, the mantlepiece well-wrought in marble, being the history of Susanna and Daniel. [6v] This college consists of deputies from Bruges, Ghent, [the] Ecclesiast[ics] and Het Vrije [=inaccurate]. Het Vrije are magistrates that govern all the country about Bruges, to Ostend, Newport, Ghent, etc.

Went to the abbey of Dunes of the Bernardites, where fine walks; an indifferent library. In the abbot's apartment three good large pictures of considerable value. Set out at nine for Ghent in the common boat. [cont. Gent]

Brugge

Population: 36,000 (1690), 30,000 (1755).

Distances: Gent 8 hours (24 miles), Nieuwpoort 7 hours (21 miles), Oostende 4 hours (11 miles), Sluis 3 hours (9 miles).

Inns, *Reisboek* (1689, 1700 and 1721): Het Hemelrijk; Het Paradijs*; De Koning van Spanjen*; 't Goude Hoofd*, daar de Barge afvaart; De vier Heemskinderen, bij 't Minne-water; De Halve Maan*; De 3 Koornbloemen, bij de Kraan; De Goude Poort, in de Vlamingstraat*; Het Hart*, De drie Monniken, De Roode Leeuw* (in de Steenstraat); De Roode Poort*, bij de Hal; 't Mandetje, op de Markt; 't Goude Tonnetje, op d'Eyermarkt. *Reisboek* (1700 and 1721) also: Den Arend*, vanwaar de Wagens op Antwerpen afrijden.

Sluis

Population: 1,200 (400 houses, 1751 T.S.).

Distances: Brugge 3 hours (9 miles), Middelburg 6 hours (18 miles), Vlissingen 6 hours (18 miles).

Inns, *Reisboek* (1689 and 1700): De Goude Poort [only 1689]; De Goude Kroon; De Roode Leeuw; De Stad Vlissingen. *Reisboek* (1700) also: In Brugge; In Ostende.

Further reading

J.B. Gramaye, *Antiquitates Belgicae*, Bruxelles-Leuven 1708.

A. Sanderus, *Flandria illustrata*, Cologne 1641-1644, 's-Gravenhage 1732, 1735 (*Verheerlykt Vlaandre*, 's-Gravenhage 1732, 1735); reprint Antwerpen-Amsterdam 1981.

J.A. van Houtte, *De geschiedenis van Brugge*, Tielt-Bussum 1982.

P. de Brock, *Sluis*, Abcoude 1991.

Brugge die scone, 1980-

Brussels

William Lord Fitzwilliam, 16 April 1663 N.S.

[5v] [coming from Mons] At last we did arrive at Brussels and took our lodgings at the sign of the Old Wolf, by a Frenchman.

Brussels lies in Brabant and in the fruitfullest and most pleasant part of it. It is situated partly on a hill, partly on even ground. The Court lies upon a hill; the fabric of it is but mean and ordinary, yet very commodious and has been formerly the residence of the greatest princes of Europe. Behind the Court there is a very ample and pleasant park. There is an ostrich kept; no other animals but dogs and cows we saw within it. Here have been likewise very [6r] curious waterworks, but now, or at least at my being there, they were all out of tune. This park serves for a walk for the ladies of this town, who ordinarily meet here in a great number every afternoon when it is fair weather. At this Court there is at present no mirth, no gallantry to be seen: a morose Spaniard resides here, Marquis de Caracena, Governor of the Spanish Netherlands.

After the Court we saw the rest of the town, its figure resembles a man's heart. It is not very big, for in two hours it may be walked about. It is fortified, but with old walls, deep ditches and some half-moons for its outworks. The river Sina [Senne] runs through the town. It has seven gates built according to the Doric manner, every gate has its own pleasure: through the Louvainish gate you go to catch birds, out of the Algidomontan's [Coudenberg gate, within the Namur gate] you go to catch fish; Obbrussel's [Halle gate] for to hunt; out of the Anderlechten's you go into cornfields; out of the Flanders [gate] you go into meadows; out of the Lovenish [Laeken gate] you go to wells [vineyards] and fountains; out of the Mechelen port you go into gardens. Every port has its peculiar walk and pleasure.

Here are seven parishes, St Gudule's is the chiefest; its church is very well-built and very richly adorned with pictures. Here are many religious and pious houses, we went only to see the Jesuits, who have here a very great college, a very well-built vestry and a very good library, filled up with very choice and curious books, and with [an] abundance of rarities, chiefly several optic glasses, the most curious that can be made or seen. The father who showed us the college was extraordinary civil and free with us. He told us that he used to be sent into Holland for to preach the gospel, to encourage the strong in his faith, to help the weak and convert others. In London he told us there are only at his knowledge two hundred of his society, who have the same employment.

After we had taken our leave of him we went to try if we could see the cham-

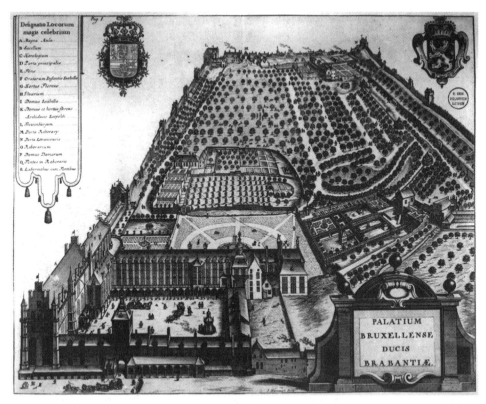

The Court, 1724

bers [6v] of the palace, but the austerity or gravity of Caracena would not give us leave to do it. We heard that two galleries are very well worth seeing, as being richly garnished and adorned with rare pictures, tables, clocks, silver globes and other rarities.

We saw the stables which are big enough to keep 127 horses; above the stable is the armoury, where we did see [an] abundance of old arms, headpieces, coats of mail, arms for horses, swords, guns, bows, etc., which the Dukes of Burgundy did formerly use, as likewise Charles V, Archduke Albert and Don John [of Austria] (who lives yet). Here we saw likewise three horses. The greater, which is a white one, served Archduke Albert at the battle of Newport [1600], where it did save him his life although it was dangerously wounded and did not die till the year after, on the very same day on which it was wounded. Some verses are made on it, and its skin remains now for a perpetual memory of its noble deeds whilst it had life in it. The grey horse served likewise the same Prince when he made his entry at Brussels [1596]. On the little one used to ride Isabella, the Archduke's wife. It was her darling, and so after its death its skin was likewise filled up for to represent it to future ages.

110

The town house of Brussels merits to be seen; there are just seven streets which lead you to it and it stands upon a fair marketplace. The architecture of it is indifferent good, not the best nor the worst. Within it is not at all garnished. Here are many other good houses as the palaces of Aarschot, Orange, Aumale, Cleve, Hoochstraten, Barlaimont, Aremberg, Mansfeld, Egmond, Solre, Furstenburg and Spinola's.

Beside the kingly magistrate who resides at the Court, the King of Spain chooses seven other (called scabini) out of the chiefest families of Brussels. Their government is only annual. To these seven are added two burgomasters, one a gentleman, the other a citizen and six counsellors; but before all these, there is a mayor who is always a very good gentleman [...]

[7r] There is a tour à la mode in the lower end of the town; all the persons of quality meet here one another in their coaches all the afternoons, and so they go out one street into another for to see and to be seen. Here we took notice how serviceable the English dogs are to this town, for they serve instead of porters and horses, two of them being put before a little waggon are able to draw a hundred pounds' weight. There are sometimes sent into Spain six of the best, which serve for to draw little coaches, and this is all which we did remark at Brussels. Our next journey was for Louvain, where we arrived about eight o'clock at night. [cont. Mechelen and Leuven]

John Walker, 27-29 August (6-8 September) 1671

[11] We [left Antwerp and] dined at Mechelen, a neat pleasant town and an episcopal see, with a fair church dedicated to St Rumbald and on the 27th, being Sunday, arrived in a waggon at Bruxelles, the usual seat of the governors of the Spanish Netherlands, which is thought most commodious, being in Brabant and edging upon the borders of Flanders. It is of a great extent, the streets steep and rising, yet spacious and well-beautified with fountains and aquaducts, the principal whereof is the Mannicke Piss, being the figure of a brass boy erected upon a pedestal, the water issuing from his privy member (at a good distance) into a stone cistern or receiver.

The palace or residence of the governors is an ancient solid building, resembling that at Whitehall but with more curiosity, excepting the part of the Banqueting House. At the front of the palace you come upon a broad space of ground encircled with pillars and rare carved stonework, on the top whereof (heretofore) stood many brass figures. But the avarice of some of their governors has now reduced them only to four, two whereof are those of Albertus and Isabella. Entering the palace, on the left hand, stood an old hall with shops, almost like that at The Hague. Belonging to it is a very sumptuous chapel and a gallery full of images of several of the Austrian and Burgundian families.

Hence we were led into the park, which [is] well-wooded but not so large as St James'. Here is a canal, paved on each side and at the bottom with smooth broad stone; many artificial rocks streaming with water, some of them composed of the roots or stumps of trees. But that which [was] most rare and delightful was a retiring place of the Archduchess Isabella, wherein was a rock, set with shells and mother of pearl, a water-organ affording great harmony; the tritons or sea-gods sounding their hollow shells; all sorts of artificers at work. Swans and [12] other fowl swimming about in a circle with a neat device of two balls running upon a string from one dragon's mouth to another and at last the water springing out of little holes in the pavement and so falling down like a shower of rain, all [of] which was performed to the great admiration of the spectators.

After this we betook ourselves to Count Marsin's [Marchin] palace (the general of the horse), heretofore the Court of the Nassaus. Part of it lies ruinous, having been a few years since beaten down by a thunderstorm which brought so much sulphur and combustible matter that it quickly consumed the timberwork. The stone hangs up at the gate in ribs of iron, which I guessed to be about 150 pound.

In the open space before the stadhouse they showed us the place where Count Egmont and Hoorne were beheaded [1568], upon which is erected a stately fountain. The stadhouse is full of ancient pictures, but that which is most prized is Solomon's Judgement, drawn by Rubens, valued at four thousand florins [guilders].

After this we went to the armoury, where we beheld very exquisite rarities, as bucklers, headpieces of carved and stained work, coats of mail, swords, pistols and guns of admirable art. The skin of the white horse which brought the Archduke Albert from the battle of Newport, with a tablet of verses in his commendation. Another of a piebald colour which the Archduchess Isabella rode on when she entered Bruxelles in state, both upon wooden frames. In all this variety we ought not to omit a buckler of Charles V, which he caused to be made for his night-sports, when he went in quest of his mistresses. In the inside was a dark lantern, the outside full of little sloping holes that if the adversary made any home pass, upon the least turn of the arm he broke off his point and at the same time might fall in and wound him with a short sword that stuck in the centre of the buckler.

From secular things we pass over to the religious, [13] viz. to the English nunnery. At the grate we discoursed with two nuns who bore the name of Russell, they were Augustines by order, the Lady Wigmore was their abbess. We went to hear their vespers but found that they chanted so miserably we could hardly refrain [from] laughing. In the chief church we saw an altar of the Carmelites, which showed them to be amorous friars; the Virgin Mary was dressed in the French mode, divers fine-dressed neat angels hanging in strings and hovering over her. It put us in mind of Venus and her band of Cupids.

After all we determined to go without the town and take a view of the works. We found it very sandy in our walking, as it is in all this part of Brabant. Many of the bastions, being grown defective and mouldering away, were undertaken by the inhabitants, whose diligence was very observable here. At one bastion you might see the Jesuits at work, some digging, others wheeling and filling the barrows. At

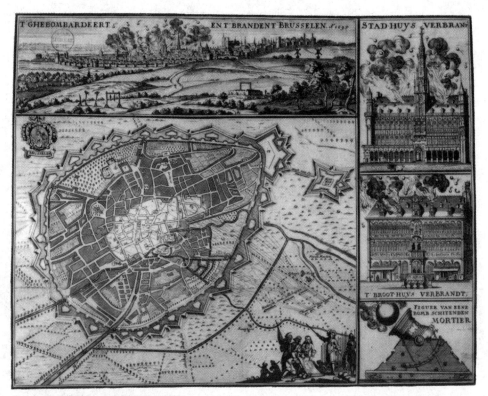

Bombardment of Brussels (1695), c. 1696

another the Capuchins and Franciscans employed after the same manner. At a third the gentry and merchants at work in their holland waistcoats, their ladies sitting by in their coaches, spectators of their lovers' labours. All endeavoured to prevent the attacks of the French. To give further encouragement to this great proceeding, the Governor of the Netherlands, Count Monterey, a person of great conduct and management, came (attended with four trumpets and forty horse) nobly equipped, about six of the clock in the evening (according to his usual custom), and very obligingly saluted the religious and the gentry labouring at the several bastions. This man by his singular diligence has so secured all roads and passages that Flanders, which for a long time was reputed a den of thieves, is now become as safe as any part of Europe and all in less than twelve months. [cont. Gent]

Anonymous London merchant, 21-23 September 1695 N.S.

[22] [coming from Antwerp] In this journey we pass by several towns and villages. The chiefest are Mechlin [Mechelen], thirteen miles from Brussels and from Vilvoorde, six. Here is a great castle almost gone to ruin and was once a prison for persons of note. In one room of it, which looks fair, as soon as you come in it, you

slide into a dungeon from whence one never returns. From Willebroek we pass about fifteen miles on [23] a canal in boats drawn by horses and from Vilvoorde runs the small river Senne close by the canal and at La Fontaine it runs under it, that place being guarded with soldiers. The canal of Brussels was made [1550-1561] by the Emperor Charles V, and cost above five hundred thousand crowns one hundred years ago.

In Brussels we found all the middle and best part of the town beaten down by the French bombs [13-15 August 1695]; a quarter part being ruined. The stadhouse, Broodhouse and several churches are blown up; only the tower of the stadhouse is standing and resembles the tower of the Exchange in London. I walked all over the ruins and found not one house standing amongst them and in all other parts round the town scarce a house touched.

The buildings are of brick except some few of stone and are very old. The town is populous but very dirty, as London is, and nothing like to the towns of Holland. The churches are large and [an] abundance of altars in them, but not so rich nor beautiful as the churches in Antwerp. The town lies on the breast of a hill, which gave the French a very fair mark from their batteries on the low side of the town; and on the upper side stands the palace of the Duke of Bavaria and the King's house [Court of Orange], wherein resides the Prince of Vaudemont. But this nor any side of the town has been damaged with the bombs.

On the 22nd September I hired three horses, for which I gave three crowns, to see the Confederate army encamped at Halle, about three hours from Brussels. At this time they happened to be upon a march from Halle to St Quentin-Linox [St Kwintens-Lennik], etc. intended to march the next day for Ninove, but by reason of the wet weather their baggage and cannon could not come up to St Quentin.

I returned the same night to Brussels, where a quarrel and some blows happened between one of my friends and the Dutch landlord about the hire of our horses, on which occasion we removed our lodging to another house. This night we had much difficulty to get lodging and victuals as we had also the night before, it being a fast-day here and the town was full of officers and others from the army, and provisions scarce. For these reasons, [24] and because my friend to whom I was recommended was gone to Antwerp, I left this town on Friday morning and came to Antwerp the same night, it having rained almost continually in this journey, as it had always done since I left England. The country about Brussels lies high, just as with us, having many woods, enclosures and cornfields and meanly built cottages much like unto England. [cont. Antwerp]

Joseph Taylor, 4-12 (15-23) August 1707

[13r] After I had written my last from Antwerp, I returned to my young Jesuits and passed the night with them very merrily. The next morning Captain Seaton and Mr Mills and I attended the Prince [of Hesse], who, after he had treated us with choco-

late and wine, took me and Mr Mills in his coach. A young German nobleman and Captain Seaton went in the coach we had hired for ourselves. Our journey [13v] was very pleasant, through a charming road all planted with trees and in several hours we arrived at Mechelen, having first passed the river Dyle. We went to hear mass in the Great Church, dedicated to St Rumbald, which is adorned with several fine altars and many oratories, and on the pillars are large images of the apostles and several of the saints as big as the life. After the priest had given the sacrament, which was the first time I ever saw that ceremony, there was a fine consort of music.

In a few hours we set out again. On the road we met a world of deserters from the French army, going to Holland, and a French party, who did not attack us. Nothing could be pleasanter than our travelling along the canal of Brussels, which is shaded by a noble row of trees for a league together, having at the same time Brussels in our view, where, by an easy ascent, we at last arrived and lodged at the Soleil d'Or. But the Prince went to the Duke of Bourgogne [inn]. You cannot imagine the pleasure I enjoyed at this place, which in all things answered the great idea I had formed of it from the [14r] description you have often given me. I need not mention to you its noble situation in a fruitful country, the fine broad streets and coffee-houses, especially those built since the last bombardment [1695]. I walked round the ramparts, which took me up above three hours. In that part of the town where the Court is, the streets are very irregular, being built upon a hill, but in the lower part the streets are very regular and straight, being all upon a flat. I observed several small carts drawn by dogs, which is very frequent in this country, though to me it was a great novelty.

The Court is a very old building, the Duke of Bavaria always resided there till it fell into our hands the last campaign [1706]. Now it is the place where the new Grand Council of the Spanish Netherlands assemble. There is a parade before it with a balustrade of stone. The first court is a large square, on the right is a piazza and on the left a great hall, where the Swiss keep guard in their proper habits with halbards in their hands, and in the front is a passage to the gardens and park. They [14v] showed us the audience room, the grand chamber and the long gallery. The floor of the antechamber is inlaid and the roof finely painted with several poetical stories, but the best is Aurora. In the dining-room is a noble marble chimney-piece, which I am informed cost a thousand pistoles. In the chamber of state the bed is divided from the room with a gilded rail.

The plafond or ceiling was painted at Paris, on which the stories of Apelles and Daphne and Jupiter and Diana are very well represented. Within this chamber is the late Elector's [Duke of Bavaria] fine closet, which I cannot but give you a particular account of, because I believe it was finished since you were there. The floor is inlaid with silver, representing the celestial and terrestrial globes, and the wainscot all round inlaid and the panels set with glass. On one side is a fine cabinet for a crucifix and a neat desk to write on, all of tortoise-shell inlaid with silver and mother of pearl, with several curious devices. On the other side is a couch to sleep on, covered with velvet and gold. On the ceiling is [15r] painted Peace and Liberty, with proper devices and Calliope and Clio, with an open book with this device: opera pacis [the works of Peace] in one leaf and on the other: Et billi stadia [=libertatis: and of Liberty], all [of] which was done by one Geoffry [Godfried] Maes. The windows are sashed from the roof even to the floor. I was informed the Duke of Marlborough generously sent the furniture, which was very rich, as a present to the Duke of Bavaria to Mons, soon after the country fell into the hands of the Allies upon the famous battle of Ramillies [23 May 1706].

In the grove next the park, is a little timber house wonderful pleasant, where the Duke used to retire to deliberate upon state affairs. There is placed on a pedestal, going down to the great garden, an old large iron gun, under which is an inscription in Latin to this effect: that a ship belonging to the enemy, being blown up in the Maese [Schelde] near Antwerp, this great gun and a young girl by the force of it, were thrown into this palace, and that the then governess of the Netherlands Isabella Clara Eugenia preserved the maid and ordered the cannon to be placed there as a memorial of that wonderful delivery.

I believe you will expect from me an account of the [15v] waterworks so much talked of, which now run to decay. I was shown first a bank of water, which, spouting from one side to the other with several jet d'eaux, made a sort of lattice, then a fountain which spouted water in imitation like a fan, and another fountain that raised a ball and kept it up several yards high for the space of a minute by the playing of the water. Next there is a little garden in which is a grotto all of shells, paved with black and white marble and arched over, from under which the water spouts very high by means of a vast number of pipes, and descends like a shower of rain. One waterwork moves several figures representing tradesmen at work, one is a butcher, another two labourers, another a carpenter. There is also a fine artificial cascade, another is two lions roaring with streams running from their mouths, with figures of two men on each side. And upon three rows of small wires descending, a ball rolls from the top to the bottom, where one figure receives it and throws it up again to the top, and the other figure at the top throws it down to the bottom, and so backwards and forwards as long as the water plays.

[16r] But this is only imaginary pleasure to that of walking in the park, which is shaded with delicate rows of trees and adorned with a fine mall, though much less than that of ours at St James's. There are three grottoes in the park, which supply the fountains and waterworks in the gardens. One is made like a mausoleum with only roots of trees piled one upon another; the others are shells. At the end of this park is a little house, where they show the room wherein the Emperor Charles V parted with all his earthly glory to his brother and son, Ferdinand and Philip [II], for the true and more solid joys of a quiet retirement. I spend many hours in this sweet retreat from the town, which so ravishes my thoughts that I could be glad to stay here much longer if my time would permit it.

Near the palace I went to visit the armoury, where I saw the rich arms of the Emperor Charles V, cap-a-pie [from head to foot] and the armour of the horse, the Archduke Albert and Duke Ernest his brother, the Prince of Parma's; likewise the fine suit of armour used by Charles V for tilts [16v] and tournaments, the plain black arms of Philip the Good, Duke of Burgundy, and his lance of two and twenty foot long; the royal standard of Francis I, King of France, with which he was taken at the battle of Pavia [1525]. Besides these there are several sorts of arms belonging to Indian princes and other curiosities, too tedious to be comprised in the compass of a letter.

Near this place is the Court d'Orange, where General [Charles] Churchill as governor of the town keeps his residence, but has nothing of grandeur in it worth taking notice of. I went next to see the Grand Place, which is an oblong square. The fronts of the houses are very high and curiously built like the sterns of ships. On one side is the town house, on the top of which is the brazen statue of St Michael, the patron of this city. The town [house] is very remarkable and over against it is a very old palace [Broodhuis or Maison du Roi]. Upon this place is the Pope's Head, a very fine tavern, where I and a Scotch gentleman that was with me drank a bottle of excellent champagne and burgundy. I mention this because in the great room I saw a very good picture of the five loaves and the two fishes [17r] done by one Janson [Victor Janssens], a Fleming. The ceiling was finely gilt and the pavement prettily composed of parti-coloured tiles. There was also a fine staircase, on the top of which was a cupola painted with several angels' heads and in the intervals a monk, a peacock and an owl, done very naturally. In this fine place is a large fountain as likewise there are several others in the streets, but the little one of Manakin Piss is particularly remarkable for its story.

I met a procession to the church next to the old palace, in honour of St Rochus, which was the first time of my seeing that superstitious ceremony. Just as I was going to turn a street, on a sudden appeared a world of wax candles and I heard a mighty jingling of bells and music. But as soon as I perceived the banners displayed and a train of priests with the host, and a vast number of people on their knees, I imagined what it was, and with as much haste as I could, retired to a neighbouring coffee-house, where I observed several gentlemen, who were then at play, throw up their cards and fall on their knees with all the outward gesture of piety imaginable. But I got by a window and [17v] had the pleasure of seeing a heretic (as they call us) well cudgelled for not pulling off his hat, which he bore very patiently rather than comply with so much folly and ridiculousness.

I visited afterwards the Jesuits' church and the Great Church, dedicated to St Gudule, the lowest step of which, I was told, was higher than the top of the steeple of the Great Church at Antwerp, though one can scarce perceive the easy ascent from one town to the other. When I returned to my lodgings, I related the story to some gentlemen how the poor heretic was beaten for his indecent action, which gave them an opportunity of telling me that last Sunday, whilst a bell was ringing in the Jesuits' church, a poor English soldier, that was got drunk, rose up with his sword under his arm and danced in the middle of the congregation, which had like to have made a great confusion had not all the English retired immediately out of the church; and the fellow being asked the reason of his behaviour, said he saw they were disposed to be merry, and though he could not sing, he had a mind to show them he could dance.

One Father Shaw, an English Jesuit, upon this occasion told me another [18r] story that on a certain time, a little after he had done service, and all the people were gone, he observed a soldier skulking behind a pillar, who, thinking the coast was clear, went up to the great altar and took down one of the wax tapers to light his pipe, after which he retired mightily pleased at what he had done. This the father gave me as an instance of his moderation, in not causing so great a profaneness to be severely punished.

I visited the church of the Recollets and many others. It would be endless to give you a description of them as well as the religious houses, of which there are above fifty, whose beauty consists chiefly in their fine altars and crucifixes, which I now began to be weary of seeing. But one evening to divert my thoughts from the reflection of the day, I went to hear [John] Abell sing at the Sablon or great tennis-court, where was a large assembly of our nation, but very few of the inhabitants. Here I became acquainted with Sir Francis Anderson, who, understanding I was displeased with my quarters at the Soleil d'Or, invited me and Mr Mills to a private house, where he and some more English and Scotch gentlemen lodged, in the Dominican [18v] Street, over against the King of Sweden's Head, to which place I removed next morning to my great satisfaction. As I was going to these new quarters I had the good fortune to meet with Captain King coming in a coach and four horses from the army. He was surprised to see me and enquiring what my design was, he invited me to go thither with him, but I excused it on account of my obligation to the Prince.

I had not been long at these lodgings, before the Prince of Hesse did us the honour of two visits, and I was so much obliged to him, that as I met him at the play, he ran quite across the parterre to me and addressed me openly with the title of *mon ami anglais*. I could not relish the French opera called the Feast of Apollo, nor the performance of it, after having so lately heard Camilla and Thomyris at home, but I was mightily taken with the comical interludes, which were performed with a world of spirit and humour. The play-house is very well, having a good stage and four galleries, one above another, all divided as it were in little boxes. I liked their custom extremely for having a file of musketeers always attending [19r] to prevent quarrels.

After all these diversions, I believe you would not think me so curious as I ought, if I had not paid my respect to the nuns, which was the business of this day. The first I visited was that of the Dominicans, commonly called the Spelakins, of which the Lady Boyle of the Burlington family is governess over about five and twenty ladies professed. It was with a great deal of pleasure that I spent several hours with Mrs Howard and the Lord Stafford's sister, who ordered chairs to be brought for us into the speaking-room and diverted us with an account of almost all the agreeable affairs of the world. Mrs Howard told us she had been almost twenty years in the house, although she was but twenty-seven years old. She not only favoured me with a sight of her fine work, but I obtained from her a heart cut curiously in vellum with wreaths of flowers painted by herself in proper colours. I must own this pretty creature moved me so much, that I was sorry to see her confined within the compass of an iron grate.

I went from thence to visit the other English nunnery [19v] called the Benedictines, where who should I see in nun's habit but two of the ladies I parted with at Antwerp. You will easily imagine I was mightily surprised to see them there. I enquired immediately whether Mrs Vaughan was with them, but they assured me she was not, but would not inform me to what part of the country she is gone. So I returned to my lodgings very much dejected, fearing her lot was the same. But I was no sooner entered the house but presently the two Mrs Vaughan presented themselves to my sight. It would be impossible to tell you the joy Mr Mills and I (who had often the pleasure of talking about these ladies) were in, at the first view. We stood speechless for some time, but at last I recollected spirits enough to go and welcome them to Brussels. My admiration was the greater that we should have the good fortune to meet a second time in a private family without the least knowledge of it beforehand.

But alas, this scene of joy presently vanished, for Monsieur Charton came that instant from the Prince to make us a visit, and told us he designed to be going tomorrow morning at five o'clock to the army, which is come to [20r] Soignies, three leagues from this place, and desired we would not fail to be ready. This was a melancholy piece of news, but having no other way of going to the army safely, I am forced to submit to so sudden a parting. However we have spent the evening very merrily, the ladies diverted us with several songs and gave me some hopes that we should meet again. But finding so many Jesuits about them, I suspected their designs, and have presumed to give them the best advice I could, to persuade them from entering into a cloister, which they assured me they would not do.

At last the fatal hour of separation drawing near, we all parted with mutual good wishes and retired to our chambers, where I am just now concluding this letter being sensible that the length of it must needs have tired your patience, and therefore that it is time to subscribe myself, dear cousin, yours, etc. [cont. The Army]

Anonymous tourist, 12-19 May 1720 N.S.

[10v] Set out from Ghent to Brussels in the diligence, ten shillings of the country apiece, and six for a hundred of baggage, ten leagues. Changed horses at Alost [Aalst], halfway. Lodged à l'Hotel de Flandre, in the street of l'Hopital (well).

Manneke Pis, c. 1700

See the collection of pictures of Mr [blank], who makes a trade of it, where an excellent family piece of Van Dyck and several fruit pieces and flowers of the best masters. The Jesuits' church pretty good, a fine and rich monument erected to St Xavier with his picture on a side of it by Rubens.

See a play acted by the boys of the fourth school. In the fifth and sixth school are some good pictures. In the sixth observed among the rules of the school that they are forbid to go and see any malefactors executed *nisi forsan esset aliquis hereticus* [unless it is some heretic]. In the same place is a picture with an inscription where the House of Austria is complimented for having destroyed heresy *flamma et ferro* [by fire and sword]. Pretty gardens, pretty good library. In the library is shown a chair of Charles V, to be carried about when he had the gout. Many editions of Stephanus, Aldus [Manutius], etc., a bible in Gothic character in folio, 1479 per Conradum de Homberg, Coloniae [printed at Cologne].

[11v] The Arsenal near the Court, where several suits of armour belonging to the

Emperor Charles V, Maximilian, the Archduke Albert, Duke d'Alva, etc. See a shield and helmet incomparably well-wrought on iron in basso relievo, with an inscription that shows the subject of both is taken out of Virgil. They are said to have been taken out of the Arsenal at Rome by Charles V [1527]. That Emperor's lanthern and chemise de maille à l'épreuve de l'épée [rapier-proof coat of mail]; another shield, worked upon they say with a point of diamond. The skins of the three horses, etc.

Inquired about the custom of the 19th January [on which the Brussels' women undressed their husbands and put them to bed]. Had an account given of it answerable to the second reason in Misson [who states that this happened when the men returned exhausted from a crusade]. Going down from the Court to the park is the cannon mentioned by Misson, but the inscription is said to be *instaurata* [restored]. The gate of Flanders; could see nothing there of what Misson relates [that there are statuettes of men armed with spits]. The Court, a pretty fine apartment, chiefly the two furthermost rooms and the closet, but not altogether furnished. The park mighty fine with fountains and waterworks very agreeable and several groves, where the Duke of Bavaria gave many a treat. [12v] The chapel common; could not see Charles V his cradle, his house being taken up by General Fale. Been at the two cours, one in the town, the other of about a mile out of the gates.

See the Great Church of St Gudula, where a very fine chapel *du sacrement des miracles*. Read in Misson the history of the consecrated hosts preserved there; the memory of which is solemnized every fifty years [on the Sunday after 13th July] and will be in six weeks or two months, great preparations made towards it. See in the chapel a picture of Rubens against a pillar at the left of the altar. In the church a picture of St Gudula, the statue of St Thomas done by Larwin [Jerome Duquesnoy], the tombs of the Dukes of Brabant.

At the Great Carmelites see a fine pulpit wrought in wood all of a piece by an artist who is now in England in order to work the King's [George I] statue. See the chapel [of Our Lady] *du bon secours*, handsomely built like a lanthern. See the town house, where very fine pieces of tapestry and good apartments. Went to Mrs [De] Voss [Vos], who has a manufacture of tapestry; were shown some pieces of the finest kind we ever see.

[13v] See the fishery house, where an excellent picture done by Rubens and three other masters, the fishing of the apostles by Christ's order. See Mannetje Piss, holds it with his left hand, which on a day of procession is clothed with a laced coat, given by the Duke of Bavaria. Brussels is a very fine town, fine walks in and about it. In winter there are many assemblies, plays and operas. Now none, but an assembly at my Lord Ailesbury's, every Saturday and a little one every day at two ladies'. Had the honour to see the Prince of Orange [Willem Hyacinth van Nassau-Siegen] and the young princess, [Maria Anna Josefa], his daughter, Mr Catterbach, a German officer, Mrs Joly and Mrs Daneant of Bruges and Mr Van Tourse, Mr Gobbé, Lieutenant-General of artillery of Antwerp, Mr Du Change, who promised a letter for Lille. [cont. Antwerp]

Population: 65,000 (1690), 58,000 (1755).

Distances: Antwerp 8 hours (24 miles), Bergen [Mons] 10 hours (39 miles), Gent 9 hours (30 miles), Liège 18 hours (50 miles), Leuven 4 hours (15 miles), Maastricht 18 hours (57 miles), Mechelen 4 hours (12 miles), Vilvoorde 2 hours (6 miles).

Inns, *Reisboek* (1689 and 1700) mentions over 30 inns, sometimes including prices of meals, e.g.: Koning van Zweden (Klooster) 14 st. In de Keizerin (beneden het Kante-steen), met wijn 36 st. In de Spiegel, 20 en 36 met wijn. enz. Misson: au Miroir; l'Imperatrice; la Fontaine d'Or.

Reisboek (1721) mentions: In den Marquis Deynse*, op de Kanter-steen; 't Schild van Vrankrijk* op de Ammans-Hofstraat; Den Hertog van Braband*, op de Koolmarkt; De Kat*, in the Bergstraat; De Koningin van Zweden*, in de Bisschopstraat; In St Katharina, op de Balie van 't Hof; Den Tuimelaar, agter 't Stadhuis; 't Wapen van Vlaanderen*, bij de Vischmarkt.

Further reading

J.B. Gramaye, *Antiquitates Belgicae*, Bruxelles-Leuven 1708.

A. Sanderus, *Chorographia sacra Brabantiae*, Bruxelles 1659-1660; 's-Gravenhage 1726-1727.

Description de la ville de Bruxelles, Bruxelles 1743.

Mina Martens (ed.), *Histoire de Bruxelles*, Toulouse 1976.

Het gewest Brussel. Van de oude dorpen tot de Stad van nu, A. Smolar-Meynart and J. Stengers (eds.), Brussel 1989.

Acta Historica Bruxellensia, 1967-1981.

Annales de la société royale d'archéologie de Bruxelles, 1887-

Ons Brussel, maandblad van de Vlaamse Club voor Kunsten, Wetenschappen en Letteren, 1980-

Delft

William Lord Fitzwilliam, June 1663

[31v] After I had been ten days at The Hague, I went to Delft, a very great and handsome town, only a little solitary. Here we found fair, broad and clean streets and the houses were well-built. Two good churches called the Old and New. In the Old we saw the tomb of a lady called Elisabeth Marnixiae [Van Marnix] and of two sea-heroes [32r] Peter Petersen Heyn's [Piet Hein] and Van Tromp's. Van Tromp's is very curiously made all of marble with this epitaph: Aeternae memoriae ... [To the eternal memory of ...].

[32v] In the New Church is the famous tomb of William, Prince of Orange, who was most treacherously murdered in this town. Here he lies buried under a stately tomb of brass with this epitaph upon it: D.O.M. et eternae memoriae ... [In honour of the most high God and ...]. Under the same tomb lies likewise his lady, his son, Prince Maurice, Prince Frederic Henry and Prince William [II], this present Prince's father.

In this town there is likewise a very handsome town house, just upon the great marketplace over against the New Church. Here is likewise an artillery house [Oorlogsmagazijn]. [33r] The ammunition house of Holland stands near this town; it is newly built. The old one was anno 1654 blown up into the air, which did a great deal of hurt to this town. It did destroy all trees, two hundred houses, churches and men. In The Hague, which is an hour's distance from hence, it broke the glass windows. At Haarlem, which is seven hours distant, it shaked the doors and windows of the town. The noise of it was heard over all Holland, at Utrecht and other places of the bishopric [Utrecht]. This town has been always obnoxious to suchlike accidents. It has been twice or thrice burnt, yet always it did rise like another Phoenix, more fairer, out of its own ashes. It is surrounded with good walls, ditches and gates and abounds with everything, as being situated in the best part of Holland. [cont. Rotterdam]

William Carstairs, 6 (16) July 1685

[159] [From Rotterdam] I went to The Hague again, where I stayed one night without going to visit any of my acquaintance. I had this day one of the oddest encounters with one that was in the habit of a very fashionable gentlewoman, that ever I had in my life. It so fell out that I sat by her in the boat, without speaking anything but one or two sentences. When we came to pay, I had no small money, and the

skipper not being able to change presently the piece I gave him, she took the opportunity of telling me with very much seeming civility, that she could serve me with small money; which accordingly she did, paying the skipper my fraught.

I kindly thanked her and put her to the trouble of changing my money, which she did; only I wanted some stivers, which made me tell them that she should pay my fraught from Delft to The Hague, and so we should be quits. When we came to the end of Delft, the Hague schuit was gone, so that being to stay half an hour and she pretending to be faint, and that some qualm [nausea] came over her stomach, we went to one of those houses where it is ordinary for people to stay and drink a glass of beer or wine, or eat any little thing that is ready, which ordinarily is only eels, till the schuit be ready to go.

I, having from somewhat of her discourse been suspicious of her being a slight person, would go into no room with her, but stayed in the outer entry where any person came that pleased. At last finding more clearly what she was and being resolved to be rid of her, I pretended I had some business in town. She told me very briskly she would go with me, and went to the door before me, which made me stay in the house. But she, finding that I did not follow, came back again. Then I told her that I must be gone. She still persisted in offering me her company, but I having answered that I was not for such company, I was glad to get away with all the haste I could, [160] she still crying she would go with me. But I was not a little pleased that she was left behind, though I had not the rest of my change from her.

Sir Francis Child, June 1697

[5r] From Rotterdam there goes every hour of the day a treckschuit to Delft, which does carry passengers for five stivers each, and for your trunk you must pay two or three stivers, more or less as it is in bigness, but whatever may be carried under one's arm pays nothing. Before I go any farther, I think myself obliged to describe this treckschuit, because it is the passageboat made use of from one town to another in this country.

It is about fifty feet long, in shape like one of our Company's barges; each side, for the more air, halfway open to the top, but has a tarpaulin which may be let down on occasion as to keep out rain and bad weather. It can hold about sixty passengers and is called a treckschuit because drawn by a horse. The boat has a mast of about ten foot high, which is to be let down at the going under a bridge, as here are many. At the stern is a rope fastened, which from thence is carried through the top of the mast and thence by a length of fifty yards is fastened to the horse's harness, which a boy rides at a usual trot upon the bank, a man all the while steering to keep the boat in the middle of the canal. As there be a great many of these boats, there is, to prevent disorders, a law which boats are to give way and how, which is either by stopping [5v] the horse, at which the rope slackens and the other boat

View of Delft, 1750

goes over it, or else by shaking the rope from the mast, by which no time is lost, the horse still drawing the boat though the rope passes under the other boat.

Near the place whence these boats go is a clock and a bell; after the clock has struck, the bell rings to warn people of the boat's going, which then must, if without one passenger, depart. It is a pleasant and easy way of travelling, and they set forward at such a constant time and are obliged to go at such a rate that if you were to go from The Hague to Amsterdam, which is more than thirty miles, you may depend upon your arriving there within half a quarter of an hour of the time allowed.

I went by one of these boats in two hours to Delft and in my way did pass through a small village called Overschie, where youth is bred up to merchants' accounts. An English mile before you come to Delft, is a magazine of powder only, well-built and moated round.

Delft, in Latin Delphi or Delphium, is a fair town, situated among meadows which may be overflowed the wind east-northeast, is said to have been so named from the canal which runs through it; for *delven* in Dutch is to dig a ditch or canal. It has the third voice in the assembly of the States, is four leagues from Leiden and one league from The Hague. Godfrey le Bossu, Duke of Lorraine, is said to have built this town. In 1536 it was almost burned down when it was observed that a stork, not able to save her young ones, flung herself with them into the flames. In 1584 William, Prince of Orange, was here assassinated by Balthasar Gerards, a Burgundian, of which I shall speak more largely when I describe his mausolée. In 1654 the magazine of powder was accidentally fired, [6r] which blew up most of the town; to prevent which danger the States have built a noble magazine for powder only at a mile's distance from the town, which I mentioned in my coming to Delft.

As you enter this town from Rotterdam, there is on your right hand a noble structure for warlike stores, with carved figures in stone over the canal, and under it in great letters [blank for VIGILATE DEO CONFIDENTES, i.e. wake and trust in God]. They brew very good beer, but are particularly famous for their porcelain or earthenware, which they paint better than the Chinese, make more large and as beautiful every way, could they but make their small ware transparent, in which the Chinese have the advantage of them. [...]

[9r] Mr [Anthonie van] Leeuwenhoek, so much esteemed amongst the virtuosi, and a fellow of our Royal Society, lives here and is very willing to show any strangers recommended to him as curious those microscopes he first invented and has since brought to that perfection that he will make it appear they magnify a million times. He showed us by them the testicles and eggs of lice, the eggs of oysters and several other dissections of the most minute insects, which anyone may be better informed of who reads his *Arcana naturae detecta*. [cont. The Hague]

Joseph Taylor, 13 (24) September 1707

[42r] I parted from Rotterdam with a great deal of regret the 13th instant and by the trackskuit arrived in two hours at Delft, which like other Dutch towns is extremely neat. I stayed to see the large armoury and magazine for guns new built [1692], and also the Old [New] Church which stands in the great place. Opposite against it is the town house, an handsome fabric. In that church I saw the most noble monument of the great William, Prince of Orange, founder of this state, who was here murdered by a Burgundian. [42v] It is a mausoleum in the front of which is placed his effigies in brass, booted and spurred and sitting crosslegged with his helmet at his feet. On each side of him in niches are two brazen figures of Liberty and Justice; behind this is his effigies again, lying at length in marble, his head placed on a pillow and at his feet lies a dog, which they say pined to death for the loss of his master soon after he was murdered. There is another figure of Fame in brass, blowing a trumpet, whose whole weight is supported by the great toe on which it is fixed, and two other figures, of Charity and Mercy [Religion and Valour], to answer those of Justice and Liberty. The frontispiece is supported by eight pillars of red [black] polished marble, but the capitals and pedestals are white; each side is adorned with several devices and inscriptions and the whole enclosed with a balustrade of iron. There is one inscription to this purpose in Latin:

> D.O.M. and to the eternal memory of William of Nassau, the greatest Prince of Orange, Father of his country, who postponed his own fortunes to those of Holland; twice maintained and led great armies most at [43r] his own charge; repelled the tyranny of Spain; the true religion and ancient laws restored, and left liberty to be established by Prince Maurice, heir of his father's virtues; a true, pious and unconquered Prince, whom Philip the Second, King of Spain, that terror of Europe, dreaded but could not conquer nor terrify; he fell by the treachery of an impious assassin; the States-General of the United Provinces erected this monument of his lasting memory.

In the New [Old] Church is the tomb of the famous Van Tromp, lying at length, and under him in bas-relievo is carved a representation of a fleet of ships at sea. The frontispiece is supported by four exquisite marble pillars, in the middle of which is a long inscription in Latin of all his life and actions to this effect:

Grafstede te Delft opgerecht ter eeren van Willem van Nassau, Prins van Oragie.

Monument to William of Orange, c. 1679

To the eternal memory of Martin Harperts Van Tromp; if you love the Dutch; if you love virtue or true labour, read and weep. The glory of the Dutch nation, the thunder of warlike valour lies here, who living never lay still. He was the love of the citizens, terror of the enemy, the wonder of the ocean. In his name [43v] are contained more praises than this narrow stone can hold, and to whom the east and western seas were occasion of triumphs. All the world was the theatre of his glory. He was the sure destruction of pirates, the happy maintainer of commerce, useful not vicious in conversation. After he had governed the sailors and soldiers (a hard generation) with fatherly and kind management, after fifty battles, in most of which he was chief, after many real victories, after meriting great honour, at last in the English War, although not a conqueror, yet certainly unconquered, he ceased to live the 10th of August 1653, aged 56 (The States-General of the United Provinces, to this most deserving hero have placed this monument).

There is another good tomb of an Englishwoman, one Colonel Morgan's lady, and another of Petrus Heins [Piet Hein], whose monument has an inscription mentioning that he was admiral at Brazil, in the sea of Mexico, in Portugal and on the French coast. That he exceeded the low fortune of his parents by the magnanimity of his mind. And the glory of his actions showed [44r] that heroes are not always born but made. And after particularizing his actions tells us that he was killed at the age of fifty-one.

I went afterwards to see the house where Prince William was shot and in one of the walls they showed me the mark of the bullet. The ruffian, whose anatomy is preserved within the town, was for the bloody fact put to death with red-hot pincers. I saw the hospital which is but small, the market and the gate called Maurice Gate [Maeslandse Poort]. From thence I came to this place in two hours more; the canal is extremely pleasant all the way. [cont. The Hague]

Population: 21,000 (1650), 24,000 (1680), 20,000 (1720), 13,910 (1749).
Distances: The Hague 1 hour (3 miles), Leiden 3 hours (9 miles), Maassluis 2 hours (5 miles), Rotterdam 2 hours (6 miles).

Inns, *Reisboek* (1689): De Verlooren Zoon. *Reisboek* (1689, 1700 and 1721): De Doelen; De Toelast (bezijden de Markt); De Stadts Herberg, De Vergulde Molen* [1721: bij de Haag Poort], De Prins van Oranje*, bij de Rotterdamsche Poort. *Reisboek* (1700 and 1721) also: 't Wapen van Amsterdam*, aan de Haag Poort.

Further reading

D.E. van Bleyswijck, *Beschryvinge der stadt Delft*, Delft 1667.
[R. Boitet], *Beschryving der stadt Delft*, Delft 1729.
I.V.T. Spaander (ed.), *De stad Delft. Cultuur en maatschappij van 1667 tot 1813*, Delft 1982.
Genealogische en historische encyclopedie van Delft, Delft 1984.
D. Wijbenga, *Delft, een verhaal van de stad en haar bewoners*, vols. II and III, Rijswijk 1986-1993.
Delfia Batavorum Jaarboek, 1991-

Dordrecht

William Lord Fitzwilliam, 29 June 1663 N.S.

[33v] From this town [Rotterdam] we went to Dordt, which is the first town of Holland and has the first voice in the States' assembly. It is a maiden city, never yet taken; it lies on the river Wahal [Merwede] and Mosa; it is very famous in Europe. It is governed by a mayor and one burgomaster, whose office is here highly valued. These two magistrates have a guard of halbardiers, which honour belongs only in this country to the governors of provinces. This city is endued with many privileges: if anyone of this town is guilty of any crime, no other magistrate but he of Dordt can take connaissance of it.

Debtors have their refuge here. They cannot be arrested, but their creditors must stay till [34r] they can make up their business. To this town did formerly belong only the privilege of coining of money, and to that end and purpose there is built a fair great house. Dordt is the staple of Rhenish wine and of all other merchandise coming down the river Rhine and Mosa. The English have here likewise their staple. Anno 1222 [1294-1295] it has been here before, in the time of one of the Edwards [Edward I] of England and Floris V, Count of Holland. From hence this wool staple was afterwards removed to Mechelen in Brabant.

Here are several fine houses and streets. Here we saw the Dool [Doelen], where anno 1619 was held the famous synod against the poor Arminians; it did little good and finished very soon. Here is likewise an exchange, town house and good great church. Here is likewise a good haven. This town has suffered much by fire and water, especially by the latter. Anno 1421 was this town by an inundation separated from firm ground. There was at that time drowned seventy-two villages, many gentleman's houses and above a hundred thousand men and women. Now some of that land is regained. [cont. Zeeland]

Anonymous London merchant, 23-24 August; 8-13 September and 8-10 October 1695 N.S.

[7] On Tuesday the 23rd we went by water to Dordt, being four hours and the next day returned by waggon to Rotterdam. This city of Dordt is very ancient, having the first voice in the States of Holland. The Exchange is much finer than Rotterdam; the air is better, and the place more healthy. It is not so large nor populous as Rotterdam, but [8] otherwise very like it, both in the buildings, pavements and sluices in the streets for ships to ride and unload. In this particular all the cities and

View of Dordrecht, c. 1700

towns of Holland are very remarkable, having great sluices in most of the streets for ships to ride and unload in at the merchants' doors, with great trees growing on the wharves between the sluices and the houses. [cont. Rotterdam]

[18] On Thursday the 8th [September] I went by water [from Rotterdam] to Dordt to settle my son there at school. I lodged with sister Bubwith, where I found a mighty good welcome both from her and her brother, Mr Irish. This gentleman is deputy-governor of the Hamburg Company and the only English merchant of any note now left in this city. After five days' stay here, in which time Mr Irish continually attended me in showing me the town, in settling my son with the rector of the Latin school, one Mr Metzler (very much to my content), he carried us in his yacht to his country house and continually supplied us with all sorts of good fruit from his gardens as my sister did likewise from hers. This Latin school, wherein are seven masters though not above twenty-nine boys, is reputed one of the best in Holland, the rector whereof gives private instruction two or three hours every day to his boarders, who are not above eight or ten, and is an ingenious person. This city being mentioned before, I say no more of it in this place.

On Tuesday the 13th September at one o'clock I went [19] in a yacht for Antwerp in company of a German Count and several persons of quality, as likewise some masons and carpenters who were going to Brussels on occasion of the late bombardment [13-15 August], and though this company was good, not one of them understood English but myself, my son being left at Dordt and my servant was returned to my brother at Rotterdam to look after my linen which happened to miscarry in coming to me the day before. Everyone in this voyage puts provision in the ship, being sixty odd miles, and is a passage sometimes of three or four days. My sister took good care of me and put me on board good store of Rhenish wine, beer, cold meat, bread, butter, a paper of salt, two plates, a napkin and pillow to lie upon, besides gingerbread and plumcake enough for a whole week. [cont. Antwerp]

[29] On Saturday [8th October] I went [from Rotterdam] to Dordt, where I spent two days at my sister Bubwith's and Mr Irish's as also at the rector's house, where Robin boarded, who made me very welcome, he and his lady being very kind to the boy and promised to be a father to him that he would tend him as his own son both as to his instruction and everything else. His entrance was on Wednesday the 5th September [October], but did not lodge there having the toothache till Friday the 7th instant.

On Sunday night and Monday morning I took leave of all friends and then returned to Rotterdam, having paid my sister for Robin's bed, etc. and left twenty guilders in her hands to be laid out for Robert's use as occasion requires. In this Latin school are seven masters, the rector and conrector are chief, having about sixty scholars. The rector gives about two hours private instruction every day to his scholars, besides their public learning with their proper masters. Their vacations are twice every year at Whitsuntide and Bartholomewtide [24 August], one month at a time. These masters are put in by the town and are allowed a house, turf and a certain sum of money yearly. The rector's salary is eight hundred guilders per annum, the boys pay but a small matter for their learning. The boarders being well-ordered both in their diet and learning. [cont. The Return Journey]

Justinian Isham, 31 May - 7 June (11-18 June) 1705

[8] Wednesday 31st. I saw the Great Church, which Guicciardini says was dedicated to the Virgin Mary, but one of the inhabitants, where I lodged who came along with me, said it was called St Ursula [Sura], from she that built it, by this miracle. This woman having in her purse three two-pence halfpenny pieces only, or two crowns as I have read otherwhere, had a vision appear to her which bid her begin this work, which she did. And these pieces being spent, others came in their room, which making the workmen think she had great riches, they murdered her, but were deceived finding only the pieces. And out of the place where she was killed came forth a spring of water. This church is a very good building after the Gothic

manner. One part of its roof is concave. There is a place which they call a chapel, where formerly they buried gratis those that had been at Rome. About the choir are carved in wood a procession of the Pope, several of the Roman triumphs, etc.

[Cornelis van] Terestein, who had been twelve times burgomaster, and Jacob de Witt, father of John and Cornelius whom the mob at The Hague tore to pieces [1672], are interred here. Nigh the gravestone of the latter, I saw [9] a stone on which is a cross, held in much veneration by the Roman Catholics of the Low Countries, it having been formerly part of an altar in the church. At the entrance of the steeple or tower is a Dutch inscription on the right hand, giving an account how it was built, June 16th 1339, over against which are two others in the same language. One that November 18th, 1421, an inundation happened in which seventy-two parishes perished; the other is under it and tells one that those of Dordt beat the Countess [Count] of Holland in a battle that was fought on the Lek in 1489. Afterwards I was up the steeple, which has 313 steps. Over the Spui-poort or gate is another inscription concerning the inundation and one how in 1413 [1418] John [IV], Duke of Brabant, besieged Dordt but was beaten by the Goths [God's hand] and forced to raise the siege.

Thursday June 1st. I went to see the Mint, which is that of Holland, the privilege of coining being granted this city by Charles V. Over the gate one reads this inscription: Moneta Divo Carolo V Caesari. Dit is de Munt des Romes Keijsers en Graefelickheit van Hollant [the Mint of Charles V, Roman Emperor, and of the Earldom of Holland]. I was in the room in which the Arminians or Remonstrants were condemned; I was also in a tower belonging to the same house, which is I think the Doelen, in which is a table with benches that they turn round altogether. I saw from this place a tower, the only remains of the 72 villages that were lost.

Friday 2nd [10] I saw a ceremony in which the burgomaster [Ernest] Van Beveren represented the officer of the Baron of Merwe, rendering the staff of justice upon the borders of the barony to the burgomasters of the town, who are now the barons. For in former times those that had committed any misdemeanour in Dordt fled to this independent barony, which was very near the town and makes now a part of it though under its former jurisdiction; and the inhabitants of Merwe fled to the town, so that the officers of justice could not prosecute them. For which reason an agreement was made between those of Dordt and the baron that any malefactor might be seized in either of their dependencies, provided that the chief officer of the baron should govern the city of Dordt and have the staff of command eight days in a year. But the magistrates, not content with that, and having a mind to get the barony in their own hands, got Daniel, then baron, in a wine cellar and gave him wine in such abundance that they got him to sell for thirty thousand florins. Some say they went to him next morning and asked him if he persisted in the same resolution and that he made answer that since he had agreed with them, a man of honour should keep his word. In the afternoon we went to the burgomaster Van Beveren's house out of town, who treated us very civilly.

Saturday 3rd. This day passed without anything of moment. Sunday 4th. I went in the morning to the French church, where I heard Mr Masson preach. After church [11] I heard the French were landed in the island and had seized some people, and amongst others a merchant of Delft coming from Breda with his wife, so that the town was in a sort of uproar, and a part of the burghers marched out against them. But they were gone before they came, for having seized two little houses upon the dike, they designed to stop all passengers which they put in effect. But two men passing that way, they took one, the other making his escape towards the town. So knowing they would be discovered if they stayed there, they went away about ten o'clock in the morning, carrying their boat upon their shoulders because it was low water, for they came in the night when it was high.

Monday 5th. We went to the head of the island to see the ducks caught, but could not have that sport, the wind being too high, so that after dinner we went round most of the island on the dikes, which are agreeably planted with trees and from which one has a pleasant sight of several little country boxes. We saw the place where the men landed, who were not Frenchmen but part of an independent company of Antwerp to the number of twenty-one.

There are a vast many windmills about Dordt and I counted forty along the road by the [Dordtsche] Kil, which is a ditch that makes the island and joins Hollandsch Diep with the Maas. When we came home we had an account that the party was taken by the neighbouring garrisons.

Tuesday 6th. Nothing remarkable happened. Wednesday 7th. I saw one of the windmills for sawing of timber, which is a pretty invention: two men being able to do more than thirty otherwise. There were three machines in which were put as many pieces of timber, which they saw in as many pieces as you will in a small space of time.

Population: 20,000 (1650), 18,000 (1732 T.S.).

Distances: Antwerp 15 hours (46 miles), Breda 5 hours (16 miles), Gouda 5 hours (15 miles), Middelburg and Veere 17 hours (50 miles), Rotterdam 4 hours (12 miles).

Inns, *Reisboek* (1689, 1700 and 1721): De Doelen, daar de Draay boven in den Tooren is; Enkhuizen*; De Roode Leeuw*; Den Engel*, aan de Rietdijk; 't Vlies*, in de Vischstraat; 't Kasteel van Antwerpen* [in 1700 Kasteel van Heidelberg]. *Reisboek* (1689 and 1700): De Paauw, aan het Groote Hoofd. *Reisboek* (1700 and 1721): 't Veer-schip op Der Veer.

Further reading

J.M. Balen, *Beschryvinge der stad Dordrecht*, Dordrecht 1677.

J.L. van Dalen, *Geschiedenis van Dordrecht*, Dordrecht 1931-1933.

Ach Lieve Tijd; 800 jaar Dordrecht en de Dordtenaren, J. Alleblas (ed.), Zwolle 1985-1986.

W. Frijhoff (ed.), *Geschiedenis van Dordrecht*, 3 vols., Dordrecht 1996-

Mededelingenblad van de Vereniging 'Oud-Dordrecht', 1893-

Dunkirk and Calais

William Lord Fitzwilliam, 10-11 July 1663 N.S.

[41v] From Newport we went directly to Dunkirk, passing only by Veurne [Furnes], a stronghold but fortified according to the ancient manner: old brick walls, one or two earth bulwarks, a great ditch and one or two half-moons about it. It has been often taken and retaken by French and Spaniard; now it is in the Spaniards' hands. We arrived late at Dunkirk.

The next day we saw the town. First we did see the citadel, built on the sands on the sea-side, just by the haven. The English laid the foundation of it and the French endeavour to perfect it, but it will be yet five years perhaps before they are able to do it. It is all vaulted; you may go below roundabout the castle under the vault. The walls are of brick, the parapets shall be of earth; roundabout it there shall be a ditch which is digged into the sandhill, and in time it may be filled up with sand as likewise the whole work spoiled by it if the wind blows but a little hard. For just by it lie the seabanks and sandhills, as high, or at least it does not want very much, as the castle, which must necessarily do a great deal of hurt to this place. Many think that the money which it does cost is but foolishly thrown into the sand.

The haven is none of the best, very narrow and not deep; at low water a man may easily wade over it. It is pretty big, but now there are no ships. Since the English left it [1662], all trading is spoiled. The walls of this town are old and of brick and very [42r] much ruinated. A great ditch with several outworks about it. Some hornworks, half-moons and ravelins: so many outworks that eight or nine thousand men will hardly suffice to defend very well this town. In the town we saw likewise a fair marketplace, a good store of old houses and ugly streets. Some religious and pious houses; a fair great church in which there are many chapels and one great altar of marble, which has cost abundance of money. On the top of this church is a very high steeple from which one may very easily see Dover. Hereupon soldiers watch for to discover if fire or any enemies approach this town. On one side of the walls the soldiers have their quarters just like at Ostend.

This town has been sometimes under the Spanish, sometimes under the French dominion. [Until] Anno 1662 it was under the English, who by Cromwell's means [1658] got it into their clutches. They could not hold it fast enough, the French [King] bought it of them, and in his power it is at present. How long it will be, God knows: he that is master at sea is most like to keep it, and this might have done His Majesty of Great Britain.

From hence we took horse for Calais, passing by Mardyck, once a very strong place. Some say it has done a great deal of good to Dunkirk; others say the contrary: rather a great deal of mischief, [42v] of whose mind was Cromwell, and therefore he rased and destroyed it utterly, so that now there remains nothing but some walls and ditches and some few thatched houses. On one side of it we saw as if it were a churchyard, full of men's bones which have been killed here. This place did lie on a sandhill not far of the sea, and was first taken [1657], afterwards Dunkirk [1658].

The next town we came to was Graveling [Gravelines], just halfway between Calais and Dunkirk. It is the frontier town of Flanders towards France, not big but very strong. The houses and streets are but mean and inconsiderable. The walls and bulwarks, of which there are five in number, deserve a traveller's curiosity, they are of good stone; good great ditches two, and three in some places, with excellent outworks likewise of stone about it. [In 1528] Charles V did build here a castle which lies on the port of Calais. It is not great but very strong and has always holden out when the town has been taken; only upon composition it has rendered itself. This town lies on the sea; it has been formerly a very great town but by continual wars between English, French, Spaniards and Burgundians it has been reduced to such a pitiful, little but strong place as it is now.

Anno 1558 there was fought a battle [43r] between the French and the Burgundians [Spanish] not far from the town at a sluice (where now people are searched which come out of Flanders) towards Calais on the seaside; the French were totally routed and defeated. Anno 1644 this town was taken by the French and few years after retaken by the Spaniards, and anno 1648 [1658] it came again under the French power, under which it is yet at this hour. So that this town has changed as often its masters as any town of the Low Countries.

From hence we went a good trot to Calais and so returned into France the same day of the [month] on which we went from it, viz. the 11th of July 1663, whereas we went from Paris the 11th of April of the same year. Calais lies on the sea-side, but seven leagues of Dover, three hours' sailing if the wind is good. This is but a little, yet a very strong town. The walls are of stone with little towers upon them according to the old fashion and as most of the towns in France are fortified. It has very good outworks, some of stone and made according to the modern way of fortifying. A great stately gate of stone leads you into the fields, another to the haven, which is very good and on one side of it defended by a little fort.

Here is likewise a very strong and well-built citadel with a good ammunition house belonging to it. [43v] Strangers have not liberty to see it, Englishmen more particularly are very much suspected, to whom this town did formerly belong as likewise the greatest part of France. It was lost in Queen Mary [Tudor]'s days, who took it so much to heart that she did use to say: 'After I am dead you will find Calais written in my heart'. It was promised it should be restored, but Queen Elizabeth, although she did all what she could, could never get it again. Since that time it was taken by the Spaniard, but presently rendered again to the French, in whose power it still remains. Here is a good, great church, a fair marketplace and good, large streets but dirty.

Here we did embark for Dover, where we arrived in very good time. And so that night we went to Canterbury; from thence to Rochester, and from Rochester by coach to London.

John Walker, 2-9 (12-19) September 1671

[17] [coming from Nieuwpoort] We landed a mile before we came to Dunkirk, the cut reaching no nearer. Being late we were constrained to be our own porters and carry our luggage through the sands up to the very gates of the town, where we found all locked fast. And had we not had the abbess of Ypres in our company (an English lady of the family of the Beaumonts in Leicestershire), we must of necessity have lain under the sand-works. But upon her prevailing we were had [allowed in] in a by-way. It was my fortune, by falling off from the works, to get first into town.

We took up our lodging that night at the Conciergerie, the chief house of entertainment in the town, and in the room where the King of France lodged his Mademoiselles. [18] Our entertainment was not to be disliked withal. In the room where we supped, the magistrates that day had sat in judgement upon two malefactors that had stolen cattle about Gravelines. The custom is they extort confession of the fact by straining of them hard upon a wooden saddle with cords fastened to their legs. On the morrow we saw them severely scourged in the marketplace, the magistrates sitting in a balcony in the stathuys and seeing execution fully performed. After they were whipped they burned them in the shoulders with a red-hot iron, made them down upon their knees to the burghers and then rang the bells and turned them out of the gates of the town.

Here is a fair church with a sumptuous altar, a neat chapel of the Jesuits, a house of Capuchins, two small English nunneries, one of the poor Clares, another of the Dames [Benedictines]. In that of the Dames we saw two beautiful Irish ladies nuns, one was named Legg; the abbess was of the family of the Carolls [Caryll] in Sussex.

The design of a fortification here is great, but it was not near finished. Several large pieces of ordnance upon the works, four hundred whereof were shamefully sold with the town by the King of England [Charles II] to the French King [1662]. Here was a gun that the King of France took from the Duke of Lorraine that was twenty-eight foot in length.

They were building here two frigates of seven hundred tun apiece. The cyclops [smiths] were making of anchors, others twisting of ropes and cables. Some working the engines to cleanse the harbour from sand. They refused to let us see the citadel. The night before we left the town, the Marquess [Louis Marie Victor] d'Aumont, Governor of Boulogne, made his entry and was saluted by the guns round the town and took up his lodging at the governor's. Upon the 5th of September we hired a waggon and took our journey for Gravelines with Father Patrick.

[19] We came to Gravelines about three of the clock in the afternoon (having passed by Mardyck, a demolished [1659] fort), that is but a small place but mightily fortified. The soldiers generally looked as if they were starved, death in their faces. Here is a large nunnery of poor Clares, consisting of about four score in number. The abbess did us the favour to grant us a view of about fifty of them at their devotion at once. From hence we went directly to Calais that night. We left our valises at the custom-house to be searched, where the shirking Frenchmen made me pay for foul linen.

Here we found very bad accommodation and nothing but thieving and exacting from a man in every corner. Here we saw the ceremony of a wedding, the priest dashing the bride with holy water as if he would have put out her eyes. This occasioned serenading for those two nights we were forced to lodge in the town.

The town has a double fortification: that which the English built and one made later [1665-1671] by Cardinal Richelieu. They refused here likewise to let us see the citadel or the old Risban or castle, built by the English and lying upon the sands or flats as you come into the town. Having stayed here two days, the wind at last served, and we went off in the packet boat and arrived safely at Dover (God be thanked) upon English ground again, and so in two days came safe to London.

Thomas Scott, 4-5 (14-15) September 1672

[8r] At our setting foot on shore [at Calais] we paid three pence apiece for our heads to a boy that stood there for that purpose. And our portmanteaus are carried to the custom-house, where they are opened, searched and then sealed by the master thereof. Which being done, going to our intended inn being the Silver Lion, we discovered the fashion of the habit and language of the place. As for the language I presume none are ignorant that they speak good French. And as to the habit of the men, they differ not from us and the women little, but going [8v] forth they wear a scarf made riding hood-like. But most of the market-women differ from ours, who instead of an old coat that ours wear about their necks in winter, go with a blue rug, with thrums [a fringe of threads] inward and turned down about their necks like a great roll.

Coming to our inn, inquiring of our passage to Dunkirk, we were informed we might go by horse, but understanding the uneasiness of horses in those countries, we resolved to go the common passage, which was by waggon and went out next morning. So that we had all the afternoon to view the town, the custom[s] of which I shall, as much as so short a time could make me capable of understanding, particularly [9r] relate, so that I shall not hereafter have occasion to speak more of it.

And first as to the manners of diet. Their meat in inns is dressed by men-cooks, who spoil it in over-boiling it to make their pottage as they call it, and stuffing those with all sorts of herbs and cabbage, etc. Their bread is pretty good and made the same way as that which we call French bread here in England, but beer none worth drinking. Their wine generally small, but well tasted; but could be furnished with but one sort in our inn, which was champagne.

Having dined we took a view of the town, guided by a poor Frenchman that could speak English, who makes it his livelihood to wait on [9v] strangers that come there. The first place we viewed was the Great Church, a stately structure, very richly adorned with images and pictures of great value, with several altars erected in small chapels very richly garnished. Where having satisfied ourselves with wonder, we went to the friary of the order of St Paul, a neat, small house with a pretty chapel very richly adorned. None of the friars whereof being English, we had no converse with them, but seemed very civil and sent a boy to show us the house, being worth our sight. From thence we went to the fortifications, by which, as far as I perceive to the contrary, the town is impregnable having only two ports or gates. One on the quay, whereon is erected an invincible fort that commands the sea. The [10r] other opposite to that, with three moats with draw-bridges over each, besides a citadel or castle, in which no one but the guards are suffered to enter. An invincible place.

From thence we went to the cloister of nuns, but were admitted to the sight of nothing but the chapel. From thence we returned to our inn, where meeting with a Calais merchant of our acquaintance, he invited us to supper at his house. Where it will not be amiss for curiosity's sake, to relate our welfare. Supper being on the table, we washed our hands (as the custom is there before meals) by standing round a dish held by the maid in one hand and a water pot in the other, still pouring out water till we had all made clean. [10v] Being set down, the meat was brought in, being but one dish, but in that several sorts of meat, but too much roasted for our palates. For sauce a dish of salad of endives, a dish of mushrooms, pickled cucumbers and capers. And after supper a dish of fruit of apples and pears, which last they eat with sugar, saying it makes them fat. During all suppertime we were continually supplied with wine, what we liked best, there being all sorts. In drinking whereof this custom is observable: they never drink to any stranger but they see themselves pledged, so that if one be not very quick you will have three glasses together. And one fashion they have which I could not accustom myself to, but admired [11r] at it. When they drink to any they take not notice by bowing or otherwise as we do in England, which we should impute to ignorance in education; and methinks they being Roman-Catholics should be more ceremonious.

Taking our leaves we returned to our inn, from whence next morning we took waggon for Dunkirk, which is distant from Calais seven leagues, or as they reckon seven hours' journey. Most part of the way to which is a sandy soil and common heath. About one of the clock we entered Gravelines; about a mile on this side of

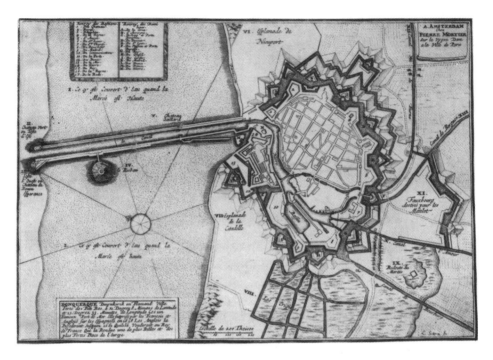

Dunkirk. Town plan, c. 1705

which town is a gate that separates France from Flanders. This town, being in Flanders though now in the French King's power [since 1658], is but a small place yet well-fortified with moats, palisades and half-moons, etc. [11v] Having eaten our dinner, which was prepared for the passengers that the waggon brings, we kept on our journey, having in all the way from Calais to Dunkirk not the appearance of so much as one tree or anything like one, but all common or heath.

About an English mile on this side [of] Dunkirk, on the sea coast, lies the Fort Mardyck, memorable since the siege [1657-1658] of Dunkirk by the English [with the French] and by them demolished [1659], there remaining at this day not above two or three houses standing. Which having on our left hand, we entered the town of [by] the South Port (as I take it [...]). This town being under the French King, daily increases its strength by the fortifications [12r] there now in agitation by the French King. At our entrance into our inn, being the Packet-boat and which I mention as to advice to those that have occasion for a commodious house of entertainment, we sent our names to the governor. But our late arrival here would not permit us the view of the town.

According to the custom of Flanders, this town being in that province, we supped with what other company the house entertained. Where I observed that whereas the French take not notice after he drinks to you, the Flemings (having something more of reason in it) bow and drink and the pledger bowing at the receipt of the cup (saying they thank us for something). [cont. Oostende and Nieuwpoort]

Sir John Percival, 14 (25) June 1718

[25v] The church (for the whole town [Dunkirk] is but one parish) is large and contains in the side-isles a great many little chapels with an altar in each, after the manner of the Romish churches. These chapels are enclosed by screens or high rails of well-wrought brass, fixed on marble bases differently carved and ornamented; and the altars within them are likewise of sundry sorts of marble, adorned with statues, pictures and other embellishments according as the zeal or purse of the particulars [individuals] who erected them would allow of; for as these smaller oratories are dedicated to particular saints, so do they belong to different gilds, fraternities and companies, or else to private persons, who in honour of their patron vie with the rest, and do their best to make them splendid, which gains to themselves respect here and is, as they think, meritorious in the other world.

In this church there are not many good paintings, but there hangs one in the chapel of Saint George, wherein the martyrdom of a saint is finely represented. He suffers with the utmost resignation, while the commanding officer through shame and regret turns his head aside. But the executioner's countenance is stern and determined; the countenances, attitudes, colouring and whole disposition of this picture is excellent.

[26r] Over the high altar is another good piece, representing the adoration of Our Saviour, but the painter is guilty of one fault common to many others of his profession and of the Romish persuasion: the representing friars in their religious habits adoring Christ, a child in the Virgin's lap, which though perhaps meant for a compliment to the orders so represented, in imposing their false antiquity upon the vulgar is a notorious affront to true history and chronology, no orders of friars subsisting till some ages after Our Saviour. Thus, St Jerome is painted in the habit of a cardinal with his red hat and scarlet robe, whereas both those parts of dress were not granted to cardinals till the Council of Lyons, anno 1245, held many ages after St Jerome died.

A third piece there is, and a very large one over the west door that represents the Last Judgment. It is so destroyed by time and in so obscure a place that I should not have taken notice of it, but that I found it commended in travellers' books. By the drawing I think it could not deserve esteem.

Anonymous tourist, 2-5 May 1720 N.S.

[2] [coming from Boulogne] Rode post through Marquise, a small town, to Calais, three and a half posts, seven leagues; paid for every post, besides the postillion, two livres five sols.

Calais well-fortified; pretty good town and cleanly. Saw the walls, where the couleuvrine of Nancy of twenty-four feet length. Saw the harbour; from thence saw plainly Dover castle. Lodged at the Lion d'Argent (well). Set out at seven in the carabas [large waggon], where every person [pays] 55 sols; every hundredweight the same; a rough voiture. At some distance rode over a road that formerly, even within forty years, was a river navigable, now sucked up by the sands blown from the seaside. Came about twelve to Gravelines, one of the best-fortified towns in France. Money raised to add a new work at the south-west side. Dined well on fish and good wine, burgundy, at the posthouse, Aux Bons Enfants. A convent of English nuns.

Set out at three and stopped at Mardyck; see the canal to Dunkirk [with] the sluice now of sixteen but designed twenty-six foot [wide]; the great sluice of forty-two [foot wide] demolished. [3] The materials lie in heaps near at hand. No forts or fortifications. The sluices won't admit ships of above eighty or a hundred tun. The canal has a winding to break the force of the sea. Both at Calais, Gravelines and Mardyck they can by these sluices set the land at a good distance under water.

Came about seven to Dunkirk at the Chasse Royale; good accommodation. N.B. All change of money very troublesome. From the 1st of May lost two and a half sols upon every thirty sols new piece; other pieces lessened also but variably in various times, which uncertainty makes everything very dear. N.B. Women very indifferent thus far, but begin to mend at Dunkirk. Dance here in May under a garland round a Maytree to their own singing. All about Dunkirk to Ypres, Gravelines, Bergen [Bergues-St Winoc], etc. would be under water had they not that outlet at Mardyck.

Seen the Great Church; two fine pictures, one made by Franciscus Pourbus, anno 1577, which expresses the death of St George, consisting of three pieces. At the right he appears commanding the statue of a pagan god tumbling down in pieces; at the other hand he appears tied to a cross; a great storm arises. His executioners in the utmost fright, one falling down. In the middle piece he is upon his knees, ready to receive the stroke [of the sword]. Himself, his executioner and the governor [4] that stands to see execution done, each in their attitude inimitable.

The other picture is the great altarpiece, which represents Our Saviour at table with his disciples, made upon wood by Rubens. The church in general is common. There is the epitaph of John Bart, died at fifty-two [1702]. Seen the Capuchins; two convents. Two convents of English nuns, one for women of quality of the Benedictine order, the other for the common sort of St Clara. In the former are three pictures whereof two very beautiful, made in 1674.

Seen the haven; the port spoiled, the jetty ruined, the three castles pulled down, viz. at the left [north of the channel] the green fort castle and the Risbank and at the right the White Fort [demolished in 1713 as agreed at the peace treaty at Utrecht]. The basin made very shallow. About it are the magazines, but all empty and fallen in ruin. The passage by which the canal of Mardyck communicates with the basin, it is made so narrow that even the smallest vessel cannot pass. The people boast here in three months they could put all this in better order than ever it was, and by finishing the canal make the town better than ever it was.

Set out for Newport in a carabas. [5] Missed the custom-house officers that would have been troublesome to us in relation to money. Rode all along the seashore to Newport, seven leagues. [cont. Brugge and Sluis]

Sir John Percival, 7-14 (18-25) June 1723

[1r] My wife being advised to use the German Spa waters as sovereign to her distemper, the colic, we resolved to experience them, and accordingly set out the 7th of June 1723 from Charlton for Dover, where we arrived the 9th, and the next day sailed for Calais in Captain Waddington's packet boat. We got thither in three hours and dined at the Lion d'Or.

The 12th we left Calais, passed through Gravelines and lay at Dunkirk. Here Mr Morelle, a gentleman made use of by the English and who speaks our language, was very serviceable to us in despatching our affairs at the custom-house and other offices, which, being set to farm to the highest bidder, are left to reimburse themselves upon tradesmen and passengers, which they do unmercifully. He recommended me to Mr De Boule at Dunkirk, who gave me a bill for 540 florins [guilders] on Mr Clement of Bruges for £54:10:10 sterling, paid by me to Mr De Boule, which precaution was necessary, the French not suffering travellers to carry gold or silver (if a considerable sum) into Flanders, though it be foreign specie, but taking the same from them in exchange of their own money, which being extremely raised, causes a considerable loss to the strangers.

We passed two nights at Dunkirk and had the opportunity of seeing an annual procession in honour of St Eloi, which put the [1v] whole city into extravagancies of noise and joy, but was to us the most ridiculous show that ever we saw. I shall not interrupt this journal with an account of this kermis, but leave it to follow at the end. [cont. Oostende and Nieuwpoort]

Dunkirk

Population: 7,000 (1676), c.10,500 (1686), 13,200 (1697 T.S.), c.10,000 (c.1720).

Distances: Brugge 12 hours (37 miles), Calais 6 hours (20 miles), Dover 40 miles, Gravelines 3 hours (12 miles), Nieuwpoort 5 hours (16 miles), Oostende 8 hours (25 miles). Inns, *Reisboek* (1689, 1700 and 1721): 't Hof van Holland*; Rijssel*; 's Lands Welvaaren; S. George*; *Reisboek* (1700 and 1721) also: Den Arend*.

Calais

Population: 6,000 (1682), c.8,500 (1721).

Distances: Dover 21 miles (4 hours), Dunkirk 6 hours (20 miles), Saint-Omer 6 hours (18 miles).

Inns, *Reisboek* (1689, 1700 and 1721): Au Prince d'Orange; Le Pinas.

Further reading

J.B. Gramaye, *Antiquitates Belgicae*, Bruxelles-Leuven 1708.

A. Sanderus, *Flandria illustrata*, Cologne 1641-1644, 's-Gravenhage 1732, 1735 (*Verheerlykt Vlaandre*, 's-Gravenhage 1732, 1735); reprint Antwerpen-Amsterdam 1981.

N. Mullard, *Calais au temps des lys*, Calais 1961; *Calais au temps de la dentelle*, Calais 1963.

A. Cabantous, *Histoire de Dunkerque*, Toulouse 1983.

A. Derville and A. Vion (eds.), *Histoire de Calais*, Dunkerque 1985.

Revue de la Societé Dunkerquoise d'Histoire et d'Archéologie, 1974-

Revue du Nord, 1910-

Friesland

William Lord Fitzwilliam, May 1663

[21v] From Amsterdam we went to see Friesland, one of the Seven United Provinces and one of the chiefest of them [...]. [22r] The assembly of the States of this province is composed of nine persons: two out of Eastergo [Oostergo], as many out of Westergo and two likewise out of Seven Wolden [Zevenwouden]; for the towns there are three representatives. The president of this assembly is the governor of this province and of Groningen, who is at present Prince William [Willem-] Frederik of Nassau. At The Hague they have likewise their deputies, two for the towns and two for the country. This country has but two natural rivers, the other are artificial and standing water. The goodness of this country consists in meadows, good store of cattle. Their oxen are but little, their cows are very fruitful, they have most commonly two calves at a time and their sheep two and three. Their horses are strong, great, good and handsome. Here is made abundance of turfs, but it is not so good as the turf of Holland. Between Hindeloopen and Staveren there is a village called Molkwerum, where they say the true Frisische language is spoken. They understand Dutch, but no Dutchman can understand them. At Hindeloopen they speak likewise a strange language.

Harlingen being the place where we did land is after Leeuwarden the greatest, strongest and most populous town of West Friesland. This town took its beginning from the ruins of two noble houses Harliga and Harns. Upon their ground [22v] it was built and called Harliga, afterwards Harlingen. There has been formerly [until 1580] a castle, but now there are some other houses in its place. A great part of this town is surrounded with the sea, against which it is defended by strong stone walls and great banks. The figure of this town is almost a perfect square, as big as Leeuwarden. It is fortified with eight bulwarks which are well flanked. She may set herself under water when she pleases.

Here is a very good haven, always full of ships. Here is much salt boiled, much paper and bricks made. The marketplace and town house are but little. The streets are great and clean, all cut through by artificial ditches. The houses are uniformly built but the greatest part of them of wood. Here is likewise a good great church and two hospitals. Five gates belong to this town, four towards the country and one towards the water. A good walk on one side of this town, all set with trees. Here we saw likewise eight men-of-war. The people of this town live by trading and fishing.

From hence we went on foot, only an hour's going, to Franeker. This town is

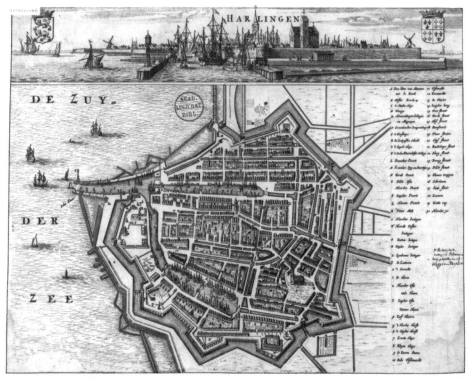

Plan and view of Harlingen, 1664

but little, more long than broad. She is surrounded with good old walls and ditches and several gates; two ditches run through the town. By the Westerport is a castle with a ditch about it, called Sjaerdema Slot. It is surrounded with stone towers, which they say can hardly be battered down by reason of their thickness. Here is but one parish church with a high steeple [23r] on it. Here has dwelled formerly a great quantity of noblemen, witness those noble houses which yet remain. This town was built anno 1191; it has the privilege to choose its own magistrates, which enjoys no other town of West Friesland except Leeuwarden, all the rest are chosen by the States of this country.

Here is a good house for orphans, a Latin school and an university which was founded anno 1580 [1585]. To it belongs a place called the Beurs, founded by the States of this province, where sixty scholars have their diet for a little money, paying only annually seventy-two guilders. Some poor students, natives of this country, are maintained for nothing. Here we saw a pretty little college, which is the university. In it are but little schools, a small library, a pretty place where scholars are graduated, called Templum Academicum, and a physic [botanical] garden. Here are three professors in divinity, two in law, two in physic [medicine], three or four in philosophy.

From hence we went by water to Leeuwarden, a great, fair, populous and very pleasant town, now it is the Court of West Friesland. Here the governor and the States of this province have their residence. Here we saw the governor's (who is Prince William [Willem-Frederik] of Nassau) house and [23v] garden, the town house and Parliament house, St Jacob's church, where William [Willem-] Lodewijk, Count of Nassau and governor formerly of this province and Groningen, lies buried with his lady, all cut out in fair marble. Here are two or three churches more. The nobility of West Friesland lives here by reason of which the people are here very civil. The women are fair, handsomer than in any part of the Netherlands.

The Court is here not very great and splendid, yet big enough for this country. Here are fair and large streets; the houses are pretty good but not so handsomely built as those in Holland. The town is fortified with good walls and some good bastions with a good broad ditch about them. Upon the walls and round about the town are the most pleasant walks, all planted with trees, that can be found in the Seven Provinces. Here are many hospitals which have been formerly convents, for the town has been superstitiously religious.

From this town we went by water likewise to Dokkum, which is one of the oldest towns of this country. In the last wars against the King of Spain this town was fortified with good walls and six bulwarks and a deep broad ditch. The town is not very great, yet fit enough for traffic. [24r] Through the town runs the river Ee. Here is a good haven, a town house, an Admiralty and a very good church, and here are likewise some hospitals. The streets are here clean enough, and the town indifferently well-built. From hence we went out of West Friesland into the Groninger Land, which is called so by reason of its green meadows and its pleasant situation. [cont. Groningen]

John Farrington, 20-22 September 1710 N.S.

[40] My last from Enkhuizen informed you that we were on the borders of North Holland expecting a favourable wind to carry us over the South Sea [Zuiderzee], which on Sunday morning September 20 presented itself to us.

We were forced to hire a whole boat to ourselves, which would have held twenty more as well as us, and about ten in the morning we set sail with a fair wind. It is but fifteen English miles or three hours from thence to Workum, but the wind taking us [41] short, we could not make it till one at noon. In our way we passed by the old and small city of Staveren, remarkable for nothing so much as the corn that every year grows upon the sands, the story whereof is this.

There was formerly in that city a very rich gentlewoman who had freighted out a ship and gave orders to the master to take in at his return the most valuable lading he could. The master thinking nothing more valuable than corn, which is necessary for the support of life, loaded his ship with it. And at his return being asked by his owner what he had brought, when he replied corn, was commanded to put off

147

to sea and to throw it over on the contrary side from that he had taken it in on, which accordingly was done. And to this day corn continues to spring up in those sands every year, as I was assured from several that had seen it.

We passed by the famous Molkwerum too, a town famous for its irregularity, being built after such a manner that it is extremely difficult for a stranger to find his way out again, and famous also for the strange language and manners of its inhabitants. I was sorry we could not see this town, but it would have hindered us at least a day's journey and therefore we contented ourselves with only seeing at the distance we were at when we passed by.

After a pretty [stormy] passage, for I think the sea was altogether as rough as the main sea in our passage from England, we came to Workum. This is a large village, in which there is nothing remarkable but the Great Church, which is indeed a very noble building, and the manner of erecting monuments over their graves in the churchyard, which are exactly like the boxes put [42] round young trees in England and much about the same height too. We dined at the best house in town on such provisions as we could get, which was very indifferent, being dressed after the Dutch fashion. After dinner we hired a waggon for Franeker, which is about five hours from this town.

The way as far as Harlingen is very good, lying on the sea coast, only the passage is extremely narrow, the sea on the left and a dyke on the right. The waggon being open, it was pretty cool travelling. Here we saw on the sea, as we rode along, incredible numbers of wild swans and wild ducks with which the sea was almost covered for a great way together. The country here lies low, but it is very fruitful and the causeway that we rode upon serves as a fence against the sea. And here, though it was Sunday, we saw the boors ploughing and sowing as if it had been any other day of the week.

About half an hour after six we passed through Harlingen, which is a pretty large but old city, situated on the sea coast, from whence is the common passage into North Holland, and there are boats that sail every day from thence to Enkhuizen, wind and weather permitting.

It is about an hour and half from this place to Franeker, but the road between those two cities is by much the worst we have met with since we left England, for the great rains had made it very wet, slippery and in some places deep. There fell so great a shower of rain and hail while we were on the way, that it wetted us through our cloaks but did us no greater damage. About eight that night or a little after, we came safe to Franeker. Lodged close to the university at the sign of the Sun, just within the gate.

Franeker is a small city, the walks round about on the walls of this town are pleasantly [43] planted with rows of trees. It is about half an hour's walk round the town, and so long we were walking of it. There are two churches of the Reformed religion, but there are no Papists tolerated. And give me leave to observe that in this and several other particulars the laws and government of Friesland are very

Franeker. The academy of Friesland, 1622

like those of England, for both their laws and ours are very severe against Papists. None of them are permitted the exercise of their religion, nay if any praetor [magistrate] whose business it is to look after these things can be convicted of conniving at them in their worship, he will be made forever incapable of enjoying any offices in the government. But these laws like ours are grown almost insignificant and now pretty much neglected.

There is still to be seen the ruins of an old castle which was formerly a considerable addition to the strength and beauty of the town but now is suffered to run to decay. The chief thing now that this city is remarkable for is its university. There are eighteen professors in it and two hundred scholars, but none of our countrymen as I could hear of. The professors, and especially the divines, are men of great reputation for learning and piety, among whom we saw the famous [Campegius] Vitringa (author of the treatise *De decemviris otiosis*, etc.) and [Johannes] Van der Waeyen, two celebrated writers as, Sir, I am not to inform you.

It happened very luckily that the day we stayed in this city, there was a degree of doctor given to a gentleman of that university. We went to the hall [church] to see the solemnity and were introduced by one of their officers and placed on chairs for gentlemen and strangers just against the pulpit. The hall is pretty large; at one end [in the choir] is the pulpit, on the left sit the professors, on the right the magistrates of the city, curators, presidents, commissaries of the Admiralty and the ministers. [44] Without the chancel sit the scholars or undergraduates. Just within are chairs for the doctors, among whom we had the honour to be placed. The disputation, which lasted about an hour, was diverting enough. They have a very good library as they told us and a gallery wherein they have the picture of every professor since the foundation of the university, but our time would not give us leave to see them.

The inn we lay at in this city gave me occasion to think of our lodgings in Wales. We went through the stable to bed, the chamber was over it and whenever I waked I heard the horses eating. This is the worst entertainment we have met with, but however, it is undoubtedly the best inn in town, and we had this one comfort we did not pay extravagantly (lodged at the sign of the Stork, over against the Waech or Weigh-house; good entertainment and good usage, the woman speaks a little English). About twelve at noon we took boat for Leeuwarden, which is three hours and a half from thence, and that ended this day's journey, September 21.

Leeuwarden or Leovardia is the chief city of this province and the residence of the Prince of Friesland. It's a large and handsome city and a place where a man might live very agreeably with good company. Here, while our dinner or supper was preparing, we hired a guide to take a view of the rarities of this place. Among the principal buildings we must reckon the palace of the Prince, the churches of the Calvinists, the Parliament House, the Spinhouse, etc.

The palace is an old building and but indifferent. Only there is one part of it that was new-built this year that is pretty good, after the English manner which I perceive is the model they all follow in this country for their new buildings. Over against the palace is a very good house where the Prince's guards lodge. [45] We were shown the palace by one they call the [blank], who spoke English very well and was mighty civil to us. In the first room, which was the antechamber to the Princess' apartment, was the picture of King Charles the First [=Hendrik Casimir II], but drawn à la mode de Frize, with such long trousers you would scarce have known him. The Princess [Maria Louise] was in her apartment so we could not see it. When we had gone upstairs, which are yet unfinished and the paintings not hung up, they brought us into a room on the left, an antechamber of the Prince's [Johan Willem Friso], where was the throne that King William sat on at Kensington. In the Prince's chamber, where he lay when unmarried, were a great number of fine pieces of small paintings, among the rest a head of Erasmus, and a great number of very good pieces in watercolours, as the head of King Charles the Second, King William, the Princes of Orange, etc.

The guard-chamber which opened into the Room of State was adorned with the pictures of officers who had been famous in war. In the state-room there was a throne on the right and, at the upper end, an admirable picture of Cain slaying Abel. The furniture of the next room was of solid silver, and in the middle hung a silver crown that served instead of a branch for lights. So also was the bedchamber furnished with silver stands, tables, sconces, screens and a large square pot of silver for orange trees.

In the cabinet in the chamber was an amber table, very large, which is said to have cost thirty thousand rixdollars. And there are also in the same abundance of curious paintings. In the Great Hall belowstairs is the picture of [46] the Prince's grandfather, father and family in one large piece. The grandfather [Willem Frederik] unfortunately occasioned his own death. He had endeavoured to fire his pistol and it would not go off, but blowing into it to see what was the occasion of it, or whether it was charged or not, it went off, shot him through the neck whereof he died. He lies buried in the Great Church. There are also two very good pieces of the Prince's father and mother, of King William in his Parliament robes, the present Prince and Princess, who is a very fine woman. At the upper end of the hall are the pictures of the ancestors of that Prince who were stadtholders of Friesland, above one hundred years ago. There were two very good marble tables, one of black marble inlaid with white, the other of a very fine brown with several curious veins in it.

The Prince was not returned from his command in the army, so I am not able to give you any account of the splendour of that Court or the figure it makes in the world.

Next to the palace may be reckoned the churches of the Calvinists in this city. There are three for their religion, and one for the Lutherans. The Papists have none allowed, though it is said that above one half of the city are Catholics. The Great or the State Church [St Jacob's] is a very good building, remarkable for the tomb of the old Prince of Friesland [Willem Lodewijk]. In the upper end of the choir lies the Prince; his statue in marble is kneeling with one knee upon a cushion. He is represented as in armour, his gauntlets on one side of him and his helmet on the other. On one side is the statue of a fine woman leaning on a pillar which is the emblem of Might, on the other a statue of a woman representing Prudence or Foresight, and overhead the arms of the family. The [47] inscription was in these words: Gul. Lud. Joh. Fil. Comes. Nassau. Frisiae. Omelandiae ... [Willem Lodewijk, son of John, Count of Nassau, Governor of Friesland, Groningen, Ommelanden and Drenthe ... died in 1620].

In the middle of the choir is the tomb of his Lady, whose statue also is in marble, she lying on the top of the tomb at her full length. Round about are these words: Anna Illustrissima Princeps. Aurantiae ... [Anna, illustrious princess of Orange ... died 13 June 1588, aged 26]. In a chapel on the north side of the church is

xli.

Leeuwarden. Monument to Willem Lodewijk, 1640

a marble coffin on a pedestal, wherein lies the body of [Hendrik Casimir II] the present Prince's father, with a golden urn on the top of the coffin. And close by him is a small coffin wherein lies one of his children.

In this church is the seat or throne of the Prince and the seat of the eighty-two, or the Parliament, of which I shall give you an account anon, which being of wainscot are a mighty addition to the beauty of the church.

The eighty-two, or the Parliament of Friesland, have a house wherein they assemble. But each member [of its four constituent bodies] has a separate room to meet in and transact matters by themselves before it is proposed in general. There is an office of the Chamber [48] of the secretaries, where they keep the papers and records of the assembly. In the chamber where the General Assembly meet is a very good picture of the present Prince and his father. Otherwise, there is nothing remarkable in them, but that they are all convenient enough for the use to which they are employed. There is a pretty garden belonging to the house with a pleasant room or house in the middle of it.

The Spinhouse or prison is a large and good building consisting of two quadrangles, in the inmost of which is the womens' apartment, who are there kept to hard labour, but certainly they are the most impudent here of any creatures in the world. The men also are kept to work according to their crimes, some rasping, others weaving, spinning, etc.

I must not forget the stables of the Prince, where are several sets of very good horses, but a great number of the finest are with the Prince in Flanders; nor the gardens of this Lord, which are at some distance from the palace.

The gardens are not quite finished, but they are already very pleasant and would be much more beautiful as well as convenient if they were laid with gravel as ours in England. And I cannot but admire why none of the great men in these countries have not brought gravel from England since they can have it brought all the way by water to them. But for want of this it was very troublesome walking, and the rain having fallen in great quantities, the walks were a perfect quag. The greenhouse or orangery is very pretty but not very large, over which there is a room large and well-painted [49] and gilt and above that the cistern, which supplies the fountain in the middle of the garden with water, which is the only way they have to raise their water in these flat countries.

In the midst of the basin where the fountain is lies an island. Round about the basin are several pretty good statues in lead, representing dancers, with castinets, timbrels, etc. The knots in the middle of the garden are of curious shapes and mighty agreeable. There is a walk round the garden, which in a little time will be covered with greens so as to defend both from sun and rain.

This, Sir, is what I have to observe of Leeuwarden, which in general may be said to be a very good city. There are a great many good buildings in it, besides those I have described. It is fortified but only with a wall and ditch, without which is a pleasant walk of trees, as there is also another within the walls, planted after the same manner, which makes the town very pleasant. And it seems to be a town of very good trade. But I must have done, it grows late, I am, etc.

Leeuwarden, September 21, 1710.

[50] Sir, the fair there was at Leeuwarden that day we arrived there afforded us no small diversion. There was a certain mountebank or stage player that had erected a booth and gave about most monstrous bills of what great things were to be performed that evening. The great brags the fellow made of the extraordinariness of the performance excited our curiosity so far that we enfin gave him our company according to his invitation. I cannot say we were disappointed or displeased.

It was, in short, but a puppet show, only Punch had assumed to himself the name of Sciambre, and he and the fiddler made the greatest part of the diversion. The show consisted in a variety of dances in the habits of Spaniards, Italians, etc., the last of which I thought were well ridiculed by the mock representation. Sciambre took a pipe very naturally and the smoke came out of his mouth. I could see no great delight in the play, but Punch and the fiddler talked and the people were very merry. I confess it is several years since I was present at a puppet show, which I should scarce have dared now to have been within the jurisdiction of my friend Isaac Bickerstaff, but I could not have thought it could have been so diverting. Next thing was a representation of the sea and the monsters in it, a mermaid, whales, porpoises, etc., two ships fighting, very well done, and at last followed divers strange and antic postures performed after this manner: between the spectators and the stage was a covering or screen of oiled paper; behind that they played all the postures of the Italian Scaramouches, who sometimes [51] seemed to leap over the stage, sometimes to the top of it, sometimes sunk under it. All sorts of shapes were represented, as boys, men, old women, dogs, etc., which, with the music of the fiddler who played tolerably well, made up the entertainment till it was time to retire to our lodgings.

You will pardon me, I hope, for giving you an account of a humorous diversion, though I know you to be so great a friend of Isaac Bickerstaff's, that you as well as he are a mortal enemy to [Martin] Powell and his puppets, and I shall endeavour to make you some amends by giving you an account of the government of this province, as soon as I have finished that of our journey through it.

September 22. At nine in the morning we left the city of Leeuwarden and took boat for Dokkum, one of the cities of Friesland, whither we came about one at noon. This I think is the least and worst city we have seen. It is governed by burgomasters as are also the greater cities, but you may be sure it is no very considerable place, since one of them keeps a public house, where we bought some provisions to carry in the boat for we could not stay to eat it on shore, but took boat for Stroobosch, which is the last place we came to in the province of Friesland.

Stroobosch is only a small village where you change boats in order to go for Groningen. Between Dokkum and Stroobosch, or Stroobus, you pass by the village of Kollum, which seems to be a large and fair village remarkable for its fair for horses, and for the butter and cheese that is made there. In the way you pass by a very pleasant seat [Clantstate] of one of the deputies of this province to The Hague (mijnheer Allingen) [Eppo van Aylva]. The banks of the canals are high and very pleasant and pretty woody. We came to Stroobosch about four, where we took boat and arrived at [52] Groningen half an hour past eight that night. So that we have been above ten hours in the boat, which, were it not for the good company that we have and the diversions of a dead friend or two [books] we carry along with us, it would be very tedious.

I shall now, Sir, give you some account of the Parliament of Friesland as I have been informed about it in this country. [...] [53] Thus you see in how many things the government of Friesland and of England are alike, where the Prince, the nobility and the people have each their share in the administration. And as the nature of their government so their language is much nearer ours than that of any of the other provinces that I have been in, insomuch that they have a proverb, that [54]

> Butter, bread, and green cheese
> Is good English, and good Frize.

And I think there is a very considerable agreement in a great many of their words, especially their monosyllables as house, hose, smith, way, rain, etc., all [of] which are pronounced just as we do. [cont. Groningen]

Leeuwarden

Population: 15,000 (1650, 1710).

Distances: Amsterdam 44 hours (via Amersfoort-Zwolle), 74 miles (via Harlingen) and 66 miles (via Workum), Franeker 3¹/₂ hours (9 miles), Groningen 14 hours (33 miles), Harlingen 5 hours (14 miles), Zwolle 22 hours (67 miles).

Inns, *Reisboek* (1689 and 1700): 't Hof van Vriesland*, over de Kasteleny, voorzien met veele groote kamers, en civil tractement; Benthem; Den Oyevaar; 't Vergulde Hoofd [also 1721: op de Markt bij de Waag]; De Toorn van Babel; 't Graauwe Paard; De Zon*. *Reisboek* (1689): Gustavus Adolphus, bij de Vischmarkt. *Reisboek* (1700 and 1721) also: bij de Poorten daar de Snecken aan komen. *Reisboek* (1721): De Valk* op den Dijk bij de Wirdumerpoort. Nugent (1749) also: The Angel*.

Franeker

Population: 3,600 (1690, 1714), 3,500 (1744).

Distances: Harlingen 1¹/₂ hours (5 miles), Leeuwarden 3¹/₂ hours (9 miles).

Inns, *Reisboek* (1689, 1700 and 1721): De Valk*; Den Oijevaar; De Zon*; De Hollandse Tuyn*.

Harlingen

Population: 8,800 (1690), 7,100 (1714, 1744).

Distances: Amsterdam 18 hours (60 miles), Enkhuizen 9 hours (30 miles), Franeker 1¹/₂ hours (5 miles), Leeuwarden 5 hours (14 miles), Workum 5 hours (14 miles).

Inns, *Reisboek* (1689, 1700 and 1721): 't Hof van Vriesland* [1721: or Heerenlogement over 't Stadhuis]; De Paauw*. *Reisboek* (1689 and 1700) also: De nieuwe Pinas. *Reisboek* (1700) adds: en daar de Snecken af varen. *Reisboek* (1721) also: De oude Pinas*; De Drie Hoefijzers*; De Ooievaar, bij de trekschuiten op Leeuwarden en Franeker.

Further reading

S.A. Gabbema, *Verhaal van de stad Leeuwaarden*, Franeker 1701.

S.A. Gabbema, *Historie van Friesland*, Franeker 1703.

Rondom de Oldehove: geschiedenis van Leeuwarden en Friesland, Leeuwarden 1952 (reprint 1989).

J.A. Faber, *Drie eeuwen Friesland*, Leeuwarden 1973.

It Beaken, tijdschrift van de Fryske Akademy, 1938-

De Vrije Fries, tijdschrift van het Fries genootschap, 1839-

Gent

William Lord Fitzwilliam, July 1663

[37v] We embarked ourselves at Vlissingen [Flushing] and passed by many strong places belonging to the States of Holland [States-General], but upon Flanders ground, as Biervliet, Philippine, Terneuzen and at last we came to 't-Sas van Gent, a mighty strong place, lying just before Gand and a key to whole Flanders. It belongs to the States of the United Provinces. This stronghold lies in marshy ground; on one side runs the sea, on the other side of which there is a little sconce, which does defend both the sea and the Sas. This town is defended with ten or eleven bastions and one piece of horn, through which runs the water which leads to Gand. Here is likewise a castle lying on the haven in which there is a very curious well-made sluice, the bottom of which is paved with good freestone. After we had seen this place and taken a shorter dinner, we went that night to Gand, the metropolis of this country.

It lies but four miles of the sea on three rivers, the Schelde, Leie and Lieve and many other little brooks which run in and about the town. This is a very great town and fortified; it has round about it suburbs like Milan, its circumference within the walls is thought to be seven Italian miles and its whole ambitus without, with all the cornfields, gardens and bleaching places, is thought to be nine Dutch miles, wherefore the King of Spain [38r] could very well say, without telling a lie, that his Gand (which is in French a glove [gant]) was big enough for to hold Paris.

At Gand the Council of Flanders has its residence in a great old house where two great statues stand before the door. This council was constituted here [1409] by John [the Fearless], Duke of Burgundy and [Count of] Flanders, consisting of a president, twelve councillors, an advocate and other officers. From this court may be appealed to that of Mechelen.

In this town there is a strong castle built [1540] by Charles V, which is surrounded with good walls, five bastions and good ditches; now it is very much ruinated. Here is a tower called the Belfort, five hundred stairs high in which do hang many bells and very excellent chimes. Upon the top of it is a copper dragon with great wings. Count Baldwin [IX] of Flanders sent it from Constantinople hither [1204]. Here is likewise a very well-built town house, without and within very fair; one great room adorned with rich pictures of Charles V and other governors of this country. Here you may see the house and chamber where Charles V was born, very poor and mean and almost as bad as the stable where Our Saviour came into the world. His cradle, which now is taken away, was not so good as a manger but like a kneading trough.

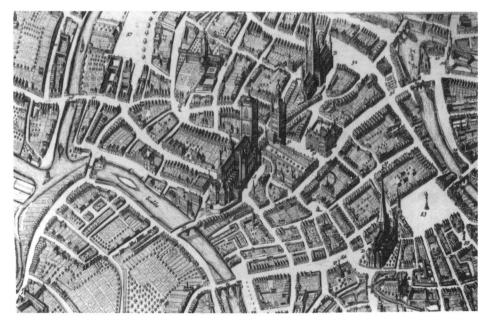

Town plan, 1641

Within Gand there are fifty-five churches, convents and other houses of piety [38v] and charity. Seven parish churches of which St John's [later called St Bavo] and St Michael's are the chiefest, in which, as likewise in St Peter's, the Jesuits' and Dominicans' church, we saw precious pictures and other very rich ornaments. In one part of this town we saw likewise a great cannon [De Dulle Griete] of a huge wide mouth and a very great bigness.

This town consists of twenty-six isles; here are ninety-eight bridges, many streets, but few very fair, several good houses but not at all uniformly built. Here are likewise thirteen marketplaces, amongst which the Friday marketplace is the chiefest on which Charles V, cut out in wood, used to stand; a new one is to be set up in the old one's place, which fell down. From hence we went directly by water to Bridges [Brugge] to eat some of the Bruges capons, having had our bellies full of veal of Gand, which is counted to be the best veal of Europe. [cont. Brugge and Sluis]

Richard Holford, 21-22 August (31 August - 1 September) 1671

[31v] We left Bruxelles Monday at seven and took coach for Ghent, and paid three guilders or florins apiece for ourselves and a rixdollar or patacoon for our man [...]. We baited at the city of Aalst in Brabant [...]. [32r] We paid for our ordinary twenty-four stivers apiece and for our man ten stivers. After we came in our coach, about a

mile towards Ghent, we crossed a little river [Dender], which divides Brabant from Flanders. All our passage this morning was very pleasant, the country being uneven and full of large hop yards and trees, as also between Aalst and Ghent.

[32v] We came to Ghent Monday, a little after seven and that night saw the town house, the largest that we had seen and of excellent good work. [...] We took a coach Tuesday morning and saw the great marketplace, and in it in the middle upon a large marble pedestal stands the picture or effigies of Charles the Fifth gilded. Then we went to the new works [fortifications] and saw the citizens, Jesuits, friars and soldiers all at their several works, levelling of great hills [...]. [33r] We saw the great gun, called the great whore of Ghent, so big that a woman may be got with child in it, being at least twenty inches in the diameter.

Mr [George] Robins fell asleep in the coach whilst we were riding about to see the town at eight in the morning [...]. The castle very large and a very large graft round it. And now the Count Monterey has made very strong new outworks, the graft or river is in many places three, one within the other, and is without all doubt a very strong place, they being able upon [33v] occasion to stop the rivers and drown the country on every side, save that where the castle stands, which is now very strong and by reason of the levelling the hills, there can be no safe approaching. [cont. Brugge and Sluis]

John Walker, 29-30 August (8-9 September) 1671

[14] On the 29th we took waggon [in Brussels] and came by dinner-time to a neat little town called Alost [Aalst], where we baited. We arrived here upon a holy day, the people in their best apparel, their shops all shut. The little time we stayed here we resolved to make use of in seeing the principal church and observe the ceremonies of the festival, knowing the priests and friars to have variety of tricks in all places.

We no sooner entered this church and came up to the choir but we were presented with a rare show: the effigies of Our Saviour in his purple robe sitting astride upon a great wooden ass on the outside of the church. He was standing under a small pent-house with a taper burning by him in the manner he was crucified, in his purple robe and crown of thorns upon his head.

Having dined we went our way for Ghant, the largest city in all the Spanish Netherlands. It is situated in Flanders, the Latins call it Gandavum or Ganda. Here we found them as industriously repairing their fortifications as at Bruxelles to keep out those locusts, the French. Considering the magnitude of the place, it is but thinly inhabited. The young women of the town appeared in a pretty antic dress in steeple-crowned hats and long feathers hanging down their waists. Their stathuys is very magnificent, in which were several portraitures of Charles V, very lively drawn; one whereof was his rescuing a lady from the savage rage of a lion. In the middle of the prime marketplace his statue is erected and likewise that of Albertus and Isabella. This [town] is noted for an English nunnery. We viewed the prime church, which contained a multitude of stately chapels; in the [Belfort] tower is a vast bell, called Rowland [Roeland], weighing above eleven thousand weight. The next day we departed from hence and proceeded on our journey to Bruges. [cont. Brugge and Sluis]

Thomas Scott, 26 September (6 October) 1672

[21v] Thursday morning we took coach for Ghent, being of the same distance from Bruxelles as Antwerp and almost as bad a way. At noon we baited at Aalst, a small ruinated town, but notable for the infinite [22r] number of hops yearly sent from thence to England and other places, known by the name of Flemish hops.

About eight in the evening we arrived near Gaunt, where being informed the gates were shut (it being customary in that country to shut the ports at seven; after which not one is to enter upon any account), we were forced (contrary to that saying 'He that has money may do what he will') to undergo great hardship, being forced to take up our lodging at a small cottage, a kind of cake-house about a quarter of an English mile from the town, where we were glad to be contented with some few eggs and butter; and the best of our cheer was a glass of wine and a good fire. And after a tedious journey we were [22v] forced to lie down on beds stuffed with chaff on which, with little sleep, we passed away the night, being fain to lie double and having for sheets I suppose tablecloths, and for a rug half of one cut in two, not covering the sheets by an inch, and those not the bed by two, and without curtains, valence or tester. [cont. Brugge and Sluis]

Thomas Bowrey, 28 June - 2 July (8-12 July) 1698

[63] Tuesday June 28th 1698. This morning at ten o'clock we arrived [from Antwerp] at Ghent. The river [Schelde] is here and for some miles lower about sixty foot wide. The tide rises at the lower end [64] of the city about four foot and makes a slack water on the flood for about three hours.

Wednesday June 29th 1698. This day dined with Mr Lodowick de Wolf, a merchant who trades to England and speaks good English. Then see the Great Church, which is the cathedral of the diocese, in which are several monuments of the dead bishops in marble, with much other marble-work and other ornaments, among which four very large brass candlesticks, curiously wrought with the arms of England on them, and were bought in England in Cromwell's time. This church is indifferent large and dedicated to St Bavo.

Then see the stadthouse, which is a stone building, one part of it very old and very good stonework, like Westminster Abbey. The house is about two hundred foot in length, three ranges of windows, within divided into many rooms for the use of the magistrates of the city, of the Council of Flanders, etc. In one room is several good pictures of Charles V, Empereur, who was born here; else but meanly adorned withinside.

Then see a nunnery called the beguinage, wherein is about nine hundred women who only vow chastity so long as they are [65] willing to continue in the nunnery; nevertheless, seldom any goes out to marry. They go abroad when they please in the day, but wear a habit of distinction and are all under a governess, but maintain themselves and live as they please, all being within one enclosure, but in several houses or communities.

Then see the house of the men vowing chastity [Alexians or Cellebroeders], whose number is a *vader* or governor, and sixteen brothers. They wear a habit of distinction, live a monastical life but not austere, have a chapel neatly adorned and have a good revenue by all burials, it being their office to bury there.

This city, I am informed, is seven miles about, walled and moated. The river Schelde runs through it and also the canal from Bruges comes here into the Schelde, and some other canals. The city is indifferent, buildings mostly two storeys high of brick, the streets broad, paved with flat stone. A great deal of ground near the wall all round unbuilt. [The city] has [66] seven parish churches and about forty other churches belonging to nunneries, monasteries, etc. Here is one English nunnery, consisting of about twenty nuns. The city and fortifications thereof are under the government of the magistrates, who are thirteen aldermen, but the citadel, which is on the east side of the town and is walled and moated, is under a governor put in by the King of Spain, to whom we paid twenty-six stivers and a half as a duty imposed.

Here is a shambles or butchery, altogether indifferent well-stocked with good veal; the mutton and beef but indifferent. Here is several marketplaces, one very large and in the middle a tall pillar with the figure of Charles V on it, gilded. Here is sometimes to be seen one hundred and fifty coaches, most gentlemen's living in the city and commonly driving about the city from five to seven in the evening. The Ghent foot is eleven thumbs or eleven inches and three quarters.

[67] Thursday June 30th 1698. This noon, the sluice at the lower bridge being opened, we passed up, paying eighteen stivers to the bridge-master. These sluices are sometimes not opened in seven days. Here [we] also hired three men at twenty-four stivers each, to help us through the city, being about two miles to the Bridges [Brugge] port. When we were got about half a mile up, the tide running very strong, we were put ashore, and the water falling, we grounded. The sluice continuing open, the tide on the flood did not rise enough to float us. Therefore in the morning at nine o'clock, [we] went to the stadthouse to request an order for the stopping the sluice to raise the water, and the bridge-master was ordered to do it tomorrow morning at four o'clock. See the office belonging to the steel-bow fraternity, which is near the stadthouse, but now much disused.

Friday July 1st 1698. This morning at five o'clock we floated and then, the tide running slack, we made our way up to the Bruges port, to which I judge to be two miles. When [we] came there, [we] hired a horse to track us to Bruges, to give four guilders. Set out at nine o'clock. Paid at the boom coming out at Ghent, two stivers and at the boom at the Bruges port two stivers.

Saturday July 2nd 1698. From the Bruges port at Ghent made the best of our way up the canal towards Bruges. [68] The canal is all the way about sixty foot broad; a great part of the way the banks on each side about twenty foot high. Found several shallow places, but four foot water; it is a still water. At nine [at] night arrived at Bruges. It is accounted from Ghent to Bruges eight hours' travel or twenty-four English miles. Passed about five drawbridges, paying one stiver at each bridge and two stivers at the boom going into Bruges.

James Thornhill, 26-29 June 1711 N.S.

[46] [Coming from Middelburg] At Sas [van Gent] before we landed, the sentinel called on us to give an account who we were and from whence, etc., and after having informed the officer of the guard, we were admitted to land. It is a place by art and nature made impregnable, a small town.

We lay at the Three Passengers, from which house we hired a waggon and two horses for one pistole to Ghent, which is about [four] leagues. Came to Ghent about noon. Lodged at Mr Hawkins' at the Diamond, an Englishman who formerly kept the Crown in Westminster near the gate-house. Along the left hand from Sas to Ghent, on the other side of the river, are several lunettes thrown up with earth. There is a fort called Red House Fort and a village called Terdonk. By Meulestede, a mile short of Ghent, are the remains of lines [of defence] from Brussels to Antwerp.

[47] No private lodgings at Ghent unless you take them for a week. Excellent pontac at Hawkins' for four permission skillings; delicate white Ghent beer and a good ordinary for four permission skillings. The great marketplace is noble and spacious and is called the Keiser Market from the great brass statue of the Emperor Charles V, who was born just by in a little poor house as they say. The city is twelve miles round the outworks. There are seven good churches, richly adorned with altars of various marbles, carvings and painting – whole doors of brass cut through with foliage very nobly.

We went to Mr Rijcard Durynck, on whom was a letter of credit, and who is a very complaisant gentleman. He has a picture of Time and Peace over his chimney in the great parlour, done by one [Jan van] Cleve, an old man and counted the best painter in Ghent. It is in a clean, neat manner, but not great nor well-drawn. In the same room is a picture of [Theodoor] Rombouts, strongly painted but in a true Dutch manner. Mr Durynck's son, a smart young gentleman, went with us to Mr Hudson's, who speaks English very well and has an excellent collection of pictures and tapestry, and is much the best house in the city, and very good gardens and orange trees.

In his parlour on the right hand are five pieces of good tapestry, done at Brussels by J[an] F[rans] vanden Hecke; others abovestairs in four pieces, after

Oskillen, and others after the original paintings of [David] Teniers. Over one door is a head by Rembrandt, equal to Van Dyck and not much unlike his manner. In his grand cabinet are two of the finest pictures that ever I beheld of Teniers. One, a merry-making, pretty large, the other an old man giving away bread and is about two feet long and a foot high. The heads, groups, lights and shadows, harmony, expressions, together with his loose easy pencil, [48] makes him justly esteem that picture at one hundred louis d'ors. [...]

St Bavo or St John's. The steeple is of an excellent Gothic gusto and very large. On one side of the church is a little niche with a taper continually burning before a picture of the Blessed Virgin. Our guide bid us observe the mole on her left cheek, which looks blackish, telling us that a Turk, coming by (accoutred [equipped]) asks what that picture meant. And being told it was the mother of Christ, he pulled out his pistol and shot her in the face. But the bullet, not being able to enter, recoiled and went through his body, of which he immediately died. The mole is the mark of the bullet on her face. [...]

[50] Chapel of the English nuns. We came hither before their service began, and found a deep silence, some people on their knees, intermixed gentlemen and commons, male and female. But after the priest began service we heard soft responses from a gallery over our heads, which came from the invisible female engines. Then a delicate soft organ played and after it a soft voice began, which was raised up by degrees into delicious music. Then the organ with several other voices formed a complete harmony. Thus we continued in the midst of service, singing and playing alternately for near an hour, during part of which time I stole privately close to a grate, through which I peeped and saw several nuns on their knees, telling their beads, etc. Amongst which was a most beautiful creature whose neat, white dress and innocent countenance added not a little to her advantage. [...]

[52] June 18/29. We set out in a berline and four good horses for Tournai, which we hired for six pistoles, about six o'clock, under the escort of my Lord Orkney, etc., keeping the Schelde on our left hand all the way, which is a pleasant road, but very close with hedges and plantations, which makes it very dangerous for partisans [soldiers], voleurs [thieves], etc. The way is sandy, the fields abound with corn, which you find better still as you advance to Lille; no mark being left of armies foraging, only here and there a mill burned down and houses destroyed, which are yet more frequent betwixt Tournai and Lille. Some of our soldiers were every now and then making little excursions to steal hens, chickens or any eatables in the boors' houses just out of the road. When we heard the women crying out, cornet Coxich rode and drove them [the soldiers] away.

John Leake, 23 June (4 July) 1712

[45r] About ten of the clock in the morning, June the 23rd, we arrived at Ghent and put up at the Golden Head. Ghent is a busy, large well-built city and may be reck-

oned among the first-rate cities of Europe. The castle, gates and all the places of strength were in the hands of the English. Here is an English nunnery of Benedictines and another convent for women of the same nation, the name of their order I have forgot [poor Clares].

We took a view of the noble arras hangings that are in St John's [St Peter's] church. They represent the history of the two great apostles St Peter and St Paul, and have had a mighty price bid for them by the present French king [Louis XIV]. The cathedral church is a noble ornamented structure and finely set off by the tombs of its several bishops. The present bishop [Van der Noot] has his tomb already set up in a little chapel behind the high altar, whether he often retires to his private devotions and to meditate upon death.

In this city are kept thirteen markets, the chief of which is that kept upon Friday. In this marketplace is placed the statue of Charles V. It was this Prince [Philip II] who erected Ghent into a bishopric [1559]. The Gentois have the character of being obliging, well-bred, observers of their laws and customs, grave and warlike. [cont. The Return Journey]

Sir John Percival, 17-19 (28-30) June 1718

[32r] On the 17th of June, we took places in the great trackscout and set out [from Brugge] for Ghent. The trackscout is a covered boat, much in the nature of our row barges that ply the Thames from London to Oxford. This sort of passage is safe from robbers or ill weather and very convenient for passengers, who are sure of arriving to their journey's end at a set hour and with their baggage are [32v] carried for a small matter. For though we hired to ourselves a very handsome cabin, we paid but fifteen stivers a head, which makes about eighteen pence English money, and ten for our servants. Neither did our dinner cost more than fifteen stivers each and yet we had meat more than enough had it been dressed to our palate.

Another pleasure and indeed advantage to strangers, which this way of travelling affords, is that persons of various nations often meet together, whose conversation beguiles the tediousness of the passage. The day I left Dunkirk and arrived at Bruges, I had a great deal of discourse with a Recollect friar of St-Omer, a Benedictine of Lille and one Monsieur Du Plessis, a canon of Ypres. The last was a gentleman of good family and a man of sense and learning, and being a secular priest had nothing in him of the monkish bigotry [...].

[34v] The church of Saint Michael is less than the others above mentioned, but contains the best paintings in the city. On the left hand, over one of the altars, is a crucifix by Van Dyck and another of the same master near it. On the other side of the church, there is a picture by Rubens, held in such esteem that they always keep it covered with a curtain, except in time of divine service.

In a little chapel dependent on the monks of St Peter's church, I observed an altarpiece where the agony of Our Saviour upon the cross and the distress of the

Virgin and of St John are admirably well expressed, but I could not learn the painter's name. [35r] Here they offered us to sale several trinkets, which were presents made to the monks by bigots of the town, and when touched by God and the Virgin (two vile images of Our Saviour and his mother) are sold to others as superstitious as themselves, for the profit of the cloister. The purchasers are assured that wearing them on their necks and repeating seven Ave Maries a day and seven prayers to God, they shall never fall sick [...].

[35v] The convent of English nuns of the order of St Bennet [Benedict] is not so strict as that of St Clare. One Mrs [Mary] Knatchbull, born in Kilkenny in Ireland, was then lady abbess, whose family is a branch of the Knatchbulls of Kent, and settled in that kingdom at the time of the Reformation. She entertained us with sweetmeats and strong waters made by the nuns of her convent and is a lady of good sense and behaviour.

They lost good possessions in England and are poor, yet she told me that she thought it unreasonable to expect the recovery of them, if ever the Catholic religion were restored. She could not forbear entering into controversy, which is the common weakness of these female societies, the men seldom touching on that point with strangers. But in the conclusion of our discourse she said that she believed Protestants who served God in a good conscience and were under invincible ignorance, whether by education or otherwise, were as acceptable to God as others who were in the right way. But then she owned this was not the opinion of many of her religion. This gave me occasion to tell her a remark I had often made, that the English Roman Catholics were generally more charitable in their thoughts of us than those of other nations. At parting she desired I would give her leave to pray for me, to which compliment I answered that though I believed her prayers would do me no good after death, I was sure they would while I lived [...].

[37r] We went one day to visit Mr Hudson, an English gentleman settled there. He was then a Protestant, but afterwards changed his religion and at his death left most of what he had to the Jesuits; the rest to a bastard daughter. He had a numerous collection of paintings, which he showed us in a very obliging manner. We were surprised to find a private gentleman possessed of so many valuable pieces, among which were several of Van Dyck, Rubens, Teniers, Velvet Breughel, Caravaggio, Corregio and other eminent hands. This house, which contains eighteen rooms on a floor, is well furnished and particularly with variety of fine tapestry. The garden was so full of orange trees in flower that the air was perfumed by them, and his greenhouse was ornamented with curious paintings after the life of horses, peculiar to several nations [...]

[37v] We met here with several British rebels and adherents to the Pretender [James Francis Edward Stuart]. The Duke of Leeds, Captain Lee [Legh] and a Scots baronet had taken up their quarters for some months in the same inn where we lodged, but we had no conversation with them. The Duke led an idle, extravagant life, treating at his own expense those of his sort who were willing to sit up the

night with him, and when drunk would dispute religion with the Papists in company, for he is still a Protestant. In this manner he disturbed my rest the first night of my arrival, for his apartment was under mine and the ceiling not being plastered, I could not sleep for him. The next night he spent in roaring out treasonable ballads in company of a lace woman and the drawer of the house. He styles himself commander-in-chief of His Majesty's navy. [38r] The Pretender, to flatter his vanity, gave him that empty title, and I saw in the house his arms and titles of quality painted and set up in a frame, after the same manner as those which are left on the English roads by the Lord Lieutenant of counties, in which that title of commander-in-chief was inserted.

Captain Lee was in Queen Anne's reign commander of the Shark man-of-war but, embarking too far in the Pretender's interest, was at King George's accession to the crown [1714], obliged to fly his country and refuge himself abroad. He is brother to Mr Lee [Legh] of Lyme, a non-juror of great estate in Lancashire [Cheshire].

Anonymous tourist, 8-11 (19-22) May 1720

[6v] Set out [from Brugge] at nine for Ghent in the common boat or barge, very convenient, drawn by two horses; dined very well in it. Came to Ghent at eight, ten leagues; lodged at the Pomme d'Or, well. Mr Shales and Mat[in] went to see Mr de Young; he was at Brussels; saw his daughters. Saw the cathedral, large church [dedicated] to St Bavon; a fine altarpiece [the raising of Lazarus by Otto Vaenius], given by a bishop of Ghent whose name [Pieter Damant], whose tombstone of marble is near it well-wrought. A fine picture of Rubens: Jesus taken down from the cross. Two pictures in the chapel of Van Dyck: the worthy and unworthy communicants. Another picture of Crayden [Gaspard de Craeyer]: the decollation of St John. Here is a cours about several streets, one salutes all the ladies and that every time. [7v] See a moving picture and the great iron cannon in the street that faces Charles the Fifth's statue in the Great Place, eighteen foot long and three foot wide, which will contain a whole man. On a bridge saw the statues in brass of the father and son (see Misson's *Travels*). A picture of it is in the town house with the inscription mentioned by Misson. The other inscription upon the statue itself is not legible.

Went to the Prince's Court; saw the room where Charles V was born. On the chimney: Matthiae Luce exiguo cubili natus Carolus Quintus [On St Matthias, 24 February, was born in this little bed, Charles V]. That room is the closet of another, and on the door is written it was adorned by Castanaga, general of the Spanish troops. Went to the council house, where the council chamber very fine. Good tapestries of Brussels. The room next [to it] handsome. Over against the judge's seat is the judgement of Solomon, beautifully done by Crayden [De Craeyer]. Went to the town house; in the large room abovestairs is the Emperor's picture under a very fine canopy. The history of Charles V in several pictures round about the room.

[8v] See Mr Hudson's house, prettiest in town, sashed, English furniture, pretty garden, fine collection of pictures in the lower room. Had a view of his mistress. Saw the English nuns, where was a draught of the Pretender as we suppose, without inscription. On the other side [his sister] Louise Mary, Princess of Great Britain, of Mrs White of Ireland. Bought some purses of their making. Went to St Michael's; at the left hand a fine cross, one side [of] the altarpiece by Rubens. The chief altar well-adorned with marble pillars. To the Dominicans; the roof of the church large and not supported by pillars; walked through the monastery. The library pretty large, some good books; treated with tolerable beer. To the convent of Beguines where there are eighteen, clean well-ordered; all work lace, dine in the same room, but have each their commons asunder to their liking. Each cook in their turns for a fortnight; each their cupboard in the dining room. They meet once a year at the superior of the whole order at Ghent to the number of seven or eight hundred.

[9v] Went to St Peter's church of the Benedictines. The church tolerable, will be fine when the additional building is finished. There [are] ten pieces of tapestry, said to be made after the designs of Raphael, very beautiful though the colours something faded. The two finest represent the vision of St Peter of clean and unclean animals and that of his walking on the sea. St Paul speaking to the Athenians is also very fine. Went to the Great Jesuits; could not see the library, which they say is tolerable. Their church is fine dedicated to St Levinus [Lebuinus]. At the right hand of the chief altar is a picture of Rubens very beautiful, representing St Levinus, whose tongue they cut and pull out, behind his neck [sic] giving it to a dog.

Ghent is a very large, neat town; old buildings, many great places; neither it nor the citadel in very great repair. No diversions in summer, people living very retired. See there Mr Le Camus from Courtrai or Lille, the Countess of Maigné, daughter to Mr Magrée and Mrs Belvere of Ypres. [cont. Brussels]

Population: 52,000 (1690), 39,000 (1755).

Distances: Antwerp 10 hours (24 miles), Brugge 8 hours (24 miles), Brussels 9 hours (30 miles), Kortrijk 8 hours (23 miles), Middelburg 10 hours (33 miles), Sas van Gent 3 hours (13 miles).

Inns, *Reisboek* (1689, 1700 and 1721): Het Goude Hoofd, op de Brugse Straat; De Swaan*; Het Hart*; Het Schild van Vrankrijk*; Den Olifant*, De Windhond (Op de Koornmarkt); 't Raadhuis van Brussel*; De Zevenstar*, in de Veldstraat. *Reisboek* (1689) also: De Gouden Appel. *Reisboek* (1700 and 1721) also: Den Appel*, De groote Sterre*, Den Haan* (op de Koornmarkt); De Spiegel, bij de S. Niclaas-kerk; De Gulde Leeuw*.

Further reading

J.B. Gramaye, *Antiquitates Belgicae*, Bruxelles-Leuven 1708.

Gent duizend jaar kunst en cultuur, [Gent] 1975.

A. Sanderus, *Flandria illustrata*, Cologne 1641-1644, 's-Gravenhage 1732, 1735 (*Verheerlykt Vlaandre*, 's-Gravenhage 1732, 1735); reprint Antwerpen-Amsterdam 1981.

J. Decavele (ed.), *Gent: apologie van een rebelse stad: geschiedenis, kunst, cultuur*, Antwerpen 1989.

Ghendtsche tydingen, tweemaandelijks tijdschrift van de heemkundige en historische kring 'Gent', 1972-

Handelingen der Maatschappij voor Geschiedenis en Oudheidkunde te Gent, 1894-

Gouda

Thomas Penson, 26 September (6 October) 1687

I left Amsterdam. But having heard much of St John's church at Gouda or Tergoud, which was eminent for the painted glass windows, I took that in my way. And being there arrived (with a silver key caused the church doors to be [69] opened) which I found to be very fine. Therein are many scripture stories with other ornaments of distinct figures, arms and inscriptions, viz.

The story of Our Saviour driving the money changers out of the Temple, which was the gift of William, Prince of Orange, anno 1567. The story of the sacrifice of the prophet Elijah and the false prophets of Baal. The gift of the Lady Margaretha of Austria [Parma], daughter of the Emperor Charles the Fifth, anno 1562. The preaching of the Apostle Philip and the baptising of the Eunuch of Ethiopia. The gift of Prince Philip, Earl of Zour, etc., anno 1559.

That of Christ's being baptised by St John in the river of Jordan and the Holy Ghost descending on him. The gift of Georgius van Egmont, Bishop of Uytrect, anno 1555. [70] That of St John the Baptist preaching to King Herod concerning Herodias his brother Philip's wife. The gift of Mr Wouter van Bylaer. That of King Solomon and the Queen of Sheba. The gift of the wife of [=Lady] Gabriel[le] van Boetzelaer, whose figure stands under the history and also that of the angel Gabriel, anno 1561.

That of the Temple of Solomon and under it in the same window is Christ at his last supper with his disciples; also the figures of Philip the Second, King of Spain and Mary, Queen of England kneeling on cushions with scepter, sword, helmet and shield of their arms lying down by them. The gift of the said Philip and Mary, anno 1557. That of Zacharias, the priest offering incense at the altar and the angel's appearing to him. Given by Dirck Cornelisz van [71] Oudewater, 30th October, anno 1561. [...]

There are many more histories and figures to be taken notice of and [72] which I could insert, but supposing these already mentioned to be sufficient for my present purpose, shall hasten forward with all convenient speed. Thus, having stayed some time in the church and taken a short view of the city, etc., after refreshing I went in the waggon from Tergoude to Rotterdam. [cont. Rotterdam]

Anonymous London merchant, 27 August 1695 N.S.

[8] On Saturday the 27th August New Style, we left Rotterdam a second time and took waggon to Ter Gouw [Gouda], which was three hours. At eleven we took a

Window with King Solomon and the Queen of Sheba, c. 1750

trackschute for Amsterdam, which is nine hours more, in all thirty-six miles English. And this journey being the finest I ever [9] took, both for the manner of travelling and the pleasure of the passage, I made the following observations as we passed along. Our waggon carried seven besides the foreman and the trackschute about sixty persons and many of them seamen who were newly arrived from India in a very rich fleet. The way on which the waggon went was paved with Flanders tiles, twelve miles together, and was covered with sand the most part to avoid the noise of the wheels. It was very narrow, not broad enough everywhere for two waggons to pass, having a broad ditch on each side and sometimes low hedges and abundance of willow trees between them and the road.

Farmhouses and cottages stand very near each other on both sides. As we passed, I observed but very few cornfields and less corn standing out, the harvest being fourteen days forwarder than in England. The cottages are thatched but much better and bigger than ours, being generally paved about their doors as are all their villages, which renders them everywhere clean and neat. These farmhouses are generally surrounded with trees, moats and ditches whereon small boats do pass, which secures them from rogues and frees them from water in their houses. The pasture ground seems to be very good and full of grass and is everywhere full of ditches or sluices, which serves both to drain the land and to distinguish every man's property. The cattle of this country are small and of divers colours, having all of them very short horns, much shorter than those in Scotland. In this passage we saw not one water mill but windmills in abundance and a vast number of schutes or boats, bigger than our yachts, going backwards and forwards both with goods and passengers. They are all drawn [10] by horses, but no more than one horse to a vessel, and the pace they go is always trot or gallop.

Tergouw is a fine city much like to Dordt [Dordrecht] and Rotterdam, having broad havens in the streets, full of great vessels and trees between the havens and the houses. The Great Church in this town, which looks like a cathedral, is famous for the glass windows, being large and curiously painted with the images of all the Scripture worthies, though I had no time to view this prospect but with the loss of my passage to Amsterdam.

Thomas Bowrey, 9 (19) June 1698

[31] At seven this morning, we having hired a covered waggon for seven guilders to carry us [from Rotterdam] to Tergou, clear of all tolls by the way, in which we went seven persons and several boxes, etc. Found the country along very low, all for hay and grazing, kept above water only by the canals which divide every field and drain the grounds. The farmhouses kept extraordinary well in repair, a small boat to every house. We travelled all the way on a bank but just wide enough for two waggons. In three hours arrived at Tergou, being then ten o'clock in the morning. I judge from Rotterdam to Tergou it is twelve [English] miles.

Tergou is about half a mile in length; several streets, indifferent [tolerably] well-built of brick. Canals through the town. [It] has a handsome stadthouse in a large open place, has a very large church in which about twenty-six large windows, all of glass finely painted and about thirteen lesser windows of the same. The window at the east end has been offered for it twenty thousand guilders.

[32] About two miles above Rotterdam [shipping] goes in a small river which comes up to and through the town of Tergou, up which come the hoys, etc. and can go this way through to Amsterdam. It is not above fifty yards wide in some places and not six foot water. The tide of flood rises at Tergou about four feet.

We embarked on the trackskute for Amsterdam, which went off precisely at eleven o'clock the forenoon, and so every day, the rate in which for each person is eighteen stivers and three quarters. We hired the after-cabin for the privilege of which, to be by ourselves, gave forty-eight stivers.

At four in the afternoon [we] stopped at a house for half an hour to eat a bit and drink. At seven came through a small town called Ouderkerk, five miles from Amsterdam. At four miles' distance from Amsterdam is a stone pillar, which is the mark for a Dutch mile from the city, and there is such a one at a Dutch mile's distance from the city on every road leading to it.

John Leake, 26 April (7 May) 1712

[24r] After having followed our studies some few weeks at Leiden, the pleasantness of the season inviting, we took a flight to Gouda, to entertain ourselves with the sight of that place and the great church of St John, so famous for the noble painted glass windows it is adorned with. It was April the 26th when we went upon this ramble, and we had the satisfaction of passing through that [25r] part of Holland where the Dutch dig most of their turf. It is for the most part so watery and morassy that there is scarce a list [strip] of terra firma left for a chaise to run along upon. They fish up in nets the slime and soil which lies at the bottom of these bogs, and then spread it about a foot thick upon a little neck of land, which every turf-digger's cottage is furnished withal, and there they let it lie till it begins to harden by the weather; and then they cut it out with an iron instrument into the shape and size of large bricks. And after letting them continue in that state some time, they pile them up hollow in the form of our brick-kilns, where after having remained a year they become saleable and serviceable.

The town of Gouda is a pleasant place and has a fine raised walk adorned with lime trees quite round it. The stadhouse and marketplace are large and beautiful, but above all the magnificence and goodness of the paintings in St John's church are worthy a traveller's observation. The church itself is beyond the common size and is kept very clean and neat. There are one and thirty windows adorned with historical paintings both profane and sacred, done by the best hands of their several times. One of the largest of them was given by our Philip [II of Spain] and [his wife] Mary [Tudor]. The upper part of the window represents the history of the consecration of the Temple by Solomon. The under part shows us Our Blessed Lord with his disciples instituting the Holy Supper. The King and Queen are represented kneeling before the table, and offering up their regalia to their great [26r] Master. The painting was performed by one Theodore Crabeth in the year 1557. There are several Latin inscriptions upon the glass in honour of the Royal Benefactors. One or two of the windows behind the choir were damaged some time since by lightning, and they are easily discovered by the faintness of the colouring of their modern repairers.

Whilst I was entertaining myself with this agreeable sight, I could not forbear reflecting upon the different tempers of the foreign Calvinists from those of that stamp in our island. Here they not only permit stories of the Old and New Testament and the figures of some signal deliverances that themselves have received at the hands of Providence to look them in their faces in the places of their religious worship without the dread of idolatry and fears of Popery. But they endeavour also to heighten their devotions by the help of the organ without ever surmising they shall become slaves again to the enchanting music of Italy. Now it is well-known our Reformation-reformers [Puritans] managed after a quite different rate when they had usurped the administration of affairs among us [during the Commonwealth, 1649-1660]. Then the churches that were most beautified were sure to be the greatest sufferers. All the historical paintings in their windows were so many painted Jezebels, and therefore to be thrown down and destroyed. All instrumental music in churches was esteemed sounding a march to Rome, and whatever was decent and tended to advance the beauty of holiness was nicknamed superstition and the trappings of the whore of Babylon, and [27r] therefore to be hewed to pieces as Samuel did Agag, etc. May latest posterity never see the second part of this Holy Farce acted amongst us. And may those who are fondest of bringing us to correspondence with Dutch models learn so much sense and religion of our neighbours as to conclude that slovenliness and inharmoniousness are far from being agreeable in places where divine service is performed.

Population: 15,000 (1650), 10,000-15,000 (1750).
Distances: Amsterdam 10 hours (30 miles), Leiden 5 hours (15 miles), Rotterdam 4 hours (12 miles), Utrecht 7 hours (22 miles).

Inns, *Reisboek* (1689, 1700 and 1721): 't Heeren-Logement*; De Doelen. *Reisboek* (1689 and 1700) also: 't Land van Belofte; 't Land van Steyn; 't Schippers- Huis; De Herbergen omtrent het Amsterdamsche Veer; en daar de Wagens op Rotterdam af Rijden. *Reisboek* (1721) also: In Boskoop*; 't Nieu Schippers Huis op de Vismarkt*; 't Huis van de Commissaris van 't Rotterdamse wagenveer.

Further reading

[I. Walvis], *Beschryving der stad Gouda*, Gouda 1714.
Gouda zeven eeuwen stad, hoofdstukken uit de geschiedenis van Gouda, Gouda 1972.
Ach Lieve Tijd, zeven eeuwen Gouda en de Gouwenaars, N.D.B. Habermehl (ed.), Zwolle 1986-1987.
De Schatkamer, regionaal historisch tijdschrift voor Boskoop, Gouda [...], 1986-
Tidinge van die Goude, mededelingenblad van de oudheidkundige kring 'Die Goude', 1954-

Groningen

William Lord Fitzwilliam, May 1663

[24r] From hence we went out of West Friesland into the Groninger Land, which is called so by reason of its green meadows and its pleasant situation, it is one of the Seventeen Provinces. The chief town in it has gotten its name from the country, and is called Groningen, a very old town, it being built, as Munsterus [Sebastian Münster] says, 378 years before Christ's birth. It is a very pleasant city, everywhere round about it fair meadows. Round about the town fair walks, part of which are curiously planted with trees. The town lies in the midst of five little lordships, which are called the Ommelanden; they make up the second member in the assembly of the States of this province, the city itself being the first.

This city is very big and very well-built, fair streets and houses. She is extremely well fortified, having seventeen of the neatest and well-proportioned bastions round about it, besides an excellent fausse braye (which is counted to be the best of the Seventeen Provinces) and brave, [24v] broad and deep ditches; all the walls set with trees; seven good gates round about them. This is the most curious piece of fortification that can be seen. Within the town we saw two good churches, three great marketplaces: the Bree-market [Great Market], fish and oxen market [and] the governor's house and garden, which is but little, yet very pretty and convenient.

Here is likewise an university. The schools are but little and the library but very mean, but the physic [botanical] garden is very well worth a man's sight. Here are only two professors of divinity, one of law and one [three] of physic [medicine], two or three of philosophy. The town house is but ordinary, yet it stands upon a fair marketplace, the Bree-market, where we did lodge. Here is likewise an artillery house, which does satisfy a curious person. Here lives for the most part the gentry of this province and here resides the Parliament likewise. This town otherwise is governed like all other towns of the United Provinces.

Every night the citizens watch, and coming to their night-quarters on the Bree-market, they give always fire, which is a pleasure to hear and see. At our being here there were twenty companies of soldiers; there had been above thirty this last winter for to keep the citizens in order, who were about to rebel against [25r] their magistrates. The ringleader was beheaded, but the chiefest actor of this play (who was a burgomaster) did escape. From Groningen we went by waggon to Coevorden, which is seven of-this-country miles distant of Groningen. [cont. Overijssel]

175

John Farrington, 22-25 September 1710 N.S.

[55] Groningen, which is the chief city of the province of the same name, is a very large and beautiful city, the finest place we have seen since Amsterdam. It is a large league round about upon the walls. The city is very well fortified and seems to be a strong place, especially according to the old way of fortification when they raised their works excessive high, but have since seen the inconvenience of it. Lodged at Peter Toelast's at the sign of the Toelast or Great Tun, just by the Great Church in the marketplace, a good house, well entertained and pretty reasonable.

The weather, September 24, was extremely good and the hottest day we have had since we came into this country, so that though in the evening and morning it was cool enough to sit by a fireside, yet in the middle [56] of the day it was very allowable to complain of heat.

I told you, Sir, the town is very strong and the fort that lies at about an English mile's distance from it on the east side of the town adds not a little to its strength. It was designed by that great engineer General [Menno van] Coehoorn, about eighteen or twenty years ago, when they had a little recovered from the ravage committed by Bernard van Galen, Bishop of Münster, in the year LXXII [1672]. The great road to the city from East Friesland lies through this fort, if I may call it so, or rather lies between two forts. On the north side of the road, the fort is the largest, consisting of five large bastions. That on the south has only two. There is a very good covered way, well defended by two redoubts, which fire all along it, and between them and the counterscarp is a large dry ditch. The counterscarp is very high and thick, and faced with brick on the outside, and the fort on the other side is after the same manner. This is a great security to the town, because it defends them in the only place they can be attacked, since by their sluices in the space of twelve hours they can lay the ground under water on every side but that to the east, which is also towards the enemy's country.

As to the fortification of the city, it consists first of a large half-moon, that will [hold] a thousand men, without the gates, surrounded by a deep and wide ditch. Then there is a very large and deep ditch, that goes round the whole town, within which there is a covered way where the breastwork is full eight yards in thickness. Above this there is a counterscarp which is [57] very steep and very high, and is about twice as thick as the breastwork of the covered way. The bastions for the defence of the curtains are very large and very strong. There are seven gates to the town, all of them under the walls and secure against bombs. The gates are about forty yards thick, and they are secured by very good drawbridges.

As to the religion it is, as you know all the provinces are, of the Reformed Calvinist profession, and there are four churches in it for the exercise thereof, besides one for Lutherans and one for Minists or Baptists and four or five Popish chapels. For though both Friesland and Groningen are subject to the same prince, yet the Papists are tolerated here, though not in that country; though I think I

View of Groningen, 1743

scarce ought to call it anymore than a connivance both of Papists and Minists. The Minists here distinguish themselves by appearing in black, which the women among them always do. The French refugees have also once a week the use of the University Church, but no place peculiar to themselves.

The Calvinist churches are very large, handsome buildings, though without ornament, except their organs and their neatness may be counted so. The steeple of the greatest church, or at least of the magistrates' church [Aakerk], fell down about eight days before Easter at nine on Saturday morning [12 April 1710], and yet did no damage to any person; only it drew down a great part of the church with it and fell with so great force as to set some of the stones that covered the graves in the church almost upright. They are now rebuilding it, which they neither design to [58] so high or so large as it was before. We walked up one of the steeples of the town, which was three hundred foot high, from whence we had a very good view of the city and the country round about.

Thence we saw on the top of one of the burgomasters' houses a fish pond. And the farmhouses in the country, which generally were defended from the weather by plantations of trees, made a very agreeable sight. The organ in that church [St Martin's] in my opinion has pipes altogether as large as those boasted of in Exeter, and the church is a very beautiful and very good one, wherein the Landtsheers and Raadtsheers [the stadholders and the States] have their seats, as the burgomasters and the rest of the governors of the city have theirs in that whose steeple fell. The University Church is not large, but is big enough for the use it is put to.

Besides the churches the Magazine, which is surrounded with a ditch, is a building well worth observing. The stadthouse is also a good building, but there is nothing remarkable within, only a very large bomb which was shot into it by the Bishop

177

of Münster, when he in vain besieged it in 1672, as there are several bullets sticking in the walls of the houses near the east gate, that were shot in during that siege.

They have a university in this city, but the buildings of it are the worst I have ever seen of that sort. There are at present but six professors and about three hundred scholars, though a man might live a great deal cheaper and the air is much better than at Leiden. One of the professors of physic [medicine], Dr Muyden [Muykens], a very civil gentleman, was so kind as to show us their botany garden, which has been for some [59] time neglected and they are now storing [stocking] with exotic plants as fast as they can. The garden is but small, but it is pleasant and in good order. There were some good orange and lemon trees, but few foreign plants.

He showed us also the anatomy theatre, where though there are no large skeletons, there are several things very curious, among which, Sir, I reckon the several embryos, one of which is a foetus of fifteen days old, which was entire in all its parts, and were valued at a hundred rixdollars. There was also a child that was born with one hand and one leg only, his right hand and left foot were off. They showed us a silver fish, called so from its shining like silver, a snake, which in Dutch they call the bril-slang from the spectacles he has upon his nose, another snake of five ells long, a white East India frog, a small tortoise and crocodile with several other curiosities of the same nature.

Now I am upon this subject I must not forget the library and curiosities of Dr [Gisbert] Eding's, a doctor of civil law, which he was so kind to show us, though the time of our waiting on him happened to be a little unreasonable. The library is very large, consisting of above fifteen thousand volumes in all faculties, and some of them, by the small view we took of them, appeared to be very scarce and valuable. Here were abundance of mathematical instruments and among the rest one to demonstrate the motion of the earth, which I shall endeavour to describe to you.

At the bottom of the instrument was a common clock or watch, that had the usual motions [60] of a clock and pointed to the hours. The sphere was projected above, and the earth in the same position with reference to the sun as it is at that hour of the day, be it what it will. The sun is represented by a golden ball that is fixed upon the top of a pole in the centre of the instrument about which the earth is to move. Now when the doctor moved the hand of the clock from three to seven, the earth moved round also towards the sun, and the different position of the earth in respect to the sun gave the time of the day.

He showed us likewise several of the paintings that are confused to the eye but either by the help of a steel [tube], or of looking through a small sight, they appear beautiful and regular [anamorphosis]. There we saw also one of the hats of the women of Strasbourg, which is exactly like the print of it in Misson. Among the rest there was also a wax baby of the bigness of a child of a month old, whose eyes rolled in its head so naturally one would almost think it to be alive, and by the help of a certain spring it would cry as loud as a child of that age could be supposed to do.

The Spinhouse in this city is a large building consisting only of one quadrangle. On the right is the apartment of the men, on the left the women. It is the worst prison I have seen, but the prisoners seem to be the most modest of any of them. As to the buildings of the town, they are generally old but good. The streets are wide, there are several canals, well-planted with trees, some parts of the city are pleasant and very agreeable.

[61] The air seems to be very good, and the people civil, though I cannot commend them for their handsomeness or gentility. Their dress is not unlike the rest of the provinces and their manner of living the same. By the entertainment we had at our ordinary, fish and flesh and wild fowl seem to be pretty plentiful and cheap, but they miserably spoil it for an English palate by their dressing.

Their trade consists chiefly in merchandise and in butter and cheese. They have no manufactures among them, but supply the whole province with what linen and woollen goods they want from Amsterdam. [...]

It was here also the time of their fair, and among the rest of the rarities brought together on [62] such occasions, was a dromedary [camel], which is a large ugly creature with a long prodigious strong neck, two bunches on his back, between which a man may sit conveniently; is very tame, but has a mighty strange tone or cry, and is of so great strength as to carry above a thousand weight.

We left Groningen Thursday, September 25th at six in the morning, for Winschoten, which is a village situated at the bottom of the Dollard sea, whither we came at half an hour past twelve noon, without changing boats. The weather was very clear and good, it having frozen in the night, and on each side [of] the canal the houses were very thick, and several very good plantations of trees. Only we were very frequently stopped by the sluices we were forced to pass, which were more in this one passage than all the rest that we had met with before.

Winschoten, where we were forced to stay till three in the afternoon, is but a very indifferent village, and nothing in it worth observing. Here we got such provisions as the place would afford (cold boiled fresh beef and part of the shoulder too), which was very indifferent, but as it was we dined on it and made ourselves very merry with our victuals. With the boat of three we went forward for Lange Acker or Nieuwe Schans, to which we came at six at night.

This is a very pretty fort, belonging to the province of Groningen, though on the frontiers of Aurich [in East Friesland]. It consists of four very good bastions, a covered way, breastwork, and a good moat. There are [at] present but ten soldiers and a governor in garrison; few pieces of cannon upon the walls, for the Dutch are too provident a people to expose their cannons and carriages to the injuries of the weather when they are under no apprehension of an enemy. There are but few houses in the fort and consequently no great choice of lodgings, but our lodging (the Prince's Head, first dinner house within the fort) was good enough, though our supper, excepting the good Rhenish we drank to it, was worse (musty eggs) than our dinner.

Population: 15,000-20,000 (1675), 20,000-25,000 (1750).

Distances: Coevorden 17 hours (52 miles), Leeuwarden 14 hours (33 miles), Nieuwe Schans 10 hours (28 miles), Zwolle 22 hours (60 miles).

Inns, *Reisboek* (1689, 1700 and 1721): De [1721: Grote] Toelast* [1721: op de Markt]; De [1721: Gulde] Jagtwagen; 't Raadhuis van Embden* [1721: daar de Treckschuiten op Delfziel afvarenl]. *Reisboek* (1689): De Vonk; 't Wijnhuis; 't Blaauw Huis, buiten de Dra-Poort. *Reisboek* (1689 and 1700): De Zeven Provinciën; De Blaauwen Engel; Winschoten. *Reisboek* (1700): De Goude Kroon; 't Blaauwe Paard; In Munster, in de Heere-Straat. *Reisboek* (1700 and 1721): De Stads Herberg*, buyte de Dra-Poort; De Valk. *Reisboek* (1721) also: De Helm* (op de Markt).

Further reading

[G.H. Warendorp], *Kort begryp [...] der seer oude ende vermaerde stadt Groningen*, Groningen 1662.

W.J. Formsma (ed.), *Historie van Groningen: Stad en Land*, Groningen 1976 (1981).

Ach Lieve Tijd, tien eeuwen Groningen en de Groningers, L. Boiten (ed.), Zwolle 1984-1985.

Groningse Volksalmanak, historisch jaarboek voor Groningen, 1889-

Haarlem

William Lord Fitzwilliam, June 1663

[26v] Having been a month at Amsterdam we went to Haarlem, which is one of the best towns of Holland. It is very big and neat and very pleasantly situated amongst woods and meadows. Here is a fair great church, counted to be the biggest of Holland. In it are very good organs and several epitaphs. Upon one of the windows you will see painted the sedition [treason] of the Casembroots [1491-1492]. Moreover, we did remark a ship hanging in this church, with a saw on the bottom of it, which in sailing did cut a chain in pieces which was extended between two castles for to hinder ships of entering the haven. This was done by them of Haarlem, helping Frederic Barbarossa against the Saracens at the town called Pelusium, now Damiata, situated in the furthest part of Egypt. By this strategem the town was taken [1219]. Every year, the 1st of January, the children of this town celebrate the memory hereof in carrying ships with saws on the bottom round about the town. Here are likewise two Damiaetgen [27r] bells, which prove this story.

Here they say the art of printing was invented and not in Germany. Laurentius Johannes Aedituus [sexton] or Costerus was the author of it, anno 1440. But his servant stealing his printing instruments and some copies, he came to Maintz and so brought printing into those parts. Laurence Coster's house stands yet on the marketplace and under his picture you will find in golden letters written these following words

Memoriae Sacrum
TYPOGRAPHIA
ars artium omnium
conservatrix,
Hic primum inventa
circa an. MCCCCXL

Vana quid archetypos et praela Moguntia jactas?
Harlemi archetypos praelaq[ue] nata scias.
Extulit hic, monstrante Deo, Laurentius artem.
Dissimulare virum hunc, dissimulare Deum est.

[Dedicated to commemoration. The art of printing, the art that preserves all the arts, was here first invented about the year 1440. Mainz, why do you

Statue of Laurens Janszoon Coster, 1810

proudly talk about the first book that was ever printed? Know that printing was born at Haarlem. With the help of God, Laurence has found out this art. Ignoring this man is equal to ignoring God!]

Here is before the town a pleasant little wood, whither the people of Amsterdam come very often to make themselves merry. Here is likewise a town house, but none of the best. Here are many brewers and the beer of this town is carried up and down this country, it is thick and very sweet, fitter for hogs than man; the Hollander loves it dearly and it makes him very fat. Here is good fresh water, which is a great rarity in Holland.

The government [27v] of this town is all the same with the government of the other towns of Holland. The strength of this town is not very great, yet strong enough to hold out for some time. It has seven good gates. By the last wars between the States and the Spaniards, this town did suffer much [1572-1573]. About this town there are many fair villages, castles and houses of pleasure. We took a waggon and did ride round about the country. We saw many of those places, but we entered into none but [Gabriel] Marselis' house, the King of Denmark's factor, who like the foolish man, has built a house [Elswout] upon the sands. It lies between sandhills, the least wind can do a great deal of hurt in driving the sand into the garden or upon the building. He is about taking away the sandhills, but that will hardly do any good. Thirty thousand pounds sterling are as good as thrown away. The house otherwise is very well-built and garnished, chiefly with very curious pictures and a little chamber full of china vessels of an inestimable price. The gardens are pretty and abounding with all sort of rarities. [cont. Leiden]

William Nicolson, 6-7 (16-17) August 1678

[12r] At our entrance into the town I took notice of their arms over the gate, which are a sword, a cross and four stars, thus [sketch], Vicit Vim Virtus [virtue has vanquished power]. [12v] These the Dutch writers report to have been given this city by the Emperor and Patriarch of Jerusalem, in remembrance of the notorious service which the Haarlemmers did the Christians in the taking of Damiata. For, they tell us (and they only) that in the siege of that place, the Christians were all baffled with a chain which the defendants had put across the river, and so hindered the passage of all their enemies' ships, till the Haarlemmers, men of longer heads than the rest, cleared the way by this strategem: they armed the keels of their ships with sharp saws, which being hurried by a strong wind, cut the chain in two. It was an ingenious invention and the historians that write of the holy war are very uncivil not to take notice of it. However, the burghers are sufficiently convinced (from infallible tradition) of the truth of the story; and to this day in remembrance of so signal an exploit, show us three ships hung up in their Great Church, which is the largest and stateliest in Holland, built [made a see] by Pope Paulus IV (A.D. 1559), who made Haarlem a bishop's see.

Here I cannot but gratefully remember the kindnesses we received from Dr Cornelius van der Sluis, physician in Haarlem, who showed us (besides his own study, in which among other rarities we saw that skull of a young Westphalian boor, near an inch thick, who nevertheless died of [13r] a small wound in his head; as also gilt letters writ by himself in imitation of and as curious as those we find in ancient manuscripts, the receipt of which experiment he communicated to me, etc.), the most remarkable things in this city as:

1. The Great Church, in which besides the aforesaid three ships I reckoned eigh-

teen of the largest brass candlesticks I had seen and forty vast pillars. 2. The library, founded by the Lords of the town. Here besides a few manuscripts, a catalogue of which I transcribed, the doctor showed us a book printed at Haarlem in the year 1485, which proves that the art of printing was made use of in this city very early, if not here invented. 3. The house of Lawrence Coster, who according to the opinion of Boxhornius and Scriverius, first invented the art of printing. Over the door of this house was formerly an inscription in honour of the said inhabitant, which is lately razed out by the owner because he would not have too many gazers upon his house. Boxhornius mentions a monument [=print] erected by one of the citizens in remembrance of this famous man and gives us the inscription thereof, *Theatrum Hollandicum*, page 137, but what is become of that I know [13v] not. Nor could I meet with any that ever heard of any such thing.

4. The wood, which some, though very unworthily, have set in competition with that at The Hague. In this wood, according to the relation of Hadrianus Junius, was printing first invented by Lawrence Coster, who walking here with some of his young grand-children, fashioned some letters of the bark of trees and made therewith an impression upon paper that he might teach the boys their alphabet. But being a man of parts and observing that his invention might be advanced far beyond what he at first intended, he improved these rude beginnings so far as quickly to print a whole [Latin grammar by Aelius] Donatus. The Lords or States of the town have, as I was informed, some of his first specimina to show.

The next morning about ten o'clock we went from Haarlem by the New Sluice [Nieuwe Vaart], which was cut in the year 1601 [1631] before which time there was no other way from Haarlem to Amsterdam but by the IJ. All along our voyage we passed by that famous dam which keeps the IJ from drowning the whole country we were carried through. By the way I took especial notice of the flood-gates which in the winter shut out the IJ, and in the beginning [14r] of summer let out the water from the meadows into the sea. About one in the afternoon we came to Amsterdam.

Anonymous Utrecht student, 29 August 1700 N.S.

[12] Next day we went to Haarlem, it is a great town and well-built; they make much linen cloth, ribbons and rich silks. There is a clock to be seen here which at every hour is made to strike by a little figure of a man, which by springs comes out at a little door which opens of itself, then he goes to a bell on which he strikes the hour with a hammer he carries in one hand, but first he sounds a trumpet which he has in his other hand. And when he has struck the hour he goes back, blowing his trumpet and when he comes to the little door he turns about and pulls off his hat and then goes in and the door shuts after him.

Without the town is a pleasant wood; there are many good walks cut in it; from hence one may have a prospect of the Haarlemmermeer. This town boasts of one

Laurence Coster, whom they pretend to have been their townsman and to have been the first that found out the art of printing. And I think they pretend to have the book he first printed in the town house; they have his statue there.

John Farrington, 17 September 1710 N.S.

[25] The next day, Wednesday September 17th, we took our [26] leaves of Leiden and went with the boat of eleven towards Haarlem, whither we came at three in the afternoon. The weather was so stormy and so very rainy that we had no opportunity of observing the country as we passed. When we came to Haarlem we had no time to dine, staying here only one hour, but however, we refreshed ourselves with some bread and fruit and wine at the Golden Lion in the marketplace just by the Great Church. French wine at twenty pence a bottle.

After which we went to take a view of the Great Church, which is the largest and best church in this province. There are three organs in the church, the largest and most harmonious is in the middle between the body of the church and the choir. The screen or chancel, that separates between them is very good work of brass. The window at the west end is well-painted after the ancient manner. They show you in the church three ships resembling men-of-war, in memory of a noble action in the Spanish war [crusades], performed by the inhabitants of that city. There is likewise still to be seen, in one of the walls of the church, a bullet that was shot into it in the time when Haarlem was besieged by the Spaniards, about thirty-six pound weight. They would not permit us to go up the tower because they told us they had an express prohibition from the magistrates to suffer anybody to go up during the time of war.

Haarlem is a pretty large and good city, very neat and clean, famous for its wood, that is just without the town, and for the hills that are on the other side of it toward the sea. Their trade is known to consist in thread and tapes and this is the most famous place in the world for whiting [bleaching] cloth, which is said to be of the best colour of any that is whited, from the peculiar nature of its water. The stadthouse of Haarlem is a very good building and so are the buildings in general. There are several canals [that] run through the town [27] but not half so many as at Leiden. This city has the privilege of keeping a scaffold for execution standing, and having their own executioner, which the other cities of Holland have, by their mismanagement of justice, lost. They boast also here of the invention of printing, and in the stadthouse is preserved under several locks the first book that was ever printed, according to their tradition. See Max. Misson *Voyage to Italy*, Vol. II, page 18, etc.

At four o'clock that afternoon, we took boat for Amsterdam [...] In our way thither, we met with an odd adventure, which I take leave to transmit to you. When the boat was upon the way, we were ordered to stop by [28] a woman that came riding at full gallop in a chaise. She came on board and immediately seized a young fellow that sat over against the entrance of the boat, and in her language called him a thousand names.

The woman, it seems, kept a public house at Haarlem. The fellow came to her house under pretence of being very poor and begged some victuals. She gave him his dinner and he in requital stole her earrings, which she said were to the value of one hundred guilders or ten pounds. She bid the fellow follow her out of the boat, which he did with all the unconcernedness that innocence itself could put on, and walked with her by the chaise side towards Haarlem.

This, you must think, put the boat into no small disorder: some began to pity, some as hastily to condemn the fellow; some accused him and others acquitted him. There was among the rest a French gentlewoman who had seen the fellow put his hand twice out of the boat when the chaise was in sight, and by a strength of imagination [she] had each time heard something drop into the water. This, however, gave occasion to some to lift up the tarpaulin and see whether anything was on the ledge of the boat, where to their surprise they found the two earrings, which were shown to all in the boat.

The skipper immediately leaves the boat and with a boat that then passed to Haarlem he went also, lest the fellow should be acquitted for want of evidence; for the Dutch are extreme strict in matters of money or theft, though murder is disregarded. But when the earrings were found, you cannot imagine the confusion that followed. He was tried and condemned and there wanted nothing but his execution. Nothing was talked of else by the inferior sort, and that with such warmth that those boats, where a great deal of decency was wont to [29] be observed, was now grown as bad as the Gravesend tilt-boats, or the noisy college of Billingsgate.

Sir John Percival 5 (16) July 1718

[77v] There are several manufactures established at Haarlem, which have great reputation. The finest silk stuffs, plain or brocaded with gold and silver, are made here in great quantities, which though not entirely equal in goodness and beauty to those of Lyon and Tours in France, are by reason of their cheapness (for they cost less by fifteen or twenty per cent) preferred by the Portuguese, Germans and northern nations, which take off great quantities of them. Other slighter silks, gauzes and flowered velvets are likewise manufactured here in great quantities. But the linen of this town surpasses all the rest in reputation and employs most hands.

It is true, great quantities pass under the name of holland, which are [78r] made out of the Provinces. But being whitened here, they may very well be called the manufacture of the country. Much of it is made in Groningen, Frise and Overijssel, where there grows great quantities of flax. But the greatest part comes from the duchy of Juliers, from whence in the spring it is conveyed brown and raw to Haarlem and there receives the best whitening on account of the sea water, which, being cleansed and purified by passing through the sand downs [dunes], occasions that particular look in true hollands, which gives them the preference to the finest linens of other countries. This great town is well situated for trade, being built on the river Spaarne and distant but one league from the sea, five from Leiden and three from Amsterdam.

Population: 45,000 (1650), 50,000 (1690), 45,000 (1720), 40,000 (1732).
Distances: Alkmaar 5 hours (17 miles), Amsterdam 3 hours (7 miles), Leiden 5 hours (15 miles).

Inns, *Reisboek* (1689 and 1700): d'Oyevaar, bij 't Haagsche Wagenveer; 't Gulde Vlies; De Haan; De Pellikaan; De Leeuw, of Engelsch Ordinaris; De Toelast. *Reisboek* (1700) also: Het Heere Logement; Altemaal omtrent de Markt. *Reisboek* (1721): De Goude Leeuw*, aan de noort zijde van de Grote kerk aan de Markt; het Haantjen, aan de zuidzijde op de Groenmarkt; het Hof van Holland*, in de Warmoes-straat; De Ojevaar in de Zylstraat; de Valk* in de Kruisstraat, daar de postwagen op Alkmaar afrijd; De Brabandse Ketting, op 't Spaarne; De Zon en Halve Maan*, aan de Sparwouwer Poort.

Further reading

Th. Schrevelius, *Harlemum sive Urbis Harlemensis incunabula, incrementa, fortuna varia*, Leiden 1647 (ed. in Dutch 1648).
J.J. Temminck, *Haarlem door de eeuwen heen*, Haarlem 1982.
Ach Lieve Tijd, 750 jaar Haarlem en de Haarlemmers, F.W.J. Kroon (ed.), Zwolle 1983-1984.
Deugd boven geweld. Een geschiedenis van Haarlem, 1245-1995, Hilversum 1995.
Jaarboek Haerlem, 1929-

The Hague

William Lord Fitzwilliam, June 1663

[29v] From Leiden we went by water to The Hague, which is one of the best villages of Europe. Although it is no town, yet it does enjoy the privileges and inconveniences [sic] of a town or city. Prince William II, Count of Holland and King of the Romans, was the first that chose this place for to be a Court. After him the States of the United Provinces, who reside here always, and three of the Princes of Orange, Maurice, Frederic Henry and William [II] have done the same, and this present Prince [William III] will likewise do so.

This town is one of the most pleasant places of Europe, partly by nature, partly by art, for here are brave great houses, fair large streets all set with trees, everywhere delightful walks out and within the town. The chiefest is upon the Vijverberg, over against the Court; the other a little lower called the Voorhout, where, every evening before supper, men and women meet in their coaches for to make the tour à la mode, and after supper, about nine o'clock in the summer only, they walk in the same place on foot till [30r] ten or eleven o'clock.

The air of this place is very good. The people civil and very conversable, chiefly the women, who are here in a great quantity. The world may be seen here in an epitome. Here reside and dwell all sort of nations and all sort of languages are spoken, chiefly the French, which the ladies have a great ambition to speak. Here are two or three good churches; a very pretty round one [New Church], newly built [1656], stands on the water [Spui] where you take boat to go to Leiden or Delft. Here is likewise a bridewell or house of correction for idle boys and women, a brave hospital for old women, half of which must be Catholic and the other half Protestants [Hofje van Nieuwkoop, 1660]. Here is likewise a new Doelen, built by the last Prince of Orange [William II].

About the new entry of the Court, on one side of the Vijver, is the palace of Prince [Johan-] Maurice [Count of Nassau-Siegen], formerly Governor of Brazil and now of Cleves, so well-built according to the rules of architecture that nothing seems to be amiss. On the side next to the Vijver, the frontispiece represents an Indian fight. Within, the house is curiously adorned with precious pictures and other rarities, which for the most part are of ivory, cedar, brazil and other precious wood. [30v] Just by this house is the kingly palace, now called the Hof, or Court of Holland. It was built by William II, Count of Holland and King of the Romans; by reason of this it is called kingly palace. This Court lies like a castle all in water, having three gates and drawbridges, where always soldiers watch. Duke Albert of

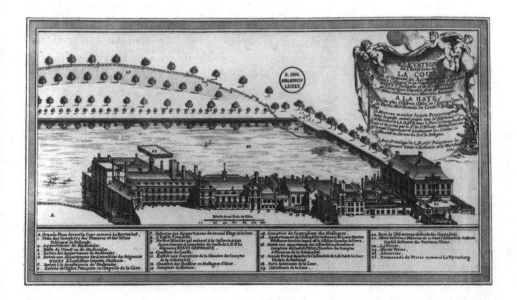

Binnenhof, 1752

Bavaria, the 26th Count of Holland, did build in this Court a chapel wherein he likewise and his lady lie buried.

On the north side of the Court is a great fish-pond or vijver, and on the other side of it a hill, planted with trees called the Vijverberg, upon which we did lodge by Mr [Johan] Hessing, the Duke [=Count Palatine] of Neuburg's agent. Within this Court meet the States of the Seven United Provinces and the Council of Brabant for law business for the towns and villages of that province belonging to the States. The hall within the Court is long and large; on both sides are shops where all sort of things are to be sold. But the greatest ornaments of this hall are the colours taken of the Spaniards. In this castle is likewise the Prince of Orange's Court and in the town is the Princess Dowager's house and garden [William III's grandmother Amalia van Solms].

[31r] Without The Hague is a little wood and pall-mall. In the wood we saw the Prince of Orange's house of pleasure, called the House in the Bosch. It is not very big or sumptuously built, but very neat and handsome. It has a fine garden and water round about it. Divers fair rooms are within it but the great hall is a most stately chamber. It is round and of a great compass and from the top to the bottom there is nothing but the rarest painting-work to be seen: the whole life, or rather the most noblest actions of Frederic Henry, Prince of Orange, are set out here to the life. On the top of this hall there is a little turret. As soon as you enter this house you will see Prince William, Prince Maurice, Prince Frederic Henry and Prince William, his son's statues, all made of very good marble.

Next to this house, Rijswijk merits very well a man's sight. It is another great house belonging to the Prince of Orange, in which there are many fine rooms, but ungarnished. There is a gallery which is adorned with precious pictures. To this house belong likewise fair gardens, waterworks and other places of delight and accommodation. We went likewise to see Voorburg, a pretty little [31v] country town. In the fields of this place there has been formerly a famous castle of a King of Friesland, called Ritzard; now it is called Koni[n]ck Eseloors Berg [Mount King Donkey's Ears]. This castle has been very big, destroyed by the Danes and Normans. Now there is nothing of it to be seen, and there grows corn where it has formerly stood. Sometimes here are found some pieces of antiquity.

From a steeple in The Hague, I saw likewise Scheveling [Scheveningen], famous because King Charles II did here embark himself for to return into England, and of a wagon which used to sail on the land. From the same steeple we saw likewise Losdun [Loosduinen], where there is nothing else remarkable but the tomb of a countess of Holland, who at one lying-in was delivered of 365 children; the basins of copper are yet kept in the church in perpetuam rei memoriam [in perpetual memory of the event]. The story is everywhere well-known, wherefore I forbear to take any more notice of it. [cont. Delft]

Sir Francis Child, June 1697

[MS 178, 15v] The Hague, in Dutch 's-Gravenhage, French La Haye, Latin Haga Comitum, is called from its having been the seat of the Earls of Holland; it is one league from Delft, three from Rotterdam, three from Leiden, ten from Amsterdam and one from the sea, and is charmingly situated, having to the north a noble wood, to the south and east pleasant meadows, and the sea to the west of it. It is accounted but a village by its not being walled round, though esteemed by all travellers, even by the Italians so fond of their own country, to be the largest, most agreeable and beautiful village in Europe, so clean and straight are the streets, so many and such noble houses resembling palaces, that no city can boast more of its buildings than this village may. Here reside the States-General and Provincial, Council of State, Chamber of Accounts, etc. Many nations have at their own charge built here stately houses for their ministers to reside in, when they have occasion to send any to these States, who are seldom without ambassadors or envoys from most of the Princes of Europe.

What remains there be of the ancient nobility, as of the Brederodes, Egmont, Wassenaar, live here and the inhabitants are more polished and sociable than in any other place of these provinces, for which they are obliged to the foreign ministers that are always here by reason it is the residence of the States and the many travellers who choose to make what stay they can here rather than in any other town of Holland. [...]

[16r] The things I did see here are: The Old [Great] Church of brick, very large,

has an innumerable sight of escutcheons against the wall and ought to be seen for the tomb of [Jacob van Wassenaer, Lord of] Obdam, that is in the choir and which I shall, to the honour of the States who erected it, describe: Under a noble pavilion supported by four pillars of reddish marble with white capitals of the Corinthian [order] is the admiral in white marble as big as the life, in armour, having his truncheon in his right hand. On each side [of] him are two boys, one holds his helmet, the other a laurel and an escutcheon on which are his arms. Behind the admiral is a Fame sitting on an eagle which stands on a globe. Fame is sounding with one hand and with the other holds a corona rostralis [crown for victory gained at sea] over the admiral's head. At the admiral's feet is a mourning cupid leaning on an urn, hourglass, etc.; all this is of white marble and as high from the ground as the top of the basis, which is about four foot. At the four corners at bottom are four figures of white marble, five foot high, as Fidelity with a dog, Vigilance with a cock, Prudence with an owl and Fortitude which has no emblem.

The monument is square, each front above the cornish making a halfround and from the middle of the top arise Roman trophies. In the halfround of each front are accounts of his actions in gold letters on black, and under each account is the action finely cut in white marble on a panel of the basis, so that, the rest of the basis being of black marble, and the sea engagements cut in white, they look like Van de Velde's sea-pieces in black frames. But the engagement in the front is the biggest and best done, which has on one side the arms [16v] of Holland and [on the other those of] the United Provinces. On the halfround in the front is [the inscription].

[... 17r] The New Church on the Spui is an oval building, very beautiful to the eye, for it has four angles betwixt four halfrounds which make the four fronts, and is as convenient within for having no pillars; all in the church may both see and hear the minister.

The palace built by William [II], Earl of Holland and King of the Romans, was formerly the residence of the Earls of Holland, but now belongs to the Princes of Orange, who have always lived here till our present King's [William III] accession to the crown of England [1689]. It is in the most open part of the town, having a great court before it [Buitenhof], a delightful grove behind it, called the Plein, and a large canal, called the Vijver, on one side it. It is pretty large, kept in good order, and its form shows it to be very ancient. [17v] Within it is a large quadrangle for the soldiers to draw up in [Binnenhof], and here most people walk [at] about ten or eleven [o'clock] who have dependence or business at Court, as our gentlemen do at Whitehall. On the left hand in this quadrangle, over the piazzas is a regular building and more modern than the rest. Beyond this was the chapel, which now is the French church.

In this Court all the States of the provinces meet, but that chamber wherein the States of Holland assemble is for its painting most to be admired. Fronting the entrance into this quadrangle is a great hall like Westminster, but not so large, and has many booksellers and toyshops in it. There are hung up a great number of standards, flags and colours that have been taken from the several Princes of Europe the States had war withal, and at the end of this hall is a High Court of Justice [of Holland and Zeeland], to which all appeals are to be made but from which none is granted.

As you go from this Court to the Plein you pass by, on the left hand, a noble house, built [1641] after the modern [fashion], by [Johan-] Maurice, Prince of Orange [Count of Nassau-Siegen], and therefore called his house [Mauritshuis]. Here King Charles II was lodged and treated by the States in 1660 when he came from Breda to embark for England. And all foreign princes who come hither on any business reside in this house while they stay. Here are pictures of most of the kings of Europe and a good collection of American curiosities. The plenipotentiaries of the States did live in this house during the treaty at Rijswijk [1697].

The statehouse by the Great Church is an old building [1564-1565]. In the first room is very good painting and under the window of the room where the burgomasters sit is this verse: Felix quem faciunt aliena pericula cautum [Happy is he who has been made careful by the risks others have run]. By this statehouse is an iron cage wherein criminals are sometimes put, to be exposed to the laughter of the mob.

Not far from hence is the flesh-hall, not to be passed by especially in hot weather, a very handsome one and well-stocked with very good meat. In the [18r] middle I observed a picture of a sheep with some Dutch under it signifying that in 1644 a sheep was here killed that weighed 340 pounds.

The house where they cast their cannon is a large handsome building of brick [1665]. In the front is this: [Latin inscription]. I took notice of the method they used in their casting and boring their great guns to be thus. The furnace in which the metal is melted is so high from the ground that any mould may stand under the mouth of it. A place of ten foot square is bricked up to the mouth; in this hole they put two or three moulds and force down the earth so tight between them that it is almost impossible for one of them to break. When the metal is melted, a man with a long pole forces open the hole in the front of the furnace, stopped with a piece of wood, and lets out the metal which by channels in the sand runs to the several moulds. To bore it they hang the cannon in an engine turned round with one horse, the mouth of the cannon being put over a tall thick spike of iron of the bigness they would have the bore brought to, and fixed fast in the ground so that the horse turns the cannon round and its own weight makes the bore.

The Voorhout is a walk boarded in like our Mall in St James's Park, but of the shape of an L. Round it is a large road with high elms on each side [of] it, where all the quality of this place appear about six at night in their best coaches and equipage, and come as constantly hither as our ladies go the Hyde Park. I have seen one hundred coaches here of a night. This Voorhout is in an open part of this town, where are many beautiful houses pleasantly situated on account of the noble trees, but more because of the noble tour the fair sex make round this place. [18v]

In a noble house by this Voorhout did the Earl of Jersey, one of our plenipotentiaries, reside and kept a table that answered his character and country.

Behind the Court is a square as big as St James's but planted so thick with limes that the sun scarce ever peeps into it. It is called the Plein. This grove is very full of wild turtles who every morning by their melancholy notes made the neighbourhood believe they slept in a delightful shade and not in so populous a place. About it are very large and stately houses, but the best are Mijnheer Odijk's, Zuylichem [Constantijn Huygens], etc., and may be called palaces. On one side of it, where there are smaller buildings, I lodged while I was here, in an apartment fronting the grove. But as it was a delightful place, it was a very dear one.

[MS 177, 11v] I must take notice of the English chapel, that I may have the opportunity to say I went there two or three times but never found above twenty besides the preacher, a Scotchman, who usually gave us but bad entertainment, as a long sermon stuffed with dull similes, to make good I suppose the old proverb that comparisons are odious.

[MS 178, 18v] As this is the only town in all the provinces for people of fashion, for pleasure and gallantry, so no rich man ever lets his family come hither before he has left off all manner of business, and designs to turn gentleman, live on his rents, and suffer his wife and children to follow the court fashions.

[MS 177, 13r] I went sometimes to the French playhouse, which was good for nothing but to draw the company of the town together. Here is an academy where is taught to ride the great horse, as the horses of this country may very properly be called, but I never found any but heavy Germans aworking at it, nor ought the horses to carry less weight.

[MS 178, 18v] In this place is every night an assembly at one house or other, where all the gay young sparks and ladies do meet to pass away the evening. Some play at basset, ombre, picquet, etc., others talk of the intrigues of the town and some of their own. Any man well-clothed is easily admitted, especially [19r] if he has fifty ducats in his pocket and he must have good luck to carry them away with him. For here are many ladies who keep a neat table and handsome equipage with what they win from strangers, who must not keep them company without playing with them. At which, being bred up to it, they are as sharp as any of our London Bowchers and Pulteneys, etc.

The Hague, though always filled with gay inhabitants, never appeared in so splendid a figure as at the last treaty of peace at Rijswijk [1697]. For the ambassadors of all the princes of Europe who assisted at it resided here, excepting the French who lived at Delft. You could hardly pass a street without meeting an ambassador with a retinue of six or twelve pages and thirty footmen, and they all used to appear at the Voorhout, where everyone endeavoured to be the most admired for richness of liveries and number of footmen, so that a nobler appearance than usually was at this place, can never be seen. Nay, sometimes the French came to this rendezvous of fine fellows with finer coats.

View of the House at Rijswijk, c. 1698

I am almost as unwilling to leave describing some part or other of this delight-ful place, as I was to leave living there. But before I do, I am in gratitude obliged to speak some of the Earl of Pembroke, our first plenipotentiary at this treaty, from whom I received favours beyond what I could have expected. He always kept a constant table after the old English manner, in which as in his rich liveries, he showed himself an English nobleman. He was well-beloved by all this country for his learning, sweet temper and easiness of access by all the inhabitants of this place, for, by paying all accounts off weekly, he never owed them much. He always made his household come to prayers and by his example taught them to be good. He never suffered any drinking to excess in his house and governed his family with that discipline that though a numerous, yet it seemed as quiet as any private family. But I must have done for he who would speak all his praises may speak to eternity; and had he then more time, might find some not spoken of.

[19v] When I had occasion to make any public visits, as to go to the Voorhout, or out of town to see any seats of pleasure nigh The Hague, I hired a handsome chariot with a pair of good Flanders horses, the coachman having a good large coat which would serve for any livery, for four guilders and a half per diem, though for the country a chaise is more pleasant. It is like a calash but halfway up your back, holds two and goes with one horse. I could have one of these for a ducatoon [*f*3:3]

194

per diem. I cannot compare these chaises to anything but an elbow chair upon wheels.

In one of these I went to see Rijswijk, a house belonging to the King and an English mile from hence by a very pleasant road. It is a very handsome stone house of thirty-three windows to the front, breaks forward in the middle and each wing; was built by the King's grandfather [Frederik Hendrik]. All the lower floors are of black and white marble, the ceilings are of wood and painted with gold foliage on a green ground. Here are some good pictures. There is a large garden belonging to it but not well kept, and a vast court and shady grove before the house. This house will be famous for posterity for the peace signed here betwixt the plenipotentiaries of the Confederate Princes and those of the French King, Louis XIV, the King of Sweden [being] mediator. Coming to the front of this house were three gates; the French entered by that on the right side, the Confederates through that on the left hand and the mediator through the middle one. The house was so fit for such a business that anyone who sees it forty years hence, will believe it to have been built for such purposes.

I went another time to the Bosch, which is a great wood that, joining to The Hague, contributes much to the pleasure of it. In this wood is a long mall, like ours, but with trees on each side so high and their tops joining that you walk as under a lofty arbour. But about two miles in the wood is the beauty of it, the King's house, called the House in the Bosch. It is but a small box, but of stone; you [20r] go up about twenty steps to it. As you enter the house there fronts you a door which lets you into the finest room of this country. It is very large and high, painted all over by the best masters; each corner breaks in, against which are looking glasses with tables, stands and sconces of looking glass. Over each looking glass unto the ceiling is on each angle flat pilasters of gold and betwixt them trophies, shields and devices curiously painted and representing the actions of this King's grandfather who built this house.

The left side of this room is one vast picture of this King's grandfather, drawn in a triumphal chariot by white horses, attended with many figures, trophies, etc. and is of Rubens [Jordaens]. The rest of the room is painted by him and other masters. It is open in the middle of the ceiling through which you see gold banisters and another ceiling on which is painted many cupids flying above the picture of this King's grandmother [Amalia van Solms], which is in the centre of it. The stairs to the apartments are very curious: crawling cupids instead of banisters supporting the rails. Here are several other rooms neatly furnished with good pieces of Van Dyck in them, and their doors were so painted with whole-length figures that I was surprised to see the maid put a key into so good a picture as some were; one I took more notice of being a naked woman and the keyhole betwixt her thighs.

Here is one curious closet made of the best sort of Indian screens, the floor inlaid and the ceiling of looking glass with gold ciphers on it. This closet was very full of fine china, which because so placed by the late Queen [Mary II Stuart], the King has ordered it not to be removed.

Belonging to this house is a large garden with a good terrace walk and a very pretty labyrinth to behold, but very difficult to get out of. It is all pretty and well-kept. This was only designed for a pleasure house for the Princes of Orange to retire to when they had a mind to be more private and free from the buzzing of courtiers or rather a [20v] place to please nature in; if so, it is a heavenly place for it.

Returning from thence I went to see the much admired gardens of Monsieur St Annaland, who has a neat dwelling on the side of this wood, about a mile from The Hague. His house [Clingendael] is small but very neat, the gardens are large and very well kept, but the beauty of them consists most in the walks and hedges, whereof there are some of Dutch elm, the highest in the country as of twenty foot high. Here are some fir trees much higher, which, growing thick and being cut like a hedge appear very delightful, besides many yew and holly hedges cut in various manner. In short, the form and design of the garden is as pretty, odd and surprising as any I ever saw, but they fall short of ours not having any gravel for walks which they supply with sand kept so hollow by the moles that in some places in dry weather you step up to your ankles.

Another time I went to Scheveling [Scheveningen], two miles from The Hague, to which place is a straight smooth road planted on each side with trees and paved with brick, over which is sand laid. Scheveling is a poor fishing town, has a battery of six guns mounted towards the sea, which by an inundation in 1574 [1570] carried away 121 [128] houses of this place, as appears by an account which hangs up in the church. Before this town, Charles II embarked in 1660 for England and in sight of this place was Obdam [Tromp, off Ter Heide in 1653] blown up. The road hither, being so very pleasant, is in an evening frequented with many coaches, especially if it's low water, for then you may ride for two or three leagues on the shore, which is of a hard sand, and view the sea, with many fishing boats always sailing up and down. About the middle of the road is a gate at which you must pay four and a half stivers passage gelt for a coach. The money arising by this toll goes to maintain the road.

As I returned from Scheveling I went to see my Lord Portland's gardens at Sorgvliet, which is not far out of the way and about a mile from The Hague. The [21r] house is very small and as old, but this Lord Portland has made some additions to it. Before the house is a handsome orangery of fifty large windows and of a half-moon form. In the middle of it is a good hall well-painted. Behind the house are many gardens, fine groves and a vast many shady walks, some terrace ones, various fountains with surprising waterworks, curious arbours and several alleys under arbours, good statues, a large aviary, two high mounts with an infinite number of evergreen trees cut in several shapes. In short, the gardens are prodigious large without two things alike in them all, and ought to be seen by everyone who comes to The Hague.

I went another time to Honselaarsdijk, a house built by this King's grandfather, and about eight English miles from The Hague. Moated round, it is a square, handsome structure with a long walk of high elms fronting the house; it is built about a quadrangle, but the front to the garden is only a piazza with banisters of stone about it. The apartments are well-furnished and have in them good pictures of several great masters. Here are two good galleries. At each end of one of them is a large picture of Henri IV [of France] and his Queen [Marie de Médicis] with a representation under each picture, of their coronation. On the sides were whole-lengths of several relations of this family [of Nassau], amongst which I observed Charles the First and Second, with their Queens. The gallery on the Queen's side had many fine pictures fixed in panels in the wainscot, and the ceiling was painted with gold on a green ground. Here are closets of choice pieces, especially one very large of japan; the ceiling of looking glass with flowers painted on it and over the chimney was fine china, neatly placed by the late Queen.

In the middle of the garden before the house is a large fountain with eight gilt statues on pedestals about it. Beyond that is a curious open arbour through which is a vista into a fine walk of trees in the park. The orangery is a hundred and fifty paces long and had before it the finest and largest orange trees I ever saw. Fronting the middle of the orange house is a fine gravel walk with a high elm hedge on each side, under which were several exotic plants.

[21v] In a neat garden on the right hand of the house is an open gallery, eighty paces long, in which are four statues in alabaster of Princes of this family, a good rape [of Proserpina by Pluto], a fine Cleopatra with other statues of brass. At the upper [end] of this gallery is a large picture of Loo, and the ceiling well-painted. In the middle of this garden before the gallery is a neat octagon, twelve foot high of arbourwork, open at top, and the entrances answering the several walks.

I walked into the park, which is a good soil and well-wooded. Here I saw a field paled in, where was an elk, an elan[d], several East India cows, very small of a red colour with bunches on their backs like camels, several sorts of sheep and deer. In a garden over against this place were many turkey, East India and West India fowl with many ducks, pheasants and peacocks of various and most beautiful colours.

As I returned from Honselaarsdijk I stopped at a poor village called Loosduinen, but famous for the miraculous birth of 365 children at one time. I went into the church to see the account of it, which is in Latin on a table, which is fixed to the wall of the church and is to this effect: [...].

[22r] In the same [church], as appears by a stone, is buried Richard Palmer [Harding], privy purse to Charles II in his exile; and under an escutcheon was in great letters: Barbara Ailesbury, who being of our nation and buried in a foreign country, I think myself obliged to take notice of, being of opinion they or their friends desired as much, who by ordering these stones to be put over them, did it to show they were English and not natives, that they might be remembered by their country people who might come hither.

Joseph Taylor, 13-22 September (24 September - 3 October) 1707

[44r] I have taken up my lodging at the Golden Lion, near the Hof van Holland, or the old palace of the Counts of Holland, at the entrance of which is a large court. In the great hall at the upper end the colours hang, taken formerly from the Spaniards and those taken lately from the French. The assembly of the States [-General] is up one pair of stairs; it is a room wherein is a long table covered with green cloth and twenty-four chairs; in the middle a great one for the president [44v] and opposite against it is one for an ambassador and at the upper end a chair for the stadtholder. There are several pictures of the House of Orange, particularly that of Prince Maurice. Over the mantlepiece is painted a figure representing Concord. The plafond or ceiling is likewise painted. There is another room for the States [Trèves zaal], more noble, which has a good prospect to the Voorhout or ring. In this is placed such another table and chairs as the former and two of the largest globes I ever saw. Over the mantlepiece is painted King William sitting in a chair, extremely like the original. The ceiling is painted with many emblems of liberty, on which is this motto: Concordia res parvae crescunt [through concord small things grow]. The cushions have the same motto. At the time when the States meet, the guards are all drawn before the palace with the trumpets and kettle-drums playing.

Prince Maurice's house, where the Duke of Marlborough used to lodge, is still in its ruins [after the fire at Christmas 1704]. There is a place called the Doelen, where the States treat the ambassadors. On the front is an inscription that Prince [45r] William [II] laid the first stone [1636]. The Great Church and cloisters are indifferent, but the New Church is a pretty round piece of building and has a good organ and also a fine monument [=in the Great Church] of Jacobus de Wassenaar, Lord of Obdam, which after enumerating some of his actions against the Portuguese and in the Atlantic seas and in the Baltic, at last gives an account that fighting most valiantly [off Lowestoft], a few ships against the Royal Navy of England, and being every way surrounded, that he might not then yield to his enemies, first a great slaughter being made and afterwards his own ship set on fire, with an Herculean example made his way to heaven through the flames in the 55th year of his age. To his memory the States-General erected this monument in the year 1667.

The canal runs through the chief street very pleasantly, but the Voorhout, railed in with rows of trees, is most delightful; the people walking under the shade like our Mall, and the coaches drive round as in Hyde Park. Here one may see a world of splendid equipages and noble appearances. I have been at a Dutch play called the Siege of Leyden, which [45v] is no better than a droll in Bartholomew Fair; and after at a French opera called L'Europe Galante, which was pretty well performed. The house is but indifferent and the company small, by reason of this time of the year the people of quality are in the army or gone to their respective provinces.

I have spent one day with abundance of pleasure in visiting the Princess' House in the Wood, to which I walked in about half an hour. We ascended by eighteen

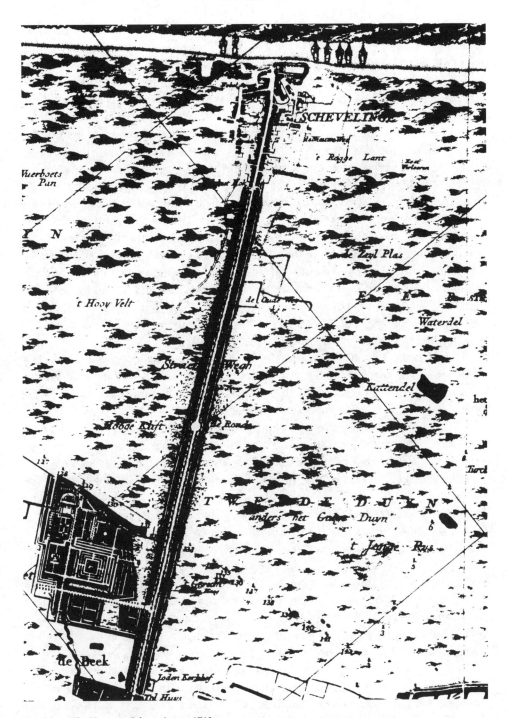

Road from The Hague to Scheveningen, 1712

steps to the house, on each side of which are figures. As soon as we entered the great door, we saw a large flight of stairs, the rails whereof are supported by little boys. We went through into the great hall, which is surprisingly noble and adorned with curious large paintings. In the front is painted the marriage of Prince Frederic Henry; on the right his triumphs on horseback with Vigilance and Death attending, and on the left his triumphs in an open chariot drawn by four white horses. This was after he had settled peace with the Spaniards; and round about are abundance of proper emblems of war.

There are likewise the triumphs of Europe, Asia, Africa and [46r] America; on the frieze [ceiling] is painted Phoebus in his chariot with Europa [Aurora] on the right and on the left a cross ascending with angels hanging about it. On the top is a cupola and the princess [Amalia], wife of Frederic [-Hendrik], painted in it, and round is an inscription that this was done to the immortal memory of that great prince. There are also pictures of the King of Prussia's father and mother, and in the several chambers I saw the pictures of the late King William when young, and his father and mother and some other of his ancestors. The India cabinet is very fine and also the bedchamber of State, the fringes to the bed and hangings are of Queen Mary's own working, and it is railed in with japan rails. In the audience room is a good picture of the angel descending to the Virgin Mary.

The house on the outside appears to be but little; on the top of the cupola is a golden sun. The gardens are not very fine, but there are in them four good statues representing the four seasons, a pretty maze and two mounts, covered with arbours, and several curious knots and green hedges.

I went a day or two ago in a [46v] postwaggon to Scheveling, a little village by the seaside about a league from home [=here]. Sure nothing can be more agreeable than the shady rows of trees thither, which makes a continual arbour. All the way is paved with Dutch bricks, wonderfully neat. The steeple of Scheveling yields a noble prospect to the sea. The seashore being a hard sand, the coaches from The Hague come hither to take the air, and indeed it is extremely pleasant. As I came back I saw my Lord Portland's fine gardens. There is a pretty avenue through a wood to a very little summerhouse, before which is an orangery in a semi-circle of almost three hundred oranges and lemons, adorned with eight fine urns on pedestals. In one of the gardens are two fine figures of Mercury and Susanna and a pretty grotto with waterworks, abundance of shady walks and several trees, cut in different shapes. The infirmary to raise trees, the mew for hawks, the fish-pond filled with several sort of ducks, and the grotto made of shells are all worth seeing. I spent the rest of the day there with much satisfaction.

Yesterday, a gentleman [47r] and I went to Loosduinen in about an hour, through a fine road, to see the famous basin wherein 365 children of Margaret, wife of Herman, Earl of Hennenberg, daughter of Florentius [IV], Earl of Holland and Zeeland, and sister of William [II], King of the Romans, were christened by Guido, suffragan of Utrecht. She was brought to bed of them at about forty years of age, anno 1276; the males were named John and the females Elizabeth, who altogether with their mother died in one day and lie here buried. This happened on account of a poor woman, who having two twins in her arms, the Countess wondered at it and told her it was impossible she should have them by one man; and so censured her that the poor woman, being very much enraged, prayed the Countess might have as many children at one birth as there were days in the year, which wonderful thing, against the course of nature happened accordingly. There is this distich on the wall:

> En tibi monstrosum nimis et memorabile factum
> Quale nec a mundi conditione datum.

> [Here you see a most miraculous and memorable event,
> which since the creation of the world never happened]

and underneath,

> [47v] Hoc lege mox animo stupefactus [lector] abibis.

> Read this [and reader] you'll straight go away amazed.

From Loosduinen we went in an hour and half to Honselaarsdijk, which has a very handsome avenue through a little paddock and wilderness. The house is moated and built with brick. In the front is a stone balustrade and on each side two wings, under which are cloisters paved with marble, and the whole makes a very handsome square court. There are two good piles of buildings for stables and outhouses with spacious yards on each side [of] the house. In the gardens I saw first a basin with an Arion of brass, supported by four dolphins with shells and jets d'eaux and eight statues in brass round the basin, two of which were Ceres and Apollo. There are abundance of urns whereon are wrought several heathenish sacrifices in basso relievo and a large gladiator, very well done. The orangery consists of about five hundred orange trees and the walk to it with high hedges on both sides is very delightful. The canal for fish is very pleasant, and the hothouse is filled with [48r] a great many Indian plants.

In the first room of the house, from the great staircase, are several landscapes of forts and prospects, in the next the pictures of the late King James [II] and his first wife [Anne Hyde], when Duke and Duchess of York, and of his son [James, Duke of Cambridge] by her and also his second wife [Mary of Modena] when Queen of England; the pictures of King William and Queen Mary when Prince and Princess of Orange; the Prince is drawn in his own hair. Likewise the Prince [George] and Princess [Anne] of Denmark, now our most glorious Queen; and over the chimney-piece are likewise King William's father and mother, all [of] which are originals and extremely well done. In one long gallery are several fine historical paintings. The audience room is hung with blue damask and the cabinet lined with Indian [Chinese] work.

In the great dining room, the plafond or ceiling is painted round with banisters and several comical pictures looking as it were, over at others playing on music. There is also a good picture of Diana hunting. In another long gallery are the pictures of the King of France's grandfather and grandmother [Henri IV and Marie de Médicis], of [48v] Philip IV [III] of Spain, the King and Queen of Bohemia, Charles the First and Second of England and their Queens and of several other princes. In another room I saw the picture of the present King of France [Louis XIV] when a boy. In another the picture of Joseph and the Virgin Mary carrying Our Saviour into Egypt, very finely drawn; another of Diana and Actaeon with a boar's head, and on the plafond is a Banquet of the Gods, with representations of Iris, Ganymede and Neptune. These I looked upon to be the chief rarities, but there being near fifty rooms, it was impossible for me to remember all.

From thence we returned by the castle of Rijswijk, famous for the last peace that was made there [1697]. It is built of stone with about thirty-one windows in front. It was all unfurnished, but I was shown the several rooms made use of by the plenipotentiaries of all nations at the time of the treaty, and the great room, where the peace was signed. All along we saw [an] abundance of pretty villas and gardens, [49r] which fill the roads on every side. I need not tell you that The Hague is one of the largest and most pleasant villages in the world; everybody that has seen it gives it that character. For my part I am infinitely delighted and wish I had more time to spend here, everything appearing with such an air of gaiety that a traveller cannot but be infinitely charmed. In a day or two I intend to set out for Leiden and Amsterdam, from whence you may expect the trouble of another letter.

John Farrington, 16 September 1710 N.S.

[21] [coming form Leiden] After we had taken a view of these gardens [House in the Wood and Clingendael] we went on to The Hague, whither we came [with] just time enough to dine at the ordinary at one o'clock (the Golden Lion, a good ordinary for a guilder, good lodging and reasonable for The Hague). As soon as we had dinner, we went to see the Court, which was the residence of the late King [William III] at The Hague. The building is not extraordinary, but the apartments are convenient. [...]

[22] The chamber of the States of Holland is a very noble large room, supported by large pillars gilt. The hangings in it are of fine tapestry. There are two very fine engravings in gold about a foot and a half square, the one representing the assembly of the States, the other a feast or entertainment. Round about the room just under the ceiling are painted men of all nations looking over a rail, as it were to see what that great and wise assembly are doing and expressing surprise and yet a great deal of pleasure, too. They showed us also three other chambers, where the magistrates meet for the dispatch of the civil affairs of that town or for the execution of the laws. The apartments of the late King, now unfurnished, they would not let us see, nor are there any great matters observable in it.

After we had seen the Court, we took a walk to the Heer Odijk's, where the Lord Towns[h]end, the British plenipotentiary, at present resides. They brought us into a large hall, where all the entertainments and balls are made. In that room hang four large crystal branches, with [a] variety of candlesticks in them, which must needs make a glorious show when the candles are all lighted. At the upper end you go up five or six steps to an alcove, where the gentlemen and ladies the spectators sit, which is adorned with several very fine paintings, among which there is one of a Dutch maid, whom old Odijk debauched, and who proved with child by him. [23] She had fifty guineas given her to suffer herself to be drawn naked, which she is, only with a due regard had to modesty, and so great was the old Lord's fancy for this woman. There is another picture of her, which was drawn when younger, and both of them show her to have been a handsome woman. In the cabinet they showed us several paintings of a very great value, one not above two foot long that cost twelve hundred guilders and another a great deal less, fourteen thousand pounds sterling as they assured us. There was also a picture of Queen Anne, which was lately sent over as a present to my Lord Townsend.

His Lordship this day set out for Amsterdam, otherwise we should have made it our business to have paid our compliments to him as a true Briton and a good and faithful minister of the Queen of Great Britain.

Sir John Percival 28 June - 2 July (9-13 July) 1718

[53v] We left Rotterdam the 28th, and passing through Delft, arrived in three hours at The Hague. The pleasantest way of travelling in Holland is in trackshouts. These boats are less than those in Flanders, but cleaner and have at the end a cabin, called the roof, where for paying a trifle more than the common rate, a set company may retire from the crowd and divert themselves with cards, books or conversation. [...]

[55r] One of the principal beauties of Holland are the country seats and gardens of persons of distinction. As many of them belong to men of business, they are for the most part situated within an hour's journey of the great towns. The roads leading to them are very well-kept, and free access is allowed to strangers. But it is only of late years that the taste for gardening is arrived in Holland to the perfection we now see it. In former times, when the inhabitants fought pro aris et focis [for hearth and home], there was no leisure to mind the luxury of life, nor were particular [private] subjects rich to an excess, when the commonwealth was in the most flourishing state. But the subject was contented with a moderate estate, and frugal management thereof. 'They still retain', says Sir Thomas Overbury, who wrote his *Observations* in the time of King James the First, 'that sign of a commonwealth uncorrupted: private poverty and public weal[th]; for no private man there is exceeding rich, and few very poor and no state more sumptuous in all public things'.

Since that gentleman wrote, corruption has crept in, and men in office have found the way to render their incomes excessive lucrative and their actions safe from question by bribing some with money and places, and terrifying others with the strength and power of their relations. [55v] Hereupon the commonwealth is sunk almost to contempt and has been forced to bear such insolent affronts from their neighbours and to do such mean things by her subjects at home, that if a stadholder be not speedily chosen, it is feared by observing men she cannot long subsist.

But all this while, the particulars [private citizens] are rich, who receding from the parsimony so commendable in their ancestors and which enabled them to establish the Republic on firm and lasting foundations, have by their luxurious example drawn all ranks of people to copy after them, and introduced a manner of life that surpasses their incomes and in time must render them uneasy with their government and liable to be corrupted by those princes and states who shall offer to repair their broken fortunes. They build them[selves] noble houses, make great entertainments, keep fine equipages, and game for large sums.

Among the rest of their luxury this of gardening is come to its height. To adorn which, and the seats to which they belong, the owners stick at nothing that is rare, though ever so dear. Yet have these gardens their defects as well as their beauties, for the whole country being a continued flat, they are destitute of prospect other than the avenues and vistas which their fine plantations afford them. Neither is there any gravel wherewith to cover their walks.

[56r] These two defects they supply the best they can. The first by high hedges of elm, etc., with which they enclose their gardens as if they despised a distant prospect. With these they likewise divide them into many parts, disposing them into [a] variety of forms. The other want is not so well supplied. Cockleshells indeed make a good covering to their walks, but it proves so dear that the finest gardens content themselves with one walk so laid. The rest have none, but use either grass kept [as] short as possible (which yet is not fit to be walked on in wet weather, in that country especially), or sand which does not bind and is very troublesome to walk on in the hot and dry season. For the rest they affect such regularity in [the] laying out of their gardens that there always appears more art than nature in them. Thus, their plantations of trees and walks are all regular and cut to a shape, and their canals, fountains and terraces answer each other with the same exactness as do their statues, urns, flower beds and lesser ornaments, all [of] which is displeasing to the eye, which in these things likes variety.

The finest gardens are near The Hague. I went one evening with my Lord Cadogan to see Sihon [Sion] near Delft, the country seat of Mr [Gijsbert van] Hogendorp, a gentleman of considerable employment under the States. The gardens are made with a peculiar [56v] good taste, consisting of fine parterres, very large canals, vistas, woods and a menagerie for fowls, most neatly finished and ornamented with high orange trees. The orchards and kitchen garden were not enclosed with walls but thick hedges, secured by broad ditches on the outside. They say these hedges break the force of the wind and preserve the fruit from blights better than walls.

I ate fine Flemish cherries there, and currants very sweet of a largeness not known in England. I was surprised when they told me the whole plantation and garden was begun and finished in seven years' time. The house is new-built and neat, but without any ornaments of pillars or pilasters; these people seeming to have no taste for the rules of architecture in their private buildings. [...]

[57v] On Tuesday the 1st July, I returned the visits of the Prince d'Auvergne and the Marquis Beretti-Landi. The former is a subject of France and enjoys many rich abbeys and preferments in the Church to the value of ten thousand pounds per annum. He dined and supped often with us at my Lord Cadogan's, and being in a Protestant country, was obliged to appear in a lay habit. At that time he prepared to go to Liège to take possession of a canon's place, lately conferred upon him.

The Marquis Beretti-Landi [58r] is an old gentleman of good sense and experience and full of intrigue. He is an Italian and was for a considerable time chief minister to the Duke of Mantua, whom he betrayed into the French King's measures during King William's wars, and was thereby the ruin of that prince. But the King rewarded well his service by conferring upon him a yearly pension of eighty thousand livres and afterwards procuring him the character of ambassador from the Court of Spain to the States. He is a polite man and pretends a great kindness for the English nation.

He could not be an Italian and want a taste to painting. Accordingly, he has a collection of pictures and other curiosities that fill one large apartment of his house. Among the rest he showed me a piece of Hannibal Caratche [Carracci], a Madonna of Paul Veronese, an Assumption of Corregio, a battle of Bourguignon, a chimney piece of Rubens, a Madonna of [Jacopo] Palma, and a piece of earthenware painted, as he believed, by Raphael Urbia [=of Urbino]. But I have seen so many of these last in Italy, pretended to be of the same hand, that a hundredth part cannot be truly so. I did not observe that style in the figures of this, so peculiar to that great man.

[58v] In the afternoon I went to see the House in the Wood, distant half an hour from The Hague. The road to it is through a fine wood with avenues regularly planted. it was a pleasant retreat in King William's time, when the gardens were kept in order, but the King of Prussia, who now owns it together with Honselaarsdijk, Loo, Dieren and Rijswijk as heir to that king, suffers the gardens to go to ruin. Nay, the house itself is uninhabited and left in the care of an ordinary man without salary, who lives in one of the offices and thinks himself well paid with a guilder or two for showing it. [...]

[59r] The finest road in the world for its length is that which leads from The Hague to Scheveling, an inconsiderable village of fishermen, built on the sea bank about a mile distant. It is paved with brick and planted with rows of large high trees on each side. Halfway on the left side, are the gardens of Sorgvliet [Zorgvliet], made by the late Earl of Portland, King William's favourite, and now the property of his widow, the Countess of Portland [Jane Temple], governess to the young [English] princesses. They take in a great compass of ground, and you see [a] vari-

ety of fine walks and vistas, with a handsome parterre and greenhouse. But now they are looked on as old-fashioned, seldom visited and but ill kept up. [59v] They have run the fate of several others, which but fourteen years ago, when I was in Holland for the first time [1706], were in high vogue, but are within this small space of time eclipsed by the later ones of Hogendorp and Sion, etc. I learned while I was there that orders were lately come from the Countess to sell both the garden and her house in The Hague, she thinking to see Holland no more, since the charge of the young princesses conferred upon her.

The Earl of Cadogan's house in The Hague is very large and handsome and the furniture answerable. He bought, while I was there, for two hundred pistoles a large piece of the Last Supper by Tintoret[to], believed to be the same that was in King Charles the First's collection, which Oliver Cromwell dissipated after the murder of that unfortunate prince.

There are few great collections of paintings in the Seven Provinces. Those who esteem the art contenting themselves with five or six good pieces, for which they give excessive prices, but they do not value themselves upon being masters of a great number. There are some good masters for fruit, flowers and landscape yet living, but scarce [60r] one eminent for history painting. Mr Whitworth, since Lord Whitworth, carried me to see the works of Mr Ruple [Roepel], a person residing at The Hague who succeeds admirably well in fruit and flowers. My Lord is a great lover of the art, and gives very great prices and had collected in Germany and Holland several good pieces which he showed us. Among the rest were four landscapes by [Christoph Ludwig] Agricola, now living in Germany, which were excellent in colour, invention and expression.

Population: 18,000 (1650), 30,000 (1690), 38,000 (1730).

Distances: Amsterdam 11 hours (28 miles), Delft 1 hour (3 miles), Leiden 3 hours (9 miles), Rotterdam 3 hours (9 miles).

Inns, *Reisboek* (1689, 1700 and 1721): De Kasteleny [1689: voor de goeden en kwaaden]; 't [1721: Groot] Keizers Hof*, op de Korte Vijverberg; De zeven Kerken van Romen,* op het Spui; De drie Snellen.

Reisboek (1689) also: De Doelen; De Keizerin, in de Heerestraat.

Reisboek (1700) also: De Princes Royaal; 't Hof van Gelderland; 't Wapen van Noord-Holland; De Keizer; De Stad Mastrigt.

Reisboek (1689 and 1700) also: Groot Gorkum, d'Oyevaar in de Kabel, De gezonde Broeder [1689: alwaar het beste Bottelbier gemaakt wordt, op het Spuy].

Reisboek (1700 and 1721) also: d' Oude en nieuwe Doelen; 't Nieuw Heere Logement [1721: op 't Buitenhof]; De Goude Leeuw* [op het Buitenhof]; De Landgraaf van Hessen* [op het Plein]; De Stads Herberg, bij het Delfsche Schuyt-veer; 't Wapen van Haarlem, op het Leidsche wagenveer.

Reisboek (1721) also: De vergulde Bal, op 't Leidse wagenveer; 't Prinsenhof, op 't Buitenhof; 't Hof van Holland, op de Plaats; Het Heerenlogement van den Roomsch-Koning op 't Spui; 't Hof van Utrecht, op 't Spui; In de Spuistraat bij Mr Herenberg.

Nugent (1749) also: The Queen of Hungary, an English House, kept by one Blunt on the Fluweelburg Wall; The Golden Lion in the Singel; The Parliament of England in the Korte Pooten; Marshall Turenne, The Imperial Crown (both in de Korte Houtstraat).

Further reading

Guide de La Haye, 's-Gravenhage 1705.

G. de Cretser, *Beschryvinge van 's-Gravenhage*, Amsterdam 1711, 1729.

J. de Riemer, *Beschryving van 's-Graven-Hage*, Delft, 's-Gravenhage 1730-1739.

H.E. van Gelder, *'s-Gravenhage in zeven eeuwen*, Amsterdam 1937.

Ach Lieve Tijd, 750 jaar Den Haag en de Hagenaars, M. van Doorn (ed.), Zwolle 1984-1985.

C. Dumas, *Haagse stadsgezichten 1550-1800. Topografische schilderijen van het Haags Historisch Museum*, Zwolle 1991.

Jaarboek van de Geschiedkundige Vereniging Die Haghe, 1889-

's-Hertogenbosch

William Lord Fitzwilliam, April 1663

[12v] From Breda we went to 's-Hertogenbosch, otherwise called Bois-le-Duc, eight hours riding from Breda. Here we saw the Great Church, called St John's, pretty big and indifferently well-built. The portal leading to the place where the [high] altar did formerly stand is all of marble with little marble statues round about it and an organ upon it. In this church are several tombs, the chiefest is a bishop's of this place, all cut out in stone, on his knees and formerly he had a mitre on his head and his hands crossed together. But at the taking of this town [1629], some over-zealous soldier did cut off his mitre and arms. Had he been caught, the Prince of Orange had bestowed a rope on him for his recompense. Upon the tomb of this bishop I did read the following epitaph:

Gisbertus Masius [...]

No religion but the Protestant is publicly exercised here; some religious women are suffered, but only for their life. As soon as they which are in it are dead, no others are to succeed but the convent is to be turned into some hospital or other. The Jesuits had here formerly a college, which now is the governor's, Mr [Lodewijk van Nassau-] Beverweerd's house, a very great building, full of great and little chambers and a pleasant garden belonging to it; the church is turned into a turf and wood house. The Papists have a free exercise of their religion three miles of this town, just by the sconce Crèvecoeur, at a village called Bokhoven, belonging to the Bishop of Leodium [Liège].

Here is little else to be seen but a marketplace where the town house stands, which is but a very pitiful building. Yet upon it there is a very curious clock, which at every time it strikes it sends out some [13r] horsemen, who ride so many times about as it strikes. The streets of this town are indifferent handsome, the houses of wood and built according to the old fashion, which now is forbidden to do any more. We lodged at the Golden Swan and lay in the same chamber where His Majesty of England, King Charles II, lay at his being here [1658].

This city is governed as all other cities belonging to the States, only it has lost its right to put a criminal to death because it did condemn and execute unjustly a poor soldier. In this case therefore it must have its power from The Hague. When here anybody dies, they put a bunch of straw with some bricks upon it before his door. By its situation this town is impregnable as lying in marshy ground. Its walls are but very ordinary, old and of no strength, but the forts, with the water round about

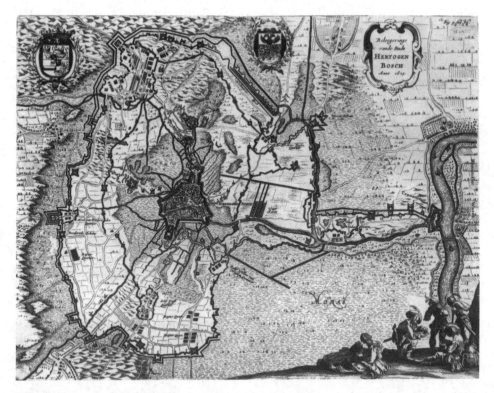

Siege of 's-Hertogenbosch (1629), 1651

it, make it invincible. There are a matter of eleven bulwarks, four great ones and seven little, with several turrets upon the courtine for to defend the bastions, which are too far one from another. The parapet is of brick, and earth in some places; a great and broad, deep ditch round about it.

At the Boom [the principal watergate] there is a citadel, built by the States for to keep the city in awe. It is all made of brick, very neat and exact. It is surrounded with five bastions and very good deep and broad ditches. Many pieces of ordnance are upon the walls. In two bastions towards the town there are twelve. By the leave of the governor we came to see this place. A league of the citadel is the fort called Crèvecoeur, built on the water [Dieze] which brings the ships into this town and on the river Mosa, which river it commands and searches all the boats or ships that pass by for to come to 's-Hertogenbosch. It is fortified with strong earth walls, seven good earth bulwarks with a double ditch, except on one side where the river Mosa runs, where it has no need of ditches.

Halfway between this fort and the town, there is a very strong sconce called Engelen, which likewise lies on the haven; no bark can come into the town, but it must come by these two forts. [13v] On the other side upon firm ground, there is a

209

third sconce called Orthen sconce, which is also extremely strong. By the Vughterport, where we came from Breda, there are two sconces more. The furthest off is called Fort Isabella, surrounded with five bulwarks of earth, good ditches and the fens. At the taking of the town [1629] the Prince of Orange [Frederik Hendrik] lost here abundance of men. The other which is nearer the town is called Fort Antoine, made all of brick, little but pretty and very neat. These two forts are built on the highway (which consists only of bridges for the rest is water), able enough to ruin a whole army. Not far from Hekelport there is another sconce on firm ground, called Petteler sconce, which is very strong and has never been taken, but upon composition surrendered when the Prince of Orange had taken the town.

Besides these six forts which defend the comings to this town, one by water and two others by land - The two land passages are so narrow, for the most part consisting of bridges (chiefly that where you come from Breda, on both sides water), that it makes a man afraid to look about him. In winter or rainy weather, there is no coming near this place but by water, all the land passages are under water. It was not quite in such a condition when the Spaniards had it, and upon that account it was taken from them. For wheresoever there was any firm ground, there the Prince of Orange made his approaches, which was about the Vughtergate, and the water he drained away with his water mills; besides, the people in the town did want ammunition. The loss of this place was so considerable that the Spaniards did not judge it fit to acquaint their king with it till a great while after, some say six years.

It is indeed a place of great importance as being the key of Brabant and Holland. The ammunition house of this town stands by the citadel, it is very strong and well-guarded. Not far from it, on the foot of the walls, there lies a piece of ordnance twenty-one foot long, which has been formerly [14r] much longer. Before it was made shorter, it was told me, they could shoot with it into Bommel, a town three leagues distant from 's-Hertogenbosch; I can hardly believe it. [cont. Utrecht]

Thomas Style, July 1669

[coming from Utrecht] [38] I observed, the nearer we came Flanders side, to see excellent good hop-grounds. The pole far lesser than ours; the fine natch weaker, generally red. They dig but once a year. Between every hill, which are small, is planted a cabbage or cauliflower. They practise here to bag them up in little bags of twenty-five and twenty pound a bag (in Flanders as we [in] England). I think in East Kent they do as they do here, in small bags; the price in general thirty guilders, about three pound, a hundred. We had very pleasant travelling in woods, six miles before we came to 's-Hertogenbosch: apples, pears and plum trees in the highways. About one we arrived.

[39] 's-Hertogenbosch, by the French called the Chateau de Bois-le-Duc, by the English the Bush, so called because situated formerly in a wood. The river Dieze runs close by it. At the gate we gave our names and country, being [customary] in

all war-towns. We were lodged at the Emperor's Head in the marketplace. That night we saw nothing, extreme weary with our journey.

The first thing next morning we saw was the Great Church, famous for the fine wrought font all of Corinthian brass, [and] a rare clock; the church is dedicated to St John. From hence we went to view the citadel, called le Chateau de Bois-le-Duc, which with much difficulty we got sight of. I find it a pentagon irregular, built with tuff brick, pointed and edged with freestone; up the bastion cannons advantageously placed. We were showed one which formerly carried eight mile. Being persuaded by a captain gained by the King of Spain to cut it, alleging it would carry twice as far, it being cut cannot kill half a league. In the castle I observed a brace of white peacocks. Here was an English captain named Lowther, who was extreme civil to us.

The other side of the town, which to the eye seems weakest, is two royal forts. That of St Anthony and Fort Isabella, besides Fort Petteler upon the river Hekel. The marketplace is very regular, adorned with stately buildings; from the middle of it, you view ten streets. The greatest strength of the town I judge to lie in their sluices, which if open drown seven mile of country round. Having stayed a day here we hired a chariot to Breda, eight hours distant.

Richard Holford, 13 (23) August 1671

[19v] After [Bommel] we came to an arm of the Mase, which having crossed, there is a very strong fortification with sconces and a great moat round it, called Crèvecoeur, built by the Hollanders when they besieged the Bosch [1629], and commands the river leading thither. And a little further is Angli [Engelen] sconce, another strong fortification. Afterwards by a great many turnings and windings for [20r] conveniency in avoiding the dikes, we came within half a mile of the Bosch, where our waggon left us and we took boat and went through the lodge to the town, where an officer of the garrison attended our landing and took our country, names and business.

We came thither about six in the evening and were carried to the main guard and there examined. And thence we went to the governor Killpatrick [Kirkpatrick], a Scotchman, to desire a soldier to show us the forts and fortifications. He complimented us and ordered us a soldier. We then went to our lodging at the Emperor upon the fish market, where came to us Captain More, a Scotchman, with whom we drank the King of England's health, the governor and the Duke of York's health and then he took his leave; and before eight we had a sentry set, which continued till the morning at eight when [we] went out.

[20v] At eight Sunday morning, the governor sent a soldier to show us the garrison [...] In the garrison [are] five companies of foot and three of horse, of one hundred each company in a very orderly manner. The soldiers having but five stivers a day.

[21r] We saw the Great Church, where there is the most stately and best organ that I ever saw, the gallery whereof is sixteen yards, and the very bellows cost 2,500 guilders this last year. It has, besides the organ notes, notes that so nearly imitate the voices of old men and women that at a little distance it will deceive the ear; as also the sound of horns and several other notes, and have thirty-eight several.

There is a very fair gallery with several curious pictures of alabaster, and in the chancel or rather a chapel, is the effigies of a priest and archbishop, with this inscription: [blank]. In the town are eleven religious houses of women, none of which but were admitted before the Dutch got the town, and by articles they are to continue during their lives, but no other admitted. And in one of these houses are twenty-five women, all about seventy-five years of age as our soldier informed us. We endeavoured to see them but could not without the stadtholder, because of abuses that had been committed.

[21v] The town house or stadhouse is by the main guard, a good handsome fabric not yet finished, and by it stands a wooden ass for punishing the soldiers. There is a large marketplace and in it, on the Sunday, abundance of apple-shops and herb-shops. The town is not so clean nor [has] so good buildings as other towns in Holland, but is a good old town, the chief trade whereof is stocking making, which they sell to Holland and Flanders. The women handsome and much more fashionable than in other parts of the Low Countries as we have seen. The wall of the town very large and two rows of trees upon the wall and lovely, pleasant walks upon the wall under the trees.

We went Sunday about five or six to see the Dool [Doelen], a place where the townsmen use to meet, and there were several people at ninepins, and in [22r] the house in two large rooms [we saw] at least twelve pair of tables and as many packs of cards; and [Sunday] seems to be the only day they have of pleasure. [cont. Bergen op Zoom and Breda]

William Carstairs, 20 (30) May 1685

[146] On the 20th in the afternoon I went from Dordt and came to the Bosch early next morning, when I had occasion at supper to discourse with a burgomaster of Amsterdam and another gentleman that had lately come from the East Indies, having been in some considerable office at Batavia.

Among other things, we came to speak about the business of Bantam and the ruin of the English factory there [1682], of which the last gentleman gave us an account showing that the old King of Bantam had willingly resigned the government to his son, but would have afterwards reassumed it. Which the son not being willing to part with, a war did thereupon ensue, the father having been assisted by the English and French, the son by the Dutch, who being conqueror would have destroyed the English, but the Dutch interposed for the preserving [of] both their persons and goods, though their factory was from that time ruined in that place.

This gentleman told us that he came in company with a Dutch ambassador from Batavia to Bantam, where they were very civilly received by the king, who was, he said, a man of understanding, but lived like a beast with his wives and mistresses and entertained him almost with no discourse but of them, and that the most immodest, even in the presence of one of the chiefest of them who was sitting by, decked richly with jewels.

He led them also to his father, who was his prisoner. And though he detained him as such, yet when he came into his presence he did him all the honour and obeisance that became a son to do to a father. But falling into discourse with him upon the late business that had been betwixt them, the old man only replied: 'Son, fortune has given you the victory, and there is no place for discoursing those things with the conqueror'. And so would undertake no discourse further upon the subject.

The burgomaster upon this occasion told me what I much wondered at, that the East India Company of Holland had very little advantage by the India trade, they having not above four in the hundred, which he had reason to know, because he himself had a stock in it. He also told me that two or three days before the time of my discourse with him, there [147] had been a friendship made betwixt the King of England and the Prince of Orange. [cont. Maastricht and Aachen]

Edward Southwell, 22-23 May (1-2 June) 1696

[65] When I had done here [Grave], I took horse and rode to Bois-le-Duc. It is six hours from the Grave; I stopped halfway to bait. I found all the roads and the country hereabouts very sandy. I undertook immediately that afternoon to make the tour of the fortifications, but found the place so large I could not do much above the better half. The walls and bastions are after the old manner and the length of the curtains very great. For the strength of the town consists in the inundation, which it commands for a mile and a half around, so that there can no approaches be made. However, I was told that there were some who knew how to drain away the water. It has a good ditch and the abundance of water causes a great deal of river fish.

The castle is a pretty pentagon and commands the town as also the canal which goes by Crèvecoeur into the Maese. There were formerly four or five forts without the town to hinder any approaches to it, but there are only two left, which are but in a bad condition. Those are St Isabella and St Antoine. The [66] first was considerable and had very good double barracks [ditches] and was a pleasant place. The road or causeway lies close to the counterscarp of these forts.

The marketplace is very spacious and has ten streets coming out upon it. The church is large and lofty and worth seeing, and from the top of the steeple you have a good prospect of the whole town and country round. On the battlements of the church are several stone figures carved, of monks and friars in several indecent postures, which they say was the ancient practice of the regular clergy thus to expose to public view the lives and practices of the secular.

This morning I took a view of the Rarityt Kamer, which are two chambers of curiosities that strangers generally visit. One room contains [a] great variety of shells, minerals and many other things of fine work, etc. The other room has nothing but skeletons of all sorts of bodies in very ridiculous postures and habits. There are three brothers who were highwaymen and hanged; two of them are playing at cards the third is smoking and drinking. There is a profuse lady who was reduced to beggary in a silk mantle. A boy that was drowned has an angling rod in his hand and is dressed up with a cravat string and ruffles. There are also pretty contrivances to make these skeletons wag their chops at you and do many antic tricks.

Population: c.12,000 (1660-1720).
Distances: Amsterdam 20 hours (69 miles), Antwerp 16 hours (36 miles), Breda 8 hours (23 miles), Maastricht 20 hours (60 miles), Nijmegen 9 hours (23 miles), Utrecht 12 hours (35 miles).

Inns, *Reisboek* (1689 and 1700): De Nieuwe Doelen; De Keizer, op de Vischmarkt; De Swaan, op de Markt; De Gans, op de Pensmarkt; De Gans, op de Schapemarkt; in Maastrigt. *Reisboek* (1721) and Nugent (1749) no inns mentioned.

Further reading

J. van Oudenhoven, *Beschryvinge der stadt ende Meyerye van 's-Hertogen Bossche*, Amsterdam 1649, 1670.

J.B. Gramaye, *Antiquitates Belgicae*, Bruxelles-Leuven 1708.

Ach Lieve Tijd, 800 jaar Den Bosch en de Bosschenaren, P.J. van der Heijden (ed.), Zwolle 1982-1983.

A. Vos (ed.), *'s-Hertogenbosch: de geschiedenis van een Brabantse stad, 1629-1990*, Zwolle 1997.

Boschboom-bladeren, uitgave van de kring voor geschiedenis en heemkunde 'De Boschboom', 1969-

's-Hertogenbosch, driemaandelijks tijdschrift voor de geschiedenis van 's-Hertogenbosch, 1992-

Ieper and Saint-Omer

White Kennett, 12-13 (22-23) October 1682

[17] Thursday. Borrowed a horse of Monsieur Le Fountaine [at Ardres] and rode to St-Omer. Many crosses and chapelets on the road. At the entrance into the town, stopped by an officer and demanded [18] an account of our names, places of habitation and business. Our horses served with hay by small single trusses at 2d each; a very small measure of oats for 3d. At night our pistols taken from us by the host, and the chamber locked at the outside to prevent our getting out in the night.

Friday. Committed an absurdity in asking for flesh to breakfast. Visited the English convent. The inscription over the gate: *Dieu convert les Anglois*. After admittance conducted by a senior Jesuit through the whole college. A very capacious theatre with an open area, several covered galleries and a convenient stage whereon upon solemn occasions they have public actings. Their school divided into several apartments for each science with a distinct master. Their dormitory in long, large galleries with single beds and each scholar's name wrote over. Their staircase so contrived that by a lamp placed at the bottom the whole ascent is enlightened. Billiard tables and bowling alleys and other conveniences for recreation allowed without liberty of going out of their gates.

After set hours of school, a public, long study for retirement; each scholar his appropriated place with a desk, an inkstand and a crucifix and some picture; the seats so placed as one candle serves four; at the upper end a repository of manuscripts and some other rarities railed off. An infirmitory [19] separate from the other buildings with an apothecary's shop at the end and all other conveniences.

Lads admitted of any age with an allowance of £25 per annum by their parents. Diet, washing etcetera prepared within their own walls by the respective officers, clad in the same apparel and called brethren. Their refectory, set round with several tables for the respective classes, adorned with several pictures. Two balconies raised on each side about the middle, where some scholastic exercises are performed every meal.

Entertained with a gentle breakfast and placed at the same table where [Titus] Oates sat, at the same time he swore to have been in England. Oates branded with many bitter epithets; his degree at Salamanca a notorious sham. He was such an unteachable dunce that to get rid of him from St-Omer they sent him off [on] some message to Valladolid in Spain, where he continued not long before he was expelled, at which time he ran back to England.

View of St-Omer, 1685

The chapel bedecked with very glittering ornaments; yet it was disowned that they paid any religious worship to any of their pictures; my objection of their occasional if not intentional idolatry replied to by an acknowledgement that the common people were to be kept in a devout kind of ignorance, and that the neglect of this piece of policy must needs be repented of by the Church of England.

Many wheedling invitations and winning proposals to tarry and be adopted into their Society being complimentarily dismissed. Visited the abbey church; the rarities most remarkable are the skin and shell of a toad and tortoise, hung opposite to [20] each other of a prodigeous bigness. The north side of the church much battered at the last siege [1677] and repaired at the King of France's charge.

A very large town and by its convenience of situation betwixt France and Flanders a mart of great trade. So great an alteration wrought in the language by its late change of master, that whereas Flemish and Spanish were the only dialects seven years ago, there is now scarce one word spoken or understood but French. Returned in the afternoon to Ardres.

Anonymous tourist, 23-25 July 1720 N.S.

[41v] Set out very early in the morning for Ypres, four leagues off; came there about ten; sandy road. Waited upon [the governor], Count La Leck, who returned us the visit and sent a sergeant with us to show us the fortifications.

Ypres is a pretty large town, but not [42v] much inhabited. It takes its name from a little river [Ieperlee] that has the same name. The works are very numerous on the rising part of the town, which cannot be laid under water; the rest may. It requires a garrison of twenty thousand men in time of siege and it must be a large army that attacks it.

See the cathedral of St Martin, very handsome. Over against the altar, at some distance lies the body of the famous [Cornelis] Jansenius, bishop of that see, who died in 1638. There were formerly ornaments over his tomb, but now nothing but a black stone with this inscription: Hic Jacet [here lies] Jansenius, anno 1638. On the left hand of the chief altar is a picture said to be the first made in oil. The Virgin Mary with Our Saviour in her arms, and this inscription: hic jacet dominus Nicolaus Migena quondam prepositus hujus ecclesiae per Johannem de Heeken, pictorem ducis Burgundiae, anno 1091 [1441] 6 of April in choro positus anno 1441 [here lies Mr N.M., once incumbent of this church; by John van Eyck, painter to the Duke of Burgundy, placed in the choir in 1441]. [43v] This picture is very remarkable upon all accounts, the more one looks at it, the more work one discovers, as many beasts of all sorts running through a wood that makes the landscape of the piece, etc.

Against one of the pillars in the middle of the church is a very curious picture [triptych] of Adam and Eve, which is kept shut up by reason of its indecency, though the natural parts are covered. The attitudes and colours and the design are very good but very ancient, some told us it was the work of Quintus Matteus [Metsys], but it appears of more ancient date. In the sacristy are very rich ornaments. Lodged at Ypres at the Cerf, pretty good house.

24 July. Set out for Cassel at five o'clock in the morning, six leagues off. Came through Poperinge, a large village. Stopped half a league from Cassel to see the monastery of the Recollets that stands on the side of a very high mount called Mount Volure [=Nieuwenbergh]. The garden is quite on the top, from whence one discovers plainly all the neighbouring country on all sides to [44v] Calais, Dunkirk, Newport, Bruges, etc. and deep into the sea, even in fair weather Dover and the coast of England. One of the finest views perhaps in the world.

There is a little place surrounded with trees on this top, where this inscription is placed: Isabella Clara Eugenia, Infans Austriaca, hic pransit [took breakfast here] anno 1627. Walked to Cassel, which lies on another mount still higher, which affords the same agreeable prospect. See the collegiate church of St Martin. Dined at the Court-House, good accommodation. Cassel is a little poor town, well-situated and though it is so high, well-supplied with water.

Set out at three o'clock for St-Omer, four leagues off. Could not find any house that would receive us; were forced to take up with the Damier, a poor house from whence we removed the next day to the Porte d'Or, pretty well. See the cathedral dedicated to St Oudemare [Audomarus], who gives by corruption to the town the name of St-Omer; nothing remarkable but the [45v] organs that are new, very great and beautiful. Over the altar is a fine chest, silver, with the body of St Oudemare.

Went to the English Jesuits, a fine seminary. They have one hundred and twenty pensioners, most of them English. Their house was founded by Philip II, King of Spain. Every year they represent a tragedy with machines, cloths and all other ornaments; we happened to be there at the rehearsal. There are thirty-four fathers and brothers together. They were very civil to us. Saw their library and the great school for their exercises, very handsome.

The abbey of St Bertin, a very large, beautiful church. The model seems to be much the same as that of the college of the canons at Mons, there being a jubé adorned with the four cardinal virtues: Strength, Justice, Prudence and Temperance in marble, well-wrought, and over it Hope, Faith and Charity, also in the marble as it is at Mons. [46v] The altar is magnificent, with fine plates of solid gold, inlaid with precious stones and figures of silver gilt. The gates that shut over it, admirably painted [on] the inside, and as we suppose by the manner done by the same, viz. John de Heeken [Van Eyck or Van der Eecke].

In the sacristy is the treasure of the abbey. Among the rest, the best piece is the head of St Bertin, wrought in silver and painted over in natural colours, admirably. Three flasks of agate, which the clerk told us served in the Temple of Solomon. The nail of a griffin, adorned with gold. In one of the chapels is a picture of St Cecilia playing on the organs, done by Rubens, and a flagellation, well-done, by an unknown master.

Set out in a handsome boat, called a carosse [=coche d'eau], to see the floating islands, about a league off, [47v] great pieces of earth with trees, etc., that float when the water is high, by a strong wind transported to and fro. A little way further is the abbey of Clairmarets [Clairmarais], belonging to the Bernardites, surrounded with very handsome walks, where the people of St-Omer come to make merry now and then. St-Omer is a large rambling town, pretty well fortified. The river Aa runs through it. The English Jesuits have another house at Watten, upon the road to Dunkirk. [cont. Arras and Douai]

Thomas Malie, 30 April - 2 May (11-13 May) 1722

[33] [Calais] Monday the 30th, Mr de Laberdoche came to us at la Table Royale with the postmaster, who procured us coaches for our journey, and to carry us to Ghent; and he gave us the following route, as the most agreeable and curious:

De Calais à Ardres	3 leagues
D'Ardres à St-Omer	5
De St-Omer à Aire	4
D'Aire à Béthune	7
De Béthune à Lille	8
De Lille à Menin	4
De Menin à Courtrai	2
De Courtrai à Gand	6

[34] We took coach at eleven a.m. and set out for Ardres, where we arrived at one p.m., where we dined. At three p.m. we set out for St-Omer and at half past six arrived very safe at our inn, called l'Hotel Royal, where we lay and supped most elegantly. And at eight, Colonel de Saint-Amand came to pay us a visit and offer his services to conduct us round the town and show us whatever was curious and worth seeing at St-Omer. He supped with us and retired at ten.

Tuesday the 1st of May, the colonel called, and breakfasted with us and we took a walk round the town and visited the cathedral and the most [35] magnificent abbey of St Bertin of St Benedict's order, which is well-worth seeing.

St-Omer is the second city in the province of Artois [...] Nature and art assist to render St-Omer strong. [36] There is a strong castle and several round towers in the antique style to be seen within the walls, which are defended by bastions well-faced; half-moons and by very large ditches, done by the famous Vauban, and [it] is one of the strongholds of that country. [...]

[37] The most magnificent abbey of St Bertin, the monks of which follow the rules of St Benoît [38] or St Benedict's order, is well-worth seeing and deserves the attention of all travellers, as it is a masterpiece of architecture. It is dedicated to St Peter [=Bertinus] and is one of the most elegant and beautiful Gothic piles in the whole country. It has a fine large steeple; it is square and very high, from the top of which you may, in a fair day, see the coast of England. It is endowed with upwards of a hundred thousand livres per annum.

The Jesuits have two colleges here: the one for the fathers of the country, and the other for the English Jesuits, both which have a fine seminary. Besides the said two colleges [39] there are several religious houses. [...] [40] Among the suburbs of St-Omer that called the Hautpont is the most beautiful and the most remarkable. It contains upwards of three hundred houses inhabited by Flemish families, who retain their language, law and dress, and marry among themselves.

Ieper
Population: 13,000 (1650), 11,000 (1700-1750).
Distances: Brugge 10 hours (31 miles), Gent 13 hours (42 miles), Kortrijk 5 hours (15 miles), Lille 5 hours (15 miles).
Inns, *Reisboek* (1689): Au Roy de France. *Reisboek* (1700 and 1721): In de Cassellery; In 't Zwaard*; Het Zilvere Hoofd*.

Saint-Omer
Population: 11,000-13,000 (1680), c.17,000 (1690-1750).
Distances: Calais 8 hours (25 miles), Lille 12 hours (35 miles), Ieper 10 hours (33 miles).
Inns, *Reisboek* (1689, 1700 and 1721): L'Ecu de France.

Further reading

J.B. Gramaye, *Antiquitates Belgicae*, Bruxelles-Leuven 1708.

O. Mus and J.A. van Houtte (eds.), *Prisma van de geschiedenis van Ieper*, Ieper 1974.

A. Sanderus, *Flandria illustrata*, Cologne 1641-1644, 's-Gravenhage 1732, 1735 (*Verheerlykt Vlaandre*, 's-Gravenhage 1732, 1735); reprint Antwerpen-Amsterdam 1981.

A. Derville (ed.), *Histoire de Saint-Omer*, Lille 1981.

Bulletin et Mémoires de la Société des Antiquaires de la Morinie, 1858-

Revue du Nord, 1910-

Bijdragen tot de geschiedenis van West-Vlaanderen, 1975-

Kortrijk and Lille

Thomas Penson, 9-13 (19-23) October 1687

[91] Sunday the 9th of October in the morning, we left Ghent and took horse to go to Kortrijk. About a mile without the city there is a very neat small chapel erected to the service of God for the following reason. [92] It happened that about six months before, there was a certain man and his wife had robbed a church and took thence two silver chalices and also eleven consecrated wafers, which so soon as it was discovered, the gates of the city were shut and diligent search made. And in the end the thief was found, who (after being shown the rack) on torture confessed where he had thrown them, which was in a ditch, whence they were taken up, and by a bishop received into the church with great solemnity. The malefactors were condemned to be burned, which was accordingly done. The man especially in a most terrible manner, being burned alive. For the fire did not consume him fast enough, that he made a most lamentable and dreadful moan for a great time. This story I heard at Ghent and saw the chapel, which is frequented by multitudes of people who go to worship there. Thus much for this accidental story.

[93] About one of the clock we came to Kortrijk, where we baited and took fresh horses and arrived at Lille in the evening. We took up our lodging at the Golden Lion, being very weary, having ridden forty and two miles in the space of eight hours.

Monday 10th of October, I was shown the church of the Dominicans and also St Catherine's and St Peter's. Tuesday 11th I saw St Maurice's church and St Stephen's, in which is well-represented the figure of Our Saviour in his sepulchre. Also I was afterwards shown Christ Church [St Sauveur], which is a curious thing. In one of these churches is kept in a gold box some of the milk of the Blessed Virgin. And in another (they tell you) is a piece of the very wood of Our Saviour's cross and divers other relics of saints, with which they go in procession round the walls of the city the first Friday of every month, about five or six of the clock in the morning.

On Wednesday I viewed the citadel or fort (which is very strong), near which is a curious garden where the officers of the guard do solace themselves. At my return from thence I met with a soldier's young child going to be christened, which was after this manner. First came four drums beating, after them a young man bearing in his hand a wax taper. Then came the midwife with the babe and she was followed by the rest of the good women in great order.

Thursday I was shown the ramparts or city-walls, which are of great breadth with walks thereon. And also there is erected a cross, very large with the figure of Our

Saviour affixed thereunto and about him stands three great figures, viz. the Virgin Mary, St John Baptist and Mary Magdalen. The city of Lille is a very ancient [95] city and was formerly in the dominions of the King of Spain. But about sixteen years ago [1667] was seized by the King of France, in whose possession it now remains.

During my stay in this city, I was courteously visited and daily attended by one Mr Haydon (a young gentleman who was placed here to learn the French language) and also by Mr Francis Bernaigain [Brannigan] and Mr Murphy, both students of the Irish college, who were likewise of his acquaintance.

Anonymous tourist, 5-7 August 1711 N.S.

[11] On Wednesday August 5th we went through Deinze, a small fortification of little consequence, and through Harelbeke, another of the same strength but conveniently situated for the river. Near to them was blown up, at a little village called [blank], the powder belonging to the Allies by the French last year. We lay that night at Courtrai, an ill-built town, a garrison town fortified a great while ago, but of no strength in comparison to the new fortifications. But it is of great consequence because it lies upon the Lys and cuts off all communication by water between the northern part of Flanders and Menin, Lille, etc.

On Thursday August 6th, we came to Menin, a very indifferent town and almost all ruined in the siege it maintained against the Allies in 1706, but the fortifications are extraordinary fine and costly. The water surrounds it so that it can't be attacked but on one side, which is defended by very regular and strong works. From thence we came the same day to Lille, an extraordinary fine-built town and a place of great trade, but much decayed since taken from the French [1708] by reason of the separation from the port of Dunkirk, where the citizens used to import their commodities and vend all over Flanders, which brought in a great revenue to the French.

[12] The streets of Lille are very pleasant and fine and the Exchange very pretty but very small. The Dominicans have a fine chapel, built of a very good sort of freestone, after the manner of the Jesuits' chapel at Antwerp, but no ways too well adorned, the west front excepted, which is extraordinary fine. The Great Church of St Peter is a very strange, old, Gothic building, but the inside looks very well; on the north side is a fine altar with the tomb of the last Count of Flanders [Louis II van Male] of brass, very costly. The Capuchins have a very lightsome chapel, consisting of only one aisle prettily adorned. The Jesuits have a very handsome chapel and very well painted, but the best thing is the building of the houses and regularity of the streets. The fortifications are very fine and strong and the citadel a very regular and costly fort, consisting of five bastions and said to be built all upon piles, but I see no signs of it but by a great work made by the French when it was besieged. It seems to be very firm ground.

John Leake, 21-22 June (2-3 July) 1712

[45r] [from Douai] Early the next morning we bent our course towards Lille. We were scarce got in the midway between these two cities, when we were stopped by a French party of the garrison of Maubeuge. They were a little rough with us at first, and one of our company had like to have been taken from us on the account of his being too militarily clothed. But after they had read our passes and found we were English, they changed their notes and were all complaisance.

The common fate of travellers, hunger and thirst, assaulting us, we made up to a little cottage in a wood to see what we could get towards the satisfying those uneasy companions. We were not long in taking our repast, for mouldy bread and some beer were the best of our entertainment.

As we drew near to the fair city of Lille, we found there had been a rencounter between a French and a Dutch party, in which the former being superior in number to the latter, they were forced to fly; which occasioned the garrison of that place drawing out under arms to sustain their companions. In the midst of this hurry we entered the town, without having the usual interrogation put to us of 'Whence did you come?' and 'Whither do you go?'. Being provided with good quarters and having bespoke our dinner, we got a guide to go about the town with us.

The first thing we did was to inquire out our banker, whom having found, [45v] we tendered our bill and had it honoured upon sight. We went next to the citadel, and having obtained leave of the commander, we were permitted to take a particular view of this beautiful and complete piece of modern fortification. It seemed to take up an English half-mile and better in compass; its outworks and buildings were in very good order and faced with good brick and freestone. The only damage it received in the late siege [1708] was upon one of its gates, where the arms of France were broken by the flight of a ball or two.

The Exchange is a small square and the walks below too much choked up with shops. Its trade is considerably abated since it fell into the Confederates' hands, and its beautiful regular streets looked melancholy and tending apace to desolation. The people here are extremely civil and well-bred, especially the women who have something inimitably sweet and obliging in their manners and carriage.

On Sunday morning June the 22nd, we got out of our inn betimes, in hopes to have reached Ghent that night, but coming to the ports we found them shut, and we were obliged to wait an hour before the guards were relieved, or we suffered [allowed] to proceed on our journey. We debated whether we should go by Menin or Courtrai; the latter was the way pitched upon, and we arrived there about noon.

This town is situated in a very pleasant country, but ill-fortified. The commanding officer here was a Scotchman and the garrison mostly English. We had some of their company at dinner, which ended, we entered our berlines again. Our horses beginning to tire and our drivers little better, we were constrained to stop short of

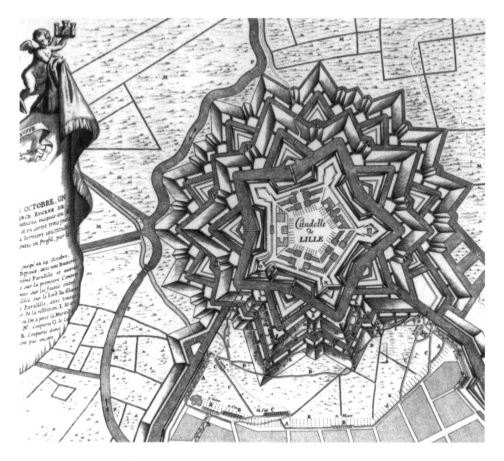

Lille. Citadel, 1709

Ghent three leagues, at a village called Deinze, [46] where we found the people very merry in a procession, and we were screened from a tempestuous night very opportunely. [cont. Gent]

Anonymous tourist, 17-22 July 1720 N.S.

[39] Set out in the afternoon [from Tournai] for Lille in a coche at four o'clock, five short leagues; fine paved road, very plentiful country for corn of all sorts and hay. Came to Lille at eight o'clock.

See the citadel, a regular pentagon with ravelins between each two bastions, a fine esplanade between it and the town. They call it here *La belle inutile*, because it is not upon a ground sufficiently raised to command the town. There is on each side a wall built with a parapet that reaches the town. In each ravelin there is *une contregarde*. The magazine of arms, sufficient for sixteen thousand men that is in the citadel, is kept in very good order.

18 July. See the church of St Etienne: ordinary; that of the Dominicans pretty fine façade, a mount in the garden remarkable for its singularity. See the library, pretty good; in it many ancient books. [40] Commentum magistri Jo. Dorp super textu summularum magistri Jo. Buridani. Impressum per Jo. Corcagni, Anno Domini 1493 [Commentary by John Dorp on the epitome of dialectics by master Jean Buridan; printed by Jean Carcain at Lyon]. An ancient Bible MS in three volumes folio, written by one of their order at Lille in 1264.

See the Conclave, which is the place in the town house where the magistrates meet [palais de Rihour], with three good pictures of Arnauld [de Vuez], who died two years ago. The convent of the Carmes Chaussés; the refectory mighty handsome paved with marble; a very beautiful picture of the same Arnauld: Our Lord at table and Magdalen wiping his feet with her hair. They were so extravagant in their expenses for this refectory and kitchen, etc. that they are not in a condition to finish their church, which remains half-built.

21 July. Dined with Mr Le Camus at his country house and Mr Devenitz. We hired a berline at Lille with two horses at sixteen florins a day and set out with it at six o'clock in the morning (22 July) for Menin, three leagues. There we arrived about ten; walked on the ramparts and saw all the fortifications; the road extraordinary good and a fine rich country. Dined with Mr [41] Beverweerd, Count [Maurits Lodewijk van Nassau-] La Leck's son, who supped with us at the Chapeau Rouge, indifferent house. The fortifications on all sides were made by Mr Vauban, and since they are in the hands of the Allies, improved by a line, behind which a whole army may encamp, and everything before it be set under water.

Menin is a little inconsiderable town; suffered much by the siege that lasted five weeks [1706]. The Lys runs through it. It was attacked at the gate of Ypres, which is looked upon to be the weak part of the fortifications, which otherwise are very beautiful. The pavilions for the officers and caserns for the soldiers are very handsome. The arsenal, in great order, contains arms for nine thousand men. [cont. Ieper and Saint-Omer]

Kortrijk

Population: 8,800 (1700).

Distances: Gent 8 hours (23 miles), Lille and Ieper 5 hours (15 miles), Tournai 5 hours (15 miles).

Inns, *Reisboek* (1689): Aux trois Rois*. *Reisboek* (1700 and 1721) also: Den Oven*; Den Gouden Appel*; 't schild van Vrankrijk; 't Schaakbord; Het Zwaard*.

Lille

Population: 45,000 (1677), 60,000 (1700), 50,000 (1709).

Distances: Dunkirk 13 hours (40 miles), Gent 13 hours (38 miles), Kortrijk and Tournai 5 hours (15 miles), Menen 3 hours (8 miles), Ieper 5 hours (15 miles).

Inns, *Reisboek* (1689, 1700 and 1721): In de drie Koningen*. *Reisboek* (1700 and 1721): De Groene Ruiter (op de Steenweg); Le Palais Royal*, bij de Place St Martin.

Further reading

J.B. Gramaye, *Antiquitates Belgicae*, Bruxelles-Leuven 1708.

Louis Trenard, *Histoire de Lille*, 3 vols., Toulouse 1970-1991.

A. Sanderus, *Flandria illustrata*, Cologne 1641-1644, 's-Gravenhage 1732, 1735 (*Verheerlykt Vlaandre*, 's-Gravenhage 1732, 1735); reprint Antwerpen-Amsterdam 1981.

N. Maddens (ed.), *De geschiedenis van Kortrijk*, Tielt 1990.

Handelingen van de Koninklijke Geschied- en Oudheidkundige Kring te Kortrijk, 1903-
Revue du Nord, 1910-

Leiden

William Lord Fitzwilliam, June 1663

[27v] From Haarlem we went by water to Leiden, the chiefest and biggest town, excepting Amsterdam, of Holland, lying as it were in the heart of it amongst very pleasant meadows; the river Rhine runs by it. Here is one [28r] of the most famous universities of Europe, not so much for colleges (wherewith Oxford and Cambridge abound), but by reason of its diligent and learned professors of all sort of sciences and their method of teaching young youth. The founder of it was William, Prince of Nassau, anno 1575, 6 [8] February. The foundation was according to this following manner. The people came all down out of the town house, a woman in white did ride before in a waggon, holding a bible in her right hand, being accompanied by the four Evangelists; this did signify Theology. Afterwards followed Jurisprudentia, riding on an unicorn, clad like Justice used to be painted. She was accompanied by Julianus, Papinianus, Ulpianus and Tribonianus, the chiefest authors of the Law. Medicina did follow afterwards on horseback, with Hippocrates, Galenus, Dioscorides and Theophrastus. Pallas with a lance and a shield in her hands followed in the last place, with Plato, Aristotle, Cicero and Virgilius. Afterwards followed the people and the professors in their order. There was likewise set a ship upon the Rapenburg, with Neptune, Apollo and the nine Muses playing and singing.

The university was founded here because the town did so valiantly hold out against the Spaniards and did rather choose to [28v] eat rats, cats or any other thing than to render itself to the cruel Duke of Alva. The money which they did use in the time of the siege [1574] was of paper with this inscription on it: Pugno pro Patria [I fight for my country], it is yet to be seen in the Anatomy School.

Here is a pretty little library, but the Anatomy School is very famous and excellent. I do not think there is any one like it in Europe; it is full of all sort of rarities. Here you will see the anatomy and skeleton of any animal, European, Asiatic, African or American, some rare mummies or embalmed bodies of a King and Queen of Egypt. Here are many idols and strange fashioned clothes and weapons, all sort of minerals and strange coins, many other rarities, which may better be seen than be written. Here we found these following verses made upon the praise of a salt herring: [poem in Latin].

[29r] The college where the university is, is but little. The public schools are yet big enough. Upon the steeple of this college we saw a curiosity in optics: things without [outside], represented within a dark chamber which has but one little hole,

Town hall, 1670

where the light comes in. Here is likewise a great quadrant to be seen. Below, within the limits of the college, there is the physic [botanical] garden, which is full of all sort of plants, shrubs and trees. For them that cannot endure the cold winter climate of Holland is heated a long gallery on purpose for to keep and preserve them. By this garden is likewise a chamber of rarities, of which some are in the Anatomy School.

In this town the Prince of Orange has a palace, a very mean one [Prinsenhof]. Here is likewise a castle, called the Burg, built, as some say, by the Romans, but others (which is more like) by Hengist, a Saxon King after his conquest of England. This place lies on an artificial hill, very pleasant: within there is a labyrinth and a very deep well and the going up to it is very pleasant.

The town house is a pretty building, but will be much handsomer within a short time. Here is a good clock to be seen and within the house many precious pictures, chiefly them of Cornelis Engelbert's [Engelbrechtsz] and Lucas of Leiden's making. Here is likewise a very great Dool [Doelen], or shooting house and yard,

three or four good churches of which St Peter's is the [29v] chiefest, all full of epitaphs. Here are likewise many hospitals and pious houses, several fair streets as
the Brede Street [Breestraat] and the Rapenburg, a great fish marketplace. For the
houses, there are a good store of great houses, all the rest well and uniformly built.
This town is likewise surrounded with good strong walls and deep ditches, but
chiefly with very pleasant walks, set with trees; and a very long and well-made
pall-mall is not far from the gates of this town; and this is all that I did observe in
Leiden. [cont. The Hague]

Thomas Penson, 21 (31) July 1687

[21] The next place we designed for was Leiden, to which we repaired by the next
opportunity, whereat when we arrived (after having refreshed), went straight to
the Academy to see those rarities which remain there.

[22] So soon as we entered the place, each person had a book given into his
hand, printed in English, containing an account of each particular thing and the
marks of the distinct places and presses wherein they were. Here I beheld the wonderful works of our Great Creator, composed and set together by the art of man. At
my first approach I was struck with an awful admiration, almost questioning within myself whether I should dare to go in or no. For as in a wood we behold trees in
great numbers stand confusedly together, so here appeared (as it were) an army of
the bones of dead men, women and children, which seemed so to stare and grin at
us, as if they would instantly make us such as themselves.

And because I would render this eminent collection worthy the observation of
any ingenious person who travels that way, I shall here insert some of the particulars, viz. [23] the skeleton of a French nobleman, who ravished his sister and afterwards murdered her; the skeleton of an ass, upon which sits that of a woman who
killed her daughter; the skeleton of a woman of seventeen years old who murdered
her son; the skeleton of a sheep stealer of Haarlem; the skeleton of a woman who
was strangled for theft; the skeleton of a man who hanged himself.

The skeleton of a pirate. The skeleton of a man on horseback. The skeleton of a
new-born child. The skeleton of a child but four months in the womb. The skeleton
of a man sitting on an ox who was executed for stealing cattle. A great bone found
in the body of a woman of ninety years old. Also the skin of a man dressed as
parchment. [...] [24] A dried arm of a blackamoor. The arm of a great Egyptian hero.
The bladder of a man containing more than two gallons of water. The skull of a
moor who was killed at the beleagering of Haarlem, made into a drinking cup. The
mummy of an Egyptian prince above thirteen hundred years old. [...]

And as if those were not terrible enough to fill up this frightful scene, there also
appears in the crowd the skeletons of two bears, the skeleton of a wolf, of a horse,
[25] a cow, a buck, a hart, a baboon, a cat, a rat, a hog, an ape, the skeletons of two
greyhounds, of a ferret, a dog, an otter. Also the heads of elephants, and of the wild

boars and the fierce lion and the rhinoceros, etc. [...] And after this, as if the earth produced not sufficient diversity of creatures, the sea contributes to this curious collection, by casting in the skeleton of a young whale taken out of the old one's belly. The head of the swordfish, enemy to the whale. The hide of a seahorse. The snout of a sawfish whose teeth are in [the] form of a saw. [...] [26] And to make this collection the more complete, there remains also: the skeletons of the eagle, the swan, the cock, the pigeon, the lapwing, the Egyptian night-owl, the shoveller, the chaffinch, the heron, the badger, the dove, etc. With many strange stones found in the heads and stomachs [27] of several creatures.

Likewise the eggs of serpents and crocodiles. Strange flies and spiders. And Roman urns above a thousand years old. With multitudes of other strange things from divers parts of the world, too tedious here to mention, but all setting forth in an extraordinary manner the wonderful works of Almighty God.

Thus, having taken a special view of those things, which I did not hastily hurry over but passed deliberately from one to the other, and not without some serious and considerate thoughts, I then purchased the book containing the particulars thereof and having gratified the young man that attended us, we took our leave. But certainly none can be spectators of these admirable works of the Great God, without a holy reverence and fear as [28] well as mortified thoughts and apprehensions. I am sure the memory of them did not soon depart from me and even now at the writing hereof make some fresh impressions of that which indeed every one of us ought at all times to keep in remembrance, viz. that we must certainly die, etc.

We afterwards took a short view of Leiden, which is a place very pleasant, then we rested and refreshed. And about eleven of the clock at night, the scuyt being ready to go off and some of our company having urgent business at Amsterdam, myself, also having letters to deliver there, went with them all night (having for two stuyvers a cushion to lay my head on) so about six in the morning we arrived safe at the famous city of Amsterdam. [cont. Amsterdam]

John Farrington, 13-16 September 1710 N.S.

[10] We came to Leiden at about eight o'clock that evening, where we got an entrance by paying sixpence for the waggon, and a penny apiece for ourselves to the porter at the gate, which is always done after the gates are shut, which is as soon as it grows duskish. Lodged at Colliard's [Colyear], a Scotch house at the sign of the Scotch Arms in the Broad Street [Breestraat], the best house in town, except the Prince of Brandenburgh, excessive dear. Colliard's pretty reasonable.

Here we stayed on Sunday September 14th and heard Mr [Robert] Milling, the minister of the English church, which is established there on the account of the gentlemen of the three nations [English, Scots and Irish] that frequent their university. The weather since we had been in Holland hitherto was tolerably good, only a little showery. On Sunday indeed it cleared up, and it was a very fine day.

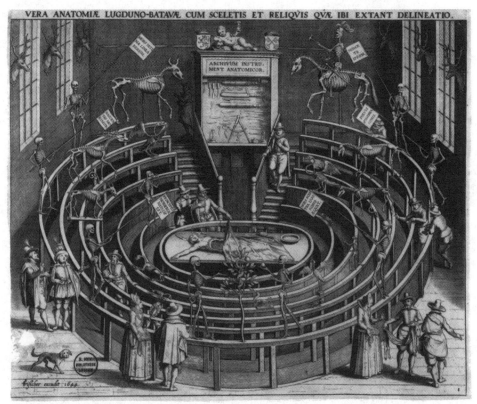

Anatomical theatre, 1644

On Monday September 15th we had determined to go to The Hague and hired chaises for that purpose, but there fell so great a rain that quite diverted us from that design, and therefore we took that opportunity of viewing several of the curiosities of this city.

The first place that we saw was the Anatomy Theatre, which is just behind the English church, which, though it was always worth seeing, yet is now made much more considerable by the large addition of professor [Govert] Bidloo's curiosities [bought in 1696]. There are indeed several very [11] admirable curiosities, both of art and nature, which I shall save myself the labour of transcribing, by transmitting you the printed catalogue of them. Next we saw the Botany Garden, which belongs to the university and is situated just behind the public schools. This garden has as great a repute for rare and [exotic] plants as most in Europe, but the time of year was past for observing several of them. There is here also a cabinet of rarities. There you see the hippopotamus or sea cow, described in [William] Dampier, to which I refer you as a very exact description; a West Indian cow, with a strange bunch like a camel's on its back, which was for some time alive since it was in the city; a large West Indian snake, taken notice of by Misson in his *Voyage to Italy*; the materia medica, which are about three hundred different ingredients, out of which the whole practice of physic [medicine] is taken.

Thence we walked up the Bergh or Mount, which is placed much about the middle of the city and said to be thrown up and inclosed with a wall by Julius Caesar. It is a considerable height, about sixty stone steps to the top of it. In the middle is a labyrinth, but the leaves, being fallen from the hedges made it not a difficult matter to find one's way out of it. It is enclosed with a wall, with a breast-wall before it, whereon you may walk two or three abreast. It was designed as a fort and was strong enough in the Roman times, while swords and slings and darts were their weapons. In this place is a well that is covered over, where they tell you in the time of the Spanish War in 1573 [1574], a fish was caught when the town was in great extremity for want of provision, which they showed to the Spaniards from their wall to let them see they had fresh fish still in town, to the great amazement of their enemy, who wondered from whence such [12] supplies should come.

The next place that we saw was the stadthuys, or the Guildhall of the city. It is a long large handsome building. In the chamber where the burgomasters meet, there is a very curious picture of the Resurrection [Last Judgement], done by Lucas van Leyden, of an immense value. Over the chimney of the same room is a fine piece of Liberty or Freedom, where is an empress who is said to have desired the government of the empire only for twenty-four hours, in which time she took occasion to cut off her husband's head. In the next chamber, which was that of the Raadtsheers or Council of State, is the famous chest of the Synod of Dort [Dordrecht], wherein lies the manuscript of the Bible [translation], which they visit with so much solemnity twice in five years. The visitation was made this year with the usual solemnity (see an account of it in Mr Locke's *Letters*, latter end). And on the top of the chest stands a noble bible that was printed from that manuscript, though it is a wonder that so noble and precious a depositum could be trusted with any prince of the world. The curators of the university have also a chamber in the same house, where there is a good piece of Pallas over the door and Prudence over the chimney.

Under the stadthuys is the Flesh-Hall where all the meat must be sold. There they have the picture of an ox which was shown for a sight and afterwards killed; it weighed about fourteen hundred pounds weight. There is a considerable quantity of flesh in that hall, but nothing comparable to the least of our markets in London. But such is the regularity of the Dutch government, all meat must be sold there, and inspected by proper officers, that no rotten or meanly meat may be sold to the ignorant or foolish buyer. And there are only such and [13] such hours in the day, when their hall is open, I think from ten to twelve in the morning and two to four in the afternoon.

The Spinhouse or prison for criminals is a very noble building. Here they put all guilty of capital or petty crimes. The former are confined, and no one is admitted to see them. The latter may be seen where they are kept to hard labour, according to the difference of their age, sex, crime, etc. Here the lewd women are confined for such a term of years as the magistrates think fit and are kept to work, so that they have no victuals if they do not earn it. But though they are confined, by their words and behaviour there is but little sign of reformation and amendment.

But the principal glory of this town is its University, which was founded by the Prince of Orange in the year 1573 [1575], on this occasion. When the Spaniards had overrun almost all Holland, Leiden was straitly besieged by them and reduced to the last extremity by famine, and the usual consequence of that, a great mortality, so that, the inhabitants mutinying within and the enemy pressing from without, the town was on the point of surrender, and had done it. Only one of the burgomasters withstood it at the hazard of his life. But the Prince of Orange, cutting the banks, and coming in boats over the lands with a supply of provisions, and a part of the wall falling down, which the Spaniards looked upon as done with a design to sally out upon them, though said to be merely casual, struck so great a terror into them, that they immediately fled in the utmost disorder, and the town retrieved, and Holland saved from [14] ravage and destruction, which would have followed the taking of that town. For the brave defence they had made for their country's liberty, and the hazard to which they had exposed themselves, the Prince offered them either to give them so many years immunity from taxes, or to found an university with several privileges annexed to it, which latter the inhabitants wisely chose as like to be of advantage, not only for a term of years, but for perpetuity; and accordingly the university was founded on the same year 1573 [1575].

The schools are all in one large building, where the several professors read their public lectures, and wherein degrees in all faculties are given. There are no colleges as at Oxford or Cambridge, but every scholar lives where he pleases. Only one Dutch college there is for the poorer sort, where every nation has two chambers for poor scholars of that nation, but few I think accept of them, except Polanders and Hungarians, and of that society Doctor [Franciscus] Fabritius is the present rector.

There are in this university sixteen professors, besides praelectors, four in divinity, law and physic [medicine], and two in languages, two in oratory. The privileges which this university enjoys, and the honourableness of the station, draw both the most valuable professors from other universities and a great number of scholars hither.

And there are at present several professors of very great note in almost all faculties, as Boerhaave for physic [medicine], Voet and Vitriarius for civil law, Perizonius for history and criticism. Divinity indeed has not so famous professors at present as it used to have when Witsius and Trigland were alive, but [15] Marck and Fabritius are very far from being contemptible. They have not yet begun their public lessons, so I cannot give you any account of them, but tomorrow there will be a funeral oration in memory of an old professor in law [Antonius Matthaeus], which, if the weather continues thus bad, I shall be present at, if not, I design to improve by seeing The Hague.

Tuesday September 16th. The happy alteration of this weather to a clear and cold day from an excessive rain has made us resolve to go for The Hague and to take a view of the curiosities round about. We have accordingly given orders to have three chaises got ready, and while preparing I shall have time to end the description of Leiden.

The city is very large and ancient, the second for bigness in Holland. It is above three English miles in circumference. Without [outside] the fortifications, which are no other than a broad and deep ditch and a wall with some bastions, is a very good cingle or walk, regularly planted with lime trees on each side, where you may walk dry in a moderate shower of rain. The buildings of this town are good, especially in the principal streets, which are very neat. The streets are for the most part broad and regular. Abundance of canals in the city, and those planted on each side with elms. These make the air damp, and the city is said to be the less wholesome, at least it was before the waters were moved, which now they are by mills which bring in fresh water in ten days' time.

As to their religion, which is the same in all this province, it is Calvinist, only there is an unlimited toleration. There are four large Dutch [16] churches; the principal is St Peter's, one English, one Dutch [i.e. German] or Lutheran church, one French and one Minist [Mennonite] or Baptist congregation, besides a great number of Popish chapels.

The trade of this town is chiefly the woollen manufactory, but since the war with France [1702-1714], their trade is dead and the town much impoverished. The chief buildings are the stadthouse, churches, University, Cloth Hall, which is the same with them as Blackwell Hall is with us. And the hofjes, or courts where the poor live, which are about twenty-five in number. These have eight or ten or some of them more apartments with little gardens to them and are mighty pleasant and convenient as well as a great advantage to the poor of this city.

I should have told you, that the music of the chimes which consist of between thirty and forty bells, is very agreeable, and that the organs in the Great Church are mighty harmonious, and as played upon three evenings in a week, afford the inhabitants a great deal of diversion. But our chaises are ready and I must lose no time, therefore I conclude thus abruptly, only, Sir, have still time to assure you that I am your very humble servant. [cont. The Hague]

Sir John Percival 4-5 (15-16) July 1718

[71v] The University of Leiden, like others of these provinces, has not any students upon foundations as those of Oxford and Cambridge have with us, but [they] lodge in private houses and repair at stated hours to the lectures held by the professors of those sciences they choose to apply themselves to. When that is over they are perfect masters of themselves, being subject to no discipline or forms. They have several small privileges, as to be excused paying the yearly duties due to the city and State

upon half a tun of beer and the quarterly duty upon forty quarts of wine.

Their greatest privilege, and which I think indeed too great, considering they are under no proper regulation, is that in case of quarrels and even murder they are exempt from the jurisdiction of the criminal court, and can be tried only before the Rector Magnificus of the university, assisted by four assessors, four burgomasters and two sheriffs or judges, who are generally observed to suffer the guilty person to make his escape.

But neither this nor other privileges are allowed them unless they cause themselves to be admitted [72r] members of the university, and their names be annually entered in the matriculate book by the Rector above mentioned and his secretary, who then engages to maintain them in their rights above mentioned. This costs the persons so admitted a very small matter.

The present professors are fifteen in number of whom three are professors of divinity, three of civil law, one of philosophy, one of the Oriental languages, two of the Greek tongue, history, eloquence and liberal sciences and five of physic [medicine]. Among the civilians Mr Noodt, a great republican, is eminent, and among the physicians Dr Boerhaave. This last, I was told, gets three thousand pounds sterling yearly by his lectures and practice, which is a great deal in a country where fees are no higher than a shilling or seven pence each visit. But the English who consult him pay him more generously. [...]

[73r] The town house stands in one of the broadest streets of the city and is a handsome old pile of building. The magistrates have therein their several offices for transacting public business and from thence issue all orders that concern the government of the city. The rooms are but meanly furnished, yet there are two or three good paintings, and among the rest a celebrated piece of Lucas van Leyden; the subject is the Last Judgement. It is extraordinarily well preserved, though of [73v] great antiquity, for that painter died in 1533. He was famous in his time though he never travelled further to perfect himself than to Flanders. There are several of his [en]gravings, in which art he so well imitated Albert Durer that they contracted a great intimacy. He fancied himself poisoned by a rival in his art and throwing himself into a milk diet, languished for six years and then deceased thirty-nine years old. [...]

[74r] The burghers (far happier in this respect than the subjects of Great Britain) without the obligation of calling lawyers to their assistance, plead their own causes before these burgomasters, and a speedy end is put to their differences. The court of sheriffs takes cognizance both of civil and criminal causes. In it the great bailiff presides, and it is only before him that the lawyers are allowed to plead. He has under him two deputies or lieutenants, who, with inferior officers called *dienders*, have charge to seize on criminals and carry them to prison. Thither the sheriffs repair to examine them of the facts laid to their charge. When they refuse to own the crime of which by several circumstances they are suspected to be guilty, they are put on the rack, which generally extorting a confession, they are afterwards execut-

ed at the instance of the great bailiff.

But sometimes persons have been known so fond of life and so courageous under pain as to bear the repeated tortures inflicted on them without confessing, by which they escaped the death [74v] they deserved. Of this there was an instance when I was at The Hague, where a desperate villain lay in jail, guilty, in the full persuasion of all the people, of several murders charged against him; for they were sworn to by eyewitnesses. Yet he, knowing that death could not pass on him by the law unless he owned his crimes, endured the rack twice before my arrival, and while I was there, underwent it a third time. He had such power over himself as not to cry out, only he fetched deep sighs. He openly upbraided his judges and executioners, bidding [them to] do their worst, and triumphed that he should be too hard for them, for that after this third and last trial they could do no more to him. But I was afterwards informed that the magistrates came to a resolution still to continue him in prison, till some pretence could be found to put him to death consistent with law.

It is justly to be doubted from such instances as these, whether the rack be a proper means of coming at the truth. Especially since it has been observed that tender and fearful persons, overcome by pain or terror, have confessed [to] crimes they [75r] were not guilty of, and thereupon been executed. I heard a melancholy instance of this when at Rotterdam, in which city a person returning home from an entertainment where he had drunk too much, laid himself down in the street and fell asleep. It happened that a murderer, fresh come from killing a man, passed that way, and observing this man asleep, thrust his bloody knife into his pocket and went his way. The night-watch going their rounds and seeing this unhappy man upon the ground, raised him up and examining his pockets, discovered the knife.

He not being able to account for its being there, was hurried before the magistrate, and nothing he could say or his friends allege in his behalf, prevent his being put to the rack, for the circumstance was pregnant against him. Under the torture he owned whatever they would have him and thereupon he suffered death. Not long after, the murderer was taken in a new crime, and being condemned confessed at the place of execution the murder above mentioned, and that he had put the knife into the innocent man's pocket. [...]

[75v] The polite arts are yet subsisting here. [76r] Mr [Carel de] Moor and Mr [Van] Mieris are two very good painters in their way. The first for faces, the other for small history. Mr Smeltzing is eminent for carving and striking medals, Mr [Johan van] Musschenbroeck for microscopes and mathematical instruments and Mr Vermey for casting busts and other figures in plaster.

Of these and other men's works, Mr [Pieter de] La Court, a gentleman of Flemish extraction and originally of the town of Lier, has an eminent collection. He is a curious man and very rich. Though entire strangers to him and his lady, he civilly invited us to breakfast and afterwards showed us three rooms full of good paintings: the works of Gerard Dou, Polemberg [Cornelis van Poelenburch],

Rubens, Carlo Lotti [Carlotti], [Jan] Velvet Breughel, Rosa of Tivoli [Philip Peter Roos], Horisonte [Jan Frans van Bloemen, alias Orizonte], [Frans van] Mieris the father and son [Willem van Mieris], etc. There are several pieces of flowers and fruit by Mrs [Rachel] Ruysch, now residing at Amsterdam, which are excellent in their kind; her price is according.

Population: 60,000 (1650), 70,000 (1690), 65,000 (1720), 60,000 (1732).

Distances: Amsterdam 8 hours (19 miles), Delft 3 hours (9 miles), Gouda 5 hours (16 miles), Haarlem 5 hours (12 miles), The Hague 3 hours (9 miles), Rotterdam 5 hours (18 miles), Utrecht 10 hours (30 miles).

Inns, *Reisboek* (1689, 1700 and 1721): Den Burgt, of 't Heeren-Logement; De Vergulde Posthoorn*, De Goude Leeuw* (both opposite 't Stadhuis); De Swaan, op de Haarlemmerstraat* [1721: aan 't Haarlemmer Veer].

Reisboek (1689 and 1700): De voorste Doelen; 't Schild van Vrankrijk (op de Breestraat tegenover 't Stadhuis); 't Schild van Vrankrijk in 't Noord Einde; 't Witte Hart of Engelsch Ordinaris, op de Paapen-Gracht. *Reisboek* (1700) also: De agterste Doelen; De Beurs van Amsterdam, aan 't Haarlemmer Veer; en bij de poorten bequame Logementen.

Reisboek (1721): De Gouden Wagen*, in 't Noordeinde; 't Wapen van Gelderland*, bij de Witte Poort; De Witte Hond en de Zwarte, bij de Hoogwoerds Poort; De Stadsherberg, De Goudse Trekschuit (both on 't Utrechtse Veer); In Rustenburg, aan de Rijnsburgse Poort; De Post in de Star, op 't Rotterdamse Veer; De Drie Haringen, bij de Waag; De Verkeerde Pot, in de Mandemakers-steeg.

Nugent (1749) also: The Golden Ball, an English House by one Macarty on the Papengraft.

Further reading

J. Orlers, *Beschrijvinge der stad Leyden*, Leiden 1614, 1641, 1760.

S. van Leeuwen, *Korte besgryving van het Lugdunum Batavorum, nu Leyden*, Leiden 1672.

[P. van der Aa], *Les délices de Leide*, Leiden 1712.

G. Goris, *Les délices de la campagne à l'entour de la ville de Leide*, Leiden 1712, 1743.

F. van Mieris, *Beschryving der stad Leyden*, Leiden 1762-1784.

P.J. Blok, *Geschiedenis eener Hollandsche stad*, 4 vols., 's-Gravenhage 1910-1918.

Hutspot, haring en wittebrood, tien eeuwen Leiden en de Leienaars, D.E.H. de Boer (ed.), Leiden 1981-1982.

Jaarboekje voor geschiedenis en oudheidkunde van Leiden en omstreken, 1904-

Liège, Spa and Namur

William Carstairs, 9-12 (19-22) June 1685

[151] June 9. I went from Aken [Aachen] to Maastricht, and next day from thence to Luik [Liège] by water, in a large boat drawn by five horses. We were seven hours long upon our way, but it is exceeding pleasant through the hills on both sides, covered either with wood or corn. One may have meat and drink aboard. I went out at a place a mile on this side [of] Liège called Herstal, from whence you can go on foot much sooner than by the boat to Liège. It belongs to the Prince of Orange, but the inhabitants are Papists.

Liège is a great and very well-peopled city. It lies part upon a plain along the river Maas, which divides it, over which there is a very fair bridge of stone, and part on pleasant hills, on one of which [152] the English Jesuits have a very fine house, and a curious garden, lying upon the side of a high hill towards the south. And that [garden lies] above the house, though even before you come to the house you must go up near fourscore steps from the ground. The garden has pleasant parterres and walks, one above the other to a considerable height.

Upon a very high hill overtopping the city, the Prince is building a citadel to keep it in subjection. There was indeed one there before, but in the year 1672 it was taken and demolished by the French in part, but wholly by the citizens [1676], who were glad to have that restraint upon their liberties taken away. But through their late divisions among themselves grounded upon their liberties, the Prince has got his will of them and has built a kind of a fort in fashion of a gate upon the middle of the bridge, in which he has some pieces of cannon and some few soldiers. This he did to keep the two parts of the town from meeting together.

He has laid a sore tax upon the city for defraying the expenses of his fortifications and other things. But it is thought that this city will not remain long in peace. They told me that it, together with its district, which is but a small bounds, can send forth upon a necessary occasion above a hundred thousand fighting men. Here I saw the iron mills; and how they make the pots, which they send in great quantities to all places. Here they also make alum and have abundance of coal and wood.

Here I saw also a solemn procession, which I bless God did convince me afresh of the folly of Popery. There are scarce any Protestants in this city. Yet I was told by one that has traded with this place near forty years, that there are many that out of fear own Popery, who if occasion did offer, would profess the reformed religion. [...] I was told that about five or six miles from Liège there is a large village the most of the inhabitants of which are Protestants.

Spa. Sauvenière, c. 1625

[153] On June 12th, I went from Liège to Spa, which is about six or seven hours. The way for some miles beyond Liège is very hilly, but afterwards it is pretty pleasant through grounds, part heathy part cornland, but within view (and at no great distance) of hills clothed with wood. When you come near to the Spa, you have for a long way a descent from the tops of high hills, which go in a range almost round the town, but pleasant because of the woods that cover them. It is true, there are in many places but short bushes of oak, yet often they are intermixed with trees, which make the place very convenient for retiring.

There are four wells: the one is in the middle of the town, of which all, almost, drink, another is about a mile and a half out of the town, hard by a wood. The other two are about the same distance from the town on the other side, in the midst of a wood, a little way one from the other. There is a pleasant garden of the Capuchiners, where drinkers of the waters generally walk, and from thence about ten o'clock, such as please go to prayers in the Capuchiners' Church hard by; and from thence to dinner, which is ordinarily ready about eleven o'clock. It is not permitted to women to enter into the cloisters of the Capuchins or their gardens; only here in Spa it is permitted for the convenience of strangers, that all persons may walk in their garden. There is a meadow at the end of the town, where generally the most of the company meet and converse; and such as please dance or otherwise divert themselves.

239

The ordinary custom is to take chambers by the night or week, which you may have for six, nine, twelve, eighteen stivers or more a night according to the goodness of them. The people of the house furnish you fire and other things for dressing your meat. But many gentlemen go to an ordinary at twelve [stuivers] to dinner. The best in the town is at the sign of the Spinet, where I stayed, and paid for my chambers and diet (twice a day) a rixdollar a day.

I met here with a very civil gentleman who was pensionary of Tournai, who, though under the French [1668-1713], was no lover of them. There was here a fashionable gentleman who could discourse well almost of everything, who was supposed to be a spy for the French King, observing the sentiments of the various companies that came to that place. The best chambers are in a great house at the sign of the Pommelet, where [154] persons of greater and lower quality are lodged, and with great convenience. It is but a small dorp Spa, and lies at the very foot of high hills.

On 16th June I came from thence to Aken [Aachen], in the company of four young merchants of Amsterdam. It is about seven hours betwixt the two places. We baited at Limburg, where as in so many other places you have the sad instances of French cruelty, for in this town there are very few houses left standing. The fortifications are demolished, and a castle, that has been a very strong and fair one, quite ruined. This town stands upon a very high hill and a river runs below it in the valley. The way is pleasant from Spa to Aken, though in some places uneasy for waggons.

When I was at Aken, I fell to be in the house with a gentleman and his lady who were both Catholics, but great enemies to the clergy, especially the regulars. Which made me take occasion to ask the lady how it came that she confessed all that she knew to such persons. She told me plainly that she did not confess all, and speaking of their lasciviousness she told me that before she was married, when she came to confess, they would have asked her questions about things that she never knew before, nor thought of. They were about lust. The gentleman told me, and she too, that the mischiefs of their unmarried life were so great that it were a thousand times better they did marry, and that he did hope in a little time to see a reformation in that matter.

We came to discourse of nuns, many of whom are young gentlewomen of good quality. He told me that many of them were forced by their parents to take that course of life, because they were not able to give them a portion suited to their quality; and that therefore the consequences could not but be sad, and the lewdness of abbeys great, of which he told me two stories from his own knowledge.

One was of a gentleman, an officer in the souldiery under the Spanish King, who was in suit of a young lady who had a kindness for him. But not having the consent of her parents [she] could not marry him, but was forced by them to enter into a nunnery, which made the gentleman think upon marrying [155] another, which accordingly he did. But his wife dying and he coming afterwards into that place where his former mistress was, old love began to revive, and it was agreed that he should come privately to her chamber, where he was hid and entertained by her a fortnight. But being at last discovered, he was taken and to his own and others' surprise he was sentenced to die. The execution of which sentence, the gentleman told me that he himself delayed for a small time (his office it seems putting him in a capacity to do it), hoping that the Marquis de Grana, then Governor of the Spanish Netherlands, would have sent a remission. But he was inexorable in that matter, and so the gentleman was executed but nothing done to the gentlewoman.

He told me that the young ladies in their abbeys have conveniences in their chambers, where they can keep a person undiscovered, and that they keep often good confections in their rooms for entertaining one another, or others where they can have them and are so inclined. But these are religious persons not of the strictest order, but who have a liberty to converse in the world. And some of them, once in a year [have] the freedom to go out of their abbeys for six weeks together amongst their friends.

The gentleman also told me another story of one of his acquaintance, who was shut up for some time in one of the young ladies' chambers in an abbey, where he had such converse with that young gentlewoman whose the chamber was, and four more of her consorts that came hither to him, that when he came out he was almost debauched to death by his practices with them. [...] These things I only mention to show how little regard many Papists have for their religious orders, and what a cheat their vow of chastity is.

Anonymous tourist, 13-20 August 1697 N.S.

13 August. About five this morning I took coach for Namur, which is [ten] hours (i.e. leagues) from Brussels. In passing I went for about three hours through the Bosch de Zoniën, which is a large wood and in many places like maidenhead thicket in others thick underwood. This place is famous for robbing and toward the latter end of it, I met a coach with about twelve people in it, all [of] which had been robbed the day before, about two leagues nearer Namur.

I dined at Genappe and passed over the place where the Allies were encamped before they removed to Cockleberg [Koekelberg], which was a large field adjoining to Genappe, which is a small village. About half an hour after dinner I passed by a castle that had been demolished by the French [at] the beginning of the war [1688] and had been a strong place. The coach stayed about two hours at Sombreffe and I made use of that time to see a house of the Count de la Monteroys [Motterie], about half a mile off, because it appeared at a distance to be the finest situated and also the best in repair of any I had seen in the country. There I saw an old castle, moated round, with fine walks of elms on all sides of it; three large courts; the building much out of repair: not a window that had any glass to it, that gave great evidences of the desolation the war had made.

View of Namur and citadel, 1748

This place had a safeguard to it, therefore the country people brought their goods for protection thither, where I saw sixty or seventy chests in a large hall. About an hour from this place, I left Fleurus about half an hour on the right hand and passed through the camp at Measy [Mazy], which is about an hour and a half from Namur. This is a very considerable pass, and it has been always thought necessary both by the French and Allies to possess themselves of it, before they make any attempt on Namur. All the way from the Bosch de Zoniën to this place is an open, pleasant country with a mixture of hills, woods and rivers, both delightful and fertile. About seven I arrived at Namur. The town and castle are commanded by Count Brouay [Bruay] under the Elector of Bavaria; the rest of the works are under the command of Mr Coehoorn.

14 [August]. The next day I went to see the castle, which stands on a rock with so steep an ascent towards the [blank] that it is inaccessible and not less than twenty yards high to the foundation of the castle. Between the castle and Coehoorn fort, which is on the [blank] side of the castle, is a deep valley, on the top of which is a fort called Orange Fort. When this was taken by the French anno 16[92], they made their entry on the upper side.

Within the walls of the castle is [a] great variety of works as bastions, etc. and also many casemates, which are caves cut into the rock, some whereof arched artificially, others only with the natural arch of stone, which are made to save the men and horses from bombs, etc. [...], which the strongest buildings of the castle could not do, they being almost all laid flat with the multitude of bombs, etc. shot into it by the Allies. It was told me that the bombs that were all shot into the castle at one time fell not far from one another and either killed or disabled five hundred men.

15 [August]. The next day I went to the Jesuits' chapel, which in some particulars exceeds that of Antwerp. From the west end to the altar are seven arches which are supported with pillars of red and white marble of the [blank] order of above

thirty foot high. The pedestals three foot and a half square and capital of composite order, both the latter of black marble polished, as also are the whole pillars and arches, over which is a frieze of red and white marble and upon that the boldest cornish of black marble that ever I saw. The roof is arched with white stone, well-carved, with square and oval spaces left for painting. The painting not so good as that at Antwerp.

16 [August]. Here I saw a more than usual procession in honour to St Roch. First there was four large banners carried by four lads on horseback, of about ten years old, which were sons to persons of quality and were assisted by servants in liveries. After these followed a long train of burghers, each carrying a white taper burning in his hand. After these, several effigies on biers. These were followed by that of the Virgin Mary in a rich Loretto habit (gold canopy over her head borne by four angels gilt with gold). This was carried by four shaven priests, several violins, etc. before them. After this was carried the host with a rich canopy over it. Here followed several priests in rich vestments. In many places in the streets were rich altars erected; boughs on each side; where the streets were narrow, garlands from one side to the other; and many fireworks although at noonday. The statue of St Roch was shown with a wound above his knee, out of which the water spouted. The remainder of the day, and also part of the night till ten of the clock, was spent after the same manner.

This afternoon I went on horseback to Coehoorn fort, which had many works underground as brewhouses, bakehouses, etc. as also casemates for the soldiers. I was in several that were cut out of the solid rock, one whereof I judged by pacing to be thirty yards in length and about five yards over; in height about eight foot. Orange Fort is on the top of the hill between Coehoorn Fort and the castle. In a casemate there, Marshall Boufflers usually was, till the taking of the Coehoorn fort, and sitting one day at dinner, a cannon shot came in at a window over the door and killed one that sat with him at dinner and made a hole in the arch, which I saw.

From this I rode to the other works, which were many and most made since the retaking from the French [1695] as also the line of circumvallation, which runs from the Sambre to the Meuse. About two miles from Coehoorn, at the northeast, was the quarters where the King lay; it was retaken from the French.

From this I crossed the Sambre on a bridge of boats under the castle; went by the town wall by Port IJsere, to which was an iron gate, to Fort Coquelet on the [blank] side of the town. At the taking of which the Allies anno 1695 lost seven thousand men. Immediately upon that the town surrendered. The several forts were made since the retaking, before which [...] there was a retrenchment only and some little forts. There is now a bastion on one of these forts, cut out of the main rock, about fifteen foot deep. Whoever is master of the forts on this hill has so far the town at his mercy that he may do with it as he pleases, it overlooking the whole town, which he may bomb, cannonade, etc., it not being distant above half a mile.

17 [August]. On Saturday about one, I took the common passageboat for Huy,

which is five hours from Namur. The French took it anno 16[93]; it was retaken anno 169[4]. In passing thither, I was shown a hermit's cell at the foot of a rock on the left hand, and another about the middle on the left. The castle of Samson, lately demolished, was on the top of a rock, just over the river. At Sell [Seilles] was a garrison of a hundred and fifty men of the Allies, at the left hand, near Andenne, which is about an hour from thence. I was stopped by a party of French, which came out of the woods, commanded the boat to come on shore; took what was valuable from such as had no French pass and would have taken their persons. But all had passes, except such as appeared to be very poor. On both sides [of] the river, till within half a league of this place, was rocks; on both sides [of] the river after, till near Huy, were woody hills, on one of which I saw the ruins of an old castle called Beaufort Castle. Near Huy the rocks on the right hand are forty yards height. One, which is next the town, has on it a fortification called Fort Picard.

18 [August]. The next day the governor sent an officer, who showed me the fortifications, the principal of which was Fort St Joseph, which is on the top of a very steep hill and I believe fifty yards high, about four hundred yards square on the top, and inaccessible on every side but one, where is a neck of land that leads to it with a steep ascent on each side. Three bastions flank this neck. On the top from the fort and on each side, one bastion is designed. A cut is designed to be made cross this neck of land of sixty foot high and thirty foot broad. Upon this neck of land, about a furlong from the fort, is a stone set into the ground which parts the territory of Spain from that of Liège. In Fort St Joseph are casemates for five thousand men to save them from bombs, etc. although five hundred men are sufficient to man it. All this work is made at the charge of the Prince of Liège.

Fort Rouge lies over the town on the same side of the Mase opposite to Fort Joseph, which is a fortification for that part. On the whole the town lies encompassed with hills on all sides but where the river runs. Here is a very rich convent of the order of St Cross [Croisiers], and the present governor is president of that order. They call him gentleman of the order. The governor of Huy is a Liègeois and is called Jambert.

About one I took the passageboat for Liège, which is about five hours. On both sides [of] the Mase are hills, which on the left are for the most part covered with vineyards, on the right with woods, which give opportunities for robbing. On both sides [of] the river, the country pays contribution to the French and not a house to be seen (except the religious houses of which there are many) but appears to be in very great decay and many falling down.

About six at night I arrived at Liège, where were several churches, but the most remarkable were (19 August) first that of St Lambert, where in the quire is a brass raised monument and on it the effigies of Marca [La Marck-Sedan], Bishop of Liège, who built the palace of the Prince of Liège. He died anno 1538. Here I saw many rich copes, some of which were embroidered very thick with silver and gilt wire, mixed with great quantities of pearl; to these were suitable antipendulums [antependiums]. They show among others a cope, antependium, etc. of the finest needlework, of figures in gold and silver mixed with silk that I ever saw, which, they tell you, were used by St Lambert, who was beheaded, where part of the church now stands, above one thousand years ago. I saw also an antependium of massy silver, the effigies of St Joseph, the Virgin with Our Saviour in her arms of massy silver also, but above all the effigies of St Lambert to the waist, with the history of his life in several figures; in their shapes, not embossed, of much greater value than the effigies, although that was of silver set with many stones and pearls of value, the lesser figures of silver only. There was also in massy gold the effigies of St George on horseback and much more altar plate to a very great value.

The Benedictines reformed have much the finest church [St Jacques] in Liège. The partition between the quire and the nave has some of the history of Our Saviour, the best cut in white marble I ever saw. Near the altar, raised about six inches above the floor, is the effigies of Curvimosanus [Jean de Coronmeuse], abbot of that place, the best cut in a large stone of black marble that is anywhere to be seen of that kind. The figures about it are many and nicely curious. He died anno 1527 [1525]. Over the cloister near the church is a gallery and in it twenty-eight arched cells for these of the order to lodge in.

20 [August]. The English Jesuits have a college here, situated on the highest ground within the walls of the town, on the side near the castle. I ascended to it by seventy large steps. They entertained me in a public room, where one of the society played the best on a bass viol that I think I ever heard. In that room were several pictures, among others Sir Thomas More's and Bishop [John] Fisher's, between which was placed the Prince of Wales' [James Francis Edward Stuart], but his was only in black and white. From this I went into the hall, where their disputations are held, where were several pictures as [Thomas] Garnet[t], [Edmund] Campion, [John] Fenwick. Under each picture was written the times, place and manner of their suffering. In their library, which is a pretty large, long room and but indifferently filled with books, I was shown a very large loadstone, Confucius's philosophy, written in the Chinese character on one side, the other in Latin by a Jesuit of the house. Several other little curiosities not well worth inserting.

They have four gardens, each higher than the other, over either of which I had a fair view of the town. They have many pleasant, shady walks, bowling green, summer houses, etc., and a dial, made by one of their fraternity, of great curiosity. This afternoon I went to the English nuns, which are called Sepulchrines; was entertained there with music, where one of them sang, another played on the lute and a Jesuit on the bass viol, all was very well performed.

Elizabeth or Mary Burnet, August 1707

[103r] We went from Maastricht at eleven o'clock to Liège, where there are few but Papists. There is an English monastery there, where my mother has a cousin, so we

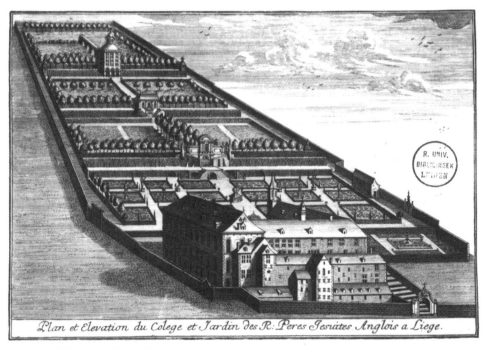

Plan et Elevation du Colege et Jardin des R: Peres Jesuïtes Anglois a Liege.

Liège. English Jesuits' college, 1738

spent some time and heard their singing the salute in the evening. Went likewise to several churches there while they were at mass, and I was very much afraid, not having seen such sights before, especially once when, as we were in the Jesuits' church, the little bell rang and [103v] everybody kneeled down, but we didn't, for we went out till it was over, and then we went in again and saw them make an end of mass. In the afternoon we went to see the Dominicans, where one of them was very civil to us and gave us some cream in an arbor in the garden. So we went home to the inn and went the next morning by five o'clock in diligences, which are the same with the others, to a cottage where they were dressing young turnips, and there we stopped to refresh the horses and eat some milk for dinner. And went on for the Spa, which is a very bad road, for you go nowhere but up and down rocks, which, if it were not so uneasy, would be very pleasant because of the little rivulets that run at the bottom.

We came to Spa at five o'clock where the first thing was to make haste to bed. My mother, thank God, bore [104r] the fatigue a great deal better than could be expected. The next day she took the waters, but we stayed two or three days first. Spa is the dullest place that ever I saw. There is no place to walk in but the Capuchins' garden, where all the company walk. There is no other but Popish churches here and none but Popish besides us except one, the Duchess of Triconnell [Tyrconnel]. Lady Napier and Lady Webb are here, which are all English, and that is all the company my mother visits.

We went once to a well called Géronstère, which waters are best for my mother as they say, in a basket drawn by two horses. It is so uneasy I never felt anything like it, it makes one's head ache, so Spa is good for nothing but eating and sleeping. For sure, if it were not for people's health, [104v] nobody would come here. For one can neither work, read nor write with the waters.

Last Sunday two of the Capuchins came to see my mother. They are dressed in brown without shirt, trousers or stocking; they look very frightful at first, but now I am used to them, they do not. They live upon charity, but they durst not touch money themselves, so they brought a man with [them] to whom my mother gave a pistole.

The second Sunday we stayed here, we heard the Capuchin preach, which is indeed worth hearing. He came up into his pulpit and said a short prayer to himself. Then he rose up and pulled off his cloak and said without naming the place or book: 'Two men went up into the temple to pray, the one a pharisee, the other a publican'. So he stopped and proceeded again, all upon prayer; but in his sermon he did not mention one word of Christ or the New Testament.

After sermon was done they carried the *hostie* in procession round the church, upon which everybody [105r] kneeled down. But we stood and looked upon it. I never see those sights but I pity them that are bred up so; nobody but those that travel can know how happy we are in England, both with respect to our religion, government and situation. For here those that have riches are foraged every year by the armies. Poorer people are taxed both by the Dutch and French, whereas on the contrary we in England have no wars but those we make amongst ourselves, and our taxes are nothing to these poor creatures'.

My mother stayed a fortnight at the Spa, and went from thence in a basket to a little village called Fraipont, where we took a boat for Liège. It is very diverting going by water, for there is [a] great many nuls [planks], and by consequence falls of water, so that you go up and down [105v] a little way and you think you are sinking; then you rise again and so it is all the way. We lay at Liège one night and the next morning went to Maastricht (where we lay the next night) in a boat, where we met with a French party, who as soon as they saw our pass, were very civil and did not search anything of ours. But there was a gentlewoman who had no pass, and they searched everything she had.

Anonymous tourist, 17 June - 2 July 1720 N.S.

[23v] [From Aix la Chapelle] Came to Spa; lodged at the Rose, chez Mme Roquelare, near the chief fountain, a pretty good house; expenses about the same as at Aix. The season begins here on St John's Day [24 June]; there was yet but few people, most English and Dutch. The great diversions here are when the Liègeois come there. The public walk is in the garden of the Capuchins (which is very pleas-

ant), who have obtained a dispense to admit women there. There is five fountains of mineral waters in or about Spa, but three only are generally frequented: the Pouhon in the town, the Géronstère three quarters of a league off and the Sauvenière half a league off. Each has a room built near it where they keep a fire for the use of people that drink their cold waters. There is a grove upon a hill at a short distance from the Spa, where people go to dance.

Spa is placed in a vale surrounded with mountains and rocks, very melancholy, a poor town. The people there and in all the country of Liège talk a sort of French, but mixed with very strange words that have no relation to any other language as I know. *Wash this glass*, they say: *Spumez le aina*. It is very difficult to understand them, chiefly the country people.

[24v] On that near Pouhon is an inscription mentioning that the Czar of Russia [Peter the Great], after his conquests in the north, came to Spa and there recovered his health [1717]. Each of these fountains has its particular quality: the Pouhon good for everything, Géronstère particularly for the stomach, Sauvenière for the gravel and the stone.

Set out on horseback to see the great cascade [of Coo]. A whole river running at the top of a hill takes its fall into another river running at the bottom of it. The fall is over a very steep rock of about sixty feet depth. The country people stop up part of the gap to keep the water in the upper river, which flows round other hills and comes into the bottom river very easily another way. But for a small gratification they take off that fence, and then the fall of the whole river with utmost violence over the rock makes a very beautiful sight. This cascade is three leagues from Spa in a very hilly and barren country.

Set out in a coach and four for Chaudfontaine, five leagues from Spa and two from Liège. Gave for the coach five crowns and a half, which is forty-four shillings. Here is a house very well-built with nineteen baths in a bottom between very high hills, all covered with green; a river runs by it with great violence and the whole is as agreeable romantic a place as any can be seen. [25v] This water for the bath is also mineral, but so lukewarm that they are obliged to mix it with some hot water to make it tolerable. They pretend it is of great virtue, particularly if one drinks some of the same water while one is in the bath. We dined there, and some bathed. Then came to Liège in a boat; gave nine shillings to have one for ourselves, which comes down the current [of the] river Vesdre (this runs into the Meuse near Liège) with a good deal of swiftness guided by two men who have a sort of oars to guide it, made of a square piece of wood fastened sideways at the end of a pole. In two hours' time came to Liège; lodged at the Mouton Blanc, pretty dear.

Liège is a pretty large and populous city; all the houses covered with slate. Vast number of churches and priests and other clergy. Besides the cathedral, where there are sixty canons, there are seven other collegiate churches with thirty canons each. See the church of St Paul's, the cleanest and prettiest in Liège; that of the abbey of Benedictines, where they show a double pair of stairs to go up from the inside of the church into the abbey, which is very handsomely contrived; the jubé is handsomely carved in marble. See the church of the Dominicans, a pretty dome, [and] that of St John, in that two very good pictures: one in a chapel for which the Elector [26v] Palatine offered two thousand crowns, the other over the great altar representing St John as they are throwing him into burning oil. Both these pictures done by a painter of Liège called Bertholet [Barthélémi Flémalle], who died a canon of St Paul's. The cathedral church of St Lambert very large.

See the Carthusians. Their old house and church was burnt down; they are building a new one much finer. There are apartments built for fourteen fathers; each has two rooms, a closet, a little gallery and a garden mighty clean and handsome and well-furnished. They are very well situated and have vines which furnish them with wine more than they want. They made us taste of it of the colour and taste of champagne, but not so strong nor so ripe. See the Minims in the highest part of the town; from their gardens they look over the whole town. In their convent they showed us some good plate for the use of their church.

The town house newly built [1714-1718], not quite furnished, nothing very remarkable in it, not too well contrived. The Dutch Jesuits, pretty church; they embellish it still. Going along, see a fine bridge over the Meuse, the coches [river boats] go to and fro under one of the arches. A pretty cours [promenade] out of the town along the river, set with trees and in the middle a fine walk.

See the college of the English Jesuits, built upon a hill. There is seventy steps to come up to the house [27v] then the gardens rise up, one over the other, in a very beautiful order, adorned with fine grottoes, groves, etc., commanding the prospect of the town. We had Mr Chapman and Sir John Shelley's brother come along with us, besides another father and the prefect of the house. In the lower garden is a set of various dials of different kinds, as one for a blind man, etc. This has been made by a Jesuit [Francis Line] who had made another more magnificent in the privy garden for King Charles II.

They showed us their library which is but tolerable; a fine loadstone well-armed [furnished with an armature]. The chapelet [rosary] of Queen Mary, Queen of Scots, and her prayer book, which is of vellum fairly written and most of the leaves adorned with very fine pictures. Two cubes of wood like dice, which grew exactly in that form in some trees in Switzerland.

Drank some good champagne at [the] Bonhommes [Minims] and that gratis. N.B. these English Jesuits teach the people of the town both philosophy and divinity. The prefect treated us with very good beer made after the English manner and some wine. They are highly valued and beloved in the town; the other Jesuits teach grammar, Latin and Greek. Met at Liège with Count Dessigny, a very civil gentleman who lives near Mons.

[28v] The bottresses of Liège are remarkable as they carry vast weights upon their back. They are very loose in their talk but at the same time very virtuous. If one of them is caught tripping, the others won't allow them to carry the hotte, a lit-

249

tle basket they wear on their backs which helps them to bear up the weights. Liège is partly built on the side of mountains and partly in a vale below; all along the hills are vines growing and hops in great quantity.

Set out at nine o'clock for Huy in a treckschuyt which mounts the Maas by the help of three horses; every person a shilling to go there, five leagues. We had the little roof, in which we found a very agreeable nun belonging to the convent de l'ordre de Cîteaux or Bernardites, which is a league from Namur on the same side of the Maas. That order has great liberties, which occasions a good deal of gallantry and sometimes something more. Came to Huy about seven. All the coasts of the river between Liège and Huy are very agreeable, having many seats and gardens and villages along its banks.

Huy is now but a poor [29v] desolate town; the fortifications and the citadel having been demolished and several houses being destitute of inhabitants. The streets very narrow; lodged at the Elephant, which will be a pretty good house when the rooms are fitted out. Went very early to see the fountain of the mineral waters, which begins to be in a very great reputation, but there is yet no ornaments made to it. Took our leave there of Count Dessigny. The waters have not so much taste as those of Aix or Spa.

Set out in a boat like that of Liège at ten o'clock for Namur, five leagues off. At Huy is the chief convent of the Croisiers, an order employed in redeeming captives from the Turks. Their general, who lives there, had been elected with great solemnity some days before we came. The sides of the river here are only rocks and hills. About midway is a [Benedictine] chapter of she-canons for ladies of quality, called the abbey [of] Andenne.

Came to Namur at seven; at the gate where we came in, the Sambre runs into the Maas. At the haven was a mob of five or six hundred people waiting for the [30v] boat and three soldiers with half-pikes to prevent any disorder. Lodged at the Little Pomelette, a pretty good house.

See the church of the Ursulines, little but very handsome adorned with a good deal of marble. That of the Jesuits is exceeding: the pavement, the pillars and the roof of very fine marble. We observed near the gate and the altar some lesser pillars not of marble which we wondered at, but were told it is the custom of these fathers never to finish their churches that some devotees may have occasion to make them gifts for the purpose. Went to the Court but could not see it, the woman that shows it being out of the way. See the cathedral very indifferent. See the copper foundry. They dig calamine near Namur, which being reduced to powder by grind-stones and sifted, they take thirty-five pounds of Japan copper and as many of Swedish, to which they add thirty of calamine and all this melted together and poured between two large stones to make it into plates, brings them forth eighty-five pounds of [31v] good copper for pins, pans, kettles, etc. They make use of Liège coals.

Took horse in the afternoon to see the citadel and other forts. Namur is a moderate town, pretty regular streets and pretty large, as they are now by the regulation of the late King of France. The houses are but indifferent; the garrison is Dutch, two or three thousand men, commanded in chief by Mr [Walter Philip] Colyear, who sent us an ordonnance to show us the forts. Without these forts the town would not be very strong, being commanded on both sides by mountains. The citadel is built on one side upon a rock and is defended by three forts that lie upon another hill. Near the Sambre is the Fort Orange; at the other side of the hill the Fort Coehoorn, and between these and the citadel is the Fort du Diable.

At the other part of the town [there] are upon the rocks three forts in this order: the Fort St Antoine, the Coquelet and the Fort Noir. On this side it was the Allies attacked Namur [1695], and the French at the other [1692].

Set out at five o'clock in the coche [32v] which sets out for Brussels every other day, Sunday excepted. The places for each gentleman twelve shillings; for each servant ten shillings one penny. Dined pretty well at Genappe, a poor village seven leagues off from Namur and five from Brussels. Most part of the road is a causeway paved. The country very good, and from Genappe to Brussels fine, large woods belonging to the sovereign; the Emperor has good revenues from it. Came to Brussels at seven o'clock. [cont. Mons and Tournai]

Sir John Percival, 25 June - 20 August (6 July - 31 August) 1723

[3r] The next day we in four hours and half arrived at Liège and spent the rest of the day there, being very rainy and bad. We lay at one of the cheatingest and most impertinent inns I ever met with: The Black Eagle, and the next day set out for Spa, whither the road all the morning was so [3v] bad that we were two hours and half getting to Beaufays, though but three leagues, a miserable cottage, which we left as soon as possible and in the afternoon arrived at Spa, four leagues distant.

The village of Spa is situated in a little valley, surrounded on all sides by mountains of rugged descent and would quickly be deserted but for the waters, which draw company of sundry nations in the summertime to cure themselves of colics, stone and lost appetite. There are two main streets, one of which is tolerable broad, but the buildings are mean and the inhabitants poor; though, being very industrious and necessaries being cheap, they make a shift to live and appear contented. To say the truth, they are very ingenious and occupy themselves in several trades as making japan toilets in imitation of those that come from thence, carving, cutting seals, making snuff boxes, mother of pearl necklaces and pendants, in painting, limning and drawing, all [of] which at the return of the season they find a good market for with the gentry that resort thither.

The inhabitants are served by one parish church and a Capuchin convent, which notwithstanding the rigidness of their order permit both men and women at all hours to walk in their garden (the only one in the place), finding their account in the presents made them by strangers for the liberty so allowed them.

The medicinal fountains or springs are five in number and have their particu-

LA FONTEYNE POVHON. *sur la marche du village* A.

Spa. Pouhon, c. 1625

lar virtues assigned them. [4r] That of the Pouhun is in the chief street, and has near it a handsome room erected at the charge of the late Czar of Muscovy [Peter the Great], who found benefit from it when here for the colic [1717]. There is a handsome inscription over it. This is the only water carried all over Europe under the name of Spa, but what we generally find in the shops in London is too often not taken from this spring, but another, some leagues distant, which comes cheaper as not being subject to the town duty of a penny a bottle and therefore tempts the importers to impose upon their customers by selling it as the true Spa; but it is nothing so good and when come home is helped by art to resemble the other. This water is chiefly drunk by persons of weak stomachs and broken constitutions.

The second spring, chiefly recommended for colics and flatulent diseases, is the Géronstère, two miles distant from the village and seated in a rocky country full of woods. These waters were recommended to my wife, but whether it was that the season was bad (as in truth I never saw a worse anywhere) or that my wife's colic was of a particular nature, she found no benefit from them. The third water is the Sauvenière, a mile from the town, only used in cases of the stone and gravel.

The remaining two I have forgot the names of, being not frequented that I know of. We lodged at The White Lamb in the house of one Chrouet, and the persons were very [4v] civil and honest, but the rooms were so noisy that were it not for the difficulty of finding a better, we should have removed. Provisions are here (both wine and meat) very cheap, as also horse meat, but the entertainments, which Englishmen wherever they meet make each other, run the week's account pretty high.

Indeed, the pleasure that persons of the same country have to meet in foreign countries prompts them to rejoice with each other, and it is impossible for them, when not extraordinary sick, to forbear enjoying each other's company, and giving marks of their mutual esteem by dinners and suppers, so much the fashion of some countries and especially of our own. Besides, cheerfulness is one main part of the cure, and that cannot be preserved where men retreat from each other's company.

In the season there comes from Liège a very eminent apothecary, Salpeteur by name, whose drugs are as good as can be, and he is of great service to the place. There is likewise a physician on the place who makes little of his business, being supplanted by a person of great note who dwells two hours off and, though a Protestant, is resorted to by all the neighbourhood, insomuch that his house is all day long thronged like a fair. His name is [Warner] Chrouet, and when sent for, the town immediately rings of it and everyone applies to him for advice [...]. [5r] He is a gentleman of learning and sense, and I have his book upon the Spa waters presented me by him, which shows him such [*La connaissance des eaux minérales d'Aix-la-Chapelle, de Chaud-Fontaine et de Spa*, Leiden 1714]. He treated more particularly of them than Dr [Edward] Browne or Dr [John] Northleigh.

At my arrival I found my Lord Ambassador [Charles] Whitworth and his lady there, who were glad to leave the public and noisy way of living at Cambrai and spend some time retired. But my Lord came also on an account of some flatulent disorders, which before we came away, he told me he was better of. He is a good master and husband, sober, religious and human, very well learned and perhaps the most experienced minister in the service, having spent twenty-seven years abroad at the Courts of Muscovy, Prussia, Saxony and Holland, and now is plenipotentiary for the treaty at Cambrai. [5v] His company there helped much to make us pass our time agreeably, and I shall always remember his civility to us with thanks.

Other company of England which came and went while we were here were Sir John Shelley and his lady and brother, Sir Gustavus Hume and his son, Mr [Arthur] Vil[l]ette[s], my Lord Whitworth's secretary, Mr Lennir, his gentleman of the horse, Mr [Moses] Rapier [=Raper], Governor [=director] of the Bank [of England], a Presbyterian, but [a] good-natured and generous man, Mr [William] Benson, son [brother]-in-law to Mr Henry Hoare the banker, Major-General [Thomas] Whetham and his lady and sister, Colonel Harrison, who has a regiment too in our service, Mr [William] Bateman and his lady [Anne], the late Lord Sunderland's daughter, a handsome and well behaved lady and not so humoursome as her husband, who did not please his countrymen, Sir James Tobin, a generous good-natured man, who being in the service of the East India Company, was by them dismissed from the command of his ship and thereupon repaired to the Emperor and laid the scheme of the new Ostend East India Company, for which the Emperor knighted him. Captain Worth, a mighty good-natured gentleman and a stout soldier, brother to Major Worth formerly mentioned, Mr Rolt of Devonshire and several others whom I have now forgotten. The only foreigners I was acquainted with were Count Wignacourt and his lady, a daughter of the Prince de Taxis [...].

[7v] The abbey of Stavelot is three leagues distant from Spa; the abbot is a sovereign prince of the Empire and has a settled revenue of twelve thousand crowns a year, besides which the abbey has six thousand more for the maintenance of twenty-five monks. They are of the Benedictine order, but the abbot, now Bishop of Tournai [Jean Ernest, Count de Löwenstein-Wertheim], is a secular priest, which is no small uneasiness to the friars, and they were then at law with him for pretending to ecclesiastical jurisdiction over them, being regulars.

I mentioned my being there. It was upon an invitation made my Lord Whitworth and the English gentry, and we were nobly entertained. Two tables were spread, the first of which had [8r] seven dishes the first course with a remove, and thirteen the second course, which was followed up by a handsome dessert. The wine was burgundy and moselle, both excellent in their kind; we were received in the abbot's lodgings (then absent) by the sub-prior and two friars, the rest did not appear. After dinner we viewed the abbey church, which is large and neatly kept. In it is a good organ with a vox humana, the best I have heard, always excepting that at Amsterdam; and there is another church underground, where they bury.

The town of Stavelot may contain about three hundred houses. Most of the inhabitants are shoemakers, and they are numerous, but the country adjacent is hilly and very barren. It is part of the forest of Ardenne and is still very woody, but the timber of it cut down. Upon a hill on the other side [of] the Amblève (which river washes the town) is the old castle of Stablo or Stavelo, built in 1540 by one of their abbots and lodged in for some time by the Emperor Ferdinand I. It is now in ruins.

A league from Stavelot is the town of Malmédi, subject to the same abbot. The inhabitants are chiefly tanners, and there are no less than 406 tan-pits. The abbey of Malmédi contains twenty-three monks of the same order with those [8v] of Stavelot, and both join their voices in the election of their abbot [...].

[10r] On the 18th August we set out for our return, and dining at Beaufays, supped at Liège at the Mouton Blanc, a very good inn. Here we stayed the following day and saw the cathedral dedicated to St Lambert, an old Gothic structure without beauty. In the middle of the quire is a fine brass monument representing an abbot [=Bishop E. de La Marck-Sedan] at his prayers and the figure of death calling him away. [...]

[10v] The inhabitants here are numerous and wealthy, carrying on a good trade and enjoying great privileges under their prince. It stands upon the Meuse and is divided by several canals into as many quarters. The country round it is extreme

fertile and rich, and formerly yielded a revenue to the bishop of one hundred thousand crowns, but being much harassed [11r] by the late wars, the most is now not above forty thousand crowns. I speak of settled revenues, for the casual, such as free gifts, aids, etc., rises to much more, as the States of the country think fit to give. [cont. Mechelen and Leuven]

Liège
Population: 44,000-57,000 (1650-1790).
Distances: Aachen 9 hours (26 miles), Brussels 18 hours (50 miles), Leuven 14 hours (35 miles), Maastricht 4 hours (12 miles), Namur 10 hours (30 miles), Spa 6 hours (17 miles).
Inns, *Reisboek* (1689): Tonnelet. *Reisboek* (1700 and 1721): Au Dragon d'Or (De Goude Draak)*; A la Pommelette ('t Appeltje)*; A l'Aigle Noir (de Zwarten Arend)*. *Reisboek* (1721) also: Au Tonnelet*.

Spa
Population: c.1200 (300 houses, c.1700).
Distances: Aix 8 hours (25 miles), Brussels 24 hours (67 miles), Liège 6 hours (17 miles).
Inns, guidebooks do not give names of inns at Spa, but provide much information on the manner and cost of staying there.

Namur
Population: 11,000 (1650), 16,000 (1800).
Distances: Brussels 10 hours (35 miles), Liège 10 hours (30 miles), Mons 13 hours (30 miles).
Inns, *Reisboek* (1689): De Koningin van Spanjen. *Reisboek* (1700) also: Au Mouton Blanc; Aux trois Barbeaux; La Chaine d'or; Au Pommelet, près l'Eglise Notre Dame. *Reisboek* (1721) and Nugent (1749) no inns mentioned.

Further reading

J.B. Gramaye, *Antiquitates Belgicae*, Bruxelles-Leuven 1708.
[C.L. von Poelnitz] *Amusemens des eaux de Spa*, Amsterdam 1734, 1735, 1737.
[P.L. de Saumery], *Les délices du païs de Liège et de la comté de Namur*, Liège 1738-1744.
M. Galliot, *Histoire générale ecclésiastique et civile de la ville et province de Namur*, Liège 1788-1790.
Leopold Genicot, *Histoire de la Wallonie*, Toulouse 1973.
H. Hasquin, *La Wallonie, le pays et les hommes. Histoire, économies, sociétés*, vol. I, *Des origines à 1830*, Bruxelles 1975.
J. Lejeune, *La principauté de Liège*, Liège 1980.
A. Dasnoy et. al., *Namur. Le site, les hommes, de l'époque romaine au XVIIIe siècle*, Bruxelles 1988.
J. Stiennon (ed.), *Histoire de Liège*, Toulouse 1991.
Bulletin de l'institut archéologique Liégeois, 1852-
Annuaire d'histoire Liégeoise, 1929-
Annales de la Societé archéologique de Namur, 1964-
Histoire et archéologie spadoises, 1975-
Chroniques liègeoises, 1996-

Het Loo

Anonymous tourist, 4-5 September 1697 N.S.

4 September. At Arnhem I baited, which is about six hours from Loo. The country for about two miles was generally planted with tobacco, after which I came into higher ground, which was a barren heath and many times several acres wholly covered with sand. I believe at one time I saw eight hundred besides several other less parcels. Sometimes for several miles together I saw nothing but heath and sand, although the country was flat. Here the King used to hunt, having several hunting seats near, as Dieren, Loo, etc. At the last of these I arrived at five. But the King was that day, before I arrived, gone to Dieren.

5 September. Loo is a very small village: those few houses that are there depend wholly on the company the Court brings there. It is seated in the forest of

The fountain of Venus, c. 1700

Gelderland, which is of great extent forty miles in length and over. It is for the most part heath and sands but has also large woods, both high and underwood, where are red-, fallow- and roe deer, wild boar and plenty of all other sorts of game. Here the King has a hunting house, built by him anno 1686. It is about thirty yards in front, seven windows in breadth and two storeys high. Each storey contains eight rooms which are about thirteen foot in height.

In the midst of the court, that is on the front of the house, is the fountain. The basin raised about three foot, in the midst of which are three fishes with their tails standing up and interwoven; the basin about thirty foot over [across]; the court divided by pitching into four green quarters; lodging rooms on the right hand and stables on the left for two hundred horses, which are generally full. The back front of the house is to the garden, in the midst of which is a fountain where is a Venus supported by four large sea-gods gilt; on each hand are four quarters; in the midst of the right hand quarter is a celestial globe placed in a fountain; of the left hand quarter a terrestrial in the like manner; from the midst of the terrace walks, which are on the right and left hand side of the garden is a cascade, which falls into three large stones cut into the shape of scallops, on each side of which are five falls for the water. There are many other gardens with [a] great variety of waterworks, walks, wildernesses, etc. One eight-square basin, each square forty foot; a hundred foot diameter; in the midst a figure that casts the water forty-five foot high.

John Talman, 11-12 September 1697 N.S.

[1] Wednesday the 11th of September, I went from Leiden to Amsterdam. From there to Harderwijk over the Zuiderzee, where we arrived the 12th [at] five in the morning. Harderwijk formerly might have been a pretty sort of a city, but now, since it has had the ill fate to fall into the hands of the French when they invested Naarden [1672], it looks most sadly. The buildings of the city are all old and the streets narrow. It has nothing to recommend itself but its church and steeple, which is of a good height but without a spire. But there seems by its top to have been one designed; but whether not finished, or demolished by the French is to me uncertain.

The city has an Academy with professors, two ports or gates, one to the sea after the Gothic fashion, square and at the top at each corner a turret. It had also a haven, but the violence of the sea has destroyed it. Some of the pilework is still to be seen. The other port is to the land; it seems once to have been pretty enough, of the Roman order with niches and pilasters but now all ruined as well as the walls about the whole city.

In this province of Gelderland you have a much different prospect from that in Holland, the country here being varified with hills and pleasant valleys all the way to the King's house at Loo, which is six hours from Harderwijk. Loo, for its fountains, grottoes and woods and lastly for its fine seat, deserves a particular description. The entrance into the court is but indifferent, the two sides of the court being joined by a silly sort of ironwork instead of a portico of marble pillars or some other ornament suitable to the majesty and dignity of a King or great Prince. At your coming up to the house you first come into a large hall which leads you to the grand staircase all painted and gilded from whence you enter the grand saloon, nobly painted and gilded with a ceiling suitable to the rest of [the] room. From thence on each hand the doors lead to the rest of the apartments: on your right to the King's, the left to the Queen's, but as for a more nice description another time shall serve.

And now for the gardens. First on the Queen's side there is a square spot of ground, bounded on one side by the Queen's apartment, the opposite side by a wall which parts it from a wilderness; the third side by a low building of offices which joins the wall and the Queen's lodgings together. On the side over against it is a terrace which runs round the grand garden, which fronts the forward part of the house, so that this garden or rather a sort of a labyrinth lies privately in a corner. At each corner is an arbour four-square which is joined by a long walk of arbour-work full of [2] openings or windows on each side to another arbour in shape like the former and so all round, so that within these living green walls [there] is a square which is divided in four small squares by handsome large walks which run through the middle of the long arbours.

In each quarter is a little round fountain whose borders are made to imitate nature, of several stones and shells of different shapes and colours, which looks very pretty, together with the pavement at bottom which is all of small pebbles for the most part of two colours as black and white, in others yellow and black, which are so set together as to make a sort of a figure which varies in each fountain. In the middle of one of these fountains is a leaden sea-bull spouting water out at his nostrils, with a triton on his back spouting water out at his shell trumpet. Both the figures are small and gilded. The second, third and fourth are just the same, excepting that instead of a sea-bull there is a sea-horse, in another a sea-lion, in a fourth a sea-leopard. In the middle is a triton something larger than the rest swimming upon the water, spouting water out of his shell trumpet, gilt with gold as the rest. [cont. Overijssel]

Anonymous Utrecht student, 4-5 September 1699 N.S.

[11] Next morning we returned [from Nijmegen] by waggon to Arnhem and dined in the camp and then went on to Loo. All or most part of the way was heathy with some wood. This heath is of a great extent and many parts of it very sandy and well-stocked with several sorts of game. Immediately on our arrival we went to see the King's gardens, which were very sweet and delightful with several very curious waterworks.

The first garden, or that next the house, consists of gravel and greens, laid in knots and figures and on each side of the garden is a grass terrace, etc. At the top on the edge of the slopes are pyramids of yew and other greens and many small pyramids in pots up and down the whole garden. There are many other places laid out in walks, parterres, etc., several curious hedges and espaliers of yew, hornbeam, box, etc. From the house there is a fine view through the first garden and a fine walk into the park, good part of which is laid in lovely walks and avenues, where are abundance of pheasants and other game kept. In another part are abundance of foreign birds and other fowl kept for the use of the King's table as well as for pleasure. There is also a bowling green, which is the only one I ever remember to have seen in these countries.

Next morning we saw the house, which consisted of a square building, at each end of which are two little square pavilions joining to the great one or body of the house. And from the aforesaid pavilions come down on each hand a long row of buildings, which make two wings, one of which is the stables and offices belonging to them. And the other side is for the several offices of the house. From each end of these two wings there is an iron work and iron gates, which, running across from one wing to the other, makes a large square court before the house. In the middle of which court there is a fine fountain. The coaches come into this court and come round to the very steps at the chief door. The whole building is brick.

Withinside it is rather neat than magnificent. The great staircase is fine, the walls are painted with history; we saw but little rich furniture. At a little distance from the King's house is the Old Hof, or Old Loo. There is another new building near the King's house, which was chiefly built for the retinue, etc. of the Duke of Zell [Celle], when he used to come hither to visit the King. All the country about Loo is generally a sandy heath with some low wood.

John Farrington, 18-19 November 1710 N.S.

[254] We hired a waggon to go [from Deventer] by way of Loo to Amersfoort, a city in the province of Utrecht, and came to that village, which is three leagues from the city [of Deventer], at half an hour after seven, the ways but indifferent no more than the weather, though about sunset it cleared up and seemed to promise better weather. We took up our lodgings at a small inn (the Half Moon) but had good beds and were well enough entertained.

Loo is no more than a hunting seat of the late King's, now contended for by the King of Prussia and Prince of Friesland, and there are only some few houses built about it for the conveniency of passengers. [255] On the 19th of November the wind continued westerly, blew pretty high, but however it held up and therefore, about eight in the morning, we went to see the house and gardens. The avenues to Loo are finely planted with trees, one of which fronts the house, the other turn to the right hand and to the left. The house is very noble. It is built of brick and fronts

Het Loo, c. 1700

the iron palisades, which make up one part of the quadrangle. In the middle of the square or quadrangle is a large fountain with several gilt images in it. There are four grass-plats, which all center in the fountain and a parade for the coach-round withoutside the grass-plats.

On the right as you enter are the offices such as kitchens, etc., which make up one part of the quadrangle. On the left the stables for hunting-horses, which with the apartments for the grooms make another part of the square and the house itself is the fourth. The middle part of the house has the room and apartments of state. On the left as you enter, are the apartments of the King and Prince of Friesland, on the right those of the Queen and Princess. Without the quadrangle are two wings: that on the left is the coach houses and stables; that on the right the orangery and the gardeners' houses. There are now no horses in the stables, but a great many deer's horns are still hung up.

You go up to the house by several stone steps and then enter into a hall, whence through an iron gate you have a fine vista through the house from the garden [at the back of the house] to the avenues, and from the avenues to the garden. On each side of that door you go up to the [256] several apartments. On the left we were brought into the Queen's dining-room. It is a fine large room, the ceiling is well-

painted and the panels are well-painted and gilt. From thence we went into the antechamber of the Prince of Friesland, and through a door on the right hand we
came into his chamber, where the furniture was very good. And through that
passed into his cabinet and returned from that into the King's antechamber, which
was furnished with blue silk laced with gold; the chairs and hangings the same.

In the room of state was very good tapestry, the table a curious piece of marble on
a frame that was well-carved and gilt and very good painting over the chimney. This
chamber was hung with scarlet damask, all the furniture the same and laced with
gold. In the first closet were several good paintings of bright colours. Through that
we passed into a second, which was hung with extraordinary fine paintings. There
was a small piece of a woman rocking a cradle, which was valued at sixteen thousand guilders; a very good piece of Erasmus; another of an English divine of 1541;
one of King Henry VIII when young, a very fine picture which resembles the pictures
we have of him, and the dress is pretty much the same. There is also an admirable
piece of an old man, mending his pen at a table, a young woman at the same table
reading by the light of the candle and a man coming to light his candle by it. A very
fine, though very small, piece of soldiers lying upon their arms upon the floor of a
church, only to be discerned by the light of a small candle that burns at the entrance
and by a fire that reflects a light from the end [257] of the church through the aisles of
it. Christ in the Virgin Mary's lap, with the Wise Men presenting their treasure to
Him, etc. But in short, they are all very fine pieces and of great value.

Through the dining-room we came into the apartment of the Princess of
Friesland, whose antechamber, chamber and cabinet are very well furnished. In the
Queen's antechamber over the chimney is a very good piece of carved work representing the Feast of Bacchus. The Queen's chamber was furnished with dark green
silk without any lace of any kind upon it, but the manner of making up the bed
made it look very well. The Queen's library is a very good collection of books in
English, Dutch, French, Italian, etc. Several political tracts, treaties of peace, alliances and the like, and amongst the rest the sermon of that great and good man
the late Archbishop Dr J. Tillotson against evil-speaking, which he presented to Her
Majesty. A very fine japan desk with silver hinges edged and tipped with silver, a
fine large and velvet chair, a fine pair of globes; on the ceiling an oval looking-
glass. In the gallery, which is adorned with several paintings, the most remarkable
is the picture of the King's father and mother, which is a very large and good piece.

In a room that leads to the King's dining-room are four large hunting pieces: the
one of the dogs at full cry; in the second the stag at bay and the death of the deer; in
the third the hunting the wild boar, and in the fourth his Majesty at dinner under a
tree. The dining-room is a large room, the table covered with red velvet, the buffet
arched, the arch supported by four pillars fluted and gilt, where stood [258] several
marble cisterns to keep the wine cool in summer.

Thence you go up a pair of stairs to the chapel, which is well wainscoted, not
unlike one of our halls in shape; at the upper end stands the communion table, in

the middle the pulpit and over against that the King's seat.

Below that we saw the apartment of the Princes Vaudemont and Albemarle, and downwards from the hall towards the garden is a small cool room, very pleasant in summer where there is [an] abundance of china. It is floored with Dutch tile, and the sides of the room are lined with the same. Beyond that is the grotto, where the fountains make a very pleasant and agreeable murmur, which would easily incline one to sleep. From thence there are steps that lead into the garden towards the bowers and orangery. The house is sash-windowed, and every window is double. I need not say that wainscot, marble, etc. are all very good.

We took a view of the gardens, but it is impossible I should do them justice, and therefore I shall be the less particular. They are very large and, at the disadvantage of the season, appeared very fine. There are a great number of fountains and waterworks, but they did not play very much at present. We walked all over the gardens, saw several cascades, a great many good statues and fountains that played. The walks of the garden are gravelled, which is more than I remember to have observed before in this country. In a large plantation of trees is the cipher of his Majesty, and a crown out of which sprang water by secret pipes. There is near that a long and fine canal, over which water plays in arches. This leads up to the [259] aviary, which is a distinct building or enclosure in the midst of a garden. The aviary is oval in the midst whereof is a fountain. On one side are the cages, on the other the dens for the wild beasts.

We saw two strange East India birds, called the kings of the Hogen's [king vulture], about the bigness of a turkey. Their bills are red, and they have great pieces of red flesh on them; their breasts are white, their wings black and part of their wings are liver colour. They have a very odd look and as odd a way of flying; their food is flesh. They showed us a deer from India; it has short horns, a spotted fur and is hardly so large as ours. Here was also a wild one, twelve years old and very fierce. In another cage was a fine crane of a very pretty colour. In a den was an Indian cow, very tame and small, her horns but short, and a beast they call an eeland, all white, a nose like a deer but something less than an ass. On each side of the fountain is a pleasure house, where they may see the fowl in the cages and the font [fountain] playing on the water. The box knots are very grand. Within the plantations are the kitchen gardens. The fine flower gardens near the house are enclosed by a wall, which on the terrace is breast-high, whereon upon white stones placed at equal distances, the greens are placed in summer.

As you go down to the garden on the left is a bowling green; on the right several bowers, well-shaded with leaves. The orangery has abundance of greens and trees in it, but I dare not say it is equal, either as to the building or the greens, to those either of Hanover or Salzdalem. We had the happiness of fair weather though windy while we saw the gardens and thence returned [260] to our inn, where we dined early and at five minutes past twelve left Loo for Amersfoort. [cont. Amersfoort]

Distances: Amersfoort 8 hours (25 miles), Arnhem 6 hours (18 miles), Deventer 3 hours (10 miles), Harderwijk 5 hours (17 miles), Utrecht 12 hours (38 miles).

Inns, *Reisboek* (1700) Jan de Boer; Moddekevuyl, anders Juffr. van Wijk, wonende naast malkanders deur.

Further reading

W. Harris, *A Description of the King's Royal Palace and Gardens at Loo [...]*, London 1699 (Dutch translation: L.R.M. van Everdingen-Meyer, *Een beschrijving van 's Konings paleis en tuinen van het Loo*, 's-Gravenhage 1985).

A.C. Kranenburg-Vos, *Het Loo: bouw, bewoning en restauratie*, Amersfoort 1986.

Maastricht and Aachen

William Carstairs, 22 May (1 June) 1685

[147] On the 22nd [at 's-Hertogenbosch] I went before four o'clock in the morning in the postwaggon, which is very commodious, and having only two wheels goes with an easiness beyond what could well be thought before trial. In those waggons we go to Maastricht from the Bosch in one day, which is near seventy English miles. We change horses six times by the way, which is most part heathy, but not without in some places groves of trees and cornfields. We dine at a place called Hamont, which is about halfway, and before we come to it, we come to a pretty large town called Eindhoven, which is well-watered. The fields about Maastricht are very pleasant, and the river of the Maas adds much to the beauty of the place. From thence there is occasion every morning at nine of the clock to go by water to Liège, where you arrive about six or seven at night. It is but eighteen miles from Maastricht, but it is against the stream.

James Drummond, Earl of Perth, 8-14 (18-24) May 1694

[23] Aix-la-Chapelle, 14/15th May 1694. My dearest sister. Seeing I know that nothing can please you better than to have an exact account of all the adventures of a brother you love so well, and seeing I can have no greater pleasure than to converse with you, I'll give you account of every step we make.

We left Antwerp the 8th instant, about eight in the morning, and came through a delightful country to Herentals to dinner, and from that to Gheel [Geel] to bed. This place is famous for the martyrdom of a prince of Ireland's daughter called St Dympna, who would not [24] yield to her father's incestuous designs, but became a Christian, fled to this place, was pursued by her father and murdered, together with her confessor. Many mad people recover here, and other miracles are wrought. There is a parish church, and this collegial one of the saint, served by a dean and eight chanoines.

We resolved to come through the Campaine [Kempen], a wild country belonging to the bishopric of Liège, to shun robbing and meeting with French parties. And indeed, a wilder country cannot be, except for hills, for the moors are barren and perfectly uninhabited. We went four hours at one time without meeting any house. We dined at a little village where we got sad fare, but we saw a marriage, which gave us some diversion.

The bride was very much avised [full of life] as ever I saw. The bridegroom a lusty young fellow. She with all her chief maids had black taffeta aprons. They had neither pipe nor fiddle, but abundance of the whitest beer I ever saw; a kind of pap like sowens [furmity] with milk; rice and milk and eggs as thick as a tancy; stewed veal with currants for the chief folks, and some roasted beef with butter and bread; and this made up the whole feast. I thought they had no dancing out of regard to Sunday, but the parish priest was as strict as any Whig in Galloway, for under pain of excommunication he would have no dancing in his jurisdiction. My wife called for the bride as I did for the bridegroom and made them and their chief folks take a glass of our sack, which pleased them most exceedingly.

That night we came through a barren heath to a pitiful village called Saint Trond; in the way there was a small village, where a pretty well-clad man came with a can of excellent beer and offered us a drink. I fancied it was to sell, and so took a little of it. He urged our man who drove the [25] berline we went into to drink, and when we offered him money he laughed at us and was so frank that nothing could be more. He told us in very good French that since the death [on 4th May] of the grand maître [of the Teutonic Order, who had been elected Bishop of Liège on 21st April by half the chapter], three chanoines of Liège were dead. He seemed to like the grand maître [Ludwig Anton, Count Palatine-Neuburg] better than the Bishop of Cologne [Josephus Clemens of Bavaria; elected on 20 April by the other half of the chapter]. He told us too that the disease that reigned at Liège cut off about three hundred a day, and that they began to fear it would turn a pest, but that Maastricht was free.

That night we lay in a most pitiful house upon straw, and had not one with us got a hen (by good luck) we had fasted. But Mary Achmuty [the Countess' servant] made us a little broth, and we lay till the under-pastor called us to mass. Next day we dined at as sad a place, where we could get nothing but eggs which were very bad, and but three or four of them, the French, to whom they pay contribution, having taken all their hens last year. We were now got within four hours of Maastricht and so we cared the less. We arrived about five at night, and (that I might see the town) we stayed there.

I deferred seeing the Great Church until next morning, resolving to hear mass there, so I went about to other places. It proved to be their chief fair and then there is so entire a freedom that nobody can be arrested. The chief thing I saw was a miraculous crucifix in a monastery of Augustine nuns.

It seems a very virtuous man had vowed to go to visit the Saint Sepulchre. At his return he gave chaplets and little relics he had brought to all his family; one poor girl, his youngest child, was abroad at mass when he made his distribution. At her return she begged her papa to give her some little token of devotion too. Alas, child, said he, all's gone save one walnut which I brought from Mount Olivet. C'est assez pour moi, dit elle, and away she runs to the garden and plants it, praying God it might grow to be a mark of his favour to her. It grew to be a tree and she

Aachen. Going to drink the waters, c. 1730

became a nun in this monastery. At last the thunder broke the tree and in the heart of it was found this crucifix, larger than a boy of about thirteen years of age.

The good nuns were reduced to a very few by a kind of plague last year. They took us into their house (for this order can [26] do that) and to their garden, which (within a town) is large. Walking there, who should I see enter but my Lord Balcarres. And so we got home to our lodging and talked and supped together.

Next day I went to the Great Church [St Servaas], which is a very ancient building. The town is all Catholic, save for a few Hollanders and the garrison. They have two churches for their meetings, but there are all sorts of religious orders in the town. It stands low, environed with hills, seated on the banks of the Meuse, is prodigiously strong and famous enough as you know.

Next day we dined at a place called Gallop [Gulpen], where a French party were within a league of us. Here we met with two servants of the grand maître, who were going to Dusseldorp [Düsseldorf] to his brother, I think to carry him an account of the design [Jean Ferdinand de] Méan, the dean, had to choose with his party the grand maître's brother, the Bishop of Breslaw to be Bishop of Liège. But

267

although they continue very stiff in their design to keep out Joseph Clement [of Bavaria], he is like to be the man, that is, his election stands fairest to be approved [which happened on 18 September].

We had thunder and rain in our way hither, which was only four hours, but the tempest was soon over. Here we found an old great town full of cloisters, [which] Charlemagne loved above all his other dominions, for it is environed with woods and hills for hunting. The fountains people drink for health are hot, and smoke terribly. When the cock is turned the water stinks terribly of rotten eggs, of which it tastes too. My wife and I began today, and it purges much.

It is pleasant to see the ladies go into their retiring places and leave their doors open and talk with one another frankly. It is true the men and they do not go to the very same lodge, but they hear all that can be heard; and indeed, necessity has no law. What effects the waters will have with us I cannot tell, but [27] now it is about noon, they have given off to work, and I never was so hungry. Sir William Dick's necessity will oblige me to drink yours and your family's and the whole house of Innerugy's healths in very good over-Moselle wine. And so far you have the history of our journey. Send it to my daughter, and believe that to your family and Earl Marischall's [Perth's son-in-law], I'm just what you would have me, with all duty and respect. Adieu.

P.S. We have here a garrison of three thousand men; yet the town pays twenty-four thousand crowns contribution to the garrison of Luxemburgh. Adieu.

Anonymous tourist, 23-26 August 1697 N.S.

23 August. About nine in the morning I took the waggon for Aix-la-Chapelle, which is eight hours from Maastricht. Near the town was a gallows with twenty-five or more criminals hanging on it. This day I passed over a pleasant and fruitful country, which for the most part was cornfields and sometimes woods, but not large. The nearer I came to Aix, the more enclosed was the country. The town stands in a valley but no hills near, except one that is about a quarter of a mile from it, shaped like a coffin about half a mile in length and half a furlong over, with a valley on every side, whereon the Jesuits have made gardens, etc. for their pleasure.

The town is encompassed with a wall, but no way fortified; the building old and streets paved. Before the stathouse, which is a fair old building, is a large open space. In the middle a fountain, on the top of which is the effigies in large of Charlemagne in brass gilt, under which is a brass basin, into which the water runs, that is at least twelve foot diameter. This empties itself at six places into a larger under it of stone.

The waters of the bath here are very nauseous, both to the smell and taste, and to both rather more cold than hot; often rises in the stomach which makes them unpleasant. They drink physically of them in very great quantities, some ten or fifteen quarts in a morning with the approbation of the physicians there, although others not above four. The baths are all in private houses, covered overhead and paved [on] both sides and bottom with stone. They are supplied with hot water by a hole on one side and emptied by one at the bottom. The colour of the water is a bluish green, clear to the bottom with a small cream at the top. It has a saltness in the taste when hot, but not cold.

The hottest springs are at Brusset [Burtscheid], a small village about a mile from Aix and parted by a hill. Here the water was so hot that I could not endure to thrust my hand into it, but could touch it with a finger. I saw a maid scald an old hen in it and skin off the feathers and I ate an egg that was boiled there in twenty minutes by a watch. The heat will immediately kill a dog if thrown into it.

Both here and at Aix they make use of that which they call the dry bath, which is thus: they have a little close place, about six foot square, in the midst of which is a round hole, about eight inches diameter, through which the steam of the bath ascends, which is so very hot as to cause violent sweating in any person that is placed naked over this hole in a chair.

At Burset [Burtscheid] is a cloister for noble women, which they call chanoinesse, where no ladies can be admitted but such as can prove themselves to be nobly descended both by father and mother for eight descents. This was founded by St Gregory [son of Nicephorus II, Byzantine Emperor] anno 978, who lies buried here. They show his face through a glass; the rest of his body is covered. They show also St Bernard's tomb, which is a black marble stone, raised about two foot with no effigies on it but an old inscription round it. There is nothing else remarkable in the chapel, which seems very old, as also does all the ornaments in it. The lady abbess has great privileges and the nuns the liberty of going anywhither and conversing freely without confinement, but may not marry, having vowed chastity.

In this place are several orders of religious, as Jesuits, Croisiers, Bernardins, etc., whose churches, although some richer than others, are generally adorned after the same manner. Their altars have three storeys of pillars carved in fruit work, the ground black and the wrought work gilt. The Jesuits' here is rather gaudy than rich. The church of Notre Dame has a very unusual figure: the body is rectangular and the quire semicircular. Charlemagne was buried here. His bones are preserved in a coffer of silver, gilt with gold. At the upper end of the quire they show the size of his arm in gold, from his elbow, which is full three foot long. In one side through a glass is shown part of the bone of his arm, also his sword with part of his scabbard of unicorn's horn and his hunting horn. The two latter, they tell you, were taken out of his tomb after they had lain there upward of three hundred years.

They show a book whereon the King of the Romans is sworn, where are the four evangelists written in a fair character in gold letters on vellum, said to be nine hundred years old. The chair where the Emperors used to be crowned. They show two pieces of the cross; the Virgin Mary's girdle of incle, Our Saviour's of leather. The reed, sponge, top of the spear and rope that tied Our Saviour when he was scourged, which is bloody. Also a lock of St John Baptist's hair, etc. Here are much the richest vestments that ever I saw, one whereof is a Loretto habit for the Virgin, which has round the bottom and down before eighty table diamonds, set in gold wrought very thick all over, either with gold and silver wire or flowers curiously wrought with a needle. Two crowns of gold curiously enameled, set with many diamonds, rubies and pearls of great value. These were not only rich, but the neatest of the sort that ever I saw and were presented [in 1629] to the Virgin and Our Saviour by the Infanta Isabella Eugenia, as were also the vestments. Here were also many rich habits for the priests. On the entrance into the quire on the left hand is a pulpit all of plate gold, about four foot high and ten foot in compass, set with many rich stones and pearl all oriental.

At this time there had been very unseasonable weather by reason of the long continued rains, which had spoiled most of the corn in the country. But on Monday the [blank] of this month, the morning being very fair, there was a mighty procession of all sorts of people to implore fair weather. The van in this procession was led by the women and children; they were followed by the priests of the several orders, each order having a cross, etc., either in wood or silver, carried before them. After these came the singing men and boys in their surplices singing; then magistrates and burgomasters with six banners of silk of several colours carried by young lads of about twelve years old. These were followed by the mob of the town. The rear was brought up by the Jesuits' scholars. The whole body that made the procession were judged to be six or seven thousand persons.

Here are many furnaces to make brass of the copper which they have from Swedeland [Sweden], the lapis calaminaris of which the brass is made being in great plenty near. 26 August. About three this afternoon I went by waggon to Alden[hoven], which is a small village and my accommodation very indifferent. I supped that night with two [blank] nuns that were going from Cologne to Aix to drink the waters. The next morning I passed through the town of Juliers [Jülich], which has but four small streets which make a cross.

Anonymous tourist, c. 1701

[28] Maastricht is capable of containing at least twenty thousand men; there are twelve thousand in it at present. The bastions are not part of the walls as in other places, but stand out by themselves; there are eighteen in all. I do not remember to have seen there one half-moon, but all are complete bastions. They are generally placed four or five together so as to defend one another. There is no ditch or palisades between them but on the outside, so as to defend them all together. On that side where the little river [Jeker] runs there is nothing but one or two bastions at a good distance. This because they can overflow the country in a few hours' time when there is occasion, and they go in a boat to those bastions. There are two hundred pieces of cannon in the town.

I wondered to see so famous a place commanded by two mountains, which are each of them about a mile off or not much more. Upon one of them they are now building a fort [St Pierre], which will quickly be finished [in 1703]. This is only one single bastion, but so large that it will contain three hundred men and be able to hold out fifteen days. There is a way to it underground, whereby the men may be perpetually relieved. It is a post for a commanding officer. They design to make another fort upon the other hill, but the place being very strong towards that, it is not so necessary.

These risings are good to bombard the town, but signify nothing to bother the walls. The fortress now raising will annoy the enemy for a great way, so that they will hardly think of attacking it on that side, which is very strong and well-fortified, and I believe [the fort] might more easily be taken than Maastricht, there being not so many outworks. But then there being a large river between, it is a new work to besiege the town, so that [fortress] must be taken first.

Anonymous tourist, 26 August - 2 September 1711 N.S.

[17r] On Wednesday the 26th we came to Louvain, a university, but for the rest an old and shattered town of no note. From thence to Tirlemont [Tienen], a less town and in the same condition. From thence to St-Trond [Sint-Truiden], all along through a very pleasant country, but so dispeopled by the war that if it were not for the churches, which being pretty thick and handsome would make one believe it well-peopled, would be the most desolate place imaginable. From St Trond the same day to Maastricht, which is counted very strong, but I suppose the strength consists underground for mines, for above it has only an old-fashioned wall and a very large and deep ditch. For the rest of the outworks, they are not very regular nor seemingly strong. This town is handsome and has a very handsome stadt-house, and the churches and convents have been both fine and numerous, but since the Dutch have been masters of it, they have made several of the churches arsenals and offices [18] for other uses. Some are shut up, some turned into Dutch, French and other Reformed churches, and the convents are decaying apace, being most of them interdicted filling up their vacancies as they happen, which is an effectual though slow way.

On Thursday the 27th we came over a very fine country, but wild and unenclosed, to Aix-la-Chapelle. But when we came within a league of this free city, the effects [of enclosure] were visible to be seen: all the hills, which make a most beautiful prospect, enclosed and improved as much as England, which I had not seen before upon the Continent. The town is nothing strong, but depends upon being supported by all its neighbours and feared by none.

In this town it is that Charlemagne lies, and they show you [an] abundance of relics necessary to the ceremony of crowning the Emperor. The cup front [shrine] (in which is some of St Stephen's blood), if I may so call it, of I know not what sort of power, very richly set with stones; the book they swear upon; a piece of Charlemagne's skull; [19] some of the Virgin's hair, set between two stones and the portrait of the Virgin and a little Jesus, cut [painted] as they say by St Luke himself (both found in Charlemagne's tomb). They also show you a leather girdle which Our Saviour used to wear, which is sealed with a great piece of wax, as they say by the Emperor Constantine, because nobody should take the length of it. Also they have a girdle of the Virgin, which seems to be beggars' inkle [linen tape]. They show likewise one of the thorns taken out of Our Saviour's crown, one of St Thomas's teeth, some of St John the Baptist's hair, a cross made of the real cross, with a great many more.

They have [an] abundance of very rich gifts made upon the account of these relics, which are of immense value. Among the rest Isabella Infanta has left her crown of great value there [in 1629], and Queen Mary [Tudor] of England has done the like, and both of them have given robes for the images of the Virgin and little Jesus, all set with pearls and precious stones of great value. Several late Emperors have done the same, and they have the robes that all the Emperors have been anointed in till of late, almost ever since Constantinus. But among other robes they show a lively blue silk one, embossed behind and before with crosses of small pearl, which, they say, St Bernard consecrated mass in five hundred years ago [1146], whereas one could scarcely [20] believe that such sort of silks have been made above a hundred years [ago]. They show you also a pulpit wainscoted with massy gold and a box, or rather chest of drawers of the same in front, wherein lie the bones of Charlemagne and St Leopold [Leopard], a Roman gentleman.

I forgot to mention a piece of the sponge which was given to Our Saviour with vinegar, and a piece of one of the nails he was nailed with.

But above all the rarities are five [four], which are not to be seen, but only the pictures of the relics. A thing like a coffin is hung over the image of the Virgin, divided they tell you into five partitions, in one whereof is, they say, a piece of the cloth that was wrapped about Our Saviour's middle at his crucifixion; in the second a piece of the cloth wrapped about him in the sepulchre; in the third a piece of the cloth that the Virgin wiped him with; in the fourth [blank]; but the fifth contains a rarity above all rarities: a bottle wherein is a drop of the blood of Our Saviour's foreskin when he was circumcised, and a piece of the small indent taken from him.

Here are several religious houses in this town. Among the rest, the Capuchins have the prettiest garden I have yet seen belonging to any of the convents, but nothing else extraordinary. I was there at the monstrous ceremony of carrying Charlemagne to his winter quarters, which is always done upon the 1st of September, the time they rejoice for the restoration of the Popish magistracy to the city [1614], which had been usurped, as they say, by the Protestants. At this time they carry about a vast figure representing Charlemagne, at least fifteen foot high, with a model of [21] the Great Church in his hand, and all the orders of the town march before him according to their seniority in the town. And first (in this order) the Capuchins, 2. the Carmelites, 3. the Augustines, 4. Dominicans, 5. the Recollets, then Charlemagne, then the chanoines of the town, the host and the burghers. Capuchins and Recollets, both Franciscan orders, dark brown habit, without shoes and stockings, only distinguished by the cap. The Carmelites white upon black; the Dominicans black upon white and the Augustines all black.

In this town (and at Burtscheid) are abundance of hot springs of all degrees of heat and different degrees of mixture with sulphur and other minerals, and the town upon the whole does not a little resemble the Bath in England.

Anonymous tourist, 3-17 June 1720 N.S.

[20v] Aix lies in a valley surrounded with hills. It is not very considerable, most houses there being for the reception of strangers in the time of the season. There was scarce any diversions this season. There is but one fountain for drinking the waters, with walks near it, pretty well-kept. There are several baths [with] different degrees of heat to suit people's various tempers.

At a short mile's distance lies Burtscheid, a little village where there are several baths, much hotter than those [21v] of Aix. There are three springs, whereof one is boiling and will boil an egg in a minute. The coolest one cannot bear one's hand in more than a very short space of time. From these three springs they let in water in the baths, but must leave it a whole night and more to cool, before it be fit for people to come into it. In most of these, men and women bathe promiscuously. At some short distance out of the village, is a fountain like that at Aix, and of the same nature, but as it is not encouraged and fitted up, few people make use of it. That little town belongs to a convent situated in it, where there are women of quality of the Minorites [Cistercian] order.

There is nothing remarkable at Aix but the cathedral, where is the tomb of Charlemagne, under a great crown that hangs over it. The structure of the church is not very good, but in the sacristy are very rich cloths for the ornaments of the altar and the priests, and many relics, richly inlaid with gold and jewels. In the choir is a pulpit most of solid gold with a beautiful and very large agate upon one of the sides. The great altar is also most of it solid gold. They showed us the four gospels, [22v] very fairly written and of great antiquity upon leaves of trees [=vellum] in golden letters, and fine pictures whereupon the Emperors swear at their coronation. In a silver-gilded chest are reposited four relics which they value highly, and expose to view only every seventh year. They were to show them this year on St John's Day [24 June] and the fortnight following. There is a shift of the Virgin Mary, the cloth wherewith Our Lord covered his nakedness upon the cross, etc.

The fair is kept in the galleries of the Great Church. We stayed at Aix a fortnight at Florentin, the Dragon d'Or, a good house, but at some distance from the fountain; things are there tolerably cheap: dinner three shillings, and two at supper; burgundy and champagne two shillings a bottle; moselle three shillings. [cont. Liège, Spa and Namur]

Thomas Malie, 20-23 May (31 May - 3 June) 1722

[85] Set out from Tongres [Tongeren] at an half an hour after three p.m. and arrived safe at seven in the evening at Maastricht, and inned at the Windmill, where we supped and lay, a very good inn. Monday the 21st of May, Captain Maat called on me and Mr le Comte [Pieter Coenraad] de Leide[n], who offered to show us the town, etc., which we accepted.

Maastricht is situated upon the Maas, which receives the Jaar or Jeker; it has six gates, besides the water-port, viz. Notre Dame, St Pierre, of Tongres or Linckel port, of Bois-le-Duc, or Hoochter port and that of Wyck, which is also called porte d'Allemagne. This is one of the best fortified towns in Europe, and a bulwark [86] of the Republic of the United Provinces or United Netherlands on this side [of] the country. It has a suburb strongly fortified called the Wyck on the east side, and both parts are united by a most elegant and beautiful bridge much admired by all judges. This bridge has nine arches, eight of which are built of freestone, and the ninth of wood so ingeniously contrived that without destroying it they can take it to pieces and cut off all communication with Wyck. This wooden arch is between seventy and eighty foot long and under it the boats pass that go from Holland to Liège.

The town is generally reckoned in the province of Brabant, but the [87] Wyck in the diocese of Liège. It is about four miles in circumference and the whole garrisoned by the Dutch. The streets are long, the buildings mostly of brick covered with slate. The marketplace is very spacious and the stadhouse built of freestone after the model of that of Amsterdam, it has one of the finest steeples in the Low Countries. It contains a very good library of books, manuscripts and other rarities worthy to be seen.

The ramparts of Maastricht consist of the old enclosure flanked with small towers and ancient bastions. But the principal strength of the place lies in several bastions, some great, some small, [88] in several hornworks and a covered way in some places double and in others triple; the whole supported with a vast number of mines. They can form two inundations round the town to prevent its being approached on the side of Liège and the other on the side of Bois-le-Duc. Besides on the Liège side there is a very strong entrenchment on the declivity of a hill, called Fort St Pierre, and is able to hold thirteen or fourteen thousand men, planted with good artillery. This fort consists of a large bastion with a very good casement [casemate], a counterscarp, and two covered ways. The whole supported with entrenchments which extend right and left to the inundation formed by the little river Jeker.

The suburbs of Wyck [89] have a rampart a quarter of a league in circumference, flanked with three large bastions joining to the body of the place. It has likewise another enclosure of earth flanked with several bastions, ravelins and a covered way. There are likewise two isles, one above the other below the bridge which are strongly entrenched and defended with redoubts and other works. In short, Maastricht is not only the strongest fortress in Europe but also the most plentiful, abounding in game, fish and all the necessaries of life at a moderate expense. Every day a boat goes from Maastricht at nine in the morning for Liège. And every day there are coaches, called diligences, which go to Aix-la-Chapelle, to Holland, to Bruxelles and to Cologne in one day. Very few towns (if any) are provided with so many conveniencies for travellers as this is.

[90] On Wednesday the 23rd of May [we] set out from Maastricht at seven in the morning and arrived at Gulpen or Gallop at eleven. We dined here very elegantly upon some fine trout and crayfish, etc., for this place is famous for trout, crayfish and all kind of game, etc.

Maastricht

Population: 15,000 (1650), 14,000 (1713), 11,000 (1760).

Distances: Aix 6 hours (18 miles), Brussels 18 hours (57 miles), 's-Hertogenbosch 20 hours (62 miles), Liège 4 hours (12 miles).

Inns, *Reisboek* (1689, 1700 and 1721): De Wintmolen*; De Halve Maan*; Het Postpaard*; En bij de Poorten [not 1721].

Aachen

Population: 10,000-20,000 (1650-1750).

Distances: Liège 9 hours (26 miles), Maastricht 6 hours (18 miles), Spa 8 hours (25 miles).

Inns, *Reisboek* (1689, 1700 and 1721): De Peereboom*, op de markt; De Klok*, in de kleine [1721: grote] Kolderstraat; De Klosbaan, in de groote Kolderstraat [not 1721]; De Gulde Poort*, in de Wasserstraat.

Further reading

Beschryving van de beroemde en van ouds vermaarde vrye Keiserlyke Ryks- en Kroning-stad Aken, Leiden 1727.

[C.L. von Poelnitz], *Amusemens des eaux d'Aix-la-Chapelle*, Amsterdam 1736.

[P.L. de Saumery], *Les délices du païs de Liège et de la comté de Namur*, Liège 1738-1744.

B. Poll, *Geschichte Aachens in Daten*, Aachen 1960.

Miscellanea Trajectensia, bijdragen tot de geschiedenis van Maastricht, H.H.E. Wouters et al., Maastricht 1962.

P.J.H. Ubachs, *Tweeduizend jaar Maastricht*, Maastricht 1991.

Ach Lieve Tijd, twintig eeuwen Maastricht en de Maastrichtenaren, P.A.W. Dingemans (ed.), Zwolle 1994-

Publications de la société historique et archéologique dans le Limbourg, 1864-

De Maasgouw, tijdschrift voor Limburgse geschiedenis en oudheidkunde, 1879-

Zeitschrift des Aachener Geschichtsvereins, 1879-

Aachener Kunstblätter, 1906-

Mechelen and Leuven

William Lord Fitzwilliam, April 1663

[7r] [Coming from Brussels] Our next journey was for Louvain, where we arrived about eight o'clock at night. The next morning we went to see this famous university, it has been the nursery of many learned men. Otherwise, its schools and colleges are but very ordinary; in respect of the colleges of Cambridge and Oxford they are but dunghills. The town is very big but not much inhabited: few houses and those very old; fields, meadows and trees within the walls (which ambitus is very great), which are of no great strength, yet it has been able to hold out against the French and to cool their courage. They lay a very long time before it and yet could not take it [1635]. I suppose they were only in jest, otherwise I should think them very great cowards, for had they but shot with sugar balls upon the town they had questionless gained it.

It is said that this town is bigger than Gand by three verges [roods], and bigger than Liège by eight verges, and bigger than Paris without the suburbs by twenty [ten] verges; bigger than Cologne by twenty-eight [eighteen] verges. The whole circuit of it does amount to eight Italian miles. St Peter's church is the chiefest of this town. Here are the Franciscans, Carthusians and Jesuits besides many other religious houses for men and women. [7v] Upon St Quentin's churchyard we read the history of a man who used to say always his Pater Noster and Ave Maria on this churchyard, and being one day at his devotion, two of his enemies came to kill him. And he being unable to defend himself, the dead bodies of this churchyard took pity on him and rescued him from his enemies. This history is written and painted and believed as an article of faith.

We saw here likewise a very well-built town house, and a castle lying upon a hill, formerly the residence of the Counts of this town. Charles V, being very young, was brought up here with his sisters. Here lived King Edward [III] of England with his Queen a whole winter [1338-1339], at his coming to demand help of this country against Philip [VI], King of France, against whom he did intend to wage war. Here lived likewise the learned [Erycius] Puteanus, who has left so many learned works behind him.

This university took its original from the University of Cologne, now it is more famous and more frequented than its mother. The governors of it are the rector magnificus and the senatus academicus; every six months there is a new rector, who is chosen by the senatus academicus. Before the rector goes always a beadle, carrying a sceptre, and [on] holy days or other days of solemnity he has eight

Mechelen. Jesuits' college, 1727

beadles before him, besides servants who follow him. It is said that Charles V should have given the wall [precedence] to the rector of this university. He has a universal jurisdiction over the scholars; the town has nothing to do with them who are in albo academico [registered students], not so much as in criminal matters.

To the university belongs likewise a chancellor whose office is to graduate or confer degrees as bachelors, doctors, etc. on scholars of worth and merit. To this office pretends the prepositus [incumbent] of St Peter's to have right, or in his absence his dean. Here are some colleges where [8r] poor scholars are maintained, but their stipends are not near so good as them of Cambridge or Oxford. The schools have been formerly a clothiers hall, whose company was once very great and numerous in this town. But their privileges being diminished and infringed, they went away in a fury and seated themselves in England.

Out of Louvain you may go to see the park, where you will find a very pretty convent of Augustin nuns. You may likewise see Heverlee, a gentleman's house, which after we had seen and all the other things of this town within and without, talked with a Jesuit who heartily did wish for our conversion, we bent our course for Mechelen, one of the fairest and greatest cities of Brabant.

It is situated in the very heart of Brabant, equally distant from Brussels, Antwerp and Louvain, only four hours of each of them. It lies on even plain ground, no hills about it, and a river [Dyle] runs by it. It has good walls about it, but the water does defend it much better, which upon all occasion may be brought round about it. The streets are here very great, big and broad, well-paved and very clean; the houses uniformly built.

The chiefest church is St Rombald's with a very high steeple on top of it, a little more than half finished, which, if it had been wholly done, the steeple of Strasbourg would hardly have equalized its height. Here are seven parishes, many religious and pious houses. The Jesuits' college and their chapel we did see, as likewise the Capuchins and their pretty garden. We saw also some other religious women, called in Dutch Begijnen, who are nuns but not obliged to such a strict life. They have their liberty to go abroad, converse with men, and to serve God at their appointed hours. In this convent they say there are sometimes twelve hundred together. There are everywhere in the popish Low Countries [8v] suchlike religious women, but scarcely anywhere in such a quantity as here.

Here is likewise to be seen the town and Parliament house, several great and spacious marketplaces, clothiers and shoemakers [butchers] hall, who make up the greatest part of this town and do enjoy great privileges. They have the liberty of hunting as well as the best gentlemen of the whole country. Besides, here are some fraternities, as that of St George. They exercise themselves in shooting with bows and arrows or with guns, and to this end and purpose they have fair great houses and gardens. We did lodge in one of them à l'enseigne de l'Allemand [Den Duyts].

This town is governed partly by the royal, partly by the city magistrate. The kingly is called the Royal [=Great] Council or Parliament. The author of it was Charles, Duke of Burgundy, anno 1473. Its form was afterwards changed by Philip I [the Handsome], King of Spain (who got the Low Countries by his wife Johanna [his mother Maria]), so that there is now one president, sixteen counsellors, two notaries and eight secretaries. The whole Netherlands may appeal to this court, but from itself there is no further appellation. All their sentences are irrevocable, only a revision is permitted, and all their pleading is performed in the French language, as most familiar and common to the people of Flanders. Before this court the knights of the Golden Fleece may be cited, which otherwise is not permitted. Here has been formerly the Court of Burgundy. Philip the Handsome, Charles the Fifth's father, made it a province by itself, and consequently its jurisdiction is different from all the rest of Brabant. The city magistrate consists of twelve men, six of the best sort of people, the other six of the meanest rank of people. Here they make the best and dearest linen. The people are extraordinary civil. This is all that which I did remark here; from hence we went directly to Antwerp. [cont. Antwerp]

Sir Edmund Prideaux, 16-21 April 1712 N.S.

[79v] April 16th, 1712. We took coach at eight for Louvain, four hours from Bruxelles, we came in about two in the afternoon, being delayed about two hours by the breaking of our axletree. We went to lodge at the Golden Sun. Father Moran and Father Caghlan came to see Mr Bellings, with whom we went to see Mr Ratcliffe and Mr Willoughby at the English nuns, where we also saw Mrs Eire, newly come from England, Mr Lind, the confessor, and Mr Jomenit his assistant. We went to see Doctor Martin, an Irish professor of the university. We passed [78r] the evening with Mr Ratcliffe and with Mr Willoughby, who live in pension with the English nuns.

17th. We went the afternoon to see Mother Plowden, prioress of the English chanoinesses regular, where we also saw the Lady Ursula Stafford, Sister Ireland and others. We supped this night with Doctor Martin in the company of the president of the divinity college, a Flemish baron, and of Mr Bellew, the Lord Bellew's nephew.

18th. Sir Thomas Gage and Mr Throgmorton came this day to Louvain. We went with them in the afternoon to see the Irish Recollets and from thence to the English nuns.

19th. We saw the handsome church of the Jesuits [1666] and the convent of the Celestines without the town, where the family of the Dukes of Aarschot, now of Arenberg, have their vault and tombs, with good marble statues of several of their ancestors. They pretend to derive their pedigree from Adam.

20th. We dined this day at the English nuns with Mrs June and all our English gentlemen; we saw the convent of the Irish Dominicans, whereof Father Magee is prior. We then saw the Irish college under the direction of Doctor Sullivan, who passes for a learned man in the university. Mr Ratcliffe and Mr Willoughby supped with Mr Bellings.

21st We set out after dinner for Bruxelles with Mr Throgmorton; we went to lodge at the Wolf.

John Leake, 11 (22) June 1712

[34r] [From Antwerp] In three or four hours we arrived at Mechelen, where after having refreshed ourselves with a moderate repast, we got a guide to show us what was most remarkable in that city. The first place he brought us to was the cathedral, which is dedicated to St Rumbold, a fine building and has a high steeple furnished with good chimes. It is an archbishop's see, whose authority is of a prodigious extent. From hence we went to the large and spacious convent of the Franciscans; we were shown their garden as a curiosity in its kind, but we could observe nothing but what was mean about it.

We took a view of the Jesuits' chapel and convent and hastened to St Catherine's gate to feast ourselves with the sight of the noble nunnery of the

Beguines, in the middle of which stands a stately church dedicated to Saint Alexius, president of their order. In this convent are constantly living more than fifteen hundred holy virgins under the tutelage and inspection of four ladies chosen from among themselves. They divide their time betwixt their devotions and making of lace. They have the liberty of going and coming from and to their cloister at pleasure, and if they think fit of altering their conditions from a single to a married life without being subject to the least reproach for so doing. Methinks an institution somewhat like this for ladies of good family, [35r] but a small fortune, would not be amiss, even in a reformed country.

We went from hence to Vilvoorde, where we first saw the dreadful tokens and effects of war. Thence we went along a fine canal in a floating house to Brussels.

Sir John Percival, 20-21 August (31 August - 1 September) 1723

[11r] On the 20th August having settled some affairs with my banker, Mr Conen, we set out [from Liège] for St Trond and in the afternoon arrived through Tirlemont at Louvain, where we lay at the Soleil d'Or, a very good inn.

Louvain is a large town, though containing but seven parishes. It has a great many religious houses and a famous university. I had the curiosity to see there a disputation in the civil law school, and there I heard [an] abundance of wrangling. It was held for taking a licentiate's degree. The hall where the divines, civilians and physicians keep their schools is neatly filled up, and painted on the sides, but the preparations in it are poor.

The Jesuits' college and church are, as everywhere else, large and handsome. The church is after the model of that at Bruges and the library worth seeing. It is a long gallery, divided into three rooms, which contains 3670 folios besides smaller volumes, but they [11v] own no manuscript ancienter than St Bernard's age, who died in 1153. The cathedral is Gothic and contains nothing worth mentioning.

Mechelen

Population: 22,000 (1668, 1700), 18,000 (1750).

Distances: Antwerp 4 hours (12 miles), Brussels 4 hours (12 miles), Leuven 4 hours (11 miles).

Inns, *Reisboek* (1689, 1700 and 1721): De Swaan* (op de Groote Markt); De Kraan*; Den Emmer*; Het Goude Hoofd*; Den Helm; Den Duits (op de Koornmarkt). *Reisboek* (1700 and 1721) also: De Keizerin*, De Ketel* (op de Koornmarkt); De Bruid, aan d'Ysere Leen. Hier zijn de karren op Lier.

Leuven

Population: 15,000 (1695, 1755).

Distances: Brussels 4 hours (15 miles), Liège 14 hours (35 miles), Mechelen 4 hours (12 miles).

Inns, *Reisboek* (1689, 1700 and 1721): De Zon*; Den Arend*.

Further reading

J.B. Gramaye, *Antiquitates Belgicae*, Bruxelles-Leuven 1708.

A. Sanderus, *Chorographia sacra Brabantiae*, Bruxelles 1659-1660; 's-Gravenhage 1726-1727.

M. Kocken, *Gids voor Oud-Mechelen*, Antwerpen-Haarlem [1981].

J.A. Torfs, *Geschiedenis van Leuven van de vroegste tijd tot op heden*, Tienen-Leuven 1984.

R. van Uytven (ed.), *De geschiedenis van Mechelen*, Tielt [1991].

Mededelingen van de Geschied- en Oudheidkundige kring van Leuven en omgeving, 1961-

Handelingen van de Koninklijke Kring voor Oudheidkunde, Letteren en Kunst van Mechelen, 1889-

Mons and Tournai

William Lord Fitzwilliam, 15 April 1663 N.S.

[5r] From hence [Valenciennes] we went to lodge at Mons, the metropolis of Hainaut, lying on the side of a hill, and the river Trouille runs under or by its walls. This place is both by nature and art very strong. It has the convenience to drown the country round [5v] about it and set itself wholly in water. It is surrounded with strong stone walls and has three ditches likewise about it. By a strategem took it Lewis of Nassau [24 May 1572], but it did not remain very long in his hands: the Spaniard retook it the same year [19 September].

Here is to be seen the college of women chanoines, who in the morning, or at any time appointed for devotion, are clad like religious women and lead likewise a solitary religious life. Yet notwithstanding when they have a mind to go abroad, they put on a worldly habit and leave with their clothes their religious manner of living, go to be merry, dance, play and do what they please. They are all noble women or persons of the greatest condition. They are maintained for nothing as long as they live unmarried, marriage being permitted and left in their choice. Which if they do embrace, they have nothing more to do with the convent.

Here resides likewise the Parliament of Hainaut, which consists of the governor of this province and four senators who decide all sort of cases without any further appellation to the court of Mechelen. Here we supped, and the next morning we did bend our course towards Brussels. We passed by Braine-le-Comte, a poor country town, where we did likewise dine. We came also to Notre Dame de la Halle, a pretty strong town, and a fair great church within it, not far from Brussels. [cont. Brussels]

Anonymous tourist, 19-21 August 1711 N.S.

[14r] Wednesday August the 19th, we came to Tournai, which is a very pretty town. The lower part of it, which has a fine river running through it, is very like the towns in Holland, and I believe mostly inhabited by Dutch. The upper part more after the Flemish way of building, but nothing remarkably fine, besides two churches, one the cathedral [Notre Dame] and the other [St Martin] belongs to the monks of St Benoît [Benedict], which are fine in the most different manners. The latter a new airy building and excellent for the air and lightsomeness, the other the most gross, solemn structure I ever saw. The windows very finely painted, but the pictures nothing extraordinary. It is adorned with the finest statues of the apostles I

ever saw, most excellently cut, as big as the life in marble, but by whom I could not hear.

But the citadel is a regular pentagon (as the citadel of Lille is also) and a wonder for strength and was as wonderfully held out in 1709 by Monsieur Surville, till all was beaten down and demolished, and the fighting came to be all underground.

From Tournai we came Thursday [15r] the 20th to Ath, a small fortification. The town [is] very indifferently built and the works nothing extraordinary for strength. Friday the 21st we came in the morning to Enghien, a miserable poor town that has been thrice lately plundered by the armies, but the castle and the gardens were saved, which belong to the Duke of Aarschot, now Duke of Arenberg.

The form of the gardens is ancient-fashioned, but mighty prettily disposed upon the brow of a hill. In the park is a stately dome of a heptagonal figure, built of marble, standing in the middle of a large basin and is extremely beautiful and costly. Seven large avenues front the middle of the seven sides and seven small ones the corners, which are each of them supported by two marble pillars. One of the avenues is a walk from the house of about three hundred paces long as I conjecture. There is also a mall of proportionable dimension and I guess half as long as that at St James', on each side whereof there is elm hedges, kept clipped, of a very great height, which makes it look very agreeable and melancholy. From Enghien we came the same day to Brussels.

John Leake, 13-14 (24-25) June 1712

[36r] We consulted [37r] with our friend Goodeau about the safest and cheapest method of going to the army. It was his advice that, being six in number, we should agree for two berlines to go with us quite to the army, and attend upon us there during our stay in it. Accordingly, we agreed with a man at two pistoles a head for the said conveniences. And after having been kindly entertained by Monsieur Goodeau overnight at his lodgings, we went into them at four o'clock in the morning, being June the 13th.

At noon we arrived at Enghien, where we had but just time to dine and take a view of the house and gardens belonging to the duke of that name. The house lies in great disorder, it being above half destroyed by fire, but the gardens look the cheerfullest of any I saw in the Low Countries. There are most stately covered walks, large remains of fine flower gardens, and in the centre of what they call the Park, a pleasure house, from whence you have fourteen different vistas. We fared the worst and paid the dearest for our ordinary here of any place since we left Holland.

In our afternoon's travelling through a desolate country and upon our frequent meeting of unhappy wretches upon gibbets, we began extremely to blame ourselves for not having furnished ourselves with firearms. As we came within sight of Ath, our coachman informed us we were very happy in having passed the worst

Enghien. The pavilion, c. 1690

ground for robbing between Brussels and the army. And indeed, a gallows hard by, with eighteen or twenty fresh corpses upon it who had suffered for their villainies in that kind, made us easily believe our guides in this point. However, under the conduct of God's good providence we found ourselves all safe in the strong town of Ath before sunset.

Ath is no large town but pleasantly situated [38r] and so well fortified as to be able to make no inconsiderable defence. Before the late wars it was the staple of these parts for linen cloth, which brought the inhabitants great gain and continually filled their streets with foreigners, who came to stock themselves with that commodity. At present the numerousness of its garrison and the conveniences it affords them for a comfortable subsistence are the chief things it has to boast of. So soon as our berlines came within sight of this place we heard a' drum beat, which continued to do so till we were entered within the gates and had shown our passes. We found that this alarm was always sounded upon the approach of any passengers to this frontier town.

The 14th, early in the morning, we steered our course for Tournai, where we arrived just as the gates were shut upon their governor's going to dinner. This circumstance, which is constantly practised in all garrison towns, obliged us to wait without until His Honour had satisfied his appetite. Our residence happening to be just where one of the attacks was made in the late siege [1709], we employed ourselves in viewing the destruction and ruins that were occasioned by the batteries and mines in those almost impregnable outworks.

Upon our entrance into the city, I was obliged on behalf of all the company to sweat after a grenadier from one officer's quarters to another, to obtain leave to refresh ourselves in an inn, which being at last granted, we had but just time enough left us to take an outside view of the strongest citadel in the world, before our coachmen called upon us to re-enter our berlines if we designed to reach St Amand that night.

Upon our passing through [39r] this place, we found it very large, and amidst all the dreadful warlike preparations and stores that it abounded withal, some faint marks of its former riches and grandeur did appear. I could not forbear having a more particular regard for this city than for any other in these parts, as having been heretofore part of the English Empire. For though it boasts an antiquity of some centuries before Christ, and it did actually once enjoy the privilege of being an independent sovereignty, yet our King Henry VIII besieged it in the year 1513, forced it to yield to his will and to pay a hundred thousand ducats to preserve itself from being plundered. However, after having added new fortifications to the place and built the citadel and made his favourite Wolsey bishop of this see, he thought fit to sell it to the French in the year 1518 for a vast sum of money. The new church of St Martin, built by the present French King Louis XIV is the most considerable building at present in Tournai. [cont. The Army]

Anonymous tourist, 8-17 July 1720 N.S.

[32v] [After a journey from Namur to Brussels] Set out at six o'clock in exactly such another coche for Mons, and dined pretty well in a village called Braine-le-Comte; extraordinary fine country; good road, being all the way a causeway [from 1705]. Arrived at Mons about eight o'clock (ten leagues). Went the next day to see the Great Church, called St [Waudru] belonging to the chanoinesses, whereof there is a chapter (their number is forty-eight [thirty]). The jubé is adorned with marble statues very well-made, among the rest the representation of Strength breaking a large club; the rent in the marble is admirably well-done.

These young ladies are all persons of quality, they are allowed to marry but forfeit thereby their order. N.B. When there is a vacant place they name three to be presented to the Emperor out of which he chooses one. But before she can be admitted she must make her proofs of nobility of sixteen quarters and illustrations, and all noble of the sword. Their revenues are about four hundred crowns each, but those that are elderly, to increase their revenues, have the liberty to board some of the young ones at four hundred guilders per annum, over whom they have an authority. There are ten houses wherein they live and there are at all of them assemblies. We were in the evening introduced into one of the assemblies [33v] by Mr O'Connor, an Irish gentleman, a lieutenant-colonel in the Emperor's service, to whom we were recommended by Mr Devenitz. The gentlemen play at cards with them as in other assemblies.

The church is very large and spacious but nothing very remarkable in it. Went to the Ursulines; their church is very neat and handsome, exactly built after the model of that at Namur. Saw the governor's (Duke of Arenberg) house and garden, which is pretty enough.

Mons is situated on the side of the hill in a fine country, pretty well fortified, an imperial garrison (two hundred men). Lodged at the Licorne, indifferent, but the best there.

Set out in the same sort of coche for Tournai; passed through a great wood where there is watches kept to prevent robberies, which used to be frequently committed in the time of war. This wood belongs to the Prince of Ligne. He has here his hunting seat, where every year he resides for some time to take the diversion of hunting the wild boar, etc. Dined in a very poor village about four and a half leagues from Mons, where no wine. As this country has been the seat of war, most of these villages have been destroyed, yet the country is [34v] very fruitful and productive of very good corn. The road is but indifferent. Arrived at Tournai about eight o'clock in the evening, nine leagues. Went the next day to Mr Wauvran's, the gentleman we were recommended to by Mr Le Camus, who received us very kindly and entertained us at his house very handsomely.

Went to see the church of the Benedictines, called St Martin's, which is a very handsome structure, being very neat and handsome within, but the roof not high enough, which was occasioned by Mr Mesgrigny's complaining if it was raised higher it would have a prospect into the citadel, but as the friars say: at their own expense. This church was built by the late French King, Louis XIV. Saw their library which is indifferent good; their gardens handsome.

Went to see the citadel (a pentagon regular, walled ramparts with a fausse braye and a ravelin à lunettes each two bastions), which has five bastions and many other strong works, and the whole has mines under it, in which subterraneous places it took us up almost two hours in walking, going under every point of the courtine [curtain], of each bastion, of every outwork and even under the glacis deep into the country. We there saw the several mines and went into some of the fourneaux [where explosives are placed]. Before the Allies took this, they were blown up three times by one of these mines, and it is believed they would not have been able to have taken it had not the enemies been almost starved for want of provisions, insomuch that for several days they were obliged to eat horseflesh.

[35v] This citadel and all its works was made by Monsieur de Mesgrigny, Lieutenant-General in the late King's service [Louis XIV], who then commanded in the citadel. Knowing that Mr Surville, who defended the town, would come and have after the surrender of the town a superior power in the citadel, he [Mesgrigny]

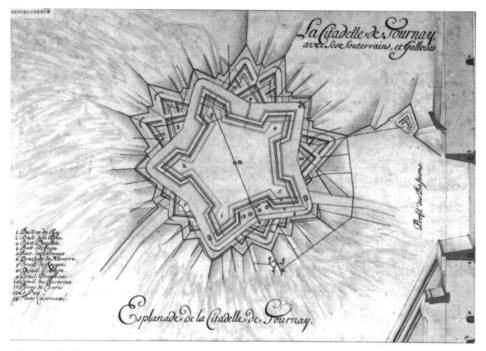

Tournai. Citadel, c. 1725

sold most of the magazines of the fortress to his own profit. He is still alive at Tournai but no more in the service. It cost the late King Louis XIV forty millions of dollars. On his viewing of it after it was finished, he found no other fault with it, but that he could not remove it to any place where he might have occasion for it.

Mr Wauvran's, after we had breakfasted with him, took a walk with us and showed us the garden of the Petit Jesuits, which is pretty enough, well-stocked with fruits. From thence to a house (of which there are several) to see a certain manufacture, which is peculiar to Tournai, of stuff which is made use of for the covering of chairs, not very unlike tapestry. Saw a couple of mills invented by Mr Mesgrigny and very remarkable, being able in one day to furnish corn for a hundred thousand men. N.B. There is a handsome quay where the Escaut [Schelde] has been made to run in a direct line through the town, and by the means of sluices makes two mills [go]. The Allies did all their endeavours to break them down with their cannon but could not succeed.

Went to the cathedral of Notre Dame, which is said to be built by one of our English kings; there is nothing very remarkable, except that it has abundance of chapels. Behind the grand autel a good picture of Rubens. Saw the library, which is a very good one, there being several curious books in it.

Took a walk the next day in the afternoon with Mr Wauvran's, Mr Beaudicher and Mr Maclean, a Scotch captain, and another gentleman to the garden of Mr

Beaudicher, which is well enough; were treated there with a cold tankard. At a little distance from thence is a mineral spring, but not much in vogue.

Not being allowed to carry out of the country more than the value of nine pistoles each, on Mr Beaudicher's offering his service, we went the next morning to leave the overplus in his hands, for which he gave us bills of exchange on his correspondent at Lille for the same value, which we received. Lodged at Tournai at the Impératrice, a very good house.

[37v] I had almost forgot, in Notre Dame at the right hand against the outside of the wall of the choir, are two monuments in marble, highly valued. And particularly a weeping child incomparably well-wrought. One is the memory of Scottus contubernio Lipsii chorus [Jean Schott, beloved among the friends of Justus Lipsius]. In the library there is a valuable collection of the best books of all sorts, as well modern as others. Several little pictures of ancient masters of 1430. Valuable. The picture of Luther when he was yet a friar. See the garden of the government, made up by my Lord Albemarle pretty well [when governor, 1709-1716]. The present governor of the garrison is Count Richtern [Van Rechteren]. See some other fruitful gardens; the fortifications. At the citadel, all the space between the wall and the fausse braye is also turned into gardens. Supped with Mr Wauvran's, his lady, Mr Hauchebord, Mr Beaudicher, a Scotch captain, Mr Maclean, etc., who the next day supped with us.

[38v] N.B. In the library at Notre Dame several curiosities such as the famous brass hand with a lizard upon the thumb and a pineapple in the middle and other hieroglyphics. An ancient pocketbook with wax and the stylus belonging to it. A dead head, made of one piece of ivory, admirably well-worked. The four gospels MS with incomparable pictures and draughts supposed to have been King Henry VIII's, by reason of the roses placed in several places, as there are several other proofs of his having been at Tournai. There is another MS where the leaves are marked with arithmetical figures in this manner: *1 2 ∿ 1 V* etc. and a book printed in , *1471* where the year is marked in the same figures. The book is Pisanus *In magistrum sententiarum*. The same figures are also to be seen at the bottom of a picture of 1466.

Tournai is a pretty handsome town, about as big again as Mons. The streets large and well-paved; pretty good houses but most of them old. The bishop's palace is nothing extraordinary. The present bishop is [39v] the Prince L[o]ewenstein of the house of Bavaria. He is also abbot of Stavelot, three leagues from Spa. Set out in the afternoon for Lille in a coche at four o'clock, five short leagues, fine paved road; very plentiful country for corn of all sorts and hay. Came to Lille at eight o'clock. [cont. Kortrijk and Lille]

Mons (Bergen)

Population: c.15,000 (1700-1750).

Distances: Brussels 10 hours (39 miles), Namur 10 hours (29 miles), Tournai 7 hours (22 miles), Valenciennes 7 hours (21 miles).

Inns, *Reisboek* (1689): St. Anthonis*. *Reisboek* (1700 and 1721) also: La Couronne Impériale*; Au Comte d'Egmont*; La Princesse d'Arenberg*; Le Pot d'Etain*; L'Ours*, à la place St Jean.

Tournai (Doornik)

Population: 20,000 (1650), 29,000 (1700), 21,000 (1750).

Distances: Brussels 15 hours (40 miles), Lille 5 hours (15 miles), Mons 7 hours (22 miles).

Inns, *Reisboek* (1689): De Faisant*. *Reisboek* (1700 and 1721) also: De Zilvere Bank*; De Zalm*.

Further reading

G.J. de Boussu, *Histoire de la ville de Mons,* Mons 1725.

[N. Poutrain], *Histoire de la ville et cité de Tournai,* 's-Gravenhage 1750.

Rolland, Paul, *Histoire de Tournai,* Paris 1964.

G. Jouret, *Histoire de Mons et du pays de Mons,* Mons 1974.

Annales du cercle archéologique de Mons, 1856-

Mémoires de la société royale d'histoire et d'archéologie de Tournai, 1980-

Noord-Holland

William Lord Fitzwilliam, May 1663

[19v] Holland being divided into North and South Holland, from Amsterdam I went to see North Holland. I arrived first at Buiksloot, which lies on the other side of the water [IJ] in Waterland, right over against Amsterdam. From hence I went by water to Monnickendam, where I found a fair great street from one gate to the other; many fair little ones. It lies by a great water in which, not far from Monnickendam, there is the island Marken.

From this town, being but an hour's going, we went on foot to Edam, lying on the Zuiderzee. In it we found a fair marketplace and a great church. In a house called the Prinsenhof we saw the picture of a very great woman, being but seventeen years old, above ten foot high, her shoe being above two spans long [c.40 cm.]. Here we saw likewise a picture of a man whose beard came down to his foot and up again to his breast, and another picture of a fat man who, being forty-two years old, was 455 pounds heavy. These three persons were born and died in this town. Here they make excellent good cheese, and this is all we found worthy our curiosity.

From hence we went by water to Hoorn, a fair great town, lying on the Zuiderzee. Here are fair and clean streets, a great church, a town- and States' house [Staten College], a very good haven, wherein we saw many [20r] good ships and eight frigates at anchor. Here we lodged a night at the White Swan, but paid too dear for our diet and lodging. The next morning we took the Apostels' post horses and so went to Enkhuizen, a great traffic town lying likewise on the Zuiderzee.

This town seems to be very great, by reason its houses are dispersedly built one from another. The chief things to be seen here are the East Indies' House and the house of Mr Steinbergen [Van Steenbergen], wherein are curious waterworks and a chamber of rarities, which is very precious and can scarcely be equalized in Europe. Here is a very good haven, which contains always very good ships, some men-of-war. And here are built abundance of ships as everywhere in North Holland. Here is likewise made very good salt, and its salt pits are very much esteemed.

From Enkhuizen we went by open waggon to Medemblik, lying like Hoorn and Enkhuizen on the Zuiderzee. We passed over the sea-banks, which made us to wonder by what art this furious element is kept in this country from the land, the sea being much higher than the land, and the banks being only of earth mixed with straw, and some stakes being driven into the sea, [20v] which break its force before

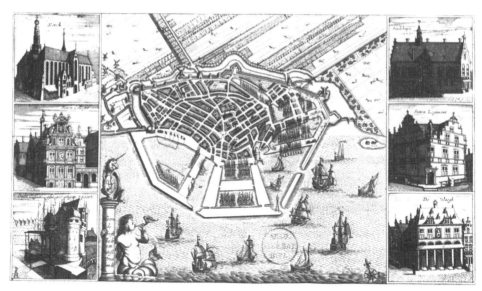

Hoorn. Town plan, 1648

it comes to the banks. In this town there is likewise a good haven and to defend it there is a strong castle. Here is likewise a town house and a great church, otherwise it is only a sea-town, a fit habitation for seamen and fishermen but for nobody else. It is very confusedly built, the houses very much distant one from another. And this is all we did remark here, and so we went from hence, having had a very short dinner, to Alkmaar, which is about four hours and a half distant from Medemblik.

Alkmaar is the chiefest and fairest town of North Holland, both within and without very pleasant. Round about the town there are very fair walks, all set with trees. The town itself is fortified with good earth walls and deep ditches. Here are many fair streets and marketplaces, as the fish and oxen. Here is a very good stad-house and weigh-house, upon which there is such a clock as at 's-Hertogenbosch upon the town house. Here are many places dedicated to a pious and religious life.

The Great Church is great and very well-built. In it we saw the seven works of mercy, very curiously painted [1504] and of an inestimable price. In fornice templi [on the vault of the church] there is a picture of the Last Judgement very well- [21r] done. Here is likewise a very old tomb of Florentin [V], Count of Holland. These following words are written upon it: 'Hier onder is ['t] inghewandt van Graef Floris van Holland, verslagen wordt van H[eer] Gerrit van Velsen.' [Below this lie the entrails of Count Floris of Holland, killed by Lord Gerrit van Velsen]

Here we lodged at the sign of the Weigh of Amsterdam, by one Cornelius van Rossen, where we were well treated and at a very good rate. This our landlord had by his wife in seven quarters of a year six children, whose picture is yet to be seen in his house. This town is very well-built and very pleasantly situated, most of the people live here on their rents; traffic and trade is here very poor.

From hence we went by close[d] waggon to Purmerend; we passed through Schermerhorn, the Beemster and the country about Purmerend, all [of] which places have been formerly water, but now they are the most sweet and delicious countries of North Holland, particularly the Beemster, now a continued meadow of seven [two] leagues long, which has been formerly a lake of so many leagues. Here are brave country houses, abundance of rich countrymen, many a hundred thousand guilders rich. Purmerend has its name from the water, which now is good land, on which it was situated: it is a little walled town. We found nothing in it worth our curiosity, wherefore we went from hence directly to Buiksloot by water and so to Amsterdam.

And so we finished our North Holland journey, where [21v] we found excellent pasture ground, filled up with good horses, cows and sheep of a very large size and very fruitful, almost every one bringing forth two and three lambs at a time. The people are here rude but neat, handsome, chiefly their women, and very industrious. They defend themselves stoutly against the sea by deep ditches and high and thick banks. Sometimes the sea encroaches upon them, and they upon the sea's limits by draining and drying up rivers and lakes. In winter it is their destiny to be always in water. [cont. Friesland]

John Leake, 27-29 August (7-9 September) 1711

[17r] The Monday following we went in a wind-schuyt to Buiksloot, and from thence in a treck-schuyt we passed by Broek [in Waterland], a village that prides itself for not having in it one inhabitant who takes alms. Thence we went to Monnickendam; thence to Edam, a small triangular city and famous for making the best cheese in Holland. Thence directly to Hoorn, where we arrived about three in the afternoon, after having been six hours in our passage from Buiksloot. We took up our quarters at the Moor's Head, where we were civilly and reasonably treated. We saw the old mansion house of the famous Counts of Hoorn [Staten College], the stadhouse, custom-house and [Admiralty] shipyard, but found nothing extraordinary in any of them.

August the 28th, at six in the morning, we went in a postwaggon for Enkhuizen, which place, though two long leagues distant from Hoorn, has a good paved causeway leading to it; which, however convenient in many respects, was particularly troublesome to us on account of the make of the Holland waggons, which are not only furnished with tire upon [18r] their wheels, but with several loose iron rings, which incessantly roar out rugged music to the no small disturbance of those who are not entirely deprived of the sense of hearing.

As soon as we arrived at Enkhuizen, we enquired for a vessel to waft us over to East Friesland, but we could get no skipper to do us that good office by reason the wind blew a stiff gale against us. This put us upon altering our measures and after having viewed the town, which seems to be the largest in Westfriesland, we went into their stadhouse, which is built à la mode romaine and is second to none in these parts but that of Amsterdam. We repassed our rattling causeway and reviewed the long row of houses which is continued almost to Hoorn. We observed that the Papists in these parts distinguish their houses from those of the Reformed by putting I.H.S. [Jesus] and a cross over their doors. There are not a few dwellings furnished with this discriminating mark. Being arrived again at Hoorn, we immediately took the schuyt for Alkmaar, where we came late that night.

The next day in the morning we traversed the town and diverted ourselves with observing the humour of the boors and boorennekies that came to the kermis, and whilst we were viewing the Great Church, we were agreeably surprised with no bad consort of music. At two in the afternoon we hired a waggon for Purmerend and by that means had the opportunity of passing through a tract of land called the Beemster, which the Dutch stole [19r] from the sea in the year 1611, and they have now made it a very pleasant spot of earth. The passage through it is either by several regular alleys of tall lime trees or upon very high causeways which both affords a good prospect of the neighbouring country, and is a good barrier to secure their acquisitions from the rage of their merciless neighbour, the sea. Having seen as much as we thought fit in Purmerend, we returned again to Amsterdam.

Richard Rawlinson, 24-27 September 1719 N.S.

[21] Set out at four for Buiksloot, where we arrived in half an hour, and paid each three stivers and went thence into another treckschuit for Purmerend, and arrived there about eight. For passage paid six stivers each, and an halfpenny each for entrance into the gate.

Monday 25 September, 1719 N.S. Walked about Purmerend in North Holland, saw the Great Church, which is large and plain with some ill-painted windows, and a stadthuys erected in 1590. Saw Myn Heer [Jacob] Spoors, who has a collection of paintings, prints, shells and books of the antiquities of Holland. He was eighty-four years of age and an old beguine, who keeps his house, eighty-two; both in good health and very hearty. When we entered his chief room he gave us a pair of straw slippers, and himself accompanied us without shoes. The reckoning came to two guilders nineteen stivers. From hence we set out about half after eleven in the morning for Hoorn, arrived at Oudendijk about one and at Hoorn in Westfriesland about half after two.

This is a small neat city, but has nothing remarkable to stay a stranger (paid seven stivers each), so that we set out [for Alkmaar] in very showery, wet weather precisely at four, and in three different treckschuits passed several villages before we arrived about nine at our inn, the City of [22] Amsterdam behind the Weigh-house. Paid for our freight nine stivers and for our entrance in, at the Frize gate, one stiver each.

View of Alkmaar, 1746

Friday 26 September, 1719 N.S. Saw this city of Alkmaar, and traversed the whole, which is neat. The Highstreet [Langestraat] is broadest, and in it is the stadthuys partly old and partly new. Over the entrance into the new part are the statues of Prudence and Justice with their proper insignia, under them this inscription in capitals: Opus hoc / Vetustate collapsum / Ex S[enatus]. C[onsulto]. / Restaurari curarunt / Cons[ules]. / MDCXCIV [in accordance with the decision of the city council the burgomasters had this building, decayed with age, restored in the year 1694].

At the upper end of this street is the church, old and built in the form of a cross, in which at the west end on the south wall are some ancient paintings on folding leaves. And at the west end on the north side of the door on a tablet in capital letters are these verses: Explicatio Hieroglyphicae Tabulae ... [23] R. de Hooghe J.V.D. et Corn. R. / Auct. D.D. 1693 [explanation of the symbols in the allegorical picture over the organs]. On the south side [of the door] on another tablet; in capitals is this inscription: In Magnificentiam / Organi ... J. Forestus / Alcmarianus [on the grandeur of the organ ... by Jan van Foreest of Alkmaar].

On another tablet, near and like the former, in capitals, is this inscription: Memoriale hujus Templi [Memorial of this church] [...] anno 1605 4 maii. [25] At the west end is a fair large organ with a small choir organ underneath. On the west wall of the south cross aisle is, on a board, this chronogram: **CLareat oCtobrIs LUX oCtaVa aLCMarIanIs** [May the light of 8th October shine over the citizens of Alkmaar, 1573]. On the east wall is a fair painting and escutcheon on which, by the painter's art, as the spectator stands on the left hand he sees the painter's face, on the right nothing. Underneath in capitals is this following inscription: Ossa hic expectant resurrectionem / Fredericus Westphalen / Enchusanus / Sac. Rom. Imp. Eques Auratus / Nec non Hierosolymitanus / post peragratam Europam, Asiam / atque Africam / diem extremum clausit Alcmariae / anno aetatis suae LXXII / a Christo nato MDCLIII / die II [XI] mens. octob. [Here the bones of Frederik Westphalen of Enkhuizen expect the resurrection. He was knight of the Holy

295

Roman Empire and of Jerusalem. After travelling through Europe, Asia and Africa, he concluded the last day of his life at Alkmaar, in his 72nd year, 2 [11] October 1653 A.D.].

Under another achievement, fixed to the north wall of that part of the church I conceive to have been formerly the choir, is this inscription in capitals: Memento mori / Felici memoriae / Nobilis ac generosi viri / Wilhelmi de Barden / domini de Warmenhuysen &c. / Equitis ordinis / [26] Sancti Michaelis. / obiit / XV Octobris Anno Christi MDCXXXI [Memento mori. To the happy memory of that noble and generous person Willem Bardes, Lord of Warmenhuizen, etc., knight of the order of St Michael. He died 15 October 1631 A.D.].

On a tomb in the middle is this inscription in very ancient characters: Hier onder leyt ingewant van Graef Florys van Hollant [die] verslagen wort van Gerrit van Velsen. Junii [Below this lie the entrails of Count Floris of Holland, killed by Lord Gerrit van Velsen in June 1296]. On another piece of black marble, joined: 1123.

In this church are several Dutch inscriptions, as there are on stones laid before several of the doors of the inhabitants, which once belonged to this church. In this town I saw ripe red and white currants, which I take to be rare at this time of the year.

Saw a handsome new hospital near the side of a canal for twenty-four women, who have each a separate house of one storey each. In the middle is a fair pump, and the area is a neat garden [Wildemanshofje, Oudegracht, founded 1714].

Went unto a painter and glazier op de Couterop [Luttik Oudorp] and saw Jacob [van Oudensteijn], admiral hollandois [commissioner of the Admiralty], who has travelled into England, Italy, Spain, and was taken prisoner into France, into whose service he afterwards listed, and was discharged from the prison of Pontaniou à Brest, 1 September 1691. He has a collection of drawings and prints of some particular masters as [Maarten van] Heemskerck, Albert Dürer, etc., and of him I bought ten views of public places in Haarlem for eighteen stivers, which were given him by the engraver himself. He is a Romanist, as I perceived by his crucifix and beads, and has about three hundred books neatly bound in vellum on various subjects.

Afterwards we went to the [27] Vischmarkt or Fishmarket, where we saw the collection of Mijnheer William Havenburgh [Havenberg], consisting of prints, drawings, etc., of which I bought two prospects of old castles: of Egmond Binnen, which lies about six miles from hence, and Den Hoef, which lies four miles and an half from this place, and a piece by Albert Dürer of Alexander's Triumphs, which cost one guilder. Saw the Waagh Huys or weigh-house, which on its frontispiece has a painting in fresco of weighing merchandizes, and over it: S.P.Q.A. Restituit Virtus ablatae jura bilancis [Courage and force gave back to the government and citizens of Alkmaar the right to have a weigh, which they had been deprived of]. Joining to it is a tower on which is a clock, and under it: Dies Extremus [alteri natalis, i.e. the last day is the birthday of the other life]. Near this place I saw a Dutch auction of chinaware, linen &c, which was in a method different from England: the auctioneer mentioning several prices, and the bidder stopping at the price he approved, and no increase to be made upon it.

Wednesday 27 September, 1719 N.S. Went to Mr Cleures in the Butterstreet and saw his prints and drawings, of which I bought four prospects of places in England on the river Thames, drawn by a Dutch soldier taken prisoner into England. From thence, directed and conducted by Claes [=Cleures], we went to Doctor Wandelaer, who has an original Dead Saviour of Vandyck, but a mean collection of prints. Paid our lodging and expenses eight guilders, and set out for Haarlem in the postwaggon about nine. Came through some wood and willows and at the foot of [28] some sandhills, which, the vulgar tradition says, were cast up from the sea in a night's time (but this is esteemed as fabulous by the more sensible people), and arrived at Haarlem about two [in the] afternoon.

Alkmaar

Population: 10,000-15,000 (1675), 5,000-10,000 (1750).

Distances: Amsterdam 7 hours (20 miles), Haarlem 5 hours (18 miles), Hoorn 4 hours (14 miles), Purmerend 4 hours (13 miles).

Inns, *Reisboek* (1689, 1700 and 1721): De Waag van Amsterdam*; 't Moriaans Hoofd*; De Toelast*; De twee Doelens; 't Paardshoofd; 't Huis van Gemak; 't Schippers Huis*. *Reisboek* (1700 and 1721) also: De Roode Leeuw*.

Enkhuizen

Population: 18,000 (1650), 14,000 (1690), 10,400 (1732).

Distances: Amsterdam 9 hours (28 miles), Harlingen 9 hours (30 miles), Hoorn 3 hours (8 miles), Staveren 3 hours (12 miles), Workum 5 hours (20 miles).

Inns, *Reisboek* (1689, 1700 and 1721): d'Oostindische Toorn; De Doelen*. *Reisboek* (1689 and 1700) also: Het Stadhuis van Amsterdam. *Reisboek* (1700) also: De Vries. *Reisboek* (1721) also: Het Heerenlogement*; Het Hof van Holland*; In Deventer*; Koning Karel III*.

Hoorn

Population: 14,000 (1650), 12,000 (1744 T.S.).

Distances: Alkmaar 4 hours (14 miles), Amsterdam 6 hours (20 miles), Enkhuizen 3 hours (8 miles), Medemblik 3 hours (10 miles).

Inns, *Reisboek* (1689, 1700 and 1721): 't Heeren Logement*; d'Oude en Nieuwe Doelen*; 't Moriaans Hoofd*. *Reisboek* (1689 and 1700) also: De Goude Leeuw. *Reisboek* (1700 and 1721) also: De Nobele Swaan*. *Reisboek* (1721) also: 't Huis van Gemak; 't Vosjen.

Further reading

[Th. Velius], *Chronijck vande stadt van Hoorn*, Hoorn 1604, 1617, 1648, 1740.

[C. van der Woude], *Kronijcke van Alcmaer*, Alkmaar 1645, 1658, 1679, 1725, 1742, 1743, 1746.

[G. Brandt], *Historie der vermaerde zee- en koop-stadt Enkhuizen*, Enkhuizen 1666, 1747.

Ach Lieve tijd: zeven eeuwen Hoorn, zijn bewoners en hun rijke verleden, J.M. Baltus (ed.), Zwolle, 1986-87.

Ach Lieve Tijd, Tien eeuwen Alkmaar en de Alkmaarders, M. van der Laan (ed.), Zwolle 1987-1988.

Oud Alkmaar, uitgave van de vereniging 'Oud Alkmaar'.

Steevast, jaaruitgave van de vereniging 'Oud Enkhuizen'.

Oud Hoorn, kwartaalblad van de vereniging 'Oud Hoorn'.

West Frieslands Oud en Nieuw, 1926-

Nijmegen and Kleve

William Carstairs, 24 June (4 July) 1685

[157] On 24 June I went [from Xanten] towards Cleves, which is most pleasantly situated, part upon a hill and part in the valley. The Duke of Brandenburg has a fair palace on the outer side of it, upon a hill from which there is one of the pleasantest prospects of a fine country, with many steeples for several miles that ever I saw. There seems to be here not a few people of good fashion. I here met with a gentleman at dinner in our ordinary, the Hof van Holland, who told me that he had several times dined with Earl Argyle and another gentleman and his son, in a private house in that town. He said that they lived very devoutly, having a minister with them that performed worship punctually twice a day; and that they checked Lord Grey for his extravagancies.

Before I came to Cleves, about a mile beyond it, there is a pleasant place called Bergendal, where the late [Johan-] Maurice of Nassau [-Siegen] lived sometimes, and where he died. The house is but ordinary, but there is a pretty park, stored with deer. Here also I saw several of the Roman urns of various shapes, with some other antiquities (as the images of Jupiter, Juno, Minerva, etc.) in stone with Latin inscriptions; most of the urns were found by the above mentioned Xanten. On this side of Cleves there is a place called the Deer garden, where you have four pleasant fountains, and upon the top of the hill, all clothed with wood, you have [158] a pleasant prospect of several fine walks through the wood. From Cleves I came to Nijmegen, which is five hours. This is a good town, and stands upon a rising hill, declining towards a branch of the Rhine called the Waal, which makes it very pleasant. This day I travelled eight hours.

James Drummond, Earl of Perth, 29 November - 8 December 1694 N.S.

[48] I left that place [Rotterdam] on Monday 29th, New Style, and was that night at Utrecht, where I stayed only one day. We left our servants and baggage to come by water hither to meet us, for, as you will see in the map, the Rhine divides itself at Schenkenschans, and one part of it, which still retains the name, goes to Huissen and so to Utrecht. The other, which passes by here, is called the Waal, and goes to join the Meuse near Dordrecht. But by ill luck for us, the wind got into the east that very day our goods should have come up hither, so that we have been lying here these six days, and may do six more if by good fortune our folks get not some waggon to hire.

You may imagine the trouble it is to us to lie in this hole, where except three Brussels gentlemen nobody is to be conversed with. We are ill-lodged, even in the best tavern in town, and weary enough. If the plenipotentiaries at the treaty [1678] had been no better accommodated, they had sooner come to an agreement, except that their honour had made them prefer their country's interest to their private ease. [...]

[50] One who were curious in matters of antiquity would find exercise in this town, for the Romans had a camp very near it, where infinite numbers of medals, Roman locks and keys, urns, inscriptions, lachrymatories, idols, buttons, buckles, etc. are daily found. One Smetius, a minister of this town, has a very large collection, made by his father and by himself. It is a pity he should be such a blockhead as neither to know the value of what he possesses nor to be able to give any satisfaction to strangers who see his rarities. He has a great collection of modern medals, too, and some very dishonorable for Britain. I saw all and heard my master [the exiled King James II] very scurvily used, for the man thought me of his own stamp. But his tongue will do no great hurt, for he is a very stupid fellow. [...]

[51] This town stands upon the bank of the Waal, but is well fortified; the east end of it is much higher than the west. From a little tower, called the Belvédère, one sees the rich country of the Betuwe like a garden to the north. The Betuwe is a country which lies betwixt the branches of the Rhine, viz. that called the Rhine and that other called the Waal. The Waal here is near thrice as big as Tay at Perth, very rapid. The town is supposed to be the Urbs Batavorum of Caesar. It is not pleasant; only it has a pretty marketplace and at the Belvédère a grove of trees, which in summer must needs be very delightful. Near it stands the castle, said to be built by Caesar, a vile ancient hole. The one half of the town at least is Catholic, but the Huguenots [Protestants] have the churches. Tomorrow is St Andrew's Eve [29 November] here, which we kept nine days since at Rotterdam.

John Talman, 15-17 September 1698 N.S.

[12] Passing through cornfields I came to Kellen and then to Cleves, where I lodged that night. This city is pleasantly situated on the side of a hill, the foot of which is washed by a small river called Wreededael [Kermisdael], over which is a neat bridge of brick, consisting of four arches. The streets are foul and narrow, but the houses are indifferent. Here are four Catholic churches, a nunnery and a Presbyterian church. The most remarkable [church] is that on [the] upper part of the city, not far from the Elector [of Brandenburg]'s palace, dedicated to the Virgin Mary, to St Peter and Paul. It is a fair Gothic building, mostly of stone. [...]

[13] The chief street, which runs through the city, is adorned with a Presbyterian church, whose front is a large and fair building of brick after the [14] new mode. A little higher stands a good old arch of brick, over which is the picture of Eumenius, the famous rhetorician. Under which is written in gold letters on an

azure field: EUMENIUS RHETOR, and under that, in a square table, an inscription after the same manner written.

From hence I turned up to the Elector's palace; it is a goodly old building of brick, it overlooks the whole city, which situation renders it very pleasant. First I came into a large square court before the palace; in the middle it is enclosed with iron rails; here stands the guard-house. From hence I passed through a narrow court and came into a spacious inner court with a brick portico round three parts of it, in the middle adorned with a pediment. In the middle of the court is a well, adorned with pillars. The third and last court is less than this; it has also its portico halfway round.

Within this palace are, as they told me, above one hundred and fifty rooms, but they show only twenty-four to strangers. They are as follows: first a noble great saloon with an arched ceiling. Over the door that leads to the next room are two heroes on horseback, armed cap-à-pied, tilting in full career at one another. [...]

[15] Next to this room [the Electress' bedroom] is a chamber designed for the lodging of strangers, not furnished. A bedchamber [is] kept for the family of the Prince of Orange, now King of England. The chamber is hung with gilt leather, the bed is of green silk. Now follows the King's apartment, the finest of them. The bedchamber, is a spacious room; the bed is of blue velvet lined with yellow silk. The bed's head and tester are finely embroidered with silk of divers colours on a white ground of silk. The table and chairs are covered with blue velvet. The chamber is hung with fine tapestry. The drawing-room is large, hung with red silk. The audience chamber is stately; the canopy is hung with red velvet striped with gold. Round the canopy hangs a rich gold fringe. Before the two doors of the chamber hang curtains of the same. The chairs are also covered with red velvet, embroidered with gold. The chamber is hung with tapestry.

Next is a bedchamber for my Lord Portland; then an antechamber, two galleries not finished, a guard chamber and a great staircase. All the ceilings of the chambers are flat and only plastered white. I saw hardly any pictures unless over the chimneys, and those only indifferent landscapes. They told me that on the top of the palace is to be seen a brass plate in which is an inscription that gives an account of the founder of this palace, who they say was [16] Julius Caesar.

Here is a great school, where they teach not only grammar, but logic and some parts of philosophy. In this city is a small garrison of one hundred and fifty foot. I walked a little out of the city to the top of the hill to see a fine lime tree. It is of a great height, and its arms spread out at such a distance from its trunk that they form a circle, seven of my fathoms diameter. This shady canopy is kept in curious order, and supported by two circles of pillars, the figure of it may give more satisfaction, it being something extraordinary [sketch].

After that I went out at another gate, of which there are six in all, to see the Elector's park and gardens. The park is very woody and well-stocked with deer. In the garden are fine waterworks, well-supplied with water from the hills above. Before this place stands a stone pillar on a square pedestal with a figure a-top.

Kleve. Lime tree in Tiergarten, 1698

From hence I rode to Kranenburg, first passing by a little village called Donsbeek [Donsbrüggen]. The country here is very pleasant. Kranenburg is such another small city as 's-Heerenberg, it is an hour and a half from Cleves. Travelling on farther, I passed over a fine clear brook, diverting ourselves with a fine prospect of the country, which is varied with hills, woods, rivers, and views of cities and towns. About an hour from Kranenburg I passed by Zefellyck [Zyfflich], a little village, the last I saw in Cleveland.

From hence I came into Gelderland, riding over a plain, where on the one hand I had a prospect of the meandering Waal (a branch of the Rhine, so called where this river divides itself at Schenkenschans), and Elter-berg on the Rhine (above mentioned) came into view, distant from hence about four hours. On the other hand, on a flat, we had fields. At last we had a sight of Nijmegen, which is above two hours distant from Kranenburg, four hours from Cleves. This city has a plain on three sides, and the Waal washes the other side. It is one of the largest cities in Gelderland and strongly fortified with high bastions and mounds of earth well palisadoed; the ditches are deep but dry. [17] The city is encompassed with an old brick wall, which I entered at three old brick gates in the chief street, which is broad. The houses are new, tall and handsome; most of the houses are covered with slate.

In this street is the stadhuys, a genteel stone building, but something after the old mode. It is six windows in front and three storeys high and flat a-top. Between

Nijmegen. Town hall, 1751

the windows of the middle storey are small stone figures standing on pedestals, supported by modillions. Before the building is a paved walk, the length of the stadhuys, at each end are five or six steps; the rails before the pavement are also of stone, at convenient distances are pillars upon which are lions supporting the arms of the city.

The hall of justice is a handsome room, the length of the stadhuys; the judges' seats are adorned with gold and white. In a white freeze is written in gold letters UTRAMQUE PARTEM AUDITE [listen also to the other party]. Over the seats is a niche in which stands the figure of Justice with a pair of scales in her hand. In a niche on the opposite side stands the figure of Charles V in armour with a globe in one hand and a sword in the other. Both the figures are of wood coppered over and tolerably well carved, above half as big as the life.

On one side of this room stands a fine clock in [the] form of a tower divided into several storeys. In the first is the picture of Atlas with the globe on his shoulders. Above it is the dial plate of brass; round the hours is a circle divided into twelve parts in which are engraven the twelve months of the year. In a broad circle without this, in twelve squares cut through the brass, are represented the twelve signs of the zodiac carved in relievo and painted in proper colours. In the outermost circle, which is broad, is a chronicle and other curiosities. This dial plate is fixed in a square panel whose mouldings and pediment are gilded, and little higher is a balcony round the tower, gilt with gold with a neat cupola with a chime of bells hanging between the windows all gilded. On the same side of the room over a door hangs a picture in which is represented [18] the story of Delilah cutting off Samson's hair, an indifferent piece.

In the marketplace, which is on one side of this street, stands a Great Church, a Gothic building in [the] form of a cross. In the choir is a tomb of a Duchess of Gelderland [Catharina de Bourbon]. The basis of the tomb is black marble, the sides are covered with brass plates on which are engraven figures both of men and women, standing as it were in niches with their arms over them. Between each figure is a little buttress of iron. On the top stone, which is of black marble, is engraven in a large plate of brass the image of a Duchess of Gelderland. On her right hand is the arms of Gelderland, on the left the arms of France with a bend sinister across the coat. Round the margent of the plate is an inscription in old Gothic letters.

The church steeple is not amiss, ascended by 250 steps it has three balconies and a clock with twenty-six handsome bells; and in time of fire there is a cistern always kept full of water; and they have a particular sort of a brass trumpet in shape of a horn which they blow on such occasions.

At the end of the town is a great old castle of stone, situated on a rising ground, as also the town. This castle was built by [the Roman Emperor] Julian the Apostate. Here they showed us a round building or temple in which the heathen used to sacrifice. Towards the middle is a gallery that runs round the building, in which are arched windows with stone pillars in the middle, through which I looked down into the midst of the temple. If I mistake not it receives no light but from an opening a-top. The roof of the gallery is arched and painted grotesque-like with green, red and yellow flowers after an odd manner. Here they showed us several earthen pots or urns in which they told us the heathens used to put the ashes of their dead.

I happened to see a burying here, which was at twelve o'clock at noon, which is the time of burial in this city. The proceeding to church with the corpse is after the same manner as in Holland, except that before the corpse went a certain person whose cloak was parti-coloured half red half black, and besides when the corpse was brought in sight of the church, there was music that played three [19] several times. First at the sight of the corpse, a second time at the company's approach to the church, a third time at their going into the church.

On the river Waal's side is a portico supported by nine pillars where they keep their Change. On this side [of] the city is a fort well-mounted with cannon, by which they have the command of the river. I must not omit saying of the manner of passing over this river: on two boats is laid a floor, which is all round accommodated with seats. The floor is large enough for four or five coaches at once. At one end are two masts kept fast by ropes; to these two at top is fastened a cross-yard in [the] form of a gallows. At the other end of the vessel, where the rudder is, is fastened a rope which lies over the cross-yard, and [which] at a great distance is fastened to several boats [anchored in the river]. On each side [of] the river are bridges which are built so far in the river till the stream begins to run strong, so that it is but freeing the vessel from the ropes by which it is held fast to the bridge. Otherwise, the force of the stream would carry the vessel towards the middle of the channel, but by a little help of the steerman it is presently at the bridge on the other side, though the river is broad. [cont. Arnhem and Zutphen]

Nijmegen

Population: 12,000 (1650), 10,000 (1700).

Distances: Amsterdam 20 hours (65 miles), Arnhem 3 hours (10 miles), Kleve 4 hours (12 miles), 's-Hertogenbosch 9 hours (23 miles).

Inns, *Reisboek* (1689 and 1700): De Toelast; Het Hart; De Swaan; De Keizer. *Reisboek* (1721): Het Rode Hart*, op de markt; De Salm, onder in de groote straat; De Goude Roos*, onder in de groote straat, bij de Kraan Poort; De Klok*, in de Sikker Straat; De Witte Swaan*, op de markt.

Kleve

Population: 800 houses (c.1750).

Distances: Nijmegen 4 hours (12 miles).

Inns, *Reisboek* (1689, 1700 and 1721): 't Heerenlogement*; De Linde Boom bij de Linde Boom*. *Reisboek* (1689 and 1700): 't Hof van Holland, De Vijf Ringen, De Diergaarden. *Reisboek* (1721): In den Adelaar*, In de Fontein*, De Moriaan*.

Further reading

J.I. Pontanus, *Noviomagum, Gelriae ducatus urbs primaria*, Harderwijk 1628.

J.I. Pontanus, *Historiae Gelricae libri XIV*, Amsterdam 1639.

J. Smetius, *Oppidum Batavorum seu Noviomagum*, Amsterdam 1644, 1645.

Chr. de Vries, *Den Cleefschen lusthof*, Cleve 1698, 1730.

C. Bruin, *Kleefsche en Zuid-Hollandsche Arkadia*, Amsterdam 1716, 1730.

[J.H. Schütte], *Amusemens des eaux de Cleve*, Lemgo 1748.

[J.H. Schütte], *Kleefsche waterlust ofte beschryving van de lieflyke vermaekelykheden aende wateren te Kleef*, Amsterdam 1752.

F. Gorissen, *Geschichte der Stadt Kleve von der Residenz zur Bürgerstadt, von der Aufklärung bis zur Inflation*, Kleve 1977.

Ach Lieve Tijd, twintig eeuwen Nijmegen en de Nijmegenaren, J. Buylinckx (ed.), Zwolle 1986.

G. Pikkemaat, *Geschiedenis van Nijmegen (Noviomagus)*, Nijmegen-'s-Gravenhage 1988.

W.A. Diedenhofen, *Klevische Gartenlust: Gartenkunst und Badebauten in Kleve*, Kleve 1994.

Jaarboek Numaga gewijd aan heden en verleden van Nijmegen en omgeving, 1954-

Oostende and Nieuwpoort

William Lord Fitzwilliam, 9 July 1663 N.S.

[40r] [From Brugge] The next morning we went to Ostend, passing by a place called Plassendaal, a village not far from Ostend, and having several sluices. And so we came to Ostend, one of the strongest [40v] places of Flanders if not of Europe, lying on the main sea, and in such a convenient place that by the means of its sluices it can drown the country round about it of a sudden. It is not properly a town for traffic, yet considering its bigness and that it is only a garrison, there is yet trading. With the permission of the governor we went to see the town. Here is a pretty little town house standing on a fair marketplace. To this marketplace there go several streets from all [of] which you may see the ramparts excepting in one place where the church stands.

About the walls, on the side where the haven is, there are the soldiers' quarters. Here is likewise a fair great church and some good houses but an excellent good haven. This town is surrounded with good walls and bulwarks, many outworks, good ditches and many. At high water you see nothing but water round about the town. It was besieged three years, three months, three weeks, three days, three hours and three minutes by the Spaniards before it was taken [1601-1604]. Anno 1658 the French did intend to take it by treason, but they were disappointed [undone] and shamefully beaten, their General [Antoine] d'Aumont taken prisoner. Within the haven their men and vessels were pitifully destroyed.

From hence we went by waggon to Newport. We went all along the sea shore [41r] on the seabanks. We saw several crosses as marks that there had been in those places some battle fought or other memorable action committed.

A league or thereabouts off Newport we saw the field where that invincible hero, Prince Maurice [of Nassau], being reduced to a great extremity, fought out of despair (if I may say so) the great Archduke Albert, killed five thousand of his men and took many prisoners amongst which was the Admiral of Aragon; and the Archduke himself was wounded and had much to do to escape. This happened the 2nd July Styl. Nov. [1600]. It is observed that on the same day the Emperor Adolph of Nassau was beaten 302 years before by another Archduke of Austria [1298].

The town of Newport is none of the strongest or fairest: it is very dirty, its fortification is very ancient, old brick walls with some outworks and other little forts not far from it, in which does chiefly consist its strength. Good ditches and water it has enough about it, it being only a mile of the sea. Here is a very good haven, bigger as some say than that of Ostend. Here is likewise an old castle and town house, a great church and some religious houses. Else there is nothing remarkable, only that there are few streets and those very dirty; few houses and those very ill-built. Formerly it has been called Sandhooft, but it having obtained town's privileges it got the name of Newport, because it was locked up with ports or gates of which she had formerly none. [cont. Dunkirk and Calais]

John Walker, 1-2 (11-12) September 1671

[16] After some difficulty in changing our boat two or three times, we were at last brought safe to the little town of Ostend, being about five hours from Bruges. We lodged that night at one of our countrymen's houses, Tom Bales by name, a drunken harmless fellow. We had not been long here, when the soldiers came in to have us before the governor, to whom we gave an account of ourselves and so were remitted to our lodging. Our entertainment here was homely and indifferent, but to qualify it, our charges were not unreasonable.

The town is for the most part the habitation of fishers, salting and drying of herrings and suchlike, but the strongest hold throughout Europe, having held out a siege against the Spaniards three years, three months and thirteen [three] days, till it was become a heap of rubbish. From the tower of the town house we viewed it. You may see from wall to wall in every street. We saw the house of the Capuchins and September the second took waggon for Newport.

[17] Our passage between Ostend and Newport was in a very homely waggon, but delightful, being upon a plain sand on the shore, where we picked up variety of coloured shells. The town is but ordinary, most of all depending upon the same trade as Ostend. Here we baited and after dinner prepared to take boat. Two of the soldiers undertook to carry our portmanteaus to the waterside, but finding us strangers and [we] wanting the lingua, they began to exact. But one of the Spanish officers standing by and observing it, took them as soon as ever they came out of the boat and caned them severely. We raised our hats to him for his great civility and so went off from the town. [cont. Dunkirk and Calais]

Thomas Scott, 6-10 (16-20) September 1672

[12r] The next morning, about an [12v] English mile from the town [Dunkirk], we took boat for Newport, distant from Dunkirk four Dutch miles, which, drawn by horses through a cut river, pleasantly conveyed us to Newport in four hours. In which passage, for want of books which would have been very convenient, we diverted ourselves by a game at cards and tables which they keep in the boat for that purpose, and sometimes in fair weather walking above deck (the boat being somewhat like the Folly [house of entertainment built on barges] on the River of Thames) to view the country, which is vacant of those pleasant elms and oaks which in England in our travels we are often delighted by.

On this cut or river is a bridge which by the help of one man, at the coming of the boat, or as [13r] occasion should serve, turns round to the shore, the like whereof I having not seen and for curiosity's sake I thought fit to mention as a convenience for my countrymen and [a] more safe way of defence than these drawbridges which those that have occasion make use of.

About twelve o'clock we entered Newport, where we dined at the Packet Boat and Prince's Arms, the landlord whereof is an Englishman. After dinner ended, having some collateral business at Ostend, being somewhat out of our way to Antwerp, our intended place of residence, we took waggon thither, being about three Dutch miles distant from Newport.

This passage is very pleasant, being most part of the way [13v] on the sea sands and the shore, affording infinite number of conies skipping up and down the sands to our great delight. About the sixth hour we arrived at Ostend, where we stayed till Tuesday following, so that we had time to make some observations on the place, being, though small, very strong, almost encompassed by the ocean with a convenient harbour which lodges ships from all parts, laden with commodities to and from Bridges, Gaunt, and Antwerp, those places lying from the seacoast. But at this time there are at least one hundred men or more at work on a sasse or sluice which will cost many thousands pounds sterling, being as great a piece of waterwork as ever was, to bring ships into a cut that extends to Bruges, by which they will [14r] bring their ships thither.

We inned here to our great convenience (having not the language of the country) at an Irishman's house: coming thither on Friday, and the next week being Ember Week, we ate very little or no flesh, they not daring to dress any but fish on any occasion whatsoever. [...]

[15r] This town being but a small place and of little or no trade, there was little of remark but the Great Church, a very stately building as most of their churches are, and the friary of the order of Capuchins, which caused our long stay here to be more tiresome. And thinking one day to take our pleasure by walking on the walls, we were hindered by the sentinels that stand there for that purpose, and the reason thereof is that the walls were measured formerly by the French for their better scaling thereof, which afterwards [1658] endangered the town.

Joseph Taylor, 31 August (11 September) 1707

[34v] Last Sunday I went down the canal in a treckschuit to visit Ostend, about three leagues from Bruges, passing by Fort Plassendaal. At the end of the canal [near the sluices], lies Fort Philip, from whence we passed in a small boat to the town, which is surrounded by the sea at high water, except on the Newport side. It has a street very handsome and regular, and a marketplace in the middle, in which is the town house with a tower. But it is still in a miserable condition by the bombs thrown into it at the last siege [1706].

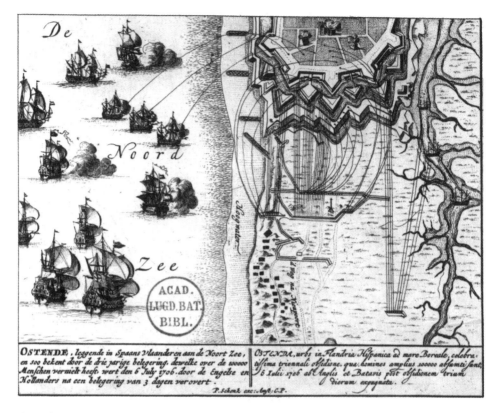

Oostende. Siege (1706), c. 1710

The Great Church is large without any manner of ornament. Here I made [35r] use of my pass from the Secretary of State for coming into the town on a Sunday. The officer of the guard, who had strict orders to examine all strangers, suspected me and sent two soldiers to carry me to the main guard, but the commandant, who was a Dutchman being at church, I could not be discharged till that was done. In the meantime another officer came to me and examined me, my man interpreting, and finding I was only travelling for my pleasure, treated me very civilly. The commandant coming afterwards to us, I showed him my pass, and he gave me liberty to go over the fortifications with a soldier, which were all repaired and very strong. Upon the ramparts towards the sea I viewed Dunkirk and the ships riding in the road. At the Capuchins they showed me a bell, which hung in the steeple melted by a bomb; and all the fruit trees were either burned or split, so that they had no fruit that year, which they mightily bemoaned, having as they said [35v] before great plenty.

At three of the clock I was to return to the trackskuit, which always goes exactly at that hour, and in order to be there by that time, took boat a quarter before. But the roguish watermen designed to keep me in town all night to get more money out of me, and scarce moved their oars, which obliged me to put myself into a violent passion and stand with my sword in my hand, and so with much difficulty made them row faster. However, the trackskuit was gone, and though it was in sight and I called out for it to stop, yet the master took no notice but kept on his pace, so I was forced to run after and could not overtake him till he had changed his horse, which was a full league and a half from Ostend, so that you may easily imagine what a condition I was in. As soon as I was got in, the fellow had the impudence to laugh in my face and tell me if he had known it was I, he would have stayed a little. However, I was heartily glad I was got aboard again and not being in a capacity [36r] to resent the affront, thought it best for me to rest satisfied.

In our passage we met Mr [George] Stepney upon his return to England. I saw the poor gentleman sitting upon deck with the face of a dying man. His death will be a great loss to our nation, for certainly no minister was ever better beloved in the Low Countries than he. I waited upon him at Brussels, where everybody bemoaned him with more than usual concern. At last I arrived at Bruges again, being never more tired in all my life. [cont. Brugge and Sluis]

Sir John Percival, 14-15 (25-26) August 1723

[1v] We left Dunkirk on the 14th and dined at Newport, six leagues distant, which we performed in four hours. While dinner was preparing, we saw the chief church and that of the Capuchins and likewise the town house, in which there is nothing extraordinary, but we were obliged to the civilities paid us by Mr Willar, one of the eschevins [aldermen], who seeing us strangers, came and offered his service to show us the town.

I could not but wonder when the priest of the parish church was about showing us the pyx at the high altar, where the wafer is kept. This gentleman took me gravely aside and asked me if I was a Christian (meaning thereby a Roman Catholic, for the name of Christian they appropriate to themselves in ordinary discourse) and upon my answering that undoubtedly I was a Christian, but yet a Protestant, he stepped up to the priest and told him that I was a heretic and that he doubted whether we would kneel to the bon dieu. The priest, who had less superstition it seems than the gentleman, replied swinging his arm: 'And what if he don't? 't Is no matter'. So we were favoured with the sight, but I will not answer that the good magistrate was [2r] not in some measure scandalized.

In the afternoon we set out for Ostend, where we arrived in two hours and twenty minutes, being twelve [nine] miles. Most of the road was over dikes hardly passable in the winter. We lay at Mr Chapman's at the sign of the Gamecocks, a very good inn.

Ostend is certainly a very strong place, situated in a moorish ground among several channels, of which the two chiefest almost encompass it. Yet such is the improvement made of late years in the art of war and especially the execution done by cannons and mortars, that in the late war [1706] it held but a few days before the army of the Allies, though Spinola in 1603 was three years in taking it and lost there seventy thousand men. The streets are regular and clean, and the town house is a very fine and spacious building lately erected. There are besides two fine marketplaces. Since the late East India Company [was] erected by the Emperor [1722], this town has exceedingly increased in riches and people and the harbour rendered very commodious.

Oostende
Population: c. 7,000 (1689), 5,000 (1723).
Distances: Brugge 4 hours (12 miles), Dover 70 miles, Dunkirk 8 hours (24 miles), Nieuwpoort 3 hours (9 miles).
Inns not mentioned in guidebooks.

Nieuwpoort
Population: under 2,500 (1700).
Distances: Dunkirk 5 hours (16 miles), Oostende 3 hours (9 miles).
Inns not mentioned in guidebooks.

Further reading

J.B. Gramaye, *Antiquitates Belgicae*, Bruxelles-Leuven 1708.

A. Sanderus, *Flandria illustrata*, Cologne 1641-1644, 's-Gravenhage 1732, 1735 (*Verheerlykt Vlaandre*, 's-Gravenhage 1732, 1735); reprint Antwerpen-Amsterdam 1981.

J. Bowens, *Nauwkeurige beschrijving der oude en beroemde zeestad Oostende*, 1792 (reprint: Handzame 1962).

R. Dumon, *Geschiedenis van Nieuwpoort*, Nieuwpoort 1989.

De Plate, tijdschrift van de Oostendse heemkring, 1972-

Bachten de Kupe, tijdschrift van de Nieuwpoortse heemkring, 1966-

Overijssel

William Lord Fitzwilliam, May 1663

[25r] From Groningen we went by waggon to Coevorden, which is seven of this country miles distant of Groningen. Coevorden lies in Overijssel, or at least on the confines of it, a frontier town towards Germany. Properly it lies in Drenthe, a part of Overijssel; the two other parts are called Salland and Twenthe. It is but a small town, but as strong as art and nature could ever make it. It lies in marshy ground; in winter it is wholly in water. The land which lies over against the bulwark called the Hollander [Holland] is much higher than all the rest. Here is a sluice, and by its means the water falls down upon all the other ground which lies about this town and so sets it in water. If they will have it dry again, there is another sluice below, which lets it out another way.

By art it is so strongly fortified that if they have but men and ammunition enough it seems to be impregnable. It is wholly regular, it has not its like almost in the world. The Venetians they say have another, which is called Nova Palma, otherwise I know of none else. It is surrounded with seven bulwarks called like the Seven United Provinces: Holland, Zeeland, Utrecht, Friesland, [25v] Gelderland, Groningen and Overijssel.

Each face of a bulwark is ninety of my paces long or thereabouts; each flank forty-five and the courtine one hundred and seventy paces. The gorge is proportionably big. The walls are sufficiently high and thick as likewise the parapets upon them, and the fausse-bray round about is of a reasonable breadth and has all its other due dimensions as likewise its parapet. The ditches are very broad and deep, all walled on one side. There are likewise seven good ravelins and seven demi-lunes, all extraordinarily well-made. Its corridor and esplanade are not so exact as where there is no marshy ground. Upon every bulwark stands a great piece of ordnance.

This town has but two gates; when you enter at one you may see the other. The soldiers, who at our being here were only six companies, have their quarters round about the ramparts excepting the place where the bulwark Gelderland is. For there stands the castle, which is fortified with four little bastions. This bastion in which it lies is separated from all the others by ditches. On one side of that separate bulwark is the haven where all boats coming from Zwolle enter.

The governor of it and the town was at our being here Lieutenant-Colonel Brosman [Broersema], who gave us leave to see this place. He has a good house and garden in this [26r] castle. Within is likewise the State's house of the province

Coevorden. Town plan, c. 1672

of Drenthe [Lands-schrijvershuis]. By the castle stands the magazine, and in the bastion Zeeland is the ammunition house.

Within the town there are only few streets and little low-built houses and one church. The States come twice a year from The Hague to visit this place for to keep it well in order, it being so near the confines of Westphalia. Anno 1592 the States took it, and as soon as they had it they did fortify it as it is at present. Formerly here was only a castle but meanly fortified, which was the reason that it was so many times taken and retaken by the Spaniards and the States. Since it has been so fortified as it is now, nobody has as yet ventured against it.

Here we lay a night, and the next day we went to Zwolle, passing by Hardenberg, where our waggoner broke an old woman's gate, not having a mind to pay an unjust tribute for passing over a bridge. At night we arrived at Zwolle, one of the chiefest towns (there being only three: Deventer, Kampen and Zwolle) of the province of Overijssel.

This is a pretty town, indifferently well fortified, being surrounded with eleven bulwarks, one hornpiece. A great church in which there is a brave pulpit almost so good as that of the New Church of Amsterdam. Here is likewise a very good haven and fair streets and houses everywhere.

[26v] From hence we went by water to Amsterdam, passing by Hasselt, lying upon a river called Zwarte Water, by Zwartsluis, a strong sconce lying likewise on the same water, and so we came into the Zuiderzee, passing by Kampen and Harderwijk. And by this means we did sail round about the Zuiderzee. [cont. Haarlem]

John Talman, c. 15 September 1697 N.S.

[3] About three hours and a half from Loo is a city called Deventer, situated on the river IJssel in the province of Overijssel. The way from Apeldoorn, a little town about half an hour from Loo, to this city is about a third part heath ground, watered with several springs. You travel the rest of the way either through broad shady roads or fields, set all round with wood, which renders them very pleasant, so that every time you go out of one field into another, you pass through a little grove. About a quarter of an hour before you come to the city, you travel over a dike which brings you to Deventer bridge, built on boats. The bridge is long and high, for the IJssel thereabouts is very broad but not deep; but now the States have given orders for the making of it deeper. The city is fortified all round, regularly with bastions and [half-] moons before the curtains, all of earth except the IJssel side; kept in very good order with a broad fosse and deep with fine walks of elms round the top of the works within the city, which afforded a pleasant sight as I walked round the city, which is about an hour's going. The city is round, excepting where it lies along the IJssel.

The inside is also pretty and neat, straight streets and well-paved, with a handsome stone Gothic church [St Lebuinus]. On each side [of] the nave are two aisles with stone pillars which support three decent arched ceilings and painted after the old way with flowers, etc. But that in the middle is finer and higher than the other two. At the east end is the choir, at the west, in one of the side aisles, is a very pretty little organ neatly painted and gilded supported by two wooden pillars of the Corinthian order handsomely painted and carved. The church steeple is after the Gothic architecture, but the cupola at [the] top is lately built of brick with handsome stone Doric pilasters on the outside and a tunable ring of bells within. From this steeple we had a very pleasant view of the IJssel and the country round about, and of Zutphen, a strong city about three hours' distance south of Deventer.

Over against the church is the stadhuys, all of stone, and deserves to be commended for a compact piece of architecture, not very fine but yet very agreeable with a handsome portico [1694], standing out before the door, of the Doric order. The Emperor's and the city's arms with the imperial crown, which the Emperor granted this city, are placed on top. There are other churches, but they must be passed over in silence as not deserving a description. The gates of the city are very indifferent. Deventer is governed by an upper and under schout, sixteen burgermeesters and a senate of forty-eight.

From Deventer to Zwolle is about six hours, all the way on a high dijck, but very pleasant. On your right hand are thick woods and fine shady walks, on your left for the most are great quantities of water with which the country abounds. On this side are also plantations, and sometimes the IJssel offers himself to view, which renders the journey pleasant.

Zwolle has also its drawbridges and fortifications, but not so strong nor so regular as Deventer, but however, the city affords a fine sight from the church tower, from whence you have a prospect of the IJssel, Zwarte Water and other pleasant places. This steeple had once a high spire, but it had the ill fortune to be burnt down [1669]; there only remains the eight piers of the window, without any top or covering where the bells hang. The church has nothing in it remarkable, excepting a pulpit canopy, which is very fine in the Gothic way, it being composed of towers one above the other diminishing to the top pyramidically, something like the sovereign's stall in the [4] choir in Windsor Chapel, but much larger and more curious, insomuch that the Bishop of Münster [who occupied Overijssel, 1672-1674] would have removed it from thence for the curiosity of it.

The stadhuys is very indifferent, but there is a particular piece of painting at the upper end of the Great Saal [schepenzaal], which is Saint Christopher carrying Christ over a river, about three times as big as the life, only worth mentioning for the size. This city has also the conveniency of the river called the Zwarte Water running through it for the passage of shipping.

The next place I saw was Kampen, about four [two] hours distant. Here we paid toll. All flat way just till we came to the city, when we rode over a dijck which leads to the city, which lies on the other side of the IJssel, on [the] Gelderland side, but belongs to the province of Overijssel. This city has had hard fate, as may be seen by the walls miserably battered and seeming, as often as you can look on them, to threaten a total downfall. All the towers and places of strength are wholly ruined and lie scattered here and there like misshapen rocks. As for the inside, there is not much stateliness: the streets are narrow and not very straight and a water in the middle of the streets stinks, and in some places you see houses and churches half in rubbish, and as Virgil [writes, in his *Aeneis*] lib. 2, vs 445: turres ac tecta domorum culmina convellunt [they tear down the towers and the roof-coverings of the houses].

There are three towers of which the middle is the best [Nieuwe toren]; it is newly built [1649-1662] and stands in the midst of a street with a very handsome gateway to go through, with a fair tower over it of a convenient height with a handsome cupola on top, in which hang thirty-five fine bells. The statehouse deserves no notice. The city is of a long shape as you see from off the tower; provision for the belly is here cheap.

John Farrington, 18 November 1710 N.S.

[254] After we had seen this house [the Earl of Albemarle's, near Zutphen], we entered our waggon for Deventer, which lies about three leagues from it. But I must give you no other than a mighty general account of this city, for resolving to reach Loo that night, we made a short stay here, and the badness of the weather hindered our making the best improvement of that.

We came to Deventer at twenty minutes past one, and as much after four took waggon for Loo. However, I may venture to tell you this city is the metropolis of the province of Overijssel and that it stands upon the river IJssel, from whence the province takes its name. To the land-side it is said to be well fortified and so it appeared to us; nor is it weak towards the river. The streets are pretty good and wide, the buildings handsome. The stadthouse is a good building and so the churches seem to be. This, Sir, is all I am able to tell you of this city. Half Moon, best inn in the city but full. We dined at the Caesar's or Emperor's Head, which is tolerably good. [cont. Het Loo]

Deventer

Population: 7,000 (1650), 6,700 (1682), 7,800 (1748).

Distances: Amersfoort 11 hours (30 miles), Arnhem 8 hours (20 miles), Bentheim 8 hours (22 miles), Zutphen 3 hours (8 miles), Zwolle 6 hours (18 miles).

Inns, *Reisboek* (1689 and 1700): De groote Kroon; De kleine Kroon; De Wildeman; Den Olden St. Olof; 't Wijnhuis, op de markt. *Reisboek* (1689, 1700 and 1721): Op 't Trapje [1721: aan de Zandpoort]; De Halvemaan, of het Wapen van Overijssel [1721: bij 't Stadhuis]. *Reisboek* (1721) also: De Kroon*; De Keijsers Kroon*, in de Nieuwstraat (van hier rijden de wagens alle middag op Zwolle); 't Haasjen, De Groene Klok* (both on the Brink); De Klok* in de Rijkmanstraat (hier komen tweemaal per week de karren van Grol, Winterswijk, Borculo, Lochem enz.); 't Posthuis, zeer bekwaam voor diegenen welke met de postwagens of post-chaisen die hier te bekomen zijn voort willen.

Kampen

Population: 7,000 (1650), 6,000 (1682), 5,600 (1748).

Distances: Amsterdam 22 hours (72 miles via Amersfoort; 42 miles by sea), Zwolle 2 hours (6 miles).

Inns, *Reisboek* (1689, 1700 and 1721): Het Tolhuis*; De Halvemaan*; Het Blaauwe Kruis*; Den Arend*.

Zwolle

Population: 9,000 (1650), 7,800 (1682), 12,000 (1748).

Distances: Amersfoort 14 hours (41 miles), Amsterdam 22 hours (67 miles), Deventer 6 hours (18 miles), Groningen 22 hours (60 miles), Kampen 2 hours (6 miles).

Inns, *Reisboek* (1689 and 1721): De witte Wan*; De Wannen, op de Markt*. *Reisboek* (1700) also: 't Wijnhuis, op de Markt.

Further reading

A. Moonen, *Korte Chronyke der stadt Deventer*, Deventer 1688, 1714.

[W. Nagge], *Weghwijser door de provintie van Overyssel*, Deventer 1724.

Th.J. de Vries, *Geschiedenis van Zwolle*, Zwolle 1954-1961.

J.G. Lugard, *De zingende stad, een historie van Deventer*, Deventer 1959.

Ach Lieve Tijd, 1000 jaar Deventer, de Deventenaren en hun rijke verleden, J. Louwen and H. Prins (eds.), Zwolle 1980-1982.

Ach Lieve Tijd, 750 jaar Zwolsen, Zwollenaren en hun rijke verleden, Zwolle 1980-1982.

H.J. Lenferink (ed.), *Geschiedenis van Kampen*, vol. 1, Kampen 1993.

Zwols Historisch Tijdschrift, 1984-

Overijsselse Historische Bijdragen, 1860-

Rotterdam

William Lord Fitzwilliam, 28 June 1663 N.S.

[33r] From hence [Delft] we went to Rotterdam, lying on the river Maas and on the mouth of the river Rotte, a great town and clean enough for a trading town. This is the country of famous Erasmus, whose statue stands to this very day upon the marketplace on a bridge. He has a great gown on and a mitre on his head, a book in his hand of which he would very willingly turn a leaf, and below used to be this inscription:

Erasmus natus
Roterodami
October 28
An. M. I.V.C. 67
obiit Basileae
12 Julii Ao
M.D.XXXVI.

[Erasmus was born in Rotterdam on 28 October 1467
and died at Basle on 12 July 1536]

[33v] The house likewise where he was born is yet to be seen; upon it are these words written:

Aedibus his ortus mundum decoravit Erasmus
artibus ingenuis, religione, fide.

[Erasmus, born in this house, embellished the world
with fine arts, religion and faith]

Here is a very Great Church and very well-built. It has lost the top just like St Paul's of London. In it is the tomb of a sea-hero called Witte Witteson [de With], who valiantly fighting against the Swedes in the Sound, lost his life anno 1658. Here is likewise a good town house and exchange. Here is likewise an Admiralty and a very good haven. Here is brewed the famous Rotterdamsche bier, so much loved by the Hollanders. [cont. Dordrecht]

Thomas Penson, 6-19 (16-29) July 1687

[7] A strange world it seemed to me when I first landed, to see people of another dress and hear another language, and the houses seemed to threaten to fall on our heads, they are built so much leaning forwards. But there soon came divers that spoke our own language to offer us entertainment in their houses. I took up my abode in the house of one Mr James Hayes, a Scotchman (his wife was a Dutchwoman), at the sign of the Ship, near the Admiralty Office in Rotterdam, where I had very good lodging and kind usage. The man was very courteous and obliging, offering his service to walk out and show me the city and the remarkable things therein, which he accordingly did.

And first I was conducted to the Beurs or Exchange, which is daily very full of merchants, who are obliged to come on at the ring of the bell (which [8] holds till about a quarter of an hour after twelve), then the doors are shut up and an officer placed at each, with a money box in his hand and whosoever will then come in must pay six stuyvers, or also stay out. About the middle of exchange time, there comes a person (whose place it is) who gives notice (first with a tinkling brass and afterwards by a loud outcry) of what sort of merchandise are in the city to be sold and where they may be seen. Also if any ships or vessels are to be sold, etc., and where they lie. [...]

[14] I was somewhat curious in my observations during my short stay in this city, which was about fourteen days, every day moving out with my guide and interpreter. And first for De Kerck oft Plaats van Godts-dienst, the church or place for the service of God. I was present at the Great Church at Rotterdam at the catechising of a woman, for it seems it is the custom if any man or woman intend to approach the Lord's Table, they shall first give an account of their faith to the minister by public examination in the church, as well as privately in their houses. And great pains the minister takes in this particular, going from house to house to instruct them well in the fundamentals of their religion as also showing them the errors and idolatry of the church of Rome (against which they stiffly labour), so that they must give very good answers in their examinations, before they are admitted to the Holy Communion.

[15] After catechising was ended, the minister stood up and made a short prayer. Then the people all drew into the body of the church, where was read twelve psalms. Then the minister ascended the pulpit, gave out a psalm, which was sung; after that a short prayer. And then a sermon of an hour and a half long and, last of all, part of a psalm was sung, and so the people were dismissed.

Gravestones: Hier lyte begraven B.W. Koopman, etc. [here lies buried B.W. merchant] Hier lyte begraven Adrian ... Skipper, etc. Many coats of arms do adorn this Great Church and almost the whole pavement is composed of great gravestones, with descriptions and arms and such kind of marks as this [sketch], within an escutcheon with a Baron's helmet and mantles, whereon are many devices to supply the place of arms, as here in the margin you may observe. If it be a merchant there is his mark; if it be a sailor that is also signified by a ship, etc. In this church are likewise two very fair monuments for two of their sea-admirals (viz.) Admiral [Witte] de With and Admiral [Egbert Cortenaer].

[16] July 18/28. At Delfshaven, not far from this city, is held a kermis or fair, to which with my landlord I walked. It consisted chiefly of gingerbread and broiled eels. There was two or three puppet shows but above all a famous mountebank, who had set out a very fine stage and thereon such diversion that he drew most of the people to himself. He had persons very aptly dressed, representing the four seasons of the year, who first danced severally and afterwards joined together in a figure, which they prettily performed. After that he began to sell his balsams and pills, etc. I spent two stuyvers in the fair and after returned to Rotterdam in a waggon for one stuyver more.

The next day (July 19/29), I repaired to Tergow [Gouda], where also was kept another fair, which was much better and in a larger place, where not only toys but all manner of good household stuff was bought and sold. [17] I went into one of the chiefest houses in the fair, where was a boor with a short cloak (so plentifully patched that it was hard to find which was the first colour) and under it a cymbal; also another with a violin. There I saw excellent sport by the dancing of the Mannekin and his Vrow, the Fryer and the Freyster, some singing, some dancing, some drunk and few sober.

Thomas Penson, 26-28 September (6-8 October) 1687

[72] I went in the waggon from Tergoude to Rotterdam, where I remained two days and took up my lodging in the same house as before, at Mr Hayes's.

I would not willingly tire the patience of my friendly reader, but hope it may not be accounted altogether impertinent to make mention of Fortune's favours and let you know there are thieves in Holland as well as in other places. It so happened that when I came to my landlord desiring to have the same lodging I had before (telling him that my intentions were for Antwerp by the next ship that sailed thither), it seems my chamber was taken up by another gentleman, but he promised I should have [73] another altogether as good, with which I was content. But in the dead of the night comes a thief in at the windows of the other gentleman's chamber; steals his coat and breeches from his bedside (wherein was all his money, I think to the value of ten pounds). Just as the rogue was got out of the window, the gentleman awaked and saw his hand; jumps out of bed and calls out: 'Thieves, thieves', but it was too late, for the rogue carried off his booty. By this time the master of the house was raised; the noise increasing I awaked and hearing of thieves, immediately felt under my pillow for my breeches, and finding them to be safe, was well pleased. Whether the robbery was designed on me I know not, but certainly if I had lodged in that chamber, the thief had been no respecter of persons. [cont. Antwerp]

Anonymous London merchant, 25 August 1695 N.S.

[8] On Thursday the 25th, we went in a treckschuit to Overschie, where we settled [the] two boys at a school (being one hour from Rotterdam) to learn Dutch, French, writing and accounts, for which we are to pay one hundred and eighty guilders per annum for each. The master, whose name is Monsieur Du Crocq, was recommended to us by Mr Huys of Rotterdam, who made enquiry of his character and found him a person very well esteemed for those matters, having one usher and sixteen or eighteen boarders, whereof four are English. After we returned from this village, where our Dutch host was very exacting, more than in any other place, making us pay him about three guilders, which is six shillings, for roasting a quarter of lamb, for which we paid the butcher but eighteen pence. Now it was we left these two boys, and the next day sent them their trunks by our servant. [cont. Gouda]

Anonymous Utrecht student, 19 (29) June 1699

[1] Rotterdam is so called from the Rotter [Rotte], a little river which falls into the canals of this town. It stands on the north side of the Maese, out of which vessels of almost any burden may come in by the canals or grafts into the middle of the city, so that a merchant may have his goods brought to the very door of his house without unlading first, which is a vast convenience. The city is large and very well-built and very populous. The canals (grafts) are commonly planted on each side with a row of fine Dutch lime trees and between them and the houses there are broad quays or causeways paved with white brick set edgewise, which are kept as clean as any of our courtyards in England, so that one may walk all over the town, even in winter, in a pair of slippers without being in the least offended with dirt. And indeed, one cannot imagine a pleasanter place, especially in summer when the trees are all green, which with the tops of the houses mixed with the masts and streamers of so many vessels as are continually here, make the most singular and agreeable prospect in the world, especially at a convenient distance.

The houses are all of brick and they have a way of painting their doors and shutters (which are always withoutside of the windows) of all sorts of colours: some red, some green, some yellow, and indeed they are careful to keep all their woodwork withoutdoors very well-painted, which is the only way to preserve it. Many of the houses lean over [page torn] be afraid of its falling and I took [page torn] [2] the buildings, but afterward I was informed that it was purposedly so contrived for the better drawing up of goods, etc.

The houses are extraordinary neat withindoors as well as without; and indeed, there is a kind of necessity of being cleanlier in this country than in some other places, because of the moisture of the air. The lower rooms of most of the better sort

Statue of Erasmus, 1694

of houses are paved with marble, and it is surprising to see such a vast quantity of it, that no country in the world has the like, except where it grows naturally. But there grows not a bit in all this country, but they have it mostly from Sweden, etc.

There are abundance of English and Scots families, and some parts of the town are almost wholly inhabited by them. And they have each of them their particular church and minister. The French Protestants have a handsome church.

The Great Church is very large; the steeple formerly leaned much on one side, but was set right again [1651] by a certain man who undertook to do it by digging under the foundation on the contrary side to that on which the steeple leaned, and so, by sinking it even with the other side, he brought it to an equal poise, and it stands straight ever since. That which they call the Boor's house [Gemeen-landshuis van Schieland, 1662-1665] is a very handsome large square building of brick. The Exchange, where the merchants meet, is very mean, consisting only in one single portico, and of no great length neither, and there are a few lime trees planted before it.

One of the greatest ornaments of this town was Erasmus, whose statue of brass in his monk's habit with an open book in his hands was erected on the great bridge in 1622, and is yet to be seen there. The house where they say he was born is but very mean, and over the door is this distich in Low Dutch and Latin:

Aedibus his ortus, Mundum decoravit Erasmus
Artibus ingenuis, Religione, Fide.

[Erasmus, born in this house, embellished the world
with fine arts, religion and faith]

Materiam superabat Opus [the work of art surpassed the material used]. One curiosity I saw which far outdoes anything I have ever seen of the same nature; which was some pieces of cut paper, done with that delicateness that I thought it very well worth anyone's while to see it. They were in a gentleman's house who cut them himself for his diversion [Gillis van Vliet]. There were sea-fights, landscapes, etc., all done to admiration. Some pieces of lace and point, so well done that one would take them to be in reality what they only represent. At the same place we saw several curious turned pieces of ivory.

Joseph Taylor, 30-31 July (10-11 August) 1707

[3r] When I arrived at Rotterdam I began to reflect on the dangers and inconveniences a stranger must needs be exposed to in travelling alone, and therefore heartily wished for a good companion. With these thoughts I was proceeding to Mr Thomas' in the Wine Street, where I was recommended to lodge, when on a sudden a merchant very civilly addressed himself to me, and seeing I was but just arrived from England and a stranger to the place, invited me to dine with him at his house, where he told me I should have an opportunity of meeting several of my countrymen. I should have been wanting to myself if I had refused this invitation, and therefore, after I had performed as much as was due to ceremony, I waited on him and had the satisfaction of seeing a very neat house, fronting the Maese, paved with marble and adorned with many pictures, more particularly with comical Dutch pieces, which as it was the first I had entered into in Holland, inspired me with a restless desire of seeing more.

After dinner, the Earl of Winton, Sir Robert Barnardiston, [3v] and one Mr Taylor, a clergyman, with some others came in. They all, as is natural, enquired of me what news from England and where I was going. I gave them as entertaining an account as I could and told them my design was for the army, if I could get good company. Upon which the Earl acquainted me that one Captain Seaton, a relation of his in the Dutch service, was going thither that day, and that he would recommend me to his care; accordingly he sent for him immediately. We soon struck up a bargain, and he promised to delay his voyage till next day at noon. All that I now wanted was a servant that could speak Dutch, which in a few hours the merchant procured for me.

So the rest of the afternoon we spent very merrily, and Sir Robert and some more of the company did me the favour of seeing me safe to my lodgings, which were very neat and, as common in this country, paved with marble. I was accommodated with very fine linen, but yet I could not sleep much, being mightily disturbed in the night by the watchmen that came about with an instrument, instead of a bell, composed of two boards like trenchers, [4r] fastened to a stick, which made a very dismal tick-tack. The next morning several of the gentlemen came to me, particularly Mr Taylor, who furnished me with letters of recommendation to Antwerp, Brussels and the army. As soon as we parted, my next business was to wait on one Mr Martin Browne, a merchant of very good repute, with my letter of credit from Mr Delamotte, which he received with assurances of giving me his utmost assistance, and immediately procured me bills of credit from Mijnheer Vollenhoven Halm of Rotterdam on the Heer Theodore Brockmans at Antwerp and the Heer Vandersteen at Brussels. With this fortunate beginning, my spirits were raised to the highest pitch, and now I thought I had good grounds to promise myself a happy progress in my travels.

I had appointed my friends to meet them at the Bourse or Exchange, but though I designed to take a more particular survey of this place at my return, yet I could not rest satisfied till I had first paid a visit to my old friend Erasmus in the great market [4v] at the head of the chief canal, where I found his brazen statue much bigger than the life, fixed on a four-square pedestal of marble, with a Latin inscription on two of the squares, encompassed with a balustrade of iron. He is in a doctor's habit, with a book in his hand; one inscription mentions that he was born at Rotterdam the 27th of October, anno 1467, but died at Basle in Switzerland July the 12th, anno 1536; the other that the people of Rotterdam had erected that statue at the public cost to the memory of Desiderius Erasmus, the great maintainer and restorer of the sciences and more polite learning, the most eminent of his time, dearest to his fellow citizens and of an immortal name by his never fading writings. I likewise saw in a narrow lane just by, the poor little house where this great man first drew his breath; over the shop on the outside by his picture is this distich: [...] [5r] which I have Englished thus:

> Erasmus in this humble cottage born
> Did with religion, arts and faith the world adorn.

While I was reading the inscription on the statue, the story you formerly told me of the Italian came into my head, who waited many hours in expectation of seeing him turn over a leaf of his brazen book, at the striking of the clock; and as I was pleasing myself with the thoughts of it, I heard on a sudden a soft voice at a small distance from me crying, 'Sir! Sir!', three or four times. I turned back, when to my great surprise there appeared to me three ladies in a very fine coach with a coronet behind it, drawn by a delicate pair of Flanders mares, beckoning to me to come to them. I could not imagine how any person of quality should know me in

Holland, being so utterly a stranger here. However, with some confusion I approached the coach door and then found they were only three of the fair passengers that came over in the yacht with me, who had hired this coach to see [5v] the town. And on this occasion upon enquiry how they came by that nobleman's coach, I understood that everyone in Holland bear what arms, crests and supporters they please, without distinction of persons or titles, and that the coaches that are hired out, of which this was one, are more particularly adorned with these emblems of honour.

I waited afterwards on Mr Simms and Captain [John] Robinson and took my leave of them. As I came over several bridges of which there are a great number here, I saw some of them lifted up, others which are fixed upon a pin are turned round, either by a boy or a woman, so that for a stiver, which is put into a shoe or some such thing which hangs down on purpose, the ships pass every bridge without lowering their masts or losing any time. Notwithstanding it had rained in the morning, the women, whose habits after the Dutch manners are very neat, walked with slippers as dry as if there had been no wet weather, the streets being generally paved with Flanders bricks.

Nothing can be more [6r] surprising than the pretty mixture of trees, masts of ships and chimneys all together, which makes it look rather like a forest than a town. Besides the pleasant canals that run through every street and the shady walks on each side of them, render the prospect so charming that I must acknowledge I was perfectly ravished with the beauty of those various objects, which at once presented themselves to my eye. I can give you a sketch of their neatness by a butcher's shop, which I observed all lined with white Dutch tiles and paved at the bottom with fine brick; every knife had its proper place, and there was even a nicety in the very chopping block, and the conveniences for carrying away the blood and bringing in water to wash and clean were extremely neat and convenient. I was also as much pleased at a barber's shop, where I was shaved, there being as great order in the disposition of everything as could possibly be contrived.

At last I got to the Bourse, which is ordinary enough, being a place only paled in and shaded with trees. When the bell [6v] rang I observed everyone crowded in, and when it ceased, those that did not come in soon enough paid a stiver. My friend presently carried me off the Exchange into a cellar hard by, where they gave me what they call Barnevelt, which is a deep glass either of bitter sack or Rhenish, for each of which is paid two stivers. I asked the derivation of that name, which they told me was taken from one Barnevelt, an Arminian in [Johan] de Witt's time, whose health in those troubles his party used to drink in that place. The custom is to go every morning to this cellar to take a whet, and of a society of friends each has his turn to pay the reckoning.

I am just now going on board the vessel for Antwerp, where as soon as I arrive, I shall be impatient to give you fresh assurances that in what place soever I am, I have no happier reflection than that of being, dear cousin, your most affectionate and devoted humble servant.

Joseph Taylor 7-10 (18-21) September 1707

[40v] I give you the following account as a supplement to what you received from me when I first landed here from England. In the Great Church I saw a good monument of Admiral [Witte] Cornelius de With, who by inscription died 59 years old. Also another of [Jan] van Braekel, another of Admiral [Egbert] Cortenaer, and there are very good organs, which I heard play. Here I first saw a Dutch wedding, which to me appeared more in the nature of a funeral, for the man wore a long black cloak and the woman looked as serious as though she had been going to a confession. The town house and the flesh market, over which is the Anatomy, are worth seeing, but especially the East India House new-built [1695], and the Admiralty [41r] and storehouse, which are all very handsome piles.

The new English church at the end of the Herring-graft [Haringvliet] is almost finished and will be extremely pretty. The arms of Great Britain and the Duke of Marlborough are very finely done and fixed up. I saw also a house now building by my Lord North and Gray's father-in-law [Cornelis de Jonge van Ellemeet]. From hence I was carried to view a couple of windmills, remarkable for their extraordinary heights. They are built with brick and cost fifteen hundred pounds apiece. The Bombkeys [Boompjes] and Scots Head [Schotse of Schiedamse Dijk] are very neat fronting the Maese. I went to see the famous works in paper [by Elizabeth Ryberg], representing King William and Queen Mary with their several palaces and other curiosities, which indeed are very curiously done.

During the few days I have been here, by the favour of Mr Martin Browne, I have been treated very handsomely at several merchants' houses and gardens, which I cannot sufficiently admire for their exquisite neatness, and the genteel entertainment I met with in a little garden out of town, full of orange, lemon, citron and jessamine trees. I had the happiness of being in company with twelve [41v] pretty ladies who spoke English. I spent the best part of the night in dancing with them; we had a noble collation in a summerhouse. I happened to have the good luck to dance with a lady who was not only the best fortune, but the prettiest woman in Rotterdam. It was my business afterwards to make these ladies my visits, whereby I had an opportunity of observing the Dutch fashions, but though I was agreeably entertained by all, yet the lady who was my partner infinitely exceeded the rest.

When I went to wait on her, I was carried up a noble marble staircase through a long dining-room paved with excellent marble and hung with Indian satin and adorned with curious china. And then through another room into a withdrawing room, where the lady was playing upon the harpsichord. It is impossible to tell you how I was delighted with her genteel reception, which was mixed with such an air of modesty and freedom that she appeared inexpressibly charming. After I had

The English Episcopal church, c. 1710

heard her sing several Latin, Italian, French and English songs and enjoyed the pleasure of a most engaging conversation, [42r] I retired home, melancholy at the thoughts of being so soon deprived of it.

Tomorrow I intend for The Hague and afterwards for Leiden and Amsterdam. I hope to return to England in a short time, where the greatest satisfaction I can receive, will be that of kissing your hands, who am, dear cousin ... [cont. Delft]

Sir John Percival, 22-28 June (3-9 July) 1718

[50v] In the afternoon we left Dordt and, ferrying over the Maas, in less than two hours arrived in a hired berline at Rotterdam, being but three leagues distant. This city lies on the same side of the Maas with Dordt, which obliged us to cross that river a second time. But it was rather a pleasure than trouble to us, the weather being fine and many delightful prospects of towns, etc. offering themselves to our view. [...]

[51r] Besides two congregations of English and Scots Presbyterians, whose number is about three hundred and whose ministers receive salaries from the government, there is also a Church of England congregation, consisting of about half that number, whose then minister was Mr [John] Mapletoft, a man well spoken of and esteemed by moderate men of all persuasions. The church lately erected for their use is handsome and large, and divine service has [51v] for some time been said in it, though not entirely finished. Fifteen thousand pounds sterling has already been expended on it.

The Remonstrants are very numerous in this town, and many of the better sort are of that persuasion. The number of the Roman Catholics is computed equal to that of the Reformed, and they have four mass houses; the established parish churches are no more. One of the latter is called the Groot Kerk, or Great Church, by way of excellence. It is large, and the isles are handsome and high. It was built in 1472, and they tell you that formerly the steeple leaning was set right again by the skill of an architect.

Within it are three marble monuments of as many admirals, who, having served their country with courage and integrity, were buried at the public expense. An example no less politic than great and worthy to be imitated by other governments. But I must observe it has not been pursued even by themselves of latter years. Whether from too parsimonious a management of the public treasure, or from faction or envy, or from a defect of merit in those who since have served the public, let others enquire.

The screen which separates the main body of the church from the quire was but lately erected. It cost sixty thousand guilders or six thousand pounds sterling, and consists of high rails of burnished brass, curiously worked [52r] and fixed in a base of wrought marble. In the middle is a brazen gate with proper ornaments over it, fixed to marble pillars. Upon it is inscribed Fr. van Douwen 1712, signifying the workman and time when set up. [...]

[52v] I went one afternoon to visit Mijnheer Vanderwerff, painter to the late Elector Palatine, who knighted [him] and allowed him a yearly pension of eight hundred pounds sterling. His works are esteemed over all Europe, and his price is according. At present being far advanced in years, he seldom uses his pencil. I learned that he was ill-satisfied with the Duke of Marlborough, whose picture he took at length, and who paid him for it no more than one hundred pounds. But

they told me withall he succeeded ill, and then I think he had no reason to complain. Indeed, history and not face-painting is his capital, wherein his figures, which are generally two foot high, are inimitably soft and graceful.

He showed us a dedication piece, designed to complete the number of sixteen emblematic pictures intended for the Elector Palatine's palace at Dusseldorp [Düsseldorf], wherein the composition is accurate, the outline correct and the colouring and painting of the faces beautiful. His works are so highly finished that it is impossible for him to preserve the spirit which the Italian masters give to their pictures; this want of life is all he is defective in. Nevertheless, the Dutch, perhaps because naturally more composed than other nations, seem to make this no objection, [53r] but give any price for his works. He received a thousand pounds for one picture not a yard square. He showed us, beside that above mentioned, two others, the subjects whereof were the Prodigal Son and the Judgement of Paris, equally fine.

There are here (which is common with other cities of Holland) several hospitals for sick persons, children, madmen and poor. There are others likewise, where such as are tired of the world, or have met with misfortunes, may for a small matter purchase for themselves a peaceable retreat during their lives. One of these, called the Old Men's House, is a fair building, very conveniently disposed and neatly kept. Thirteen old men are there charitably maintained by the public. But as many more as please may buy a place therein, with good diet allowed them and a bedchamber, conveniently furnished. These last eat together in a room separate from the others, who have likewise their common room and lodge together in a long gallery, like the King's scholars at Westminster, but in a more cleanly and decent manner. They are all under the direction of four persons appointed by the magistrate, who use them so humanely that they appear to pass their time with the utmost content.

Population: 30,000 (1650), 50,000 (1690), 45,000 (1720).
Distances: Amsterdam 14 hours (37 miles), Antwerp 18 hours (52 miles), Brielle 5 hours (15 miles), Delft 2 hours (6 miles), Dordrecht 4 hours (12 miles), Gouda 4 hours (12 miles), The Hague 3 hours (9 miles).

Inns, *Reisboek* (1689, 1700 and 1721): Het Swijnshoofd* [op de Markt]; St Lucas* [op de Hoogstraat]; De Doelen. Reisboek 1689: 't Schild van Vrankrijk; De Sleutels; Het Goude Laken; 't Ordinaris van de Weduwe H. Otten. *Reisboek* (1700) also: Maas-Dijk. *Reisboek* (1700 and 1721) also: 't Schippers Huis, op 't Zeeuwsche Veer [1721: op de Spaansche kaai]. *Reisboek* (1721) also: Sommelsdijk, op 't Stijger; De Postelijne Kom, De Zwarte Leeuw (both in de Wijnstraat); De Maarschalk van Turenne*, in de Schrijnwerkers-steeg [Nugent: on the South Blake]; Pennington bij de Wijnhaven, voornaam logement voor de Engelse Lords. Nugent (1749) also: Mrs Caters in the Wine Street, Mr Edwards in the Gelders-key, 'much the genteelest and very reasonable, considering the goodness of the accommodation in which everything is the best of the kind'.

Further reading

G. van Spaan, *Beschryvinge der stad Rotterdam*, Rotterdam 1698, 1713, 1738.

H.C. Hazewinkel, *Geschiedenis van Rotterdam*, Zaltbommel 1974-1975 (reprint).

Ach Lieve Tijd, zeven eeuwen Rotterdam en de Rotterdammers, R. Feringa (ed.), Zwolle 1986-1988.

Rotterdams jaarboekje, 1888-

Utrecht

William Lord Fitzwilliam, April 1663

[14r] [coming from 's-Hertogenbosch] We passed in a ferry the river Wahal [at Zaltbommel], having passed by Crèvecoeur the river Mosa; and before we came to Utrecht we passed likewise the Rhine. At Utrecht we arrived very late. The next day we went to see the town. It has been formerly a bishopric and its bishops have been very famous in the world. Now it is one of the Seven United Provinces and is a free state. The Papists of this town acknowledge always a bishop, and when one dies they make presently another; he is only known to them and to nobody else.

This town is pleasantly situated: it lies higher than any of the towns of Holland and in a very good air. Its strength is inconsiderable: there are old brick walls and a good broad ditch about it. Without, the town is surrounded with brave, pleasant walks and set with trees. There is likewise a very curious long pall-mall; on each side of it trees and fair walks. Within the town we saw the cathedral church, called the Dom, which is a great and rare building and of very great revenues, as having many prebendships, which are not quite abolished. Some particular persons possess them, and when they are dead others buy them.

[14v] The steeple of this church is four hundred and fifty stairs high; from it you may see in a clear day Amsterdam. Within the precincts of this church is the university. The schools and auditoria are but very mean yet very commodious. The university library is in St John's church. In St Mary's, which is the English church, there is likewise a library but of very old books, very reverend for their antiquity. In it we saw a manuscript of the Bible, written in several volumes by one man. In the same church we saw likewise three unicorns' horns, found by somebody after the great deluge and presented by one of the Emperors of Germany to this town. If all is true what is reported of these horns they are inestimable and must needs be the greatest rarity of Utrecht.

Here is a town house indifferently well-built. Here all the town's business is examined. The country affairs are brought before another senate [Provincial Court], who keeps court in the abbey of St Paul, and the States of this Province have their meeting where formerly has been the convent of Minims. The streets of this town are very clean and large, the houses very uniformly built. The whole town is one of the fairest and well-built places of the Low Countries. It is very big and has very great suburbs about it. In the town we saw yet the horse market, which is a very spacious, brave, open place, and here has been formerly the castle [Vredenburg] of this town.

The Catholic religion is here not publicly exercised, all the convents are put down, several of them are destined to a secular use, others to be hospitals and pious houses. In some of the old monasteries there live yet some religious women, and there are yet some prebendships allowed to noble women, but for the most part they are Protestants. Out of the town we saw Count Solms' house. Here live abundance [15r] of gentlemen, and all the people are very civil and conversable.

From hence we went to see Vianen, which belongs to the Lord of Brederode. It is but three or four [two] hours going from Utrecht, a little pleasant town; the above-said Lord is absolute lord over it. Here have all rogues and knaves their refuge: nobody can take them from hence or offend them in the least manner without the Lord Brederode's permission, in whose power it is to pardon or punish them. So that this town is composed only of broken merchants and other wicked persons, who dare not live in any other place. Here they enjoy great privileges and live at an easy rate. Very enormous transgressors, it was told me, had here no shelter, the Lord would not suffer them to dwell here. We dined here at the sign of the Angel. I fear he was a member of this venerable society of knaves, for he made us to pay an unreasonable price for our dinner. But where should we have found any honest person? Diogenes himself, if he had been with his lantern, would have lost his pains if he had looked for one.

Here we saw the house of Brederode, which is not very magnific, but yet sumptuous enough; a pretty wood, gardens and water belonging to it. We saw in it most of the pictures of the House of Brederode. This place is surrounded with walls and ditches and is pretty strong. Here we saw likewise the church and in it the tombs of the family of Brederode. In the town there is one great street, extending itself from one gate to the other; and this is all which we did remark in this place. From hence we returned to Utrecht and the next day to Amsterdam. [cont. Amsterdam]

Richard Holford, 11 (21) August 1671

[15v] Friday 11 August at seven in the morning, we left Amsterdam and took boat for Utrecht. For about one league, went up the river Amstel, which at Ouderkerk we left and turned up a cut on the left hand, where we made a quarter of an hour's stay. We then came by Abcoude, the first town in Utrecht, where is a pretty church and steeple. Here four times in the year is a very great horse market, at least two thousand horses. Here lives the marshall van Abcoude, in a stately structure. He is a kind of justiciar in the country and can for offences commit the offender to prison, which he has in his own house. The house of brick [is] seated very low, but handsomely fenced with trees, a square house with four towers with battlements.

We saw Nigtevecht, a steeple (town) about a mile to the right [left] hand and came through Baambrugge. We saw a fair town, called Weesp about a league on the left hand. We also came by Loenersloot and Loenen, where is a double [16r] government, one part under Holland and the other under Utrecht, and accordingly

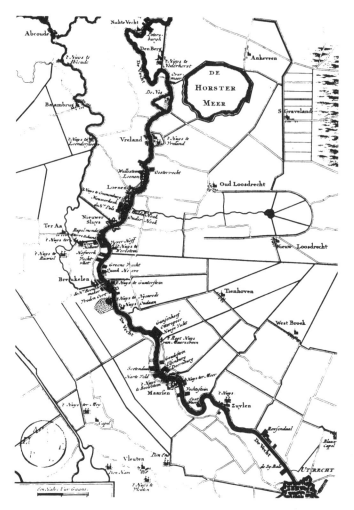

River Vecht, 1719

they have two schouts. Here is the house of the late Grave of Cronenbergh, one of the Lords of Cronenbergh being Earl of Holland, was killed by Van [=Gerard] van Velsen for having debauched his wife [=Floris V, Count of Holland, was kept prisoner at Cronenburgh by Gijsbrecht IV van Amstel]. And for this, Van Velsen was put into a barrel full of nails and drawn two leagues and then the head of the barrel opened, and he leaped out, having by the very strength of his body kept his head and his feet so firm that he received no hurt. But then they took him and put him in again and nailed the ends full of nails and shut him up again and so killed him.

We dined at Nieuwersluis upon the Vecht and paid twenty stivers apiece for our dinner and nine stivers for our man, and went up the Vecht river and by Breukelen, a pleasant passage with fine gardens and garden houses on both sides, where is Gunterstein, a good brick house, where [Johan van Olden-] Barnevelt dwelled and was fetched thence when he was beheaded. Also a little further [16v] is a very fine house called Nieuwenland [Nijenrode], the house of the Heer van Sadtsfeilt [Saesveld]. A little further is an indifferent good house called Oudaen, where a little river, part of the Rhine, comes into the Vecht. At Arnhem, within two years last, passed the Rhine so dry that an old man at that place ploughed in the place where the main stream did run.

A very pleasant fair house [Goudestein], belonging to Maarsseveen, a burgo-master of Amsterdam. He is a gent and has arms on his door, but is not of an old stam [lineage]. From hence by a dorp called Maarssen, which is the best between Amsterdam and Utrecht, in which the Lord van [de] Werve's house [Huis ten Bosch]. In this dorp the Jews have a house and came hither this night to observe their sabbath the next day. A monastery called the stone kamer, now a merchant's house.

The next village upon the Vecht to Utrecht is Zuilen; behind the church is the house of the Lord of Zuilen; upon the church is his coat of arms. [17r] We came to Utrecht Friday about half an hour past three to Mrs Glover's at the Jerusalem Cross. We saw St John's church, where the English formerly preached. This church is built with a stone called tuff stone, square like brick and of incredible hardness, the art of making which stone is forgotten. The Jews of Amsterdam have proffered to build a church, as good and as big again, if they may have the stones of this, for that they make cement with this stone.

Thomas Penson, September 1687

[65] My friend Mr Norris (whose civilities I must ever own), though his business would not permit him to go [from Amsterdam] to Utrecht with me, yet he gave me a letter to a particular friend there, one Mr [Nicolaas de] Vries, a watchmaker against the stathouse. I arrived there at about nine of the clock at night and took up my lodging at the sign of the Jerusalem Cross, a good house, where I found divers English gentlemen had lodged by their names written in the glass windows (and to follow their example, I pulled off my ring and wrote mine likewise and so also I did in other places).

In the morning Mr Vries attended me with [66] great respect and kindly enter-tained me at his own house, and afterwards went and showed me what was re-markable in this ancient city, particularly the Dom, which is a vast high tower or steeple (the church having been torn from it in a storm or earthquake [1674]). It contains three hundred and eighty steps, but they are deep ones, and indeed, I take it to be much higher than the Monument in England [311 steps]. At the top of this tower is affixed a great iron barrel, about ten foot diameter, whose motion causes the chimes to go in pleasant tunes. Above that is a room where Mr [Carel van] Falkin [Valbeeck] (who is a very ingenious master of music) played on the bells with his hands and feet as with an organ. He played several English and Dutch tunes by book for the space of an hour on purpose to oblige me (being a stranger).

Afterwards I was conducted to the English church which is called St Mary's. [67] It appears very ancient, for time has set his teeth therein. It is said to be of six hundred years' standing and was built by the Emperor Henry IV, whose figure is there preserved both in carving and painting. Adjoining to this church are kept the ancient books, etc., particularly nine great manuscripts in Latin, six whereof contain the Old and New Testaments and the other three the Psalms. All [of] which are very curiously written on vellum by the monks in the hand called German Text. Several of the great letters being laid with burnished gold and leaves, adorned with divers colours, etc. There are likewise many other printed books when printing was in its infancy. Being led into another room, I was shown two molten images of brass which the heathens worshipped, and a white surplice, which they say was made by the wild heathens. It is woven throughout and without seam. Likewise two [68] horns of unicorns for the altar (in the ends of which stood wax candles) and an elephant's tooth, made like a hunter's horn, which was to call the people to worship.

Anonymous Utrecht student, 6 July 1699 - 8 October 1700 N.S.

[5] We went by water [from Leiden] to Utrecht, which is nine hours, reckoning the time the boat stays by the way for the passengers to refresh themselves. In our way we passed by Woerden and Bodegraven, at which place the French committed most shameful extravagances when they overran these countries in 1670 and 1672 [only 1672]. Besides these two places we passed by a small fort [Wierickerschans], very regular and neatly fortified, encompassed with a large ditch and all the works planted with lime trees.

Utrecht is a pretty large town, though not so big as Leiden. The university is not so flourishing as it has been formerly. It has an old wall with a pretty good ditch; there are several old towers on one part of the wall, the other part has three or four sorry bastions, one of which serves for the garden of simples, which is but small. And one of the towers on the wall serves for an observatory; the rampart is very broad and good part of it planted with fine lime trees.

The planting without the town is very fine and pleasant; the mall is fine and of a good length and planted with four or five rows on each side. The cingle (from the Latin word cingulum because as a girdle it encompasses the town) goes round the outside of the town and is as fine a walk as one need desire, it being about three short miles in circuit. The present King of France [Louis XIV], when he was hereabouts with his army in 1672, thought the planting about this place so well worth preserving that he forbade any of the soldiers to cut or destroy any of it on very severe penalty. The Rhine runs through the town ditch and so goes away to Leiden.

The Great Church, called the Dom, is very remarkable for its tower or steeple,

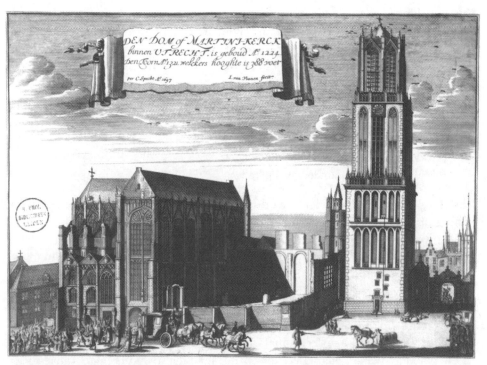

Great Church, 1697

which is very high and stands some score of paces from the church as now it is, and was divided from it by a strange accident. Above twenty years ago [6] in the night time, there was a most terrible storm of wind with dreadful thunder and lightning [1674], which threw down all the west part of the church from the cross to the steeple, leaving standing the east end and the cross together, and so the steeple remained by itself. And the noise of the storm was so great that nobody perceived the fall of the church till they found it down to the ground in the morning, though there are houses all round the church and at a very small distance. The places for public lectures which the professors give are in the cloister of the Dom. There is one room where are the pictures of all the professors that have been ever since the founding of the university [1636]. And there is the table at which the Union of Utrecht was signed in the year 1579 by the States of Holland, Zeeland, Gelderland, Friesland and Utrecht; into which afterward entered also the provinces of Overijssel and Groningen.

The church called St Mary's is allowed for the use of the English, who have a minister who is maintained by the States of Utrecht. I think he has about one thousand guilders a year pension. This church was founded by the Emperor Henry III [IV], whose statue is to be seen on the top of it. They keep here a pretended smock of the Blessed Virgin: it is without seam and looks like a sort of muslin. Perhaps if

337

this smock were in the hands of some cunning popish priest, it might be made to work some profitable miracle in time. There are two or three little ancient brass idols and an elephant's tooth or two in the same chest. In a room just by are several old manuscripts of Latin bibles, but none of any great value. On one of the pillars in the church is this:

> Accipe posteritas quod per tua saecula narres
> Taurinis cutibus fundo solidata columna est.

> [Posterity see this and tell it to your children,
> this pillar is solidly founded on bull hides]

The story of it goes that when they dug to lay the foundation of this pillar, there sprang up a source of water which they could not stop till one found the way of laying raw oxhides there, on which they laid the foundation of this pillar.

Within this church and in the place before it, they hold the kermis or yearly fair, which begins about the latter end of July and lasts three weeks. During a stated number of days any are permitted to come into the town, without molestation, that have been banished the town or voluntarily have left it upon the account of any crime. At the end of which time there is a bell rung to give notice that the time is expired. And if any of the said criminals are found within the town after the ringing of the bell, any person has power to seize or take them, and they are liable to be prosecuted for their former crime. Whilst I was there, a man was seized whom they said had committed a murder; he was got so drunk that he did not take care to retire before the ringing of the bell. And so being known, was taken and carried to prison, and soon after was executed for the crime he had committed eight or ten years before.

The church of St John stands in the middle of a large square which is planted with pleasant walks of Dutch limes. In this square is a great [7] building called the Stadts Cammer, where the States of Utrecht hold their assembly. In the church of St John there is a public library; I did not see it, being told it was very inconsiderable. The largest square in the town is that they call the corn market [Neude]. There are many Roman Catholics in this town, and I was told there are eight or ten places where mass is said. There are many persons of good fashion, and Utrecht is called the Ape of The Hague. There are but four principal gates beside several small ones or sally-ports; the handsomest of all the gates is that called the Witte Vrouwen Port. Without the Leiden Gate [=Katharijnen-Poort] was formerly a citadel with five bastions, but it has been long demolished [1577]. The firearms made here are in good esteem, they make good quantities of them.

About two hours or six miles from Utrecht lies Vianen, a little sovereignty by itself. There is a little town, walled round, and the remains of an old castle and a dwelling house. There is a fine wood; they have good fish out of the Lek or Rhine, which is hard by. It is very pleasant coming from Utrecht hither by water in the summertime. And there is a public house in the wood where one may have good pike or carp at any time, they keeping them always ready in a pond, so that one may always depend on a pretty dish of fish.

About halfway between Utrecht and Vianen, about a mile from the canal, is Heemstede, where is a house belonging to one who takes the title of Heer van Heemstede. It is a very pleasant place. The house stands surrounded on all sides with wood in which are very delightful walks and avenues, ponds and a small park with some deer. The house itself is moated round; the gardens are not great but very pleasant having abundance of fine greens and several very pretty water-works and wetting places. At the further end of the garden is a pretty large basin and deep and well-kept.

About two hours as one goes towards Amersfoort heath is a village called Zeist, where Monsieur Odijk, who is one of the States-General, has a very pleasant seat. The house together with a fair garden is moated round with good running water. But without the moat are very fine avenues and parterres with curious greens and several very good statues and urns.

John Leake, February 1712

[21r] The advances towards a peace made by the Courts of Great Britain and France having been [22r] the subject of most people's conversation the latter months of this year, and Utrecht being the place pitched upon by the contending powers to transact this great affair, we resolved, upon the arrival of the Bishop of Bristol [John Robinson, the English ambassador] in these parts, to decamp for some days and make our personal appearance among the rest of our countrymen at Utrecht who came along with that Great Man, to wait upon him during his embassy.

And accordingly, February the 22nd we went [from Leiden] to the said place in company with my dear friend, Mr Henry Leslie, Mr Macnaughton, and Mr Beard. We were conveniently lodged in a private house near the market square. Here I found my good friend Mr David Cunninghame upon his return from Italy. Among many other things I was obliged to him in particular for bringing me acquainted with the honourable Sir William Wentworth, a person of great accomplishments and who was upon his return home, adorned with all the good qualities of each country he had passed throug.

The 23rd there was to be a general assembly at the stadthouse of the ministers of the several Allies, as well as of those of France. We could not slip this opportunity of gratifying our curiosity, and therefore, about ten in the morning, we placed ourselves as conveniently as we could to observe the cavalcade, and view the politic faces of these arbitrators of the fate of Europe. In the evening we were introduced by some English gentlemen to my Lord Strafford, second plenipotentiary at this treaty for Great Britain, and were courteously received by his Lordship. There were with his [23r] Lordship at the same time, the Counts [Ernst] of Metternich [Prussian envoy at Vienna], [Annibale] Maffei [ambassador of Savoy] and Tarouca [ambassador of Portugal], with a minister of Tuscany, diverting themselves at cards. After staying some time in this noble company, we took our leaves and retired.

One of the greatest satisfactions I had during my stay here was the opportunity of going twice a day to the Bishop's, to hear divine service. His Lordship was not content with the common privilege of ambassadors of having the service of God performed in his own private chapel according to the rites and ceremonies of the Church of England. But by his interest he procured leave of the magistracy to have the English service read, the sacraments administered, and preaching by his own chaplains in St John's Church.

It is true in most of the chief cities in the United Provinces there is an English Presbyterian Church settled, and the same stipend allowed the pastor of it by the States-General as the Dutch *dominees* have; and such a settlement we had at Leiden, the care of which was committed to one Mr Milling in my time. But this was no advantage to us nor any of our countrymen, who thought we had reason to scruple their mission and dislike several of the tenets they embrace purely upon the authority of John Calvin. The Episcopal churches at Amsterdam and Rotterdam were at too great a distance from us to go every Sunday to, and therefore that place [Utrecht] could not want agreeableness that delivered us from these inconveniences and gave us though but a transient view of the beauty of holiness.

During our stay in these parts we made an excursion over the river Lek to Vianen, a [24r] sort of lordship or baillage, where people of desperate fortunes fly for security when they have committed any enormous crimes and are ready to fall into the arms of justice. The famous Huguetan, who had cheated his master the French King of so many millions of livres, purchased the sovereignty of this asylum. And to my thinking he was a proper head for such a band of wretches who seemed to have such large characters of villainy of all sorts written in their foreheads.

We went also to see the house of the Baron van Heemstede, which is antique and situated in a moat. Its apartments are rather convenient than magnificent, and the chief thing it has to boast of are its gardens, in which are a fine orangery, waterworks and vistas of a prodigious length.

We could not take our leave of Utrecht without making a view of its stadthouse and the several apartments in it that are allotted to the ministers of the Allies and France to negotiate the great affair of peace. They have nothing of fineness or magnificence about them, but are as dark and melancholy as the transactions within them have hitherto been.

Population: 30,000 (1650), over 25,000 (1675-1750).

Distances: Amersfoort 4 hours (14 miles), Amsterdam 8 hours (23 miles), Arnhem 12 hours (32 miles), 's-Hertogenbosch 12 hours (35 miles), Leiden 10 hours (30 miles), Rotterdam 11 hours (25 miles).

Inns, *Reisboek* (1689, 1700 and 1721): 't Veerschuitje, buiten de Waert Poort [1721: Catharijne Poort]; 't Wapen van Amersfoort, De Witte Swaan (buiten de Witte Vrouwen Poort); Den Arend, buiten de Catharyne Poort [1721: Witte Vrouwen Poort]; Den Hulk, buiten de Tollesteeg Poort. Binnen de Stad: 't Kasteel van Antwerpen*, bij de Bakker brugge; De Plaats Royaal, in de Minnebroers-straat; De Doms-toorn*, op 't Oude Kerkhof.

Reisboek (1689) also: De Weduwe van Stamme, op de hoek van de Nobelstraat, tegenover St. Jans Kerkhof. *Reisboek* (1689 and 1700) also: De Toelast, over de Bezem-brug; 't Witte Paard, op Vreeburg. *Reisboek* (1700) also: De Kroon, mede op 't oude Kerkhof; Het Witte Poortjen. *Reisboek* (1700 and 1721) also: De Engel, buiten de Catharyne Poort. *Reisboek* (1721) also: 't Nieuwe Kasteel van Antwerpen, De Maagt van Gent* (both on the Ganze Markt); La Cour de Loo*, 't Hof van Holland* (bij de Witte Vrouwe Brug); 't Wapen van Jerusalem*, op de Voorstraat; De Stad Groningen*, De vergulde Wagen* (both on Vreeburg).

Further reading

[C. Booth], *Beschryvinge der stadt Utrecht*, Utrecht 1685, 1715, 1745.
J. van Staveren and J. Kievid, *Utrecht negentienhonderd jaar historie*, Utrecht 1948.
Ach Lieve Tijd, dertien eeuwen Utrecht en de Utrechters, M.W.J. de Bruijn (ed.), Zwolle 1985.
A. van Hulzen, *Utrecht: een beknopte geschiedenis van de oude bisschopsstad*, Utrecht 1994.
Jaarboek Oud-Utrecht, 1925-
Oud-Utrecht: tweemaandelijks tijdschrift, 1926-

Valenciennes and Cambrai

William Lord Fitzwilliam, 14-15 April 1663 N.S.

[4v] Some leagues from this town [Péronne] we came into the Spanish dominion, and at supper we arrived at Cambrai, the frontier town of France, very well-built and fortified. Charles the Great [Charlemagne], it is believed, did first surround it with walls, and Charles V built the castle, which lies upon a high hill and is very well fortified. It has a Spanish garrison within it. It is so exactly guarded that no stranger is permitted to come in for to see it. Yea, they are so jealous that they will not suffer anyone to look upon the walls or ditches of it. They have liberty to kill anyone that does it.

By this town runs the river Scalde [Schelde], which is here very small as likewise at Valenciennes, whereas it is about Antwerp much broader than the Thames is about London. Our Lady's church of this town deserves very well to be seen and its rare clock. It is a metropolitan church. Here are nine parishes, three abbeys, many pious and religious houses, amongst which St Lazare's hospital, a place for leprous people, is one of the chiefest.

This town lies in the bishopric of Cambrésis. The bishop has here a very fair palace, and here is likewise a fair town house, on the outside of which all the electors' coats of arms are cut out in stone. In the midst of them stands Charles the Fifth's statue, with his golden fleece about him. Here are many bridges and several fair marketplaces. Here is made the best sort of cambric.

This town has sometimes belonged to the States of the Low Countries, sometimes to the French, sometimes to the Spaniard. It pretends to be a free imperial town, [5r] but yet it is under the Spanish dominion. Anno 1581 it was a long time and very straitly besieged by the Spaniards, that the inhabitants were forced to eat horses, cats, rats, anything that they could get; everything extraordinary dear: a cow did cost two hundred guilders, a sheep fifty, a pound of butter twenty-four stivers, a pound of cheese thirty stivers, an egg eleven stivers and an ounce of salt eight stivers. It was at last relieved by the French as Thuanus writes in the 74th book of his history [*Historia sui temporis*].

After a bad night's lodging, we were forced to rise soon the next morning for to be at dinner at Valenciennes, a town of the county of Hainaut, seven leagues distant of Cambrai. It lies on the river Scalde, fortified with deep and broad ditches, strong walls and bulwarks. In the last war between France and Spain it did hold out a long siege [1656]. Its enemies were forced to make a very shameful retreat. Here is the church of Our Lady to be seen; the convents of Franciscans and

342

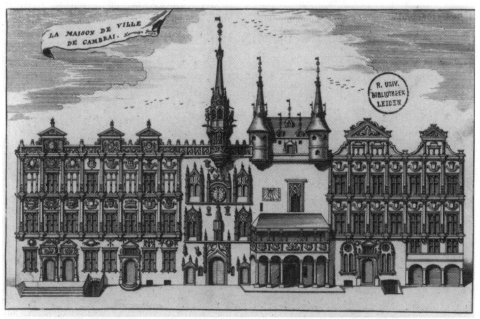

Cambrai. Town hall, 1716

Dominicans, in whose church you will find some princely tombs. Here is likewise the Counts of Hainaut's palace, an ammunition house and a maison de ville, which is very spacious and comprehending within its confines a corn marketplace, a wool marketplace, drapers' shops, a fencing school and a public prison. Upon the town house is a rare clock, showing not only the sun's, but moon's and all the planets' motions, the seasons of the year and the length of days and many other pretty curiosities. Here are likewise many bridges inhabited. The town's jurisdiction is different from that of the country. The Archbishop of Cambrai has some power over the town, whose archdeacon resides here most commonly. The chief magistrate is now the King of Spain, whereas formerly the Dukes of Burgundy have had this right. [cont. Mons and Tournai]

Sir John Percival, 17-19 (28-30) July 1718

[93r] On the 17th of July, we set out for Paris and at three leagues distance passed through Halle, the first town in Hainaut, to Braine-le-Comte, where we dined. In the afternoon we proceeded in sight of Mons, which we left a mile on our left and [93v] makes a handsome show at that distance, to Cuveren [Quiévrain], an inconsiderable village, and the last on this side subject to the Emperor, where we lay the first night, having made fourteen leagues.

Hainaut is one of the Seventeen Provinces and contains in length twenty leagues, in breadth sixteen. It is watered by several rivers as the Schelde, the Dender, the Sambre, the Haine, the Trouille and the Hanneau [Honnelle]. There are large forests in it with mines of iron and lead, and marble quarries. There is also near Mons a good coal mine, but the ordinary people burn turf. Within this circumference there are no less than twenty-four walled towns of which Mons and Valenciennes are the principal and about nine hundred and fifty villages, besides castles and private seats.

We left Cuveren the 18th after having been narrowly searched to prevent our carrying tea or other East India goods into France, which are either prohibited or pay so high a duty as almost amounts to the same. We set out about five o'clock designing to lie at Cambrai that night, and in half an hour entered French Flanders, where at a barrier we were stopped by a parcel of commis on the like occasion as at Cuveren. But they behaved more civilly, for having satisfied them without search, we proceeded to Valenciennes, where [94r] at half an hour past eight, we arrived.

This is an ancient city and received its name, as some pretend, from the Emperor Valens [Valentinianus I], who in 378 was killed by the Goths. The Scalde passes through it and is here navigable, which proves of great advantage to two considerable manufactures carried on by the inhabitants, one of stuffs and camlets, the other of fine linens called batiste, transported to France and Spain and even to the Indies. In 1677 the King of France took this city the seventh [tenth] day after opening the trenches and added strong fortifications thereto, though irregular.

The situation is commodious in respect of water, wherewith private houses are well supplied, and there is a handsome marketplace, but the streets are narrow and crooked. The form is round. The number of houses is four or five thousand and the inhabitants about twenty-five thousand. The citadel is an irregular fortification, but well defended by ditches both wet and dry.

The city is governed by a chief governor, who has under him a lieutenant du roy, a major, two aide-majors and a captain of the gates. This is the military government of most places of strength subject to France. Monsieur de Saint-Just, a brigadier of foot, was at that time commandant or governor of the citadel. Monsieur de Champeron, likewise brigadier, the king's lieutenant in the city, and the Prince de Tingry, Lieutenant-General, [94v] an officer of distinguished note, was governor. He was born in 1673 [1675], is fourth son of the famous Duke of Luxembourg, and esteemed a devoted friend of the Regent [Philippe d'Orléans].

At entering the town the sentries obliged me to go before the commanding officer to acquaint him with my country, name, quality and business, which ceremony being over, I had a second trouble with the custom-house officers, who constrained me to carry thither my trunks in order to be opened and strictly examined. By the help of a very wealthy gentleman, a banker residing here and the only Protestant professing his religion, I was dispatched in two hours, and to prevent the plague of frequent searches, took his advice which was to cause a note of my things to be entered upon a written ticket and when replaced in their trunks, weighed and the king's seal set on them. This they call plumbing. Then signing the ticket, my goods were free to pass to Paris, the only place where they might again be opened. At the same time my friend gave security that I should not break the seal.

By the time I returned to my inn, the day was so far spent that we resolved to dine there, the rather because I learned there was no good place to stop at till [95r] I arrived at Cambrai. Accordingly, after dinner at half an hour past twelve, we set out for Cambrai, where we arrived in six hours, the computed distance being but seven and the road extremely good.

Cambrai is the capital of a small county, about ten leagues in length and five or six in breadth, though in some places not above two. The soil is not over-fruitful in corn, but abounds in pasture for horses and sheep whose wool is fine and much esteemed. The inhabitants have a good traffic for their linens.

Cambrai was in early times subject to the King of France; afterwards the Emperors of Germany subdued it and appointed their own counts or governors. These in process of time became hereditary and would have been absolute sovereigns if after the death of [Emperor] Arnold [Arnulf], the bishop had not obtained of the Emperor either to suppress that dignity or to unite it to the church, which last was by the Emperor complied with in 1007. Neither the kings of France not the descendants of Arnold were pleased with that disposition. However, the bishops of Cambrai found means to appease both and remained absolute lords of the city and county, till Charles the Fifth (Emperor) in 1543 built a citadel on a place called the Oxhill [Mont-des-Boeufs], which he pretended belonged to him as lying within the precinct of Bouchain, [95v] though so near the city as to command it. From that time the archbishop ceased to exercise princely jurisdiction there, and their sovereign authority was no longer acknowledged, except in Cateau-Cambrésis, a small city five leagues distant.

At length Louis the Fourteenth put an end to the old disputes and prevented any new, when [in] 1677 he conquered the whole country. For from that time the archbishops have acknowledged the King of France for successor to the ancient sovereigns of Cambrai, swear fealty to him and are nominated by him. Nevertheless, the title of Duke of Cambrai and Prince of the Holy Empire remains to them, and it is a dignity of handsome income, no less than one hundred thousand livres per annum. Six hundred parishes are under him.

The city is built on the Scalde [Schelde] and well fortified, especially on the east side, where lies the citadel, a regular pentagon with ditches cut out of the rock. Part of this citadel is enclosed by the city wall and stretches down by a gentle slope to the river, where is another citadel which secures the city on that side and may, on account of its low situation, be laid by means of sluices, under water. Maréchal [de] Bezons is governor. The streets of Cambrai are handsome and broad, the principal of which end in a very large marketplace, where the town house makes a handsome [96r] appearance.

A stranger without the help of a map may know when he enters the territories of France on the Flanders side, from the face of misery which everywhere appears. One of the principal inns of Cambrai was where we took up our quarters, and yet it is inconceivable how dirty and ill provided it was. We had not met before with such bad beds, meat, light or attendance. The floors of all the rooms had, I believe, been never washed from the time they were first laid, and the pavement was so uneven with clods of dirt from men's shoes, they could not safely be paced. Neither did the bedding seem to have been beat[en] or washed, and the dirt on the curtains and underneath the bed was insupportable.

Moreover, this being summertime produced such a multitude of fleas that we were obliged to rise several times in the night and give them chase. Nay, we had been in the inn but half an hour, when the ladies were obliged to undress themselves to remove those vermin that sported themselves under their petticoats, pleased I suppose with the warmth of that climate.

This sort of treatment we met in almost all the places we lay at, till our arrival at Paris, and I may venture to affirm that even our common Irish are cleanlier than the French of much better rank and substance. Nevertheless, though the accommodation we met with in all respects upon this road [96v] was so bad, the innkeepers made more extravagant bills than even the Dutch. For which reason whoever travels in France must take care to bargain for everything beforehand and that before they put their foot into the house. For provisions and living are cheap enough, and rather than suffer you to go elsewhere, they will come to a reasonable agreement.

Anonymous tourist, 4-6 August 1720 N.S.

[53v] Set out [from Lille] at six o'clock in a coach and four, which we gave for every day one pistole. Came to Saint-Amand, eight leagues off, about one o'clock; the road bad but a pretty good country. St Amand is but a little town, watered by the river Scarpe. The fortifications are demolished by the barrier treaty. See the abbey of St Amand, very large and handsome of the Benedictine order. The church is the finest we yet saw; from the nef is an ascent to the quire and great altar [54v] of many marble steps, under which are buried those friars of the house who were put to death by the Normans under the reign of [Emperor] Charles le Gros. Dined at the Coup d'Or.

Set out in the afternoon for Valenciennes, three leagues off. Lodged au Cygne, pretty good house but dear. Went to the opera; the chief actress very good, Mademoiselle Des Jardins; the second Mademoiselle De Jars, a very good dancer; the rest but indifferent.

August 5. See the citadel, which makes a part of the fortifications of the town, very high placed and commands the town. It has a great hornwork exterior to it, very beautiful and ravelins, beyond it five bastions. There is a mill [that] brings the

King three hundred thousand livres revenue. Mr le Comte de Simier, aged 104, is governor of it.

August 6. Set out in the afternoon for Cambrai, six leagues off. Lodged au Palais Royal, pretty well. Observed at the steeple upon the Great Place, Martin de Cambrai and his wife striking the hours, made of metal at the town house. [55v] Two leagues on this side of Cambrai, see the [Benedictine] abbey of Haspres, belonging to the abbey of St Vaast of Arras; very civil to us.

See the citadel, a square with very high walls; within round. The body of the place is a high cavalier from which they command the country and the town. See the bishop's palace, unfurnished and out of order. They expect orders to furnish it against the congress. See several churches but nothing extraordinary: l'Eglise de St Sépulchre, the Jesuits, the cathedral. Cambrai is but a moderate town, very narrow streets. They say it is well peopled; a large marketplace. A circular town.

Valenciennes
Population: 20,000-25,000 (c.1700).
Distances: Cambrai 4 hours (12 miles), Mons 5 hours (15 miles), Tournai 5 hours (15 miles).
Inns, *Reisboek* (1689): A Notre Dame*; Le Duc d'Orléans*; Le Prince de Condé*.

Cambrai
Population: 12,000 (c.1700).
Distances: Arras 7 hours (20 miles), Douai and Valenciennes 4 hours (12 miles).
Inns, *Reisboek* (1689): Au Grand Roi de France*; Au Dauphin*.

Further reading

J. Le Carpentier, *Histoire de Cambray et du Cambrésis*, Leiden 1664.

J.B. Gramaye, *Antiquitates Belgicae*, Bruxelles-Leuven 1708.

L. Trenard (ed.), *Histoire de Cambrai*, Lille 1982.

H. Platelle (ed.), *Histoire de Valenciennes*, Lille 1982.

Revue du Nord, 1910-

Zeeland

William Lord Fitzwilliam, 30 June - 1 July 1663 N.S.

[35r] In coming from Dort [Dordrecht] to this country, we saw Tholen, Zierikzee and Ter Goes. We did not land in any of them, but went directly to Terveer, which lies in the isle of Walcheren, which although it is not the biggest (its compass being but ten leagues), yet it is the chiefest, richest and most populous isle of all the eight.

Terveer is the third walled town of Walcheren, having the sixth and last voice in the assembly of the States of this province. This town took its original from fishermen and mariners, and so it continues to this present hour its being. The Scots have here their staple and residence of merchants. It was begun here [1444] in the reign of James I, King of Scots, whose daughter was married to one Wolfaert, son of Henry of Borselen, Lord of this place, and from that time it does continue to this present. The magistrate has given them a fair great house for the use of the company and the old parish church for to serve God in their own language.

Next to the Scottish church you will see a brave, great church with two steeples on it, built of pure white stone. On the marketplace, which is fair [35v] and large, is the town house, built likewise of a white stone. On the outside of it, the statues of the Lords and Ladies of this town are cut out in stone. On the steeple is set a gilded ship, which signifies the means by which they live. Here is likewise an ammunition house, three dools [doelen], where the citizens exercise themselves in shooting. Here are likewise some hospitals, one fair street and very mean houses. Here is a very good haven and two good sluices. The town is indifferently well fortified.

From hence we went to Middelburg, the chiefest town of Walcheren as likewise the metropolis of whole Zeeland, and it has the first voice in the assembly of the States of this province. This is a very great city, environed with good walls and bulwarks, deep and broad ditches and several good gates leading into it. This town is by her own situation very proper for trading, but the two good havens belonging to it make it more commodious, for the greatest ships can harbour here and lie at shelter upon a standing water which is within the town. By this means this town traffics all the world over, and always its havens are full of ships.

Here are many fair [36r] buildings as the Abbey, which now is the house where the States of this province hold their assembly. This place is built in oval, round about it good houses; the court all set with trees and four doors leading to it. The town house is another noble building, having a fair, curiously made clock upon its tower and on the outside of it the statues of the Counts and Countesses of Zeeland,

MEDIOBURGENSIS CURIA

Middelburg. Town hall, c. 1650

all cut out in stone. Before its doors a great marketplace, where every Monday is kept a great market, as big as an ordinary fair. Here is likewise to be seen a dool, or shooting house, the Exchange and the houses of the East- and West India Companies, three churches but of a very mean fabric and some hospitals or pious houses. Within and without this town there are fair and pleasant walks, chiefly the foot-way between this town and Terveer.

From hence we went to Vlissingen [Flushing], the second town of the island Walcheren and having the fifth voice in the assembly of the States. This town, it is very like, took its beginning from poor fishermen's houses, and so by little and little, by reason of the conveniency of its situation, it became to be a town of great traffic. This town is one of the strongest, and has the most commodious haven of Zeeland. It lies as if it were in the jaws [36v] of Neptune, the sea does almost surround it. Before the haven is made a great bank, which is with very great cost maintained. It breaks the waves so that they can have not so much strength to come near the town. She is almost invincible by water, and by land she cannot so easily be attacked, being well defended with good walls, bastions and ditches.

Amongst the public buildings of this town, the town house is the chiefest. It is a model of that of Antwerp, not so big and great but lesser and very like it. It stands on the great marketplace. Afterwards you may see the Prince's house and garden and the old parish church with its steeple and clock. The Prince of Orange [William III] is Lord of this town, his great-grandfather Prince William [I] bought it. It has been formerly pawned to Queen Elizabeth [1585]; King James restored it to the States [1616].

We arrived at this island the 30th of June 1663, and the day before there was a man executed who had committed a very enormous crime. He was only arrested for some debts and conducted by two sergeants to the town of Terveer for to be imprisoned, or upon payment of his money to be released. This wicked fellow going free and unbound (as debtors and suchlike prisoners ought to be) between [37r] these two men, he took a long knife out of his sleeve (of which nobody did dream) and presently stabbed with it one of these fellows to the heart and in the same instant cut the other's throat. He was presently taken and eight days after executed. First his right hand was cut off and with the same knife with which he had killed the two sergeants his heart was only touched, not at all wounded; afterwards half strangled and so broken upon a wheel. [cont. Gent]

James Drummond, Earl of Perth, September 1694

[44] We stayed only a day and a half at Bruges, and went by tractscout upon a canal to Sluis (the first town that way that belongs to Holland), to take our leave of the Catholic part of Flanders. We went and heard mass at a little fort which belongs to the Spaniards about a little English mile from Sluis, where the tractscout stopped (for it goes no further and passengers must foot it to Sluis). My wife walked it bravely, and seeing we could get no dinner at Sluis, we resolved to fast till we came to Flushing in Walcheren (Blair [Drummond]'s famous island). So we crossed a little ferry, near half as broad as the Queen's Ferry, in an open boat. It blew furiously, but we got safe over and took the only voiture the island afforded, which is an open cart. The land is called Cadzand, where [Georg] Cassander, who would have reconciled Catholics and Protestants, was born.

Our cart carried us the nine miles, which is the length of the island, in two hours' time, but it rained, with thunder and lightning, one half of the way. We had a ferry of open sea (for the ocean branches in towards Flanders, betwixt [45] Cadzand and Walcheren), as large as Bruntisland Ferry [on the Firth of Forth], to get to Flushing; but yet we got over pretty well and very hungry to Flushing, about six o'clock at night.

Our inn we were directed to was a good one, but we could get nobody could speak French, and none of us have Dutch as yet. At last the goodman's son came home, but such a lump I never saw: he was about Andrew Drummond's height, twice as big as Humbie and a head like a turnip for littleness. He says he is twenty years of age, has been bred at Bordeaux, and was very sparkish in his black suit, which is a Dutch gallantry for a vear.

Next day, as it had proved all night, it blew furiously with thunder, rain and great lightning. I went and saw the whole town in the forenoon so soon as it grew fair. There is a new dock made there, the finest imaginable: it can hold a hundred and twenty men-of-war. In the evening we went through the worst part of the island to a brave city, Middelburg. Near it the country is like a garden. There we stayed two days, and found here a Catholic chapel.

On Sunday afternoon we went to Camphire [Veere], where one William Gordon, a young man who has married a rich, handsome Dutch lass, carried us to his house and lodged and entertained us most nobly. His wife is the genteelest, best-bred Dutch woman I ever saw. Next day he carried us round the island to Domburg, a fine village, where he treated us at dinner, and then showed us Westkapelle, where the dike is that preserves the country from the sea. It is odd to see how securely they dwell when there is so small a business betwixt them and destruction. The work is great, but what can resist an enraged sea, or a deluded multitude?

After this day's pleasant promenade (for in our return we saw a most admirable garden of a Raadsheer, or one of their States-General, at a place called Poppingdoun [Poppendamme]), we took the scout for Zierikzee, a town in an island not far off, but it took us too much time, the weather being calm, to suffer us to go any further. So we stayed at this town from three in the afternoon to next [46] morning. It proved mighty hot, but yet we walked about all the town, which is large and pleasant. Next morning in an open cart we went three hours to a place where once stood a town called Bommenede, near Brouwershaven, where we overtook the burgomaster of Zierikzee going to Rotterdam.

Our way lay by Helvoetsluis; we were to go betwixt Goeree and Somerdyke [Sommelsdijk], but a dead calm overtook us about a musket shot from the shore, and we lay three hours for the tide. At last the tide came, but a contrary gale sprang up, and we turned up to get through the flats betwixt the islands. But all would not do, we came aground on the Halls [de Hals] and, the heat increasing and the clouds gathering, we would gladly have been ashore to lie in a boor's house. Our skipper told us there was but an open cart to carry us to Sommelsdijk, and we would be better aboard. But the burgomaster with a cousin of his and another man who spoke English, with their wives, waded through the sleek and salt water near half a mile, took a cart and were wet to the skin, for such thunder and lightning I never saw.

We sent our honest young man, captain of a ship, one Gordon, ashore to get us some meat; for we were made believe we would be only three hours on the water, and now it was about seven o'clock at night, and both my wife and I fasting. He got a piece of an old ham, two dozen of hard eggs and some brown bread and beer, and in my life did I never eat meat that relished better than that ham did to me. My wife ate heartily too, and in the storm of thunder and fire we spent the evening and lay still until twelve o'clock, when we set sail and arrived at Helvoetsluis about three in the morning.

We got into an English house, one Howie's, he says he is cousin germain to the Earl of Buchan, a very honest man. Next day we came to the Briel by waggon, for it lies in the same island. Helvoet is a place where lie many of the States' men-of-war, and here the English packet boat goes off and come on. It is but one row of houses on each side of the harbour, but they are very prettily built. The Briel is a pretty large but unwholesome [47] place, bravely fortified. We stayed here until next day about twelve o'clock. My wife walked round the walls, which I am persuaded is three English miles. Next day in a huge storm of wind we went up to Rotterdam, three hours up the river.

Sir Francis Child, 5-6 (15-16) June 1697

[1r] About noon, June the 5th, we came to an anchor before Ter Veere, a seaport town in Zeeland. Ter Veere is two leagues from Flushing, one from Middelburg, has two gates, some old fortifications, a small garrison of soldiers and is governed as other towns in this country are. It was taken by the Prince of Orange in 1572. Here are three old churches with as old a statehouse, but neither worth the being visited. Many inhabitants of this place are Scotch and are called free houses, not for their hospitality to strangers, but because they pay no excise for what drink they sell at home, wherefore they are severely fined if they send any abroad.

We went out at the Middelburg [Zandijkse] gate and for twenty-two stivers did hire to ourselves a waggon to Middelburg, but those who can endure bad tobacco and worse company may go for three stivers each. The road thither has a causeway in the middle whereon all waggons are obliged to go, which is so furiously that we expected to be disjointed before we should reach happiness, I mean our journey's end.

[1v] The many pleasant houses, which with as delightful walks of lime trees do front this road, gave us some satisfaction in our misery, especially Mijn Heer Monk's house, which is an English mile from the road, small but very neat, with

fine gardens, waterworks, statues, etc., of all [of] which we had a view through a noble pair of open iron gates. We had stopped to have seen this place, but a due consideration of the time we should require to recover the use of our limbs carried us to Middelburg, where we gave God thanks for his delivering us from the fury of the waggon, reposed our wearied joints and then went to see the town of which take the following account:

Middelburg, in Latin Metelli-Castrum or Medio-Burgum, is so called from its situation in the middle of the island of Walcheren, of which it is the capital; it is one league from Flushing, two from the Rammekens and five from Sluis. In 1561 [Pope] Paul IV made it a bishop's seat in favour of Nic. de Chatain [Castro], who was the first bishop of this place. In 1572 Mondragon most bravely held this town twenty-two months for Spain against the Prince of Orange and did not, till forced by famine, surrender it [in February 1574].

It now is a rich, populous and beautiful town, has many merchants which trade to all parts of the world, has a share in the East India Company and has, during this war, sent out many capers [privateers], whereof some have carried thirty guns. Here are five good churches, an old irregular court, where the Heer Odijk lives, who is Lord [representative of William III] of this province and is much respected. In the marketplace, which is large enough to be a good one could the country well furnish it, is the statehouse, an ancient, noble pile of building, the front whereof is adorned with above forty [25] niches in which are statues of the Counts of Flanders [Zeeland].

From Middelburg I returned to Ter Veere and from thence went in the scout-boat to Dordt, paying eighteen stivers for my passage. Two leagues on our left hand from Ter [2r] Veere, we were shown a token of Providence's love for these people, as a steeple and a vast tract of ground submerged by the sea, which was formerly called Wolphaartsdijk. Had I not been told it was a steeple, I should have taken it for a beacon, the whole country around it being become a sea. Two leagues further on our right, we had a view of Ter Goes. In eighteen hours, being always within land, if one may so say in this country, we arrived at Dordt.

Anonymous tourist, 16-21 July 1697 N.S.

16 July. At eight in the afternoon we landed at Terveere, a small town in the province of Zeeland; saw nothing remarkable there; went the next day (17) to Middelburg, the principal town in Zeeland and has in it five churches. The town is well-built, encompassed with an old fortification of earth on which are several trees planted in walks, and moated round with a large fosse into which the sea rises every tide.

18 July. From thence I went to Flushing, where are built the best ships in this province. On the side toward Middelburg is a large dock, newly made at a very great expense: about two furlongs or more in length and seventy yards over; opens

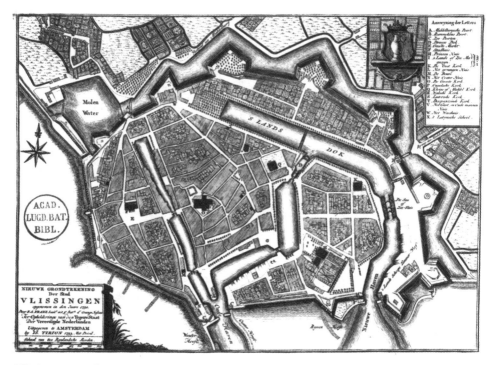

Vlissingen. Town plan, 1753

into the sea, the bottom, as I was informed, covered with oak plank; the water twenty-five foot deep with sluices to keep the water to what height they have occasion. Over this dock is a bridge of timber, which is made to open that large ships may go through. In this dock lay several men-of-war, as the Koning [van] England, Zeeland, etc., some of which carried a hundred guns. This dock was newly finished, having been eight years making. Returned at night to Middelburg.

19 July. About five in the afternoon, I took boat for Antwerp. In the passage thither I saw the church of Ouskinkerk [possibly Oostkerk, near Borssele, inundated in 1532] and one chimney only appearing above the water, the Scheldt having overflown the town anno 1617. About ten the next morning (20 July), I saw a whirlwind which first appeared on the water like a smoke which was driven by the wind about half a league from the vessel where I was. It continued for about half an hour, in which time the wind had driven it about three leagues. About a quarter of an hour before it expired, there appeared a spout into which the water seemed to be gathered that was exhaled, which made a very large, dark cloud. The sailors told me if the vessel had been in its way, the force of the whirlwind would have torn the sails and broken the mast, if not sunk the vessel.

About twelve o'clock we arrived at Lillo, a small town that belongs to the Dutch, inhabited only by fishermen and those that depend on the garrison, kept there to exact passage money from those that pass and also to search for goods prohibited, etc. Being on the frontier of the Spanish Provinces. About half an hour from this place, we arrived at Fort [St] Marie, a small fort belonging to the Spaniard, where we were searched, but paid no passage money. About five of the clock (21 July) we arrived at Antwerp.

Joseph Taylor, 3-4 (14-15) September 1707

[38v] We found it cheaper to take a vessel from Sluis to Flushing than to go in a waggon over the land of Cadzand, to which we might have passed for a stiver apiece in the ferryboat which goes from Sluis. But being informed there was no place of accommodation before we could arrive at Breskens, from whence we must have sailed over to Flushing, we chose rather a voyage altogether by sea, though [39r] something exposed to the dangers of privateers; and so sailed round the land of Cadzand and, having a brisk westerly wind, in about four hours got safe to Flushing, where the people, who live most by privateering, were on the shore welcoming with huzzas several privateers just come from the West Indies with great prizes, who in return fired all their guns to salute the town.

It is walled towards the sea and has several windmills about it, which with the fine tower to the Great Church makes a very good prospect upon the water. I quartered at the Golden Pear, and after I had refreshed myself a little, I went to see the town house, which stands in a handsome place. It has several pictures of famous heroes, one whereof is the great Prince of Orange [William I], and under it is written this distich in the nature of a chronocon [chronogram], by several letters showing the year of Our Lord: aUrIacUs prInCeps hIspanI fraUDe tyrannI oCCUMbIt, VInCI non aLIter poterat [1584], which I have Englished thus:

By Spanish fraud the Prince of Orange fell
No otherwise they could his conquering arms repel.

There is nothing more remarkable but the large graft and [39v] the buildings and streets, which are extremely neat. Here I parted with the ladies, who went directly to Rotterdam, whilst I took a waggon to see Middelburg, about a league from Flushing. I paid twenty-one stivers having hired it to myself, but with passengers the fare is only three stivers and a half. I had a very pleasant journey over a fine causeway with a great row of trees all along, and saw many pretty villas and gardens with delightful avenues.

I lay one night at Middelburg at the Golden Lion in the Long Delft. It is a very neat town. I saw the kirk wherein is the monuments of the Evertsen [Cornelis and Johan], killed in the war between England and Holland in 1672 [1666]. There is another church in [the] form of an octagon and three or four others, English and French, of which one is called the New Kirk, but they have nothing remarkable in them, except the great number of achievements against the walls, whereby one would judge most of the families in Holland were noble by the coronets and supporters to their arms, which they thus generally hang up and dedicate them to the memory of their ancestors instead of monuments.

In the Simplehuys (as they call it) or hospital for idiots, I saw forty-five miserable objects of the defects of nature, and there is [40r] a good hospital for sick people, another called the Weeshuys, containing about four hundred boys and girls, much like our Christ's Hospital at London, and another for old men and women, containing about a hundred; some of them, as they informed me, were a hundred years old. The town house is a good piece of building with a large place before it. On each side [of] the great door is a cage fixed upon [iron] pins, to turn round. In one they kept an eagle, in the other they put scolding women, turning them about as fast as they can, which is a punishment answerable to our ducking stool in England. The place where the merchants assemble is like an amphitheatre. I judged the town, as I walked round it, to be a mile about.

Middelburg

Population: 30,000 (1650), 25,000 (1700-1750).

Distances: Antwerp 14 hours (42 miles), Bergen op Zoom 8 hours (26 miles), Brugge 8 hours (25 miles), Rotterdam 21 hours (50 miles), Sluis 5-6 hours (18 miles), Veere 1 hour (3 miles), Vlissingen 1 hour (3 miles).

Inns, *Reisboek* (1689 and 1700): De Doelen; De Florentijnsche Lely; Het Huis van Domburg; De Hooge Deur; Het Wijnhuis* [1721: bij de Dambrug]; 't Hof van Bourgondiën* [1721: op de Rouaanse Kaai]. *Reisboek* (1700) also: Graaf Lodewijk; De Soutkeet. *Reisboek* (1700 and 1721) also: De Goude Leeuw* [1721: in de Lange Delft]; Het Hof van Holland* [1721: bij de Beurs, is vooral gerecommandeerd]; Den Helm [1721: bij 't Stadhuis]; Het Fortuintjen [1721: bij de Oosterse Kerk]. *Reisboek* (1721) also: 't Schild van Vrankrijk in de Bellinkstraat; De Retorijkkamer, op de Markt; De Zwarte Leeuw*, op de Beestemarkt; St. Pieter, op de Wal; De Verginjes, bij de Segeers Brugge. Nugent (1749) also: The King's Head, an English House kept by one Wilson.

Vlissingen

Population: 5,000-10,000 (1675-1750), 8,000 (1750 T.S.).

Distances: Middelburg 1 hour (3 miles), Sluis 4-5 hours (14 miles).

Inns, *Reisboek* (1689, 1700 and 1721): De eerste Peer*; De Peer, aan de Beurs*; De Bykorf; Den Engel*. *Reisboek* (1689): De Granaadappel. *Reisboek* (1700 and 1721) also: De Goude Appel*; De Oranje Appel*; Water-Vliet.

Veere

Population: under 2,500 (1675-1750), 700 houses (1700 T.S.).

Distances: Dordrecht 16 hours (50 miles), Middelburg 1 hour (3 miles).

Inns, *Reisboek* (1689, 1700 and 1721): De Trouw; De Goude Harp*; St. Joris; Den Toorn; d'Oranjeboom*. *Reisboek* (1700 and 1721) also: De Goude Kroon*; De vier Heemskinderen; Zierikzee*.

Further reading

M. Smallegange, *Nieuwe Cronyk van Zeeland*, Middelburg 1696.

M. Gargon, *Walcherse Arkadia*, Leiden 1715, 1717, 1746, Middelburg 1755.

C.H.J. Peters, *Vlissingen in de tijd: geschiedenis in kort bestek*, Vlissingen 1982.

P. Sijnke and W. Riemens, *Middelburg*, Middelburg 1988.

J. Bruijns and J. Jilleba, *Middelburg, haar geschiedenis en mooiste monumenten: stadsgids*, Middelburg 1988.

Ach Lieve Tijd, Zeeland, G. van der Ham (ed.), Zwolle 1996.

De Wete, gedaan aan de leden van de Heemkundige Kring Walcheren, 1971-

Zeeland, uitgave van het Koninklijk Zeeuwsch Genootschap der wetenschappen, 1991-

The Army

William Mure, 13-27 June (23 June - 7 July) 1696

[174] I went to Bruxelles in a dragscute, where I passed by Mechelen and Vilvoorde, where the King of Spain has a room for those liable to his inquisition, with strange engines of torture. The one is the picture of a lady, shaped of iron, who by her embraces squeezes them all in pieces. Others are broken on a mill. But it is locked up since our wars that the inquisition ceased. At the Fountain tavern near Vilvoorde suffered [William] Tyndale [1536], the reformer who first translated our Bible, whose last words were: 'Lord open the eyes of England.'

There I found the Duke of Wurtemberg's camp, consisting of ten thousand men encamped along the canal, where I accidentally met with Major [William] Bortwick and Captain [James] Cranston, who entertained me kindly and lodged me all the night, where I had the major's tent to lie in.

June 14th. They furnished me horses to Brussels, some four hours riding from that, a town where the last [year] houses were burned by the French and near four thousand families dislodged; but it is speedily rebuilding. There the streets are but narrow. I viewed the whole town off one of their churches. There is the palace where the King and Court of Spain used to reside. It is a great building, but much after the old fashion, with a handsome park and garden, in which are very fine waterworks. The Duchess of Bavaria resided then there. The Duke [=Prince] of Vaudemont has likewise a house [Court of Nassau], where sometimes he dwells.

[175] The Court mostly speaks Italian, but the town French. There is upon the back stair of the palace a cannon with a very fabulous inscription that it was preserved by a miraculous chance of a maid's sitting upon it, while the ship in which they were was blown up. But she, praying to the Virgin Mary, was brought ashore alive upon the cannon, which inscription is of some two [one] hundred years' date.

17th June. From Bruxelles I got in a bread-waggon, with near two hundred more in company, with bread and provisions to the army. We went that night to Louvain, under convoy of about five hundred horse and foot, on our way to the King's grand camp. It is a considerable town, less hospitable than any in Flanders to Huguenots, they are all so bigotly Popish. Here there are divers convents, nunneries, and Irish universities of all professions. In one of their convents one of our fellow travellers got an acquaintance of several of the priests, who made all our company drink very heartily. And from that [town] is, just by, Park, a little small country village, where our camp lay for near two summers there and thereabout.

Against night I came at the grand army, but the King caused meet us within

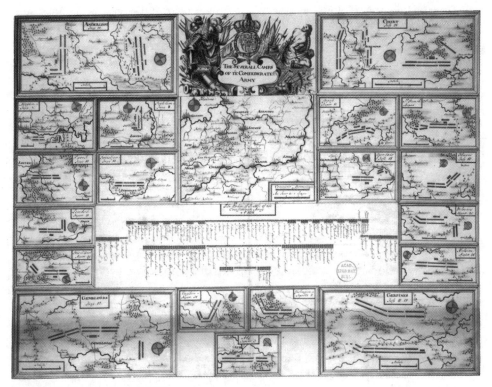

Camp of the Confederate army, 1691

four hours of it, with four or five hundred more horse and dragoons, for fear of the French partisan parties. The reinforcement was commanded by Colonel Capell [Keppel, later Earl of Albemarle], a great favourite of His Majesty. So we safely arrived there, having marched the most of that day through a country much wasted and destroyed by their provisions. I lodged at the quarter at Korbeek, where my friend Mr [William] Carstairs and Mr [Robert] Pringle, the then Scots sub-secretary, stayed in an old boor's house. Within a day or two after, I kissed the King's hand, being introduced by the Earl of Selkirk, one of the bedchamber men. And once a day, while there, I rode along, still with the King, in viewing the lines.

26 June. I went to Gembloux, being reinforced the night before with the Duke of Wurtenberg's army, which then made us, of horse, foot and dragoons, eighty thousand. We had the most charming march, being favoured by both the way and the day. I marched along with the King in the midst of the four columns, entertained the whole way with trumpets, kettle-drums and hautbois and drums. When we encamped I quartered [176] still with my friends in a little village near to an abbey where the King lodged. That village is pleasantly situated on a river, which is rare there for good springs.

359

27 June. I went to Colonel Ferguson's regiment near to the rear of the lines and heard worthy Mr [Alexander] Shields preach.

28 June. The opportunity of a convoy offered, going to Mechelen for money and beer, I returned in a beer-waggon thither by Louvain, and from that to Mechelen without any convoy. That night came to Mechelen, a most pleasant town. I lodged well and cheap in it. It is famous for good beer and fine laces. There I saw the nunneries that did them.

Joseph Taylor, 12-27 August (23 August - 7 September) 1707

[20r]   *From the camp of Soignies, August 16th, 1707.*

Dear Cousin,

I parted with the ladies and the rest of the good [20v] company at Brussels the next morning (after I wrote to you my last) with a great deal of reluctancy and not without some apprehension of the dangers I was to undergo before I could arrive here. The French army lying at Cambron but a league distant from ours, I had the precaution to get the French King's pass before I left Brussels.

The Prince very often upon the road discoursed with me about those English ladies, for he had heard by Mr Charton [his governor] such a character of them, that he seemed to be all on fire and told me he had wished he could have stayed to enjoy the company, and said he was resolved to visit England, where such charming angels are to be found. We had a very entertaining prospect, all along the great causeway, and met with but one party of French, who plundered some waggons, but did not attack us.

By Halle we met with the bread-waggons coming from the army to Brussels, under a strong guard, which were above an hour passing by us. We did not stay at Halle, it being a town of no great consequence, only remarkable for the unfortunate battle of Steenkirk [Steenkerken, 1692], fought by King William. But passing through it we arrived at Braine-le-Comte, where we dined. An old Swiss [21r] partisan was then in the house and came to us, but when he heard the Prince's name, he retired with a great deal of respect. There I saw one of the Flanders stage-coaches, with great baskets before and behind. It held a great many passengers and is much like our coach-waggons.

About two we set out again and passing by a place which our soldiers call the burnt village (having formerly destroyed it by fire for refusing to pay contributions), we at last came to the top of a hill which commanded a view of the town of Soignies. It is impossible to tell you the pleasure I took in this noble prospect; I am altogether incapable of giving you any manner of idea of it, but upon the whole I can only tell you that I think myself sufficiently recompensed for the pains and trouble I have undergone. We passed by a vast number of tents and sutlers' booths before we arrived at Soignies, which with the vast crowd of people about them, something resembled a fair.

The British guard encamped near the town, where is my Lord Duke's [Marlborough's] headquarters, it being in the centre of the army, so that we are a league distant from the English troops, which lie on the right of the line. [21v] Here the Prince set me down, and I was immediately directed to Captain Seaman's quarters in a poor little thatched house near the battalion. I found an empty house, but his servant went presently to call him, and the captain, who had before notice of my coming by a letter I wrote him from Brussels, soon came in, and he received me with all the civility that might be expected from your recommendation and his own good nature. In a few minutes his house was full of officers, and after a glass or two of wine I thought myself a perfect soldier.

We afterwards walked out to a neighbouring hill, where they showed me the army and in the evening, for two or three hours, I saw all the foragers come in, which was very diverting. You will scarce believe what vast quantities of corn, hay, clover and other things they brought in. Every horse had his load, besides a great trooper on his back with a scythe over his shoulder and a large pipe in his mouth. From hence I heard the troops sing psalms throughout the army, as they do constantly every evening at the sun setting. A gun fires from the train of artillery, which is the signal for the tattoo to beat. The drum [22r] major of our guards, with all the drums beating, marched backwards and forwards in the front of the battalion. As soon as they begin, it is received from them by the next regiment and so immediately from one to another through the whole army. Nothing can be more pleasant than to hear all the drums, trumpets and hautboys, playing for an hour or two in the evening, which has been my diversion ever since I have been in the camp; the enjoyment of so much harmony makes me forgetful of the danger.

This evening I saw the picket-guard turn out, and then returned to the little cottage, where I found a very good supper, and Captain Seaman and about half a dozen officers kept a handsome table. Our beds are made in the same room, like a little hospital, and I have slept as well as ever I did in my life. We often drink your health and our friends' in England. I hope you will give yourself the trouble to acquaint them with it, and be assured that I am always with the greatest sincerity imaginable, yours, etc.

[22v]   *Ghent, 27 August 1707*

Dear Cousin,

since my last I am grown almost a soldier, the many hardships I shall acquaint you I have endured, are enough to make me weary of campaigning. During my stay at the camp of Soignies, my business was in a morning to ride through the lines, and visit the English, about a league from us. And I assure you, the redcoats, as they lay encamped on a rising ground, made a far more glorious show than the rest of the army, clothed in white and blue. The French were within a view of our outguards, finely encamped on the pleasant plains of Cambron. Nothing certainly can be more entertaining than the extraordinary regularity of the lines extending over the plains of Soignies, across the causeway from Brussels to Mons. It is impossible to describe the glorious appearance of four score thousand men, or the curious order of the train of artillery belonging to them.

John Leake, 14-20 June (25 June - 1 July) 1712

[39r] [coming from Tournai] As we went deeper into the country we found more visible marks of the calamities of war. Before our arrival at St Amand, we began to hear the cannon that were playing upon Quesnoy, and our eyes as well as ears were everywhere made sensible of the power of fire and sword.

We came to St Amand just time enough to see the glorious church of St Steven and to furnish ourselves with beds, scarce preferable to clean straw. As we were viewing the noble convent of [the] Benedictine fathers and the stately temple of St Steven, our guide showed us the marks of an inundation upon both those buildings, which were occasioned by the Confederates turning the course of a river the last year. The water had risen in the church above six foot [40r] in height, and the fathers were obliged to row up to the high altar in a boat, where were several carps caught during this deluge. The paintings in this church are the history of the saint to whom the church is dedicated and are all from Rubens' pencil, consequently of a value inestimable. In short, the church both within and without is an exquisite piece of workmanship and would be an additional beauty to the buildings even of London, Paris or Rome.

June the 15th we came within sight of the army, the advanced guards of which we found at Marchiennes, where was a great convoy of all manner of provisions. We passed the Scarpe over a bridge of boats and got to the Earl of Albemarle's quarters about noon, where, after having refreshed ourselves, we proceeded on our journey between the two lines of the army, till we came to Cateau-Cambrésis, the Duke of Ormonde's headquarters. In this day's journey we had not only the pleasure of viewing the encampment of the grand army from nine of the clock in the morning till sunset, but of seeing in transitu Valenciennes, Cambrai and part of the French army. We supped in one of the Duke's tents, and by reason one of our company was acquainted with Captain Crow, the quarter-master, we had very good lodgings in a mercer's house in the town allotted us, where we remained during our stay in the army.

The next day we went into the coffee- and gaming-tents, the better to learn the humours and manner of living of the gentlemen of the army. We made enquiry after such officers as were our friends, and succeeded so well that by the assistance of Captain Foster, Captain Gouge, Captain Vicars, etc., we wanted no manner of information that might render this part of our travels useful and delightful.

Tuesday the 17th, under the direction of Captain Foster, we all of us went to the

DE PAR LE ROY.

LAiſſez librement & ſeurement paſſer & repaſſer *Edward Soudterell engloris de Nation Demeurant à Bruxelle alans aued Deux Valets, sur en terreci dans cer Ville, ec france deppasnece don aleier à chiual ou toute autre Commoedite aued Contre ces Volleuur*

ſans ᶜᵘ donner aucun empêchement, ains toute Sauvegarde & affiſtance, ſi vous en êtes requis; à la charge de ne rien faire de préjudiciable à nôtre ſervice & à nos Sujets; & à condition de faire preſenter le preſent Paſſeport aux Gouverneurs & Commandans de toutes les Villes & Places cloſes de nôtre Obéïſſance avant d'y entrer; à peine de nullité. Le preſent Paſſeport valable pour *3n mois* —— à commencer du jour qu'il ſera collationné; & ne pourra ſervir pour aller au-de-là de la Riviere de Somme. Donné à Verſailles le vingtiéme Avril mil ſix cens quatre-vingt-onze. Signé, LOUIS: Et plus bas,

LE TELLIER.

Collationné à l'Original par Nous DANIEL FRANÇOIS VOYSIN, Chevalier Seigneur du Meſnil, Conſeiller d'Eſtat, Intendant en la Province de Haynaut, Païs d'entre Sambre & Meuſe, & d'outre-Meuſe *assou* —— le *Vingtième*
jour *De Juillet* —— mil ſix cens quatre-vingt-ſeize.

Le ſouſſigné Commis à la diſtribution des Paſſeports au Bureau de *Mons* a reçeu pour le preſent Paſſeport la ſomme de *Ceule ſuile...ce* FAIT audit *Mons* ledit jour

French pass for Edward Southwell, 1696

siege of Quesnoy. Mr Wright, [41r] Mr Clayton and myself were furnished with horses from the Duke of Ormonde's stables to perform this expedition. The town was about eight or ten English miles from our quarters, and we were forced to have leave from the advanced guards to pass two or three rivulets before we entered the lines of circumvallation. Upon our approach to the trenches, we found the entrance into them very safe and good. After having ridden along them some way, we dismounted and left our horses with our servants and then proceeded to the more advanced trenches, and had the curiosity to mount a battery of eighteen cannons. There was but little firing whilst we were there, there having been hot work some few hours before our arrival.

Quesnoy is but a small place, for whilst we were upon the aforementioned battery, another, which was on the other side of the town, flung balls over our heads which we saw light at some distance and graze along the ground. The town was within a few days of surrender when we were before it, the Confederates having carried on their works within a few paces of the palisadoes. It pleased God not to make us pay for our curiosity, but to bring us all safe again out of these dangerous windings.

The only blood which was drawn during our stay in the trenches was from the hip of a young Hanoverian soldier, who, having been a-foraging a little too near the town, had the misfortune to receive a contusion from an almost spent drake-shot, which he brought to us in his hand. And one of our company gave him a six stiver piece for it, with an intention of carrying the leaden ball home with him, but it proving too heavy for his pocket, he dropped it by the way. We went to a sutler's tent at the extremity of the lines of circumvallation, refreshed ourselves with a crust of bread and a glass [42r] of champagne and moved towards our quarters again. Upon our return we rode up to the English train of artillery, which, we were told, was the best and most numerous of any of the Confederates. Captain Foster invited us all to a cold collation upon our arrival at his quarters, and all things were managed calmly and gently, till the wine began to exert its power about midnight, when we thought fit to retire and betake ourselves to rest.

The 18th a detachment of above thirty thousand of the Confederates were ordered out a-foraging. They went deep into Picardy and ravaged as far as Péronne and St Quentin, and brought off subsistence for their horses for about a fortnight. Some of the English horse having fallen into the enemy's hands, and being known by their docked tails, were sent back again in the evening to the Duke's quarters, which occasioned no small murmuring among the other Confederates who had met with the like misfortune with ourselves, but were not considered in the restitution. [...]

[43r] Having pretty well satisfied ourselves with the humours of the army, we began to have some thoughts of looking homewards, and accordingly, Friday the 20th instant, having paid our landlords for our lodgings (which by the way was unusual enough, where free quarters are always claimed), we went towards

Bouchain, where we arrived about noon. The marks of the foregoing year's siege [August-September 1711] were very visible, there being scarce a church or building of any sort repaired since the Confederates took the place. [cont. Arras and Douai]

Further reading

F.J.G. ten Raa, *Het Staatsche leger*, vol. vii (1688-1702), 's-Gravenhage 1950.

J.W. Wijn, *Het tijdperk van de Spaanse Successieoorlog, 1702-1715* (*Het Staatsche leger*, vol. viii), 's-Gravenhage 1956-1964.

J.B. Hattendorf, *England in the War of the Spanish Succession*, New York 1987.

Customs

[43] The common people of Holland, especially inn-keepers, waggoners (foremen they call them [voerman]), boat-men and porters are surly and uncivil. The waggoners bait themselves and their horses four or five times in a day's journey. Generally, the Dutch men and women are almost always eating as they travel, whether it be by boat, coach or waggon. The men are for the most part big-boned and gross-bodied.

The first dish at ordinaries and entertainments is usually a salade, *sla* they call it, of which they eat abundance in Holland. The meat they [44] commonly stew, and make their hotchpots of it. Puddings, neither here nor in any place we have travelled beyond sea, do they eat any, either not knowing the goodness of the dish, or not having the skill to make them. Puddings and brawn are dishes proper to England.

Boiled spinach, minced and buttered (sometimes also with currants added) is a great dish all over these countries. The common people feed much upon cabiliau (that is cod-fish) and pickled herrings, which they know how to cure or prepare better than we do in England. You shall seldom fail of hung beef in any inn you come into, which they cut into thin slices and eat with bread and butter, laying the slices upon the butter. They have four or five sorts of cheese; three they usually bring forth and set before you: 1. Those great round cheeses, coloured red on the outside, commonly in England called Holland-cheeses. 2. Cummin-seed cheese. 3. Green cheese, said to be so coloured with the juice of sheep's dung. This they scrape upon bread buttered, and so eat. 4. Sometimes angelots [small size camembert]. 5. Cheese like to our common country cheese.

Milk is the cheapest of all belly-provisions. Their strong beer (thick beer they call it, and well they may) is sold for three stivers the quart, which is more than three pence English. All manner of victuals, both meat and drink, are very dear, not for the scarcity of such commodities, but partly by reason of the great excise and impost wherewith they are charged, partly by reason of the abundance of money that is stirring here. By the way we may note that the dearness of this sort of provisions is an argument of the riches of a town or country, these things being always cheapest in the poorest places.

Land is also here sold at thirty or forty years' purchase, and yet both houses and land set at very high annual rents: so that were not the poor workmen and labourers well paid for their pains, they could not possibly live.

Their beds are for the most part like cabins, inconveniently short and narrow; and yet, such as they are, you pay in some places ten stivers a night the man for them, and in most six. There is no way for a stranger to deal with inn-keepers, waggoners, porters and boat-men, but by bargaining with them beforehand.

Their houses in Holland [45] are kept clean with extraordinary niceness, and the entrance before the door curiously paved with stone. All things, both within and without, floor, posts, walls, glass, household-stuff marvellously clean, bright and handsomely kept. Nay, some are so extraordinarily curious as to take down the very tiles of their pent-houses and cleanse them. Yet about the preparing and dressing of their victuals our English housewives are, I think, more cleanly and curious than they [...].

In the principal churches of Holland are organs, which usually play for some time after the sermon is done. The collections for the poor are made in sermon-time, a purse with a bell hanging at the bottom of it, and fastened to the end of a pole, being by the collector reached to everyone. The psalm to be sung is marked upon slates, which are hung up and down the churches. The people of these countries buy and sell small commodities, and travel by waggon or boat upon the Lord's days. Their travelling waggons are some covered and some open; few travel on horse-back.

No beggars to be seen in all Holland, care being taken to set on work all that are able, and provision made for the aged and impotent. There are, in this one province of Holland, three or four and twenty walled towns and cities, and six of these at least, beside Amsterdam, bigger than any we have in England, except London; and Amsterdam, by this time, well approaches to the bigness of London.

Thomas Scott, September 1672

[25v] Of Flanders. Flanders is situated on the English Eastern Seas, being for the most part under the King of Spain and governed by the Count Monterey. The towns therein well-fortified with walls, palisades, half-moons, etc. No town therein considerable but is well fortified. The houses built altogether of brown brick [26r] very uniform, about two storeys high for the most part. The lower rooms are by the inhabitants strewed with sand, by which means they are always clean, the sand drying the dirt of the shoes. But this is so used in some places in England. The streets therein very clean by reason of the high paving thereof with a flat border stone [kerbstone].

The inhabitants, both men and women, generally gross and fat, and as far as I perceive are good-natured and well-conditioned. But the common sort of women generally wear the breeches, they keeping shop and selling commodities while their husbands look after house-keeping, and not unparallel [26v] to our oyster-women for tongue. Their language is called Flemish, which is a revived Dutch and not so broad pronounced. The common sort of men retain their old fashion of wide-kneed breeches and broad-skirted doublets, and the gentry only differ by wearing French, or close-kneed breeches. The gentlewomen differ not from us, and the common sort only by wearing on their heads a short coiffe with the corners stretched out to either ear and there fixed with pendants such as their ability affords; and in the summer go in their hair and the poorer sort without stockings with wooden shoes, cut out of the whole piece, a great commodity in that country.

[27r] Their religion is Roman Catholic, but not altogether so superstitious as more easterly countries, some using holy water and others not. Yet as to devotion, no country [is] more devout, the meanest and ignorantest boor not presuming to go to work till he had offered himself to God in his holy temple, the church. And though there are many that ignorantly bow to images, not knowing what they do, yet the real intent is no other than to put them in remembrance of such saints as it resembles, and so consequently of the goodness of God, whereby all evil thoughts or actions may be prevented: for, say they, who can have God in mind and do evil? And therefore in order thereto, at the corner of [27v] every street there is erected the image of our Blessed Lady, and in many other places crosses in memory of the Passion of our Blessed Saviour. And the bowing thereto signifies just as much as our bowing with our face towards the east end of the church at our entrance thereof. Therefore those that dissent from the Church for outward ceremonies therein used, as there are too many, that do, in my opinion, lie under a great censure of doing evil.

And yet it is strange to hear the daily complaints of the laity against the Church by reason of the sufferance of so many begging friars, which are there very numerous and [28r] permitted to go about the country begging. Who having vowed both poverty and chastity, never carry about them or handle one farthing of money. Insomuch that a gentleman there said before us that we in England had our pockets picked by lawyers and they were eaten up by friars. Yet surely that man did not consider that our lawyers and their friars, by reason of their daily concourse of people to and from them, are the only means of their and our trading. For we shall easily find that where there is no concourse of people, there will be but dead trading. Witness a vacation in London and the dissolution of monasteries in other parts of England.

They have sermons but once [28v] a day and that in the afternoons before prayers, saying that the life of the church consists in prayer. And I question not, if we in England had not so much preaching, we should be more devout, too many of us being of opinion that religion consists in hearing of sermons.

As far as I could learn, there is but one court of justice for deciding of all differences. The chief whereof is held at Bruxelles [Mechelen] to which all parties grieved by courts in other towns (there being a court kept for every town) may appeal. It consists first of the Lords of the town who are judges of the court. Next [29r] of advocates or counsellors who without doubt, as appears by the sequel, are deep philosophers: two of them disputing one full hour pro and con at the arrest of a gentleman of my acquaintance at Bruxelles, whether the prosecutor or defendant should pay the officers for the arrest, and at length concluded either should pay hal.

Next to advocates are procurors or attorneys, through whose hands goes all the business. Next to them are public notaries or registrars, who enter all letters of attorney in their books, to be made use of as there shall be occasion. Also all records and proceedings are entered in books, parchment there being very scarce. [29v] They arrest with writ all, except burghers, which are those who have kept any trade one year and a day in the town where they dwell, who are first summoned. But if you send the defendant to prison you must allow him reasonable maintenance till the discharge. And if one commit any offence and absconds, after delivery about the town [of] notice thereof in print, he is prosecuted and sentence passed and present punishment when apprehended.

They punish malefactors by hanging them in chains till they rot. [...] [30r] If a man dies, his estate to be divided between the wife and children, but in what manner I could not learn.

They keep good hours, going to rest generally about nine at night, but no watch kept in the streets. For want thereof much mischief is done, insomuch that at Bruxelles many have had their cloaks and hats taken off in the streets and some their throats cut. The boys there, though apprentices, are permitted to beg for play-money, and there is [30v] no law for restraint of begging, insomuch that every road is full both of lusty men, women and children. Their firing generally wood, having no coals, but what they have from England.

Their diet is for the most part fish and herbs, three parts of the year being fasting days. And as we count flesh the substance of diet, so they count fish. And it is observed by them that the disease called the rickets, incident to children of our nation, is occasioned by too much eating of flesh, that disease being never known among them. The common diet on flesh days is mutton and fowl, there being very little beef in that country. And that they generally [31r] over-roast or boil, with which they make pottage stuffed full of cabbage and other herbs. And it is observable here that they seldom or ever have any pies or tarts or the like.

Their bread is of wheat made up in small cakes, one whereof will serve a meal, which is much like ours, but [they] have a coarse sort for the servants, which is made of rye or barley. And whereas the French put several sorts of meat in one dish, the Flemish strive to have as many several dishes as the table will conveniently hold. Beer of two sorts, that is white beer being of the colour of whey, which is almost [31v] of the taste of our ale, and also brown beer, which is in the nature of our mild beer in England.

Wine is very much used there at meals, being for the most part a sort of French wine, both white and red, but [they] have no sack but what comes from England. But by way of advice it will not be amiss to inform the reader that for every bottle of sack that now goes out of England thither, the party to whom they are consigned is to pay twenty stivers. It is observable there that though all alehouses serve wine, yet no house has above one sort.

Besides what meats before [32r] related used with them, they entertained us with several other dishes, namely a dish of boiled salt fish and turnips; a dish of old French beans and apples; a dish of pullets boiled with pottage, cock's combs and ox palates, etc.; a dish of eggs fried together in a pan with spice as ginger, cinnamon and the like and crumbs of bread; a dish of small birds boiled, to eat bones and all, with quinces. But commonly the first dish is mutton and cauliflowers or other things according to the season. But it is to be observed that they always eat the cauliflowers or other things by themselves [32v] and before their meat.

It is also observable that at meals they lay three or four plates one upon another, that you may give the foul one away at your pleasure. Never eating meat without forks and spoons, wondering at our indecent eating with our fingers. And always in drinking, give everyone a several glass; the right meaning thereof being, though now not so much observed as formerly, that no one should drink after another in the same cup, for which they very much discommend us in England; and are so cleanly at meals that they constantly wash their [33r] hands immediately before meals, lest any should before have handled any noisome thing such as the handling dogs, making water and the like.

Tis observable also that whereas they seldom drink to friends or strangers but they see themselves pledged, so, lest that custom should sometimes disoblige the pledger, they observe never to drink to anyone in any sort of beer.

For salads, the chiefest herbs they feed on, are lettuce and cold cabish [cabbage], but many other excellent salads as endives and celery which are so much esteemed in that country. [33v] For fruit, which they commonly eat at every meal according to the season, are apples, which are but mean and harsh; also pears, pretty good; grapes very delicious and also walnuts which they have in great store. Most of the churchyards of villages being planted with walnut trees, and of these many are transported into England and other places.

Women servants seldom or never wait at table but we are generally attended by men. It is also observed that very few in their [34r] houses keep dogs, and an English dog there is very much esteemed. Only herb-women, blacksmiths and suchlike trades do keep great mastiffs, which they employ in drawing their goods in small carts about the towns.

It is also observable that for convenience of dressing their meat, they have several sorts of jacks, some whereof are in the nature of a watch [clockwork] so that it needs no weights; others there are that go without line, being contrived with an nicked [notched] iron, which with a weight at the end [34v] goes down by degrees and is much more serviceable than, though not commendable as, the first, the first being more incident to disorders. Another contrivance is a tin thing set before the fire, in which the meat is contrived to go round and by reason of the sudden heat thereof is a very speedy way.

The ingenious contrivance of a pump that affords both rain water and spring water may also be commended, being contrived with two sockets, the one bringing up spring water [35r] and the other rain water from a cistern underground into which rain from the top of the house is by spouts contrived to run and there by reason of the coolness never decays.

That country in many other things than what is before related differs from us in England, which will not be much impertinent to note: first in their tillage of ground: first ploughing it, then sowing and instead of harrowing, cover the same by throwing the earth over it with shovels, which certainly is much more laborious. But what more profit they may reap by it, [35v] I leave to the skilful farmers, my countrymen, to judge. Also the shepherds, instead of driving their sheep, go before them and whistle, at which they all follow him.

Ringing of bells little used in that country, but have chimes erected in every town hall there; in casting whereof they surpass all the world; the music whereof being able to glad the most sorrowful heart.

In charity they far exceed us, most of their public houses keeping a poorbox, so that men out of their extravagancies may bestow something on the poor. And also in [36r] some inns they make certain orders, which are hung up in the common dining-room, that whosoever puts his hat off at table shall pay something to the poor's box. And also in the passageboats there are boxes kept under lock and key for passengers to extend their charity for the release of Christian slaves.

Also in taking tobacco more moderate than our countrymen, they thinking it much to take above three pipes a day, but instead thereof use much snuff. Here it is to be [36v] noted that they pay for clean pipes, about two stivers for three, which we in England have gratis.

The Low Countries as well as England is yet famous for trading, and in ancient time the staple trade for cloth and the like was kept at Antwerp, but now they have most of it from England, and it is there a great commodity. Also hair camlets are there made; the chief places for that commodity are Antwerp and Bruxelles. Hops in great abundance grow in that country and especially about Aalst. Guns made there are very much esteemed. Lace, called Flanders lace, and point de Venise is most of it made in these countries, [37r] every woman and maid at leisure employing themselves in [the] making thereof.

Matches, not worth speaking of but for curiosity's sake, are different from ours, being made of hemp stock, but more convenient. Old shoes are mended and sold again there, and are very convenient for the poorer sort that are not able to buy new, leather being very scarce in those parts, which may satisfy those that wonder what the broom-men do with the old shoes they give brooms for in London, which otherwise would be thrown away. Pictures a good commodity and cheap, worth transporting, the inhabitants being very excellent at the art of limning. [37v] Gilded leather printed [is] a good, great commodity there, used by the inhabitants, being very commodious for hangings for which they use it.

The least piece of money used in that country is an orekin [oortje, i.e. two doits], five of them being an English penny and four of them a Dutch stiver. A stiver is one penny but ten make an English shilling and six a Flemish skelling. A skelling is six stivers, twenty of which [schellings] make a Dutch pound. They have a certain piece called a ducatoon, which is ten skelling and is worth 5s:6d English, and also a patacoon [Albertusdaalder], which contains eight skelling and is worth 4s:6d English. But note that it goes there [38r] for more or less according to the exchange.

They have also several other pieces as two stiver pieces, three stiver pieces and two skelling pieces. Also till lately, all Spanish and Dutch money were current but are now cried down. English money is also current there, but if you have an acquaintance, change it at the first town you come at for Flemish, otherwise you will lose by it in the exchange, whether gold or silver, which is the whole of my knowledge as so short a time as one month has furnished me with. In which, if I have erred, I question not there are those of this [38v] nation who have so much knowledge of that country (though not opportunity to relate) as to correct the errors therein.

William Mountague, August-November 1695

[219] [After a visit to a music-house in Amsterdam] These women attend the service of the public and, when agreed with, will go where you please and do with you what you please. These things are connived at by the magistrates, who say it is unavoidably necessary to prevent worse things: violations, rapes, etc., they abounding with strangers, travellers, and mariners, long absent from women. They have many of these houses, as we were informed, between forty and fifty. They generally go under the name and shadow of music-houses, but we were content with seeing but two, taking [220] their words for the rest; nor did we hear any music there. The state makes an advantage of these light ladies, for each for her admission must pay three pence, by laying out of which she hopes to get more.

In summer the principal diversion here is to keep (as some) or to hire (as most do) a chaise, and take their mistresses (often) or wives (sometimes) abroad into the country, and give them the air and a handsome treat, returning home for the most part in the evening. We have seen three or fourscore of these chaises, or small chariots, abroad at one time and together, though almost all of different company.

[221] In winter the ladies, or better sort of women are, when the frost is hard and the streets slippery with hardened snow (which is often), taken abroad by their gallants (often) or husbands (seldom except when first married) in Polish sleds or sledges, richly gilt and carved, covered with embroidery of gold or silver or rich silk or tapestry, drawn by a fine horse, richly harnessed, with which they are very swiftly driven from street to street, from one burgwal to another for about two hours and then brought home. Whence, after a little rest and a dish of tea, they are attended to the play-house, and so home, and to tea (not cold) again, and then to

cards, [222] which they use much and hold long, both before and after supper, which they rarely fail of, loving their bellies as well as any people in the world, though they would be thought to do the contrary.

The ordinary sort of people divert themselves but little in the summer, except in walking (chiefly out of the city in Sunday's afternoon) and in winter in skating, which they do very much and promiscuously, boys and girls, young men and maidens, and some few of the better sort are sometimes seen on the ice at that sport.

The merchandise in this city [Amsterdam], even the heaviest, viz. huge fats of Rhenish wine, is drawn on sledges, very low, and consisting [223] of two pieces of wood in length about ten to twelve feet, held together by two pieces across, and covered with iron at top. And on this they lay the goods, having no great, heavy lumbering cars like ours. The brewers also carry their drink abroad thus, all having a little tub of water upon the sledge, which they often spill on the ground to make it go the glibber. The drivers of these, as also of their travelling waggons, are (like our car-men and coach-men) often rude, and affront folks. But then upon complaint to the burgomaster they shall be punished by suspension or otherwise, very severely.

[224] They have no coaches like our hackneys that ply in the streets, but you may hire a sledge, which is the body of a coach upon a sledge without wheels and drawn by a horse. The coach is a handsome one, and the horse a good one, and the fellow in very good habit. And thus the better sort are carried to church and to the play-house and to visits; the price reasonable. But then at The Hague, Amsterdam and other places, you may hire (as we did often) a handsome coach on wheels and a pair of good horses, to carry you anywhere out of town.

The Dutch everywhere observe a great decency in their funerals, all the men following [225] the corpse (two by two, in handsome black cloaks), which are brought to the church (upon a forfeit of twenty-five guilders the first, and fifty the second half hour, to be given to the poor) at two or thereabouts, the doors being locked up at three. The dead body must lie three days in open view to satisfy the relations that it was a natural death. And in some places in these provinces, when anybody dies, there is a truss, or bundle of straw laid at the door, where it continues till the day of the burial, and is great or small according to the age or sex, there being a very large bundle for a man, less for a woman, and much less for a child.

[226] The Dutch are the worst nurses in the world, they cannot make a little good, common broth, gruel or caudle; they are hard-hearted too and careless of the sick. If you can recover by strength of nature and a small help from your doctor, so; if not, you may die, they are very indifferent in the matter.

In the public houses we pay for pipes, candles and everything. The excise is very high and heavy, so that it cannot be avoided. But then you are served with very fine pipes (which you may break if you please) and large, white, tall candles, made of pure tallow, but bad wick, and so they do not burn extraordinarily.

The Return Journey

Anonymous London merchant, 18-22 October 1695 N.S.

[30] On Tuesday morning the 18th October N.S., the wind coming fair, Mr Raworth hired a yacht, and having laid in provision, we sailed to the pits below the Briel, where all the yachts lay to take in the King [William III]. We went on board the William and Mary yacht, Captain [William] Sa[u]nderson, who showed us all his rooms and the King's bed, and gave us a bottle of wine and after sent us in his boat, with Captain Guy and Harris, on board the [31] Mary yacht, where we supped and lodged that night.

The next morning early, we went on board the Admiralty tender who was to carry us on board Sir Clowdishly Shovell, on the Northumberland, who then lay with the other men-of-war two leagues at sea. On Wednesday forenoon at ten o'-clock, the King came on board the William and Mary, the yachts and other vessels firing their guns and the people on them shouting huzzas. Presently after, we all set sail, but our hoy upon hauling his anchor broke his cable, and it cost us half an hour to get it up and [this] put us the last in the fleet. However, in two or three hours we came up with them and the men-of-war, who fired their guns upon joining the King, the standard being set on the top of the main mast of the William and Mary. Here we intended to go on board the Admiral, but the wind being fresh at east-northeast and the sea high, we could not do it.

My Lord Lovelace and six or eight more came also on board our hoy to pass into the Admiral or the Essex prize, but could not; whereupon we were obliged to go in the said hoy for England, being a small vessel of fifty tun, but a good sailor. This disappointment gave us some trouble, having no accommodation for passengers as the master told us and as we found afterwards by experience. Here my Lord Lovelace and I and everybody else were sick, the sea rolling very high, though the weather was good and moonlit nights.

For my part, I expected every moment to be devoured by the waves, and this thought was increased by the meanness of our vessel, which appeared to me little bigger than a coal-lighter in the river Thames. Towards morning the Admiral hailed us and ordered our tender to advance forwards and make the land. Here we used all our sails, and being now the foremost in the fleet we spied the North Foreland at six on Thursday morning, and at nine the King went on shore at Margate, and all the guns were again fired, both at sea and land, the Dutch men-of-war having fired theirs an hour before and returned home, being seven or eight in number.

[32] On Friday morning 11th October, I landed at Gravesend, and after a refreshment of two hours with my Lord Lovelace, etc., I hired a boat, which cost us twenty shillings, being myself and servant and six officers. And at twelve arrived at London, where I found that George Alder, my clerk, died in my absence of a consumption; whereupon at my arrival, my family removed from Putney to London. And thus ended my voyage to Holland, Brabant and Flanders, which proved agreeable to my health and very diverting, having placed my son and Richard Grosvenor at two schools to satisfaction.

Anonymous tourist, 10-29 October 1697 N.S.

10 October. Thursday about five in the morning, I went on board a vessel with Major-General [Thomas] Erle and others, which we had hired for forty-five pounds sterling. But the wind not serving, we lay that night at the Briel; we returned on board by six in the morning.

12 October. About eight in the morning we were taken by a French privateer of Dunkirk called the Dragon [d'Or]. She carried twenty-five guns and four patararoes [small guns]; the captain's name was François Dimitor [De Mitter]. She had one hundred men on board. We surrendered as soon as she had fired two cannon shot. She carried some of our passengers and all our seamen on board her and sent us others in exchange.

13 October. About eleven we were ransomed for four thousand crowns, to be paid if we proved prize. Captain [William] Cadogan and Captain Gibbon were carried to Dunkirk for the ransom. This night there happened a terrible storm as we lay at anchor near the Kentish Knock [sand northeast of the North Foreland], where the bowsprit and forecastle were broke, the herring fishers lost their net about our anchor, which had like to have done us much mischief.

14 October. The sea was rough and wind contrary all this day and night. 15 October. The sea ran high till near night. When it was abated, we threw overboard a horse of Major-General Erle, that was killed in the last night's storm. This night we anchored at [blank]. The wind blew hard, but toward the morning it abated, and about nine this morning (16 October) we saw the North Foreland. But the wind grew so high by eleven, and we were forced to drive by one. It abated again about nine and was quiet about twelve.

17 October. We saw the North Foreland by seven in the morning; hoisted sail; stood out to sea to get the point. The weather blowing high, [we] lost the sight of land by ten and were forced to drive to sea. About one we discovered, about a mile from us upon the Whiting Sands [off Orford Haven], a fresh wreck of a large ship, whose mast stood high above the water and her boat floating at her stern. The seamen concluded she foundered in the storm the night before. The wind easing, we recovered the sight of land at Orford Ness about three in the afternoon, but the wind blowing hard again we were forced to sea and take down our sails with the

best speed we could, for our main mast cracked in the partners and the main stay gave way at the same time. This night the wind blew harder than at any time during the voyage, which, being at west, forced us to sea.

18 October. The wind and storm continuing, we drove all this day to sea. 19 October. The wind and storm continuing, we now made for the coast of Holland. This night were nine of Major-General Erle's horses killed in the storm and the vessel often overrun by the sea. 20 October. Sunday. We hailed a dogger [fishing vessel] about five, which relieved us with beer and biscuit, after we had lived four days on stinking water, not a pint to a man, no beer for five days nor a pennyworth of bread in a day among six men for the last four days. We agreed with him for twenty pounds great, which is about eleven pounds sterling, to wait on us till he could send a pilot on board to conduct us into some port.

21 October. The sea being calm, the dogger sent two men on board us, who exacted five guineas more than the last night's agreement, which we were forced to give; and they brought us into Helvoetsluis about four in the afternoon, after having been eleven days at se.

25 Friday. About twelve at noon we went on board the Centurion, Captain [John] Price commander. 27 Sunday, four in the morning we weighed anchor, lost sight of land about four in the afternoon; made land at Aldeburgh the next morning (28) by sun rising, the wind hitherto blowing very fair. But afterward abating, it became a calm about nine, at which time, being about three leagues from land, we went into the pinnace belonging to the Centurion and landed at Aldeburgh about eleven; that afternoon went on horseback to Ipswich. The next morning (29) took post for London, where I arrived about a quarter after four.

John Farrington, 9-13 December 1710 N.S.

[278] Not doubting you will be pleased to hear of our safe arrival at Harwich, I date this from thence, which will be with you two days sooner than I can be. My last told you that, on December 9th at eleven in the morning [in Rotterdam], we hired a yacht for Helvoet, where we arrived December 10th about eight in the morning. We went on shore to the English house and bought us some provisions, and had it dressed there but dined [on board]. We were informed Helvoet was so full of soldiers and other passengers that there were no beds to be had in town. Therefore we hired a yacht which had four large beds and a good cabin, a stern and a good cook-room in the forecastle. We agreed with our skipper besides his fraught to pay him four guilders a day for his yacht, while we stayed there and he to dress our victuals and find us linen, fire, small beer, etc. In the day we brought her to shore, in the night we lay at anchor at some distance from it. Here we stayed till Thursday, December 12, when the wind coming pretty fair we sailed aboard the Marlborough [packet], commanded by Captain [Henry] Cole.

[279] We spent our time here in viewing the fortifications of this town; they are very beautiful and very strong. We went on board a large Dutch East Indiaman of eleven hundred tun. The weather, while we stayed here, was mizzling, so we kept pretty much on board our yacht, where we had the good company of Mr South of Rotterdam, who with Mr Murrison returned to Rotterdam in the yacht.

The wind [on] December 12th was pretty fair and at eleven we sailed. We had hired cabins of the captain at Rotterdam, and it was well we had, otherwise, as our company proved numerous and the night stormy, we should have had but indifferent lodgings. Our packet, though one of the smallest (seventy tun) had near two hundred passengers, soldiers and officers aboard, thirty of which were officers. As soon as we had passed the Goeree, a privateer gave us chase pretending to be a Dutch dogger, but finding ourselves able to outsail her and being well-manned, we kept our way and lost sight of her towards night. The wind rose very high and all night blew hard, and the seas ran perpetually over us, so that we were forced to ply our pumps all night. We could not carry much sail, but were forced to slack what we might have carried, for fear we had come too soon upon the English coast.

With the morning light we made Orford Ness and, the wind taking us short, we beat off at sea till Friday, December 13 at four in the afternoon, when we reached Harwich. We are returned to our old quarters [the King's Head], have hired a coach for tomorrow morning (John Long, civil fellow, paid eight pounds), but shall not reach London till Monday night, designing to lie at Chelmsford all Sunday. I am, Sir, your very humble servant,

Harwich, Friday night, December 13, 1710.

John Leake, 25 June - 9 July (6-20 July) 1712

[46r] June the 25th we proceeded [from Gent] for Bruges along the canal cut [1613-1622] by Spinola. It is of a great length and of depth enough for ships of bulk to go along. The track-schutes of Flanders are nothing near so convenient for a quick passage as those in Holland, but their slowness is made amends for by the conveniences you find on board, which consist in variety of apartments and all the advantages that a good ordinary can afford.

It was night when [47r] we came to Bruges, and we had but just light enough to see the decaying beauties of a once renowned city. Here we lost sight of the military world again, there being none of that profession in this place. Upon our arrival we lodged at the Golden Gate, took our leave of good burgundy, [and] ordered ourselves to be called betimes the next morning to embark for Ostend.

Accordingly, we fell down to that port June the 26th, in hopes of getting aboard the packet boat for England the next day. But we were not able to accomplish our ends till nigh a week after, by reason of contrary winds. After having lain without the gates once or twice to no purpose, we did at last sail on Saturday morning July the 3rd. But the wind did us so little service that we were obliged to anchor within sight of Ostend. At daybreak we hauled our anchors and were beholden to the tide for what way we could make the second day.

At the same time we put to sea, Admiral [Sir James] Wishart, Mr [George] Gordon and some other gentlemen belonging to the Admiralty set sail in a yacht, under the convoy of the Lark man-of-war. As we stood before Dunkirk, we spied two privateers plying towards us. We crowded all the sail we could, and made towards our man-of-war, but they were too nimble for us and came so near us as to fire at us in order to make us lay by, which we did. But not much to their satisfaction, for having sent our master aboard with the French King's pass, they were obliged to dismiss us, after we had satisfied their curiosity about the yacht and man-of-war.

As we passed by the Downs we saw Sir John Leake's squadron of men-of-war in a line, which were designed to go and take possession of Dunkirk [as agreed at the peace negotiations at Utrecht]. Monday July the 6th in the afternoon, we [48r] got sight of Dover castle, and after having suffered the impertinences of the Deal tide-waters, we left the packet boat, went on board a Dover-wherry and by God's assistance, we safely landed in that port, about four of the clock in the afternoon.

The next day we went to Canterbury and the Thursday following to London, where, at the vicarage house in Stepney, I surrendered a charge which had not been always over-agreeable to me. Laus Deo Tri-uni [Praised be God the Trinity] J[ohn] L[eake].

Financial Accounts

Richard Holford, 28 July - 30 August (7 August - 9 September) 1671

[41r] A shilling Dutch	6 stivers
a stiver is	1d and more
five [stivers] is	6d English
ducatoon	63 stivers
patacoon	50 stivers Holland
	48 in Flanders
ducat	5 guilders
A guilder is	20 stivers
	2 shillings English
pistol	9 guilders
ten stivers is	1 shilling English
rixdollar is	the same with a patacoon

	£ sh d
[42r] Mr Astrey, Mr Geo. Robins and myself to our expenses into Holland.	
At the salutation at Billingsgate on Mr Long, Mr Clerk, Mr Doddrington,	
Mr Gooderich and Mr Bresland	0:14:6
a cheese	0:1:6
two neat's tongues	0:5:0
by water to Gravesend	0:5:0
to see Tilbury Fort and by water	0:2:0
spent at Gravesend	1:2:6
going aboard the passageboat	0:1:0
paid to the customer [customs official] for our heads	0:4:6
given the boy of the Lion	0:0:6
our passage, twenty shillings apiece	3:0:0
given the skippers	0:3:0
going ashore at the Brill [Den Briel]	0:0:6
given the waggoner to Brill	0:0:10
	[subtotal] 6:0:10

	ducatons stivers
[42v] At the Brill [Friday 4 August]	
given at the Great Kirk	0:0:6
carriage of the cloakbag	0:0:9
dinner	0:0:48
wine, etc.	0:0:30
our passage up the Mase to Rotterdam	0:0:12
at the gate there	0:0:3
that night spent	0:0:25
Saturday morning	0:0:19
over the water and fruit	0:0:1
at the coffee-house	0:0:11
our dinner at Mr Searle's [at the Colchester Arms in Cow Street]	0:0:60

gave Searle's two boys	0:0:4
paper and thread	0:0:1
carrying our things to the water	0:0:6
English beer	0:0:4
scout to Delft	0:0:12
carrying our things at Delft	0:0:4
at the Old Kirk there	0:0:4
at the New Kirk	0:0:6
Rhenish at the Dool [Doelen]	0:0:12
277 stivers, which is	[subtotal] 0:4:25
	ducatoons stivers

[43r] At Delft at Mr Appleby, the coffeeman, Saturday night and Sunday morning [6 August] spent four guilders and sixteen stivers in all	0:1:33
gave the maid there	0:0:6
carrying the cloakbag to the water	0:0:3
to the scout to The Hague	0:0:6
carrying the cloakbag to Mr Brown's [coffee-house near the Prince's Court]	0:0:4
at Mr Brown's before sermon	0:0:8
1sh:2d given to the poor and the sexton	
our dinners at Mr Brown's fourteen stivers and five stivers extraordinary apiece	0:1:2
spent at Scheveling [Scheveningen]	0:0:19
passage to and fro at the tollhouse	0:0:4
to the waggoner	0:0:22
to Prince Maurice [Johan Maurits van Nassau-Siegen] his gardener	0:0:6
our lodging at the Scotch ordinary and wine at night and breakfast	0:0:36
to the servant there	0:0:3
a map	0:0:9
Rhenish wine	0:0:21
Monday [7 August]: to go up and seeing the steeple and tower and chimes, etc.	0:0:14
to the boy at the church to see up Obdam's tomb	0:0:3
	[subtotal] 0:5:11

[43v] To the gardener at the [House ten] Bosch	0:0:12
coach hire to the Bosch	0:0:30
paper and an almanac	0:0:2
our dinner at Mr Brown's ordinary, and extraordinary	0:0:58
and a bottle of ale	0:0:4
to see the States' chambers	0:0:12
2sh:6d to the Prince of Orange his servant, John Weele	
to Mr Martin our guide	0:0:24
spent with Mr Browne waiting for the boat	0:0:22
to the scout to Leyden	0:0:18
paid at the gate at Leyden, being past nine at night	0:0:3
carrying the cloakbag	0:0:3
we lay at Mr Andrew Dryon, a Frenchman, at Leyden at the French Arms	0:0:0
spent at the White Hart, the English house	0:0:16
	[subtotal] 0:3:15

[44r] Gave at the physic [botanical] garden	0:0:6
at the anatomy school	0:0:8
at the Borough [Burcht] or castle	0:0:4
spent at our lodging	0:1:52
gave the maid	0:0:4
carrying our cloakbag to the scout	0:0:4
the scuit to Haarlem [Tuesday]	0:0:33
spent by the way	0:0:3
the porterage through Haarlem	0:0:5
the scuit to Amsterdam [Tuesday]	0:0:15
Amsterdam our supper	0:0:59
to the wheelbarrow man	0:0:10
porterage to the porter	0:0:3
in the morning	0:0:21
entering the Rasphouse	0:0:10
weighing there	0:0:6
to the [poors'] box	0:0:2
almshouse	0:0:6
Wednesday [9 August]: dinner ordinary fifteen stivers and extraordinary in all	0:2:4
steeple in the Old Church	0:0:24
the woman at the stadhouse	0:0:12
steeple at the stadhouse	0:0:12
New Stadt Harber [Herberg]	0:1:33
in the Long Stiver [Cellar i.e. Kelder]	0:0:4
at our neighbours	0:0:24
supper	<u>0:0:42</u>
	[subtotal] 0:10:28

[44v] Thursday: spent at Sardam [Zaandam]	0:0:15
paid a boat thither	<u>0:0:62</u>
Thus far Mr Robins	[subtotal] 0:1:14

Our man's name Sextus Dove of Amersfoort near Utrecht. Mr Wood changed
    us six guineas and gave us eleven guilders and five stivers for each guinea.

[45r] Thursday August 10th, 1671

paid our breakfast	0:0:24
ourselves and our man's ordinary and extraordinary	0:1:19
given at the Bethlehem or place where distracted people	0:0:5
gave there	0:0:1
to see the Spinhouse	0:0:10
gave a handsome wench there	0:0:2
given at the playhouse	0:0:24
given at the East India House	0:0:6
by water	0:0:2
spent at the Great Vat	0:0:24
at the New Wine Vat or best bawdy house	0:0:8
our supper	0:0:21
Mr Robins his bed three nights	0:0:18
our lodging three nights	0:0:24

our man's lodging	0:0:8
our breakfast Friday morning [11 August]	0:0:25
gave the maids there	0:0:12
	[subtotal] 0:4:44

[45v] Our passage to Utrecht seven leagues eleven stivers apiece	0:0:44
given to the riders that drawed the boat	0:0:1
our dinner at New Sluys [Nieuwersluis] twenty stivers apiece and our man's nine stivers	0:1:6
gave at Br. Church at Utrecht	0:0:6
our supper and breakfast at Utrecht, where our ordinary was sixteen stivers and our man's six stivers	0:1:52
at several ferries between Utrecht and The Bosch [12 August]	0:0:18
our dinner at Geldermalsen fourteen stivers our ordinary and ten st. our man's	0:0:52
way-money at Bommel	0:0:2
paid our waggoner from Utrecht to Bosch seven leagues	0:2:34
paid a ferryman at the Bosch	0:0:4
gave a soldier that brought us to the main Vauxhall	0:0:2
	[subtotal] 0:7:32

[46r] To the guards in the Papenbrille [citadel]	0:0:12
to the sexton of the Great Church	0:0:12
to organ keeper there	0:0:12
to the soldier that showed us the garrison	0:0:25
sugar	0:0:4
spent at the Keizer or Emperor at The Bosch, Saturday night, Sunday and Monday morning, our ordinary being a guilder and our man's twelve st.	0:5:19
our passage from Bosch to Gorkum, eight stivers apiece	0:0:32
our ordinary at Gorkum and extraordinary there sixteen stivers apiece and six stivers for our man	0:0:54
for fruit yesterday and this day	0:0:5
gave the skipper's boy for beer	0:0:2
our passage from Gorkum to Dort [Dordrecht] by the same vessel four apiece	0:0:16
gave the ship boy	0:0:3
	[subtotal] 0:8:17

Changed with Mr Goodenough £5 English and had for it 22 rixdollars at 48 stivers each rixdollar.	
[46v] Paid for our supper and lodging at Dort, Monday night [14 August]	0:1:10
gave at Mr Goodenough's	0:0:36
paid our passage to Moerdijk [Wednesday]	0:0:42
our dinner at Moerdijk	0:0:26
our passage by cart from Moerdijk to Breda	0:1:7
our passage by ferry over Breda haven	0:0:4
our supper and breakfast at Breda	0:2:4½
to see the Great Church	0:0:12
to see the tower	0:0:12
to see a little wench there	0:0:2
powder and shot at Breda	0:0:5½
our passage into the Buss [Mastbos] of Breda	0:0:2
spent at our bait at Zundert	0:0:29

spent at Berscoad [Brasschaat], two leagues from Antwerp	0:0:12
paid our waggoner from Breda to Antwerp [Thursday] six rixdollars	0:4:48
paid our way-money into Antwerp	0:0:3
sugar	0:0:5
	[subtotal] 0:12:20

[47r] Paid our barber	0:0:25
at Plantin's printing house	0:0:6
spent staying to see the procession of St Austin	0:0:4
gave the poor	0:0:1
gave at the Castle poor	0:0:4½
gave to the soldier that showed us	0:0:12½
gave the sergeant at the guard	0:0:6
and to the sentry	0:0:2
spent in the castle	0:0:13
gave to see the Great Church tower	0:0:18
paid for our eating and lodging for two nights and one day	0:6:10
gave the servants there	0:0:12
our coach or waggon to Mechelen [Saturday]	0:1:24½
gave a man to carry our cloaks, etc. to the waggon	0:0:6
for drink by the way to Mechelen and gave to the poor by the way	0:0:3
our dinner at Mechelen	0:0:30
paid for drink by the way to Brussels	0:0:2
gave the poor by the way	0:0:1
paid our waggoner from Mechelen to Brussels	0:1:24½
	[subtotal] 0:11:16

[...]

[48r] Brussels. sugar	0:0:5
our supper and lodging Saturday night and breakfast Sunday [20 August]	0:0:36
draught of Rhenish	0:0:12
gave to see the park	0:0:6
to see the fountains there	0:0:12
to see the echo house	0:0:6
to see the armoury	0:0:30
and the girl there	0:0:4
to the groom of the chamber	0:0:18
to a fellow that brought us to and fro	0:0:24
paid our ordinary twenty stivers apiece and fourteen stivers extraordinary and ten stivers	0:1:49
	[subtotal] 0:4:22

Received of Mr Robins eight ducats at 96 stivers per ducat. Gave the coachman in hand for Gaunt [Gent] for which we pay three guilders apiece and a patacoon for our man	0:0:50
[48v] our supper, lodging Sunday night and breakfast Monday morning [21 August]	0:0:50
gave the servants	0:0:12
gave the coachman's man	0:0:3
our dinner at Alost or Aelst twenty-four stivers apiece and our man ten stivers	0:1:19
given to the poor	0:0:4

paid our coachman in full, besides the patacoon in hand	0:2:54
our ordinary at Ghent at supper eighteen stivers apiece and 10d our man and wine, lodging, etc.	0:2:24
paid for a coach to see the town	0:0:48
gave the servant there	0:0:6
gave to see the town house at Ghent	0:0:12
our passage from Ghent to Bruges ten hours by boat fifteen stivers apiece [Tuesday 22 August]	0:0:60
spent in the boat	0:0:16
spent at the Old Hooft at Bruges	0:0:18
	[subtotal] 0:5:26

[...]

[49r] Paid our supper Tuesday night, dinner Wednesday and breakfast Thursday morning at Bruges; twenty stivers our ordinary, twelve stivers our man's; four beds six stivers per night and extraordinaries	0:4:33
gave the chamberlain	0:0:8
gave the maid there	0:0:6
paid our passage by boat from Bruges to Ostend [Thursday] four hours eight stivers apiece	0:0:24
paid carrying the cloakbag and cross the river to Ostend and after	0:0:11
paid our dinner at the Crown at Ostend [Mr Bowen's]; ordinary and extraordinary eighteen stivers apiece	0:0:54
paid our waggon from Ostend to Newport three hours [Thursday] twelve stivers apiece	0:0:36
gave the waggoner	0:0:1
paid our supper and lodging at Newport and breakfast and dinner	0:2:6
gave the maid there	0:0:12
	[subtotal] 0:9:2

[49v] Ten patacoons at sixty sols	patacoons sols
paid our passage from Newport to Dunkirk by boat [Friday 25 August] seven hours, nine stivers apiece and two stivers drink	0:0:29
gave a boy to carry our cloakbag from the boat to Dunkirk	0:0:6
spent at the Angel in Dunkirk, our supper Friday night, thirty stivers apiece and our lodging and morning draught	0:2:18
gave the servants there	0:0:6
baited at Gravelines, Saturday, where I gave the maid three stivers	0:1:23
paid our coach from Dunkirk to Calais seven hours	0:5:0
gave the coachman	0:0:3
received of Mr Robins two guineas at thirteen guilders apiece	
our morning draught Sunday at the Bras d'Or at Calais	0:0:6
spent Sunday at Mons. La Force his house with Captain Guy, the master of the Henrietta	0:1:35
paid at the Lion d'Argent for our eating and lodging, Saturday, Sunday and Monday morning, twenty-one livres and three sols; gave him	0:7:3
gave a shipboard by L. A[strey] and R[ichard] H[olford]	0:0:24
paid a boat to bring us on shipboard	0:1:12
gave more to the boys du Lion d'Argent by Mr Astrey	0:0:6
	[subtotal] 0:19:51

[50r]   £ sh d

	£ sh d
Gave the master and boatswain and seamen a guinea	1:1:0
gave the cabin boy five shillings English	0:5:0
gave the captain's boy	0:1:3
gave the boatmen that brought us on shore 2sh:6d	0:2:6
gave Captain Guy, captain of the Henrietta, two broad-pieces [old twenty shilling pieces] A.H.	2:6:0
spent at Deal, where we landed Tuesday morning [29 August] about 3, paid the clerk 4sh:6d English	0:4:6
paid Mr Smith, master of the passage at Deal, eighteen pence English	0:1:6
received of Mr Astrey a crown	
paid to the postmaster at Deal, to Canterbury fourteen miles, fifteen shillings English	0:15:0
at Canterbury gave to see the Great Church one shilling	0:1:0
paid for our horses from Canterbury to Sittingbourne, fifteen miles, twelve shillings	0:12:0
paid our bait there two shillings English	0:2:0
paid our horse hire from thence to Gravesend, eighteen miles 13sh:6d	0:13:6
[...]	[subtotal] 6:5:3

[50v] Paid a pair of oars to Upnore Castle and to the ships, etc. four shillings	0:4:0
paid for our horses and our own eating at Rochester eleven shillings English	0:11:0
spent at Gravesend, where we lay on Tuesday [29 August] night, six shillings English	0:6:0
by water from Gravesend to London [30 August] five shillings, whereof received of Mr R. three shillings	0:5:0
spent at the Beehive on St Mary Hill nine pence, and paid a porter seven pence	0:1:4
	[subtotal] 1:7:4

Paid our man Sextus Dove (Mr Robins gave him one shilling)	1:15:0

[51r] Mr Robins is now out in all	23:1:6
Mr Astrey is out	13:8:6
R. Holford is out	11:15:6
Divide 48:4:6 into three parts; the third is 16:1:6	[total] 48:4:6

[52r] We went from Gravesend to the Brill in the passageboat
from Brill to Rotterdam by boat and sail, 4 leagues, 4 stivers apiece

- Rotterdam to Delft, every hour, 2 leagues, 4 stivers
- Delft to Hague, every half hour, 1 league, 2 stivers
- Hague to Leyden, every two hours, 3 hours, 6 stivers
- Leyden to Haarlem, every two hours, 4 hours, 11 stivers
- Haarlem to Amsterdam, every hour, 2½ [hours], 5 stivers
- Amsterdam to Utrecht, at 7 and 2, 7 hours, 11 stivers
- Utrecht to Geldermalsen and thence to Bosch by waggon, 7 hours, 8 guilders and to several ferries 18 stivers
- Bosch down the Mase to Dort, every morning at 9, 8 hours, 12 stivers, whereof 8 to Gorkum and 4 to Dort
- Dort to Moerdijk by boat, 12 stivers a man, and thence to Breda by cart, 3 guilders and a half, it is in all 10 hours

- Breda to Antwerp by waggon, 10 hours, 15 guilders
- Antwerp to Mechelen and so to Brussels by waggon, 8 hours, 3 guilders a man
- Brussels to Ghent by coach, 10 hours, 3 guilders a man, baited at Alost [52v]
- Ghent to Bruges, at 9 in the morning, 10 hours, 15 stivers apiece
- Bruges to Ostend at 7 and 2, 4 hours, 8 stivers
- Ostend to Newport at 8 and 2, by waggon, 3 hours, 12 stivers apiece
- Newport to Dunkirk, 7 [5] hours, 9 stivers apiece, every day at 1 [in the] afternoon
- Dunkirk to Gravelines and thence to Calais, by coach, 7 hours, 5 patacoons at 60 sols the patacoon

William Carstairs, 9 May - 16 June (19 May - 26 June) 1685

[161] For passage to Gravesend for myself and a friend	£ 0:1:6
for coach to Rochester	0:1:6
for dinner at Rochester	0:1:2
for coach to Canterbury	0:6:0
spent by the way, having paid for some in the company	0:1:2
spent at Canterbury	0:0:6
for post horses from Canterbury to Dover	0:8:0
to the ostler	0:0:9
to the postboy	0:0:6
spent at Dover	0:2:0
for passage and for a pass, together with money for the searchers and carrying my goods aboard	1:3:0
[10 May] for my bed aboard and drink money to the seamen and carrying my things ashore at Newport	0:7:0
for supper and dinner next day, and lodging that night I landed, having also paid for a poor Englishwoman that came from England with us, and given drink money to the maid	ƒ 3:6:0
[11 May] for fraught from Newport to Bruges	0:14:0
for my expense by the way	0:6:0
for carrying my things through Bruges	0:6:0
for supper, lodging, a small breakfast, and drink money to the servant	1:10:0
[12 May] for carrying my things from my quarters in Bruges to [the] Sluis boat	0:8:0
[162] to the barber	0:6:0
for fraught from Bruges to Sluis	0:4:0
for the fraught of my portmantle	0:1:0
for carrying my things from the place where we landed, being a quarter of a mile from Sluis	0:10:0
for carrying my things from the waterside at Sluis to the other end of the town, where I was to ferry over to Cadzand	0:7:0
for ferrying over thither	0:1:0
for waggon through that island [Cadzand] to the place where we took water for Flushing	1:2:0
for ferrying over to Flushing	0:6:0
for waggon from thence to Middelburg	0:4:4
for carrying my things through Middelburg	0:4:0
for diet at Sluis	0:9:0
[13 May] for lodging and diet at Middelburg and some other occasional expenses	3:4:0
for fraught to Dordt from Middelburg	0:19:0

for carrying my things	0:7:0
for a convenient place in the boat from Middelburg, and for beer and diet when aboard	1:3:0
[14 May] for carrying myself and things ashore at Dordt	0:4:0
[..]	
[162] [22 May] for the post waggon from Den Bosch to Maastricht, whither it goes in one day	6:6:0
for my baggage	0:18:0
by the way for diet	0:18:0
for carrying my things twice, and letting me see the town	0:12:0
at Maastricht for diet and lodging	8:17:0
for drink money	0:6:4
[23 May] for the waggon to Aken [Aachen]	1:4:0
for a glass of wine	0:5:0
for bathing	0:6:0
for wine in the bath	0:3:0
to the poor	0:2:4
to the barber	0:6:0
for gloves	1:16:0
[...]	
spent in Putsen [Burtscheid], a place without Aken, where there are also baths and those very good	0:18:0
to the barber	0:6:0
for bathing at Putsen and some other expenses	1:5:4
to the maids of the bath	0:6:0
for wine	0:4:0
[164] for rings, curiously made of horse hair, and another conceit	1:10:0
for needles of all sorts, which are curiously made here	3:15:0
for two books explaining the nature of Aken baths	1:16:0
to a doctor of physic [medicine]	1:16:0
for a place in a waggon to go to church	0:6:0
for letters	0:8:0
to the barber	0:6:0
for bathing fourteen times	4:4:0
for beer at the several times of my bathing	0:12:0
drink money to the servants of the bath	0:9:0
for fourteen days lodging and diet with other extraordinary expenses	28:16:0
for bathing again and drink in the bath	0:15:0
spent more at Aken	0:5:0
[...]	
[12 June] for a cart from thence to Spa, not having any company, and spent by the way	6:6:0
given to the foreman	0:3:0
for four nights at Spa	9:15:0
for bracelets	1:16:0
for buttons	0:9:0
given at the several wells, of drink money, to fillers of water according to custom	1:4:0
drink money to the servants	0:12:0
[16 June] for passage betwixt Spa and Aken	2:16:0
spent by the way	0:6:0

[165] to the barber	0:6:0
spent upon an extraordinary occasion in company	2:8:0
for three days at Aken	6:12:0

Two Anonymous gentlemen, 1 September - 5 October 1712 N.S.

[2] New Style, September	Guilders stivers doits
1st Day, The Hague, for dinner	02:16:01
for seeing the States' rooms	00:16:00
for supper	02:16:01
Day 2nd, for our beds	00:12:00
for breakfast	00:18:00
for dinner	01:08:00
in the afternoon for tea	00:07:00
betwixt that and Delft	00:08:00
from that to Rotterdam	00:11:00
at the ports [gates] of Delft and Rotterdam	00:03:00
Rotterdam, for a boy to show us the way to lodgings	00:02:00
for supper	01:17:00
Day 3rd, for breakfast	00:16:00
for a pair of stockings	08:00:00
to the barber	00:08:00
for dinner	01:09:00
[3] for twelve shifts	97:00:00
for supper	02:00:00
for the plays in the kermis	01:00:00
for a boy to go some errands	00:06:00
Day 4th, for six pair of gloves	03:12:00
in the coffee-house for breakfast	00:16:00
for dinner	01:04:00
for beer and supper	02:19:00
Day 5th, for the poor at the church door	00:10:00
for breakfast	00:08:00
for coffee and sugar	00:08:00
for dinner	01:04:00
for tea in the afternoon	00:06:00
for passing the river	00:01:00
for supper	01:10:00
Day 6th, for breakfast	00:16:00
for mending my shoe	00:02:00
for getting into the Exchange	00:02:00
for dinner	03:00:00
for supper	02:00:00
for three nights lodgings	01:16:00
Day 7th, for breakfast	00:16:00
for the barber	00:15:00
for a crystal [glass] for the watch	00:18:00
for buttons for my sleeves	00:15:00
for dinner	02:14:00
for carrying our baggage to our new lodgings	00:06:00

for seeing the Great Church	01:00:00
for seeing the Surgeon's Hall	00:16:00
for the washerwife	01:16:00
for a string to the watch and seal	02:03:00
for a lead pen	00:06:00
for the poor	00:02:00
[4] for a nightcap	03:10:00
for mending a lock and key	00:10:00
for a lad	00:04:00
for a porter to carry our baggage to the ship	00:16:00
betwixt Rotterdam and The Hague	02:03:00
for carrying our baggage from the scute	00:06:00
for supper	02:00:00
[...]	
[5] Day 13th, for breakfast	00:16:00
for seeing the House of the Wood	00:11:00
for seeing Honselaarsdijk and Rijswijk	01:16:00
for dinner at Honselaarsdijk	08:18:00
for Mr Grant	23:00:00
for the comedy	00:18:00
for supper	01:06:00
for a chaise out to Honselaarsdijk	03:00:00
[...]	
[6] Day 18th, Amsterdam, for passage at the port [gate]	00:04:00
for the poor	00:02:01
for supper	02:03:01
Day 19th, for breakfast	00:14:00
at the Exchange	00:08:00
for dinner	02:16:00
for seeing the East India House	01:08:00
for seeing the Hortus Medicus	00:16:00
for supper and for the lass and lad of the house at Leiden	02:19:01
Day 20th, for breakfast	00:18:00
for seeing the Stadhuis	01:14:00
for oil and [powder] pluff [for wigs]	01:10:00
for dinner	03:00:00
for supper	02:00:00
for seeing the Rasphouse	00:14:00
for lodging	01:00:00
[...]	
[8] October. Day 2nd, for seeing Fort Lillo	01:08:00
Day 3rd, for breakfast	00:18:00
Antwerp, for lace for ten shifts	52:00:00
for seeing the tapestry manufactory	00:07:00
for our beds in the ship	01:01:00
for beer in the ship and carrying our baggage out of the ship	00:18:00
for passage at the port [gate]	00:01:01
for seeing the Academy of painting	00:14:00
for seeing the Great Church and the comedy	02:02:00
for seeing the Capuchin church	01:08:00

for seeing the Dominican church	00:14:00
for seeing Bedlam and for the poor there	03:02:00
for dinner and supper	07:08:00
[9] Day 4th, for seeing the famous picture of Rubens	01:01:00
for seeing the famous steeple	01:01:00
for seeing the Jesuits' church	00:14:00
for a pair of gloves	00:14:00
for lodging	01:08:00
for seeing the Citadel, church and poor there	02:14:00
for breakfast, dinner and supper	08:19:00
for seeing the Abbey of St Michael	01:00:00
for seeing Nunciature	00:14:00
for seeing the Franciscan convent	00:14:00
for seeing the Virgin Mary's statue of silver	00:07:00
Day 5th, for passage between Antwerp and Brussels	18:18:00

John Tillard, July-August 1716

[9] A petit pièce	3 patons or 2 liards
livre	16 patons or 20 sous
paton	5 liards French or 4 of the Emperor
sept liards	7 liards
crown	5 livres
French crown	9 schellings and 2 stivers
ducatoon	10 schellings
guilder	20 stivers
florin	20 stivers
French guinea [louis d'or] in Flanders	12 guilders 12 stivers 2 liards sometimes 13 guilders
French guinea in Holland	11 guilders 6 or 8 stivers
schelling in Flanders [permissie schelling]	7 stivers
schelling in Holland (if it be what they call good)	6 stivers
if bad [malle schelling]	5½ stivers
doublet	2 stivers
doit	⅛ stiver
pistol current in Flanders	10 guilders, in exchange 9 guilders
pistol current in Holland	9 guilders 9 stivers
three crowns and two schellings make a pistol	
a sovereign current	18 guilders 10 stivers, in exchange 15 guilders
a sovereign in Holland	15 guilders 15 stivers
crown current	3 guilders 5½ stivers, in exchange 2 guilders 16 stivers
ducat in exchange	5 guilders, in Holland 5 guilders 5 stivers

There are likewise double schellings, pieces that go for 3 guilders, others for 4 stivers, others for 25 stivers, others for 28 stivers. Note: 15 crowns is 42 guilders. Ten guilders in Flanders and eleven in Holland is one pound sterling.

Chronological List of Travellers

with itineraries[1]

1663 William Lord Fitzwilliam (1643-1719), later Member of Parliament. *The Voyage of the Low Countrys and of Some Part of France, ann° 1663*. Northampton, Northamptonshire Record Office, Fitzwilliam Misc., vol. 234.

He set out from Paris on 11th April N.S. and travelled via *Cambrai, Valenciennes* and *Mons* to *Brussels*. From here his itinerary was *Leuven, Mechelen, Antwerp, Bergen op Zoom, Breda, 's-Hertogenbosch, Utrecht, Amsterdam, Noord-Holland, Friesland, Groningen, Coevorden, Zwolle, Amsterdam* (by ship). Here he remained from mid-May until mid-June. Then he journeyed via *Haarlem, Leiden, The Hague* (10 days), *Delft* and *Rotterdam* to *Dordrecht*, where he embarked for *Veere*, arriving 30th June. After visiting *Middelburg* and *Vlissingen*, he crossed the river Schelde to *Sas van Gent*, and then travelled via *Gent, Brugge, Sluis, Oostende, Nieuwpoort, Veurne, Dunkirk* and *Calais* (11th July) back to London (mid-July).

1663 John Ray (1627-1705), naturalist. *Observations Topographical, Moral and Physiological; Made in a Journey through Part of the Low Countries, Germany, Italy and France*, London 1673.

He set out from Leeds in Kent on 17th April O.S. with his student Philip Skippon and picked up two more friends and servants at Dover, from where they made the crossing to Calais. From here the itinerary was Gravelines, Dunkirk, Nieuwpoort, Oostende, Brugge, Gent, Brussels, Leuven, Brussels, Mechelen, Antwerp. Next they sailed to Middelburg, saw Vlissingen and sailed to Bergen op Zoom. From here the itinerary was Breda, Dordrecht, Rotterdam, Delft, The Hague, Leiden, Haarlem, Amsterdam, Utrecht, Vianen, Zaltbommel, 's-Hertogenbosch, Eindhoven, Maastricht, Liège, Spa, Aachen (28th June), Cologne ... [*customs*]

1669 Thomas Style (c.1650-1672), law-graduate. *A Voyage through the Low Countrys, Germany, Italy and France, 1669-1671*. Charlottesville, Virginia, University of Virginia Library, Special Collections Department, Thomas Style Manuscript (#6846-DL).

He set out from London on 4th July O.S. and made the crossing from *Harwich to Hellevoetsluis*. From here the itinerary was Den Briel, Rotterdam, Delft, The Hague, Leiden, Amsterdam, Utrecht, *'s-Hertogenbosch, Breda, Bergen op Zoom*, Dordrecht, Utrecht, Nijmegen (21st August) ...

---

[1]   Italics in the itineraries mark passages printed in this book.

1671 Richard Holford or Halford (knighted 1695; d.1718). *Account of a tour in the Low Countries*. Trowbridge, Wiltshire Record Office, MS 184/8.

Together with two friends he set out from London on 28th July O.S. and made the crossing from Gravesend to Den Briel. From here the itinerary was Rotterdam, Delft, The Hague, Leiden, Haarlem, *Amsterdam, Utrecht, 's-Hertogenbosch*, Gorkum, Dordrecht, *Breda*, Antwerp, Mechelen, Brussels, *Gent, Brugge*, Oostende, Nieuwpoort, Dunkirk, Calais, Deal, Canterbury, Gravesend, London (30th August). [*accounts*]

1671 John Walker, lawyer, from 1669 to 1703 Usher of the Exchequer. *A Voyage Begunn in August Ann° 1671*. Taunton, Somerset Record Office, MS DD/WHb 3087.

He set out from London on 5th August O.S. and made the crossing to Rotterdam. From here the itinerary was Delft, The Hague, Leiden, Haarlem, *Amsterdam*, Utrecht, Arnhem, Kleve, Grave, 's-Hertogenbosch, Gorkum, Dordrecht, Breda, Bergen op Zoom, Antwerp, *Brussels, Gent, Brugge, Oostende, Dunkirk, Calais*, London (9th September).

1672 Thomas Scott, lawyer. *Iter Breve, or a short and plain narrative of a journey from London to Antwerpe in Flanders*. London, British Library, MS Add. 18722.

He set out from London on 2nd September O.S. and sailed to Gravesend, then travelled to *Dover* and made the crossing to *Calais*. From here the itinerary was *Dunkirk, Nieuwpoort, Oostende*, Brugge, Gent, Antwerp, Mechelen, Brussels, *Gent, Brugge, Nieuwpoort, Margate*, London (2nd October). [*customs*]

1678-1679 William Nicolson (1655-1727), student at Queen's College, Oxford; later Bishop of Carlisle. *Iter Hollandicum*. Oxford, Queen's College Library, MS 68, edited by P.G. Hoftijzer, *Lias*, 15 (1988), pp. 73-128.

He set out from Greenwich on 16th July O.S. and made the crossing to Rotterdam. From here the itinerary was The Hague, Leiden, *Haarlem*, Amsterdam, Utrecht, Nijmegen (12th-28th August), Wolfenbüttel, Leipzig, Hamburg, Rotterdam, Den Briel, Harwich, London (24th March).

1682 White Kennett (1660-1728), student at Oxford; later Bishop of Peterborough. *Un voyage à Calais, Guines, Ardres & Saint-Omer en 1682 extrait du journal de White Kennet*, C. Landrin (ed.), Paris 1893.

He set out from London on 3rd October O.S. and made the crossing from Dover to Calais. From here the itinerary was Ardres, *Saint-Omer*, Ardres, Calais, Dover (24 October O.S.).

1685 William Carstairs (1649-1715), minister of religion; later adviser to William III and principal of Edinburgh University. Journal and expenses of a journey in Holland and Flanders. *Selections from the Family Papers Preserved at Caldwell*, W. Mure (ed.), Maitland Club, new ser., vol. VII, Paisley 1883, pp. 144-166.

He set out from London on 9th May O.S. and sailed to Gravesend, from where he travelled to Dover. After the crossing to Nieuwpoort the itinerary was Brugge, Sluis, Cadzand, Vlissingen, Middelburg, Dordrecht, 's-Hertogenbosch, Maastricht (Aachen v.v.), Liège, Spa, Aachen, Cologne, Nijmegen, Gorkum, Dordrecht, Rotterdam, Delft, The Hague (6th July) [breaks off]. [accounts]

1687 Thomas Penson (born 1652), arms-painter. Penson's Short Progress into Holland, Flanders and France, with Remarques. Edinburgh, National Library of Scotland, MS 3003. Other MSS in Leeds University, Brotherton Library, MS Trv. d2, and London, British Library, MS Harl. 3516 (rough copy); (Cf. C.D. van Strien, 'Thomas Penson: Precursor of the Sentimental Traveller', Travel Fact and Travel Fiction. Studies on Fiction, Literary Tradition, Scholarly Discovery and Observation in Travel Writing, Z. von Martels (ed.), Brill's Studies in Intellectual History, vol. 55, Leiden 1994, pp. 194-206; an edition is in preparation by the present editor).

He set out from London on 30th June O.S. and made the crossing to Rotterdam. From here the itinerary was Delft, The Hague, Leiden, Amsterdam, Utrecht, Amsterdam, Gouda, Rotterdam, Antwerp, Gent, Kortrijk, Lille, Paris (19th October - 10th November), Calais, Dover, London (22nd November).

1693-1694 James Drummond, Earl of Perth (1648-1716), politician. Letters from James Earl of Perth to His Sister, W. Jerdan (ed.), Camden Society, vol. XXXIII, London 1845.

He left Scotland as an exile in the beginning of October. Together with his wife and servants he made the crossing to Rotterdam. From November till 8th May O.S. they lived in Antwerp. From here the itinerary was Maastricht, Aachen, Maastricht, Leuven, Antwerp (Brussels v.v.), Gent, Brugge, Sluis, Vlissingen, Middelburg, Hellevoetsluis, Den Briel, Rotterdam, Nijmegen ... Italy.

1695 Anonymous London merchant. An Account of My Two Voyages beyond Sea, in the Years 1695 and 1699. New Haven, Yale University, Beinecke Library, the James Marshall and Marie-Louise Osborn Collection, Osborn MS b.155.

He set out from London on 3rd August O.S. and sailed to Gravesend, from which he made the crossing to Hellevoetsluis. From here the itinerary was Den Briel, Rotterdam, Dordrecht, Rotterdam, Gouda, Amsterdam, Noord-Holland, Haarlem, Leiden, The Hague, Rotterdam, Dordrecht, Antwerp, Brussels (army v.v.), Antwerp, Rotterdam, Gouda, Utrecht, Rotterdam (Dordrecht v.v.), Den Briel, Gravesend, London (11th October O.S.).

1695 William Mountague (born 1645), lawyer. The Delights of Holland: Or A Three Months' Travel about that and the Other Provinces, London 1696.

He set out from London on 14th August O.S. with two friends and servants and made the crossing from Harwich to Hellevoetsluis. From here the itinerary was Den Briel, Maassluis, Rotterdam, Delft, The Hague, Leiden, Haarlem, Amsterdam, Naarden, Loenen, Utrecht, Soestdijk, Utrecht, Amsterdam (Alkmaar v.v.), Haarlem, The Hague, Rotterdam, Dordrecht, Middelburg, Vlissingen, Veere, Hellevoetsluis, Harwich, London (19th November). [customs]

1696 William Mure of Glanderstone (c.1650-1728), landowner. *Selections from the Family Papers Preserved at Caldwell*, W. Mure (ed.), Maitland Club, new ser., vol. VII, Paisley 1883, pp. 170-180.

> He set out from Edinburgh on 24th April O.S. and travelled to London. From here he sailed to Gravesend (24th May) and made the crossing from Harwich to Hellevoetsluis (3rd June). From here the itinerary was Den Briel, Maassluis, Rotterdam, The Hague, Delft, Rotterdam, Antwerp, *Brussels, Leuven (the army at Gembloux v.v.), Mechelen,* Antwerp, Gent, Brugge, Sluis, Vlissingen, Middelburg, Veere, Rotterdam, Leiden, Haarlem, Amsterdam, Gouda, Rotterdam, Hellevoetsluis, Harwich (22nd July), London, Edinburgh, Glasgow, Glanderstone (12th August).

1696 Edward Southwell (1671-1730), government official, son of Sir Robert Southwell, Secretary of State for Ireland. '*A Visit to the United Provinces and Cleves in the Time of William III, Described in Edward Southwell's Journal*', K. Fremantle (ed.), *Nederlands kunsthistorisch jaarboek,* 21 (1970), pp. 39-68 (BL, MS Add. 21495). *Letters written in July and August 1696.* The Hague, Koninklijke Bibliotheek, MS 133 C6.

> He set out from London on 2nd May O.S. and travelled via Canterbury to Margate, from where the crossing was made to Maassluis. From here the itinerary was The Hague, Utrecht, Amersfoort, Het Loo, Dieren, Kleve, Nijmegen, Grave, *'s-Hertogenbosch,* Breda, Antwerp, Brussels, Gent, Brugge, Oostende, Nieuwpoort, Dunkirk, Dixmuide, Brussels, Gembloux (army), Namur, Liège, Maastricht, 's-Hertogenbosch, Utrecht, Amsterdam, Noord-Holland, Leiden, The Hague, Rotterdam, Zeeland, Dordrecht, Kleve, Dieren, The Hague, Rotterdam, Hellevoetsluis, Lowestoft, London (29th August).

1697 Sir Francis Child (1642-1713), banker and in 1699 Lord Mayor of London. *A Short Account by Way of Journal, of what I Observed Most Remarkable in My Travels thro' Some Part of the Low Countrys, Flanders and Some Part of Germany which is on the Rhine.* London, London Metropolitan Archives, Ac. 1128/177. *A Journall of My Travells through the United Provinces.* Ibid., Ac. 1128/178.

> He set out from London on 2nd June O.S. and made the crossing from Gravesend to *Veere.* From here the itinerary was *Middelburg, Vlissingen, Veere,* Dordrecht, Rotterdam, *Delft, The Hague,* Leiden [breaks off].

1697 Anonymous tourist, probably a member of the Penruddocke family of Compton Chamberlayne near Salisbury. *Account of a journey in the Netherlands.* Trowbridge, Wiltshire Record Office, MS 549/46.

> He set out from London on 12th July N.S. and made the crossing to *Veere.* From here the itinerary was *Middelburg, Vlissingen,* Antwerp, Brussels (the army at Koekelberg v.v.), *Namur, Huy, Liège,* Maastricht, *Aachen,* Düsseldorf, Cologne, Düsseldorf, Wesel, Kleve, Nijmegen, *Het Loo,* Utrecht, The Hague, Delft, Leiden, Haarlem, Amsterdam, The Hague, Rotterdam, *Den Briel, Helvoetsluis, London* (29th October N.S.).

1697-1698 John Talman (1677-1726), student at Leiden, son of the architect William Talman. *Journall from Leyden to Loo in Gelderland and throw the Province of Overyssel, 1697* and *Diary of a Journey in Holland, 1698*. Bedford, Bedfordshire County Record Office, HY 941 (1697) and HY 939 (1698).

He set out from Leiden on 11th September 1697 N.S. for Amsterdam, and crossed the Zuiderzee to *Harderwijk*. From here the itinerary was *Het Loo, Deventer, Zwolle, Kampen*, Hasselt, Blokzijl, from which he returned by ship to Amsterdam, Leiden (19th September).

He set out from Leiden on 11th September 1698 N.S. for Amsterdam. From here the itinerary was Weesp, Muiden, Hilversum, Laren, Soestdijk, Soest, *Amersfoort*, Barneveld, *Arnhem, Velp, Middachten, Zutphen*, Doetichem, Emmerik, *Kleve, Nijmegen, Arnhem*, Rhenen, Zeist, Utrecht, Leiden (21st September).

1698 Thomas Bowrey (c.1650-1713), merchant. *The Papers of Thomas Bowrey, 1669-1713*, R.C. Temple (ed.), Hakluyt Society, 2nd ser., vol. LVIII, London 1925.

He and a friend set out from Greenwich on 28th May O.S. for Calais in his own yacht. From here they sailed to Dunkirk, Oostende, Vlissingen, Dordrecht and Rotterdam. Here they left the yacht and travelled to *Gouda*, Amsterdam, Haarlem, Leiden, The Hague and back to Rotterdam, where they embarked again. From here the itinerary was Dordrecht, Antwerp, *Gent*, Brugge, Oostende, Dunkirk, Calais, Greenwich (12th July O.S.).

1699-1700 Anonymous Utrecht student. *Notes of several passages and observations in Holland, etc., part of France, Savoy, Piemont, Italy and Part of Germany, from June 1699 to July 1702*. Huntingdon, County Record Office, M 36/19.

The traveller and his brother (probably accompanied by a tutor) set out from London on 15th June 1699 O.S. and made the crossing from Gravesend to *Rotterdam*. From here the itinerary was Delft, The Hague, Leiden, *Utrecht* (6 July N.S.). From Utrecht excursions were made, particularly to Amsterdam (24th-27th July), to *Arnhem*, Nijmegen, Grave, Arnhem, *Het Loo*, Amersfoort, Utrecht (1st-5th September N.S.) and to Naarden, Amsterdam, *Haarlem*, Noord-Holland, Amsterdam, Utrecht (27th August - 1st September 1700 N.S.). On 8th October the travellers left the United Provinces: Dordrecht, *Breda*, Antwerp, Mechelen, Brussels, Mons (19th October), Paris (27th October).

1701 Anonymous tourist. *Journal kept during a continental tour*. Plymouth, West Devon Record Office, MS 280/1.

The traveller arrived in *Maastricht* at the end of a journey through Italy, France, Switzerland and Germany. From here the itinerary was Nijmegen, Arnhem, Naarden [breaks off].

1704-1705 Sir Justinian Isham (1687-1737), studied at Utrecht together with his cousin Edmund Turner under the supervision of Monsieur Masson; afterwards they studied at

Wolfenbüttel; later Member of Parliament. *Account of a Tour on the Continent.* Northampton, Northamptonshire Record Office, Isham (Lamport) 5275.

He set out from London on 2nd May 1704 O.S. and made the crossing from *Harwich to Hellevoetsluis.* From here the itinerary was *Den Briel, Rotterdam (Dordrecht v.v.)*, Delft, The Hague, Leiden, Haarlem, Amsterdam, Utrecht (2nd July O.S.). On 16th April 1705 N.S. the travellers went (via Woerden and Gouda) to Rotterdam. From here the itinerary was Dordrecht, Veere, Middelburg, Vlissingen, Goes, *Tholen, Bergen op Zoom*, Breda, 's-Hertogenbosch, Grave, Nijmegen, Arnhem, Dieren, Zutphen, Het Loo, Amersfoort, Naarden, Amsterdam (4th-25th May N.S.). From here they toured to Haarlem, Alkmaar, Hoorn and Enkhuizen from where they crossed into Friesland (Staveren). From here the itinerary was Workum, Bolsward, Leeuwarden, Dokkum, Groningen, Delfzijl (3rd June), Embden, Bremen, Wolfenbüttel (10th June).

1706 Anonymous military officer. *Account of a Journey to the Army in Flanders.* Oxford, Bodleian Library, MS. Rawlinson D. 1004.

He set out from London on 1st May O.S. and made the crossing from Harwich to Hellevoetsluis. From here the itinerary was Rotterdam, *Breda*, Antwerp, Gent, Brugge, siege of Oostende (16th June; surrender 25th June O.S.).

1707 Joseph Taylor (1679?-1759), lawyer, later Member of Parliament. *A Relation of a Voyage to the Army. In Several Letters From a Gentleman to his Friend in the Year 1707*, C.D. van Strien (ed.), Leiden 1997.

He set out from Greenwich on 28th July O.S. and made the crossing to *Rotterdam.* From here the itinerary was Antwerp, Mechelen, *Brussels, Soignies (army)*, Ath, Oudenaarde, Gent, *Brugge (Oostende v.v.), Sluis, Vlissingen, Middelburg*, Bergen op Zoom, Dordrecht, *Rotterdam, Delft, The Hague*, Leiden, Amsterdam, Rotterdam, London (10th October O.S.).

1707 Daughter of Gilbert Burnet, politician and Bishop of Salisbury; she travelled with her stepmother, Elizabeth Burnet (1661-1709), who after finding lodgings for her sons at Leiden, travelled to Spa for her health. *Diary kept during a journey with Mrs Burnet.* Oxford, Bodleian Library, MS. Rawlinson D. 1092, ff. 100-106.

The travellers set out from London on 29th May O.S. and made the crossing to Rotterdam. From here the itinerary was The Hague, Leiden, Amsterdam, The Hague, Rotterdam, 's-Hertogenbosch, Maastricht, *Liège, Spa, Liège*, Maastricht, Leuven, Brussels, Antwerp, Rotterdam, The Hague (October) [breaks off].

1710 'John Farrington', possibly a London merchant. *An Account of a Journey through Holland, Frizeland, Westphalia, etc., in Severall Letters to Mr N.H.* London, British Library, MS Add. 15570. The passages concerning the United Provinces have been published by P.G. Hoftijzer (ed.) and C.D. van Strien (introduction), Leiden 1994.

He set out from London with some friends and servants on 28th August O.S. and made the crossing from Harwich to Hellevoetsluis. From here the itinerary was Rotterdam, Delft, *Leiden (The Hague v.v.)*, *Haarlem*, Amsterdam, Hoorn, Enkhuizen, *Workum*, *Harlingen*, *Franeker*, *Leeuwarden*, *Groningen*, *Nieuwe Schans* (25th September N.S.), Bremen, Hamburg, Hannover, Wolfenbüttel, Osnabrück, Kleve, Nijmegen (11th November N.S.), *Arnhem*, *Rozendaal*, *Dieren*, *Zutphen*, *Deventer*, *Het Loo*, *Amersfoort*, Utrecht, Amsterdam, Leiden, The Hague, Delft, Rotterdam, *Hellevoetsluis*, *Harwich*, London (15th December N.S.).

1711 Sir James Thornhill (1676-1734), artist. *Sir James Thornhill's Sketchbook Travel Journal of 1711. A Visit to East Anglia and the Low Countries*, K. Fremantle (ed.), Utrecht 1975.

He set out from London with three friends and two servants on 21st May O.S. and made the crossing from *Harwich to Hellevoetsluis*. From here the itinerary was *Den Briel*, *Maassluis*, Delft, The Hague, Rotterdam, Dordrecht, *Sas van Gent*, *Gent*, Tournai (30th June O.S.) [breaks off].

1711-1712 John Leake (born c.1682), clergyman, non-juror, governor to Hickson Wright, son of the vicar of Stepney; both enrolled as students at Leiden on 4th September 1711. *A Diary of Occurrences and Observations Begun June the 15th O.S. 1711*. Oxford, Bodleian Library, MS. Rawlinson D. 428.

The travellers set out from London on 15th June O.S. and made the crossing from Harwich to Hellevoetsluis. From here the itinerary was Rotterdam, Delft, Leiden, Amsterdam (Haarlem v.v.), Utrecht, Leiden (The Hague v.v.), Amsterdam, *Hoorn*, *Enkhuizen*, *Alkmaar*, *Purmerend*, Leiden (1 September). From here excursions were made to The Hague, *Utrecht* and *Gouda*. On 3rd May 1712 they journeyed (via Rotterdam and Dordrecht) to *Antwerp*. From here the itinerary was *Mechelen*, Brussels, *Enghien*, *Tournai*, *St Amand (army)*, *Cateau-Cambrésis*, *siege of Quesnoy*, *Douai*, *Lille*, *Kortrijk*, *Gent*, *Brugge*, *Oostende*, *Dover*, London (9th July O.S.).

1711 Anonymous tourist. *Journal of a continental tour, 1711-1712*. Leeds University, Brotherton Library, MS Trv. 3.

He set out from London on 29th June O.S. and made the crossing from Harwich to Rotterdam. From here the itinerary was Delft, The Hague, Amsterdam, Bergen op Zoom (28th July N.S.), *Antwerp*, Gent, *Kortrijk*, *Lille*, *Douai*, *Tournai*, *Ath*, *Enghien*, Brussels, *Leuven*, *Maastricht*, *Aachen* (27th August - 2nd September N.S.), Cologne ... Italy, ... Hannover.

1711-1712 Sir Edmund Prideaux (1647-1720), lawyer, later Member of Parliament (1713). *Journal of a continental tour*. Manchester, John Rylands University Library, English MS 1153.

After a journey through Germany the travellers arrived at Nijmegen on 26th October N.S. From here the itinerary was Gorkum, Rotterdam, Delft, Leiden, Haarlem, Amsterdam, Utrecht, Leiden, Rotterdam, Antwerp, Lier, Mechelen, Brussels (1st January - 16th April 1712 N.S.), *Leuven*, Brussels, Gent, Brugge [breaks off].

1712 Two anonymous young gentlemen. *Accounts of expenses on a tour on the continent.* Edinburgh, Scottish Record Office GD 345/843.

> The travellers set out from their home at Gogar near Edinburgh with their servant or governor Mr Grant on 5th August O.S. and made the crossing from Leith to Hellevoetsluis (19th August O.S.). From here the itinerary was Den Briel, Maassluis, The Hague, Delft, Rotterdam, The Hague, Leiden, Haarlem, Amsterdam, Utrecht, Gouda, Rotterdam, Antwerp, Mechelen, Brussels, Gent, Brugge, Nieuwpoort, Dunkirk, Lille, Paris (18th October - 5th December N.S.), Calais, Dover, London (17th December). [*accounts*]

1716 John Tillard (1690-1774), lawyer. *Tour through Flanders and Holland.* Leicester, Leicestershire Record Office, 6D 43/1/3.

> He set out from London in a yacht on 14th July O.S. and made the crossing to Dunkirk. From here the itinerary was Nieuwpoort, Brugge, Gent, Brussels, Antwerp, Breda, Utrecht, Amsterdam, Noord-Holland, Haarlem, Leiden, The Hague, Delft, Rotterdam, Dordrecht, Willemstad, Hellevoetsluis, London. [*accounts*]

1718 Sir John Percival (1683-1748), politician, created first Earl of Egmont in 1733. *My Journy to France, Holland, and Flanders in 1718.* London, British Library, MS Add. 47059, ff. 19r-158v (the passages concerning the United Provinces have been edited by Margriet Hagenaars, MA thesis English, University of Leiden, 1996).

> On 12 June O.S. he made the crossing from Dover to Calais. From here the itinerary was *Dunkirk*, Nieuwpoort, *Brugge, Gent, Antwerp, Breda*, Dordrecht, *Rotterdam*, Delft, *The Hague, Leiden, Haarlem, Amsterdam*, Utrecht, Gorkum, Breda, Antwerp, Mechelen, Brussels, *Valenciennes, Cambrai*, Roye, Paris, Amiens, Abbeville, Boulogne, Calais, Dover (30 August O.S.).

1719 Richard Rawlinson (1690-1755), lawyer and antiquary. *Account of a journey to Paris and the Low Countries.* Oxford, Bodleian Library, MS. Rawlinson D. 1191.

> He set out from London on 2nd June O.S. and made the crossing from Rye to Dieppe. From here the itinerary was Rouen, Paris (27th June - 17th September N.S.), St Quentin, Valenciennes, Mons, Brussels, Antwerp, Rotterdam, Gouda, *Amsterdam* (Utrecht v.v.), *Noord-Holland*, Haarlem, Leiden, The Hague, Delft, Rotterdam, Den Briel, Willemstad, Hellevoetsluis, Greenwich, London (17th November N.S.).

1720 Anonymous tourist. *Account of a continental tour.* London, British Library, MS Add. 60522.

> He set out from London on 18th April O.S. and made the crossing from Dover to Boulogne. From here the itinerary was *Calais, Dunkirk*, Nieuwpoort, *Brugge, Gent, Brussels, Antwerp*, Mechelen, Brussels, Leuven, Tongeren, Maastricht, *Aachen, Spa, Liège, Huy, Namur*, Brussels, *Mons, Tournai, Lille, Ieper, Saint-Omer, Arras, Douai*, Lille, *Valenciennes, Cambrai*, Rheims, Chalons, Lunéville (17th August - 8th January N.S.), London (22nd January 1721 O.S.).

1722 Thomas Malie MD. *Memorandum of the rout from Leyden to the Southern Netherlands.* Birmingham City Archives, 607387 DV912.

He set out from London as physician to the Countess of Burlington on 16th April O.S. and made the crossing from Dover to Calais. From here the itinerary was *Saint-Omer*, Lille, Kortrijk, Gent, Brussels, Leuven, Tongeren, *Maastricht*, Aachen (23rd May O.S.) [breaks off].

1723 Sir John Percival (1683-1748), politician, created first Earl of Egmont in 1733. *My Expedition to Spa 1723*. London, British Library, MS Add. 47059, ff. 1-18r.

He set out from Charlton on 7 June O.S. and made the crossing from *Dover to Calais*. From here the itinerary was *Dunkirk, Nieuwpoort, Oostende*, Brugge, Gent, Antwerp, Brussels, *Liège, Spa (Stavelot, Malmédy v.v.), Liège, Leuven*, Brussels, *Antwerp*, Gent, Brugge, Nieuwpoort, Calais, Dover (7 September O.S.).

List of Illustrations*

* Most of the illustrations have been made available by the Collectie Bodel Nijenhuis (Coll BN) of Leiden University Library (UBL).

LIST OF ILLUSTRATIONS

p. 228 [Leiden] *HET RAADHUYS.*
Print belonging to the decorative border of the large town plan of Leiden in 18 sheets by J. Dou and C. Hagen. 1670-1674. Etching. Coll BN P 330 N 58.

p. 231 *VERA ANATOMIAE LUGDUNO-BATAVAE CUM SCELETIS ET RELIQUIS QUAE IBI EXTANT DELINEATIO.*
[J. Woudanus del.; W. Swanenburg sculp. 1610]. Amsterdam: C.J. Visscher, 1644. Engraving. Coll BN P 315-III N 17.

p. 239 [Spa] *LA FONTEYNE SAUVENIER.*
[Detail from] *VICUS SPADANUS AMOENISSIMUS ET SALUBERRIMUS.* Joannes Breugel delineavit; Guil. van Nieulant fecit. Antwerpen: Theodorus Galle, c. 1625. Etching. Coll BN M31-18-5651-110/1.

p. 242 *De Stad en Kasteel te Namen langs de Maes en Sambre brug te sien.*
J. de Beijer ad viv. delin. 1748 et fecit 1748. Pen and watercolour. Coll BN P 314-I N 36.

p. 246 *Plan et Elevation du Colege et Jardin des R: Peres Jesuites Anglois a Liege.*
R. le Loup fecit. From: *Les délices du païs de Liège.* Liège: E. Kints, 1738. Coll BN M31-18-7411-532 Jes/1.

p. 252 [Spa] *LA FONTEYNE POUHON.*
[Detail from the print mentioned under no. 43].

p. 257 [Het Loo Palace near Apeldoorn] *de Groote Fontein van Venus.*
[Amsterdam]: Cornelis Danckerts, [c. 1700]. From a set of prints showing Het Loo Palace, published by Danckertsz. Coll BN P 329 N 248.

p. 261 *het Koninglijck Huijs van Vooren op 't Loo.*
From the set of prints mentioned under no. 47. Coll BN P 329 N 245.

p. 267 [Aachen] *De Groote Vergaader-Plaats van alle gebrekkelyke Menschen, die sig na de Fonteinen begeeven om de Wateren te Drinken &c.*
[c. 1730]. Etching. Coll BN M33-19-9032-350/4.

p. 278 *COLLEGIUM MECHLINIENSE SOCIETATIS IESU.*
R. Blokhuyse fecit. Etching. From: J. le Roy, Groot kerkelijk toneel des hertogdoms van Brabant. 's-Hage: Chr. van Lom, 1727. Coll BN M31-23-0334-532 Jes/1.

p. 285 [Enghien Park] *12. Het groote Pavilloen. 13. Groot Rond [...].*
From a set of 17 prints by Joannes van Avele, published at Amsterdam by N. Visscher, c. 1690. Etching. Coll BN M31-17-7063-722/27.

p. 288 *La Citadelle de Tournay avec ses Souterrains, et Galleries* [upper part].
[c. 1725]. Pen and watercolour. Coll BN P 75 N 10.

p. 292 *Hoorn de hooftstadt van West Vrieslandt.*
Etching. From: Th. Velius, *Chroniick van Hoorn.* Hoorn: Isaac Willemsz., 1648. Coll BN P 30 N 85.

p. 295 *Alkmaar.*
C. Pronk del. ad viv.; J. Punt sculpsit. 1746; Ph. & J. Losel excudit. From: G. Boomkamp, *Alkmaer en deszelfs geschiedenissen.* Rotterdam: Ph. & J. Losel, 1747. Coll BN P 316 N 104.

Index of Personal Names

Index of Geographical Names

417

Index of Subjects

In this selection of topics we have indexed remarks on (1) travel and accommodation, (2) sightseeing, (3) leisure activities, (4) government and justice, (5) trade, industry and farming, (6) religion, (7), customs and finally (8) some anecdotes.

1. Travel and Accomodation

banker (bills of exchange, letters of credit) 73, 84, 143, 162, 223, 253, 281, 289, 325, 344; **changing money** 46, 142-3; **coins** 372, 379, 390; **customs formalities** 13-5, 19-20, 57, 60, 138, 143, 289, 343-5, 355, 379, 386; **gate-money (head money)** 14, 21, 45, 50, 78, 138, 160, 230, 294, 379-80, 388-9; **pass** 7, 15, 18-9, 69, 223, 244, 247, 285, 310, 360, 378, 386; **passage money** (way-money) 45, 78, 196, 355; **toll** 55, 60, 77, 92, 171, 196, 316, 380; **inns** passim; detailed comments 22, 27, 35, 89, 91, 137-8, 150, 160, 162, 165-6, 179, 208, 211, 215, 251-3, 274, 292, 308, 320-1, 325, 346; cost of lodging and meals 21, 158, 185, 202, 240, 273-4, 297, 322, 326, 334, 367

travelling on foot 21, 56, 60, 145, 238, 291, 350; **(post)-horses** 114, 136, 138, 213, 215, 221, 243, 248, 250, 291, 358, 364, 367, 376, 385-6; **vehicles**: basket 247; beer-waggon 360; berline 71, 96, 163, 223, 225, 266, 284-6, 329; bread-waggon 358, 360; calash 194; carabas 142-3; cart 92-3, 115, 350-2, 370, 382, 385, 387; chaise 172, 185-6, 194-5, 231, 234, 318, 372, 389; chariot 14, 57, 89-91, 194-5, 200, 211, 372; coach (coach-waggon, post waggon, stage-coach, travelling waggon, waggon) passim, described in some detail 21, 27, 35, 111, 148, 171, 198, 241, 248, 265, 275, 293, 308, 325-6, 346, 352, 360, 373; coche 224, 251, 286-7, 289; diligence 119, 246, 275; hackney 13, 373; sledge 35, 44, 373; **vessels**: boat passim; coche 218, 249; ferry 91-2, 304-5, 329, 332, 350-1, 355, 382, 385-6; fishing boat 16, 196, 376; packet boat 4, 13, 15-21, 102, 138, 140, 143, 309, 352, 376-8; sloop 18; tender 374; tilt-boat 186; trekschuit (trackscout etc.) passim, described in some detail 101, 124, 164, 166, 171-2, 186, 203, 250, 294, 308, 336, 371, 377; wherry 17, 378; yacht 17, 67, 130-1, 171, 326, 374, 376-8

accidents 13, 16, 91, 137, 280, 364, 375; **calm** 13, 18, 351, 376; **caper** (privateer) 15, 102-3, 353, 355, 375, 377-8; **convoy** 15, 17-8, 358, 360, 362, 378; **French party** 7, 115, 163, 223, 247, 265, 267, 359; **robbers** (thieves) 113, 138, 163-4, 221, 241, 244, 265, 285, 287, 321; **running aground** 56, 161, 351; **sea-sickness** 15-6, 18, 21, 60, 374; **shower** 148, 230, 294; **shutting of city gates** 91, 102, 160, 221, 223, 230, 285; **storm** 13, 16, 21, 60, 148, 185, 337, 352, 375-7; **whirlwind** 354

2. Sightseeing

tourist guide (interpreter) 1-9, 68-9, 79, 131, 139, 150, 163, 223, 280, 285, 320, 362, 380, 382-3, 387-8; **guidebook** 1-11, 27, 35, 52, 141, 229, 253, 387, see also Misson

admiralty 32-4, 52, 147, 293, 319-20, 327; **anatomy hall** 31, 178, 227-8, 231, 327, 381; **arsenal** (armoury, magazine) 6, 53, 79, 86, 110, 112, 117, 120-1, 123, 125-6, 142, 177, 224-5, 271, 288, 314, 383; **citadel** (castle) 7, 53, 62-3, 67, 70-1, 79, 84-9, 92, 98-9, 113, 135-9, 142, 145-6, 149, 157, 159, 161, 164, 167, 181, 183, 188-90, 202, 209-11, 213, 219, 221-5, 228, 238, 240-5, 250-1, 254, 277, 284, 286-7, 289, 292, 296, 300, 304, 307, 313-4, 332, 338, 342, 344-7, 378, 381-3, 385, 390; **Court** (residence) 74, 79, 109, 111, 115, 120-1, 147, 151, 166, 188-9, 191, 193, 196, 202-3, 250, 257, 358, 380; **exchange** 6, 32, 35, 37, 44, 51-3, 57, 64, 67, 71, 114, 129, 222-3, 319-20, 323, 325-6, 349, 388-9; **fort** 7, 13, 57, 60, 66, 72, 91, 99, 136, 138-40, 142, 162, 176, 179, 201, 208-11, 213, 221-2, 232, 238, 242-4, 250-1, 271, 274,

3. Leisure Activities

5; Croisiers 244, 250, 269; Dominicans 65, 72, 99, 118, 158, 167, 221-2, 225, 246, 249, 273, 280, 343, 390; English churches, see England; Franciscans 113, 273, 277, 280, 342, 390; French churches, see France; Jesuits 6, 40, 55, 57 61, 66, 68, 71, 83-4, 86, 98-120 passim, 137, 158-9, 165, 167, 208, 215, 218-9, 222, 238, 242, 245-6, 249-50, 268-70, 277-81, 288, 347, 390; Jews 31, 35, 41, 46, 335; Lutherans 25, 27, 31, 40, 51, 79, 151, 176, 234; Minims (Minorites) 83, 249, 273, 332; Norbertines 65, 72; Paulinians 31; Persian church 52; Presbyterians 25, 76, 253, 300, 329, 340; Puritans 9, 173; Recollets 83, 86, 118, 164, 217, 273, 280; Reformed 59, 96, 148, 176, 271, 294, 329; Sepulchrines 245; Socinianism 47; Tiresians 68; Ursulines 250, 287

abbeys 6, 9, 60, 62, 72, 85-6, 100, 104, 107, 160, 205, 216, 218-9, 240-1, 248-50, 254, 332, 342, 346-8, 359, 390; **Catholics in United Provinces** 25, 40, 52, 79, 87-9, 96, 109, 132, 148, 151, 176-7, 188, 205, 208, 267, 294, 300, 329, 333, 338, 351; **Protestants in Southern Netherlands** 165, 238, 246, 253, 272, 344, 358; **discussion about religion** 59, 105-6, 165, 238, 278, 311; **divine service** 1, 6, 8-9, 17, 68, 85, 91-2, 106, 115, 133, 164, 173, 193, 246-7, 262, 266, 320, 329, 340, 350, 360, 367-8, 380, 387; **Catholics criticised** 58, 65, 95, 101, 106, 112, 117, 139, 141, 159, 164-5, 173, 214, 216, 238, 240-1, 311, 358, 368; **fasting** 62, 114, 309, 369; **hermit** 244; **holy water** 62, 138, 368; **incense** 6, 62, 169; **tapers** 118, 159, 163, 221, 243; **miracle** 58, 83, 106, 121, 131, 197, 201, 265-6, 338, 358; **procession** 61-2, 71, 117, 121, 132, 143, 221, 224, 238, 243, 247, 270, 383; relics 61, 85, 105, 221, 266, 271-3; English, Irish and Scottish churches, colleges, convents, clergy, see England, etc.

7. Customs

burial (churchyard) 27, 41, 54, 62, 100, 136, 148, 161, 277, 304, 370, 373; **cleanliness** 21-2, 25, 34, 43-4, 78, 123, 126, 145-7, 171, 185, 190, 279, 291, 312, 319, 322, 326-7, 332, 355, 367, 370; lack of it 75, 78, 84, 114, 137, 212, 300, 307-8, 316, 346, 362; **diet** 22, 81, 139, 142, 160, 164-5, 179, 212, 249, 254, 309, 366-7, 370; **dress** 27, 34, 40, 44, 62, 102, 115, 138, 154, 159, 177, 179, 219, 243, 247, 270, 273, 283, 320, 326, 368; **wedding** 52, 138, 265, 327; **women** 22, 34, 41, 44, 98, 105, 107, 121, 138, 142, 147, 159, 177, 188, 192-3, 212, 223, 240-1, 248-9, 268, 273, 293, 326, 361, 366-8, 372; **various customs** 15, 22, 35-6, 39, 41, 44-5, 60, 111, 115, 118, 121, 137-40, 221, 159, 210, 239-40, 250, 320, 326, 366-73, 387

8. Anecdotes

Bantam, King of 213; clapperman 89; crime 185, 221, 236, 321, 338, 350; prostitute 44, 123; Protestants in Catholic setting 59, 117, 240-1, 311; surprise meeting 104, 119, 325; travelling incidents 15-6, 18, 46, 56, 90, 160-1, 165, 308, 310, 352, 375

historical anedotes: **Antwerp**, Brabo 55; picture of the Virgin 163; Quinten Metsys 72; Rubens 55; **Brugge**, leaning spire 100; **Brussels**, cannon 116, 121, 358; miracle 121; **Cambrai**, siege 342; **Delft**, explosion 123; **Dordrecht**, St Sura 131; barony 132; **Douai**, miracle 83; **Geel**, St Dympna 265; **Haarlem**, printing invented 184; Damiata taken 181, 183; **Leeuwarden**, Willem Frederik 151; **Leiden**, Lucas van Leyden 235; siege 233; **Loenen**, Gerard van Velsen 334; **Loosduinen**, miracle 200; **Leuven**, churchyard 277; **Maastricht**, crucifix 266; **Staveren**, gentlewoman 147; **Utrecht**, St Mary's 338; church collapsed 337